# STUDIES IN
# PAUL'S TECHNIQUE
# AND THEOLOGY

# STUDIES IN
# PAUL'S TECHNIQUE
# AND THEOLOGY

## Anthony Tyrrell Hanson

WILLIAM B. EERDMANS PUBLISHING COMPANY
GRAND RAPIDS, MICHIGAN

Library of Congress Cataloging in Publication Data

Hanson, Anthony Tyrrell.
Studies in Paul's technique and theology.
Bibliography: p. 305
1. Bible. N. T. Epistles of Paul — Criticism,
interpretation, etc. 2. Bible — Criticism, interpre-
tation, etc. — History — Early church, ca. 30-600.
I. Title.
BS2650.2.H36 1974     227'.06'6     74-7491
ISBN 0-8028-3452-3

*In grateful memory of*
*the Reverend Canon J. E. L. Oulton, D.D.*

late Regius Professor of Divinity in the University of Dublin

*a fine scholar and a fine Christian*

# CONTENTS

# ACKNOWLEDGEMENTS

I wish to acknowledge with much gratitude the very great help given to me by Mr Christopher Huggett, B.A., a research student in my department, in reading the proofs for this book. I would also like to thank my wife for help in compiling the indexes.

I would like to acknowledge the helpfulness and consideration shown me by Mr R. J. Brookes of SPCK in all the negotiations which preceded the publication of this work.

A.T.H.

Thanks are due to the following for permission to quote from copyright sources:

T. and T. Clark: *Church Dogmatics*, vol. II, by Karl Barth, tr. G. W. Bromiley and T. F. Torrance.

Irish University Press: *The Thought of Rudolf Bultmann*, by André Malet, tr. R. Strachan.

Biblical quotations from the Revised Standard Version of the Bible, copyrighted 1946, 1952, and 1957 by the Division of Christian Education of the National Council of the Churches of Christ in the United States of America, are used by permission.

# FOREWORD

The first seven chapters of this book represent separate studies on the theme indicated by its title. They have however in common the fact that they all originated from a close study of Romans and Galatians. This is true even of the first chapter, which is concerned with a passage in Colossians. It was an examination of Gal. 3.13 that led me on to Col. 2.14–15. The last five chapters are concerned with drawing out implications and arriving at conclusions based largely on the evidence presented in the first seven chapters, though some fresh evidence is presented in these later chapters also. The last two chapters in particular may be said to give its unity to the book: its theme is the significance of Paul's interpretation of Scripture.

Some indication is called for as to which of the Pauline Epistles I take to be authentic. Throughout the book I assume that all the Epistles usually attributed to Paul are really his except Ephesians and the three Pastoral Epistles. But Ephesians I take to be from the hand of a direct disciple, and therefore as reflecting Paul's mind and method much more accurately than do the Pastorals.

When a commentary on a Book of the Bible is first cited the date and place of publication is given in a footnote. After that it is taken for granted that the comment cited occurs in the part of the commentary concerned with the passage of scripture under scrutiny, so references are not given.

*University of Hull*                                                       A.T.H.

# ABBREVIATIONS

| | |
|---|---|
| AV | Authorized Version |
| BT | Babylonian Talmud |
| *Bibl. Ant.* | *Biblical Antiquities* of Pseudo-Philo |
| *Bibl. Heb.* | R. Kittel's *Biblia Hebraica* |
| e. | edition |
| *ET* | *Expository Times* |
| ET | English Translation |
| ICC | International Critical Commentary |
| *JBL* | *Journal of Biblical Literature* |
| *JTS* | *Journal of Theological Studies* |
| LXX | the Septuagint |
| MT | Masoretic Text |
| NEB | New English Bible |
| *NTS* | *New Testament Studies* |
| *Nov. Test* | *Novum Testamentum* |
| *RdHPR* | *Révue d'Histoire et de Philosophie Religieuse* |
| *RB* | *Révue Biblique* |
| RV | Revised Version |
| RSV | Revised Standard Version |
| S-B | Strack-Billerbeck: *Kommentar zum Neuen Testament aus Talmud und Midrasch* (3 e., Munich 1961) |
| *TWNT* | *Theologisches Wörterbuch zum Neuen Testament* |
| Vg. | Vulgate |
| *ZATW* | *Zeitschrift für die Alttestamentlichen Wissenschaft* |
| *ZNTW* | *Zeitschrift für die Neuentestamentlichen Wissenschaft* |

# TRANSLITERATION OF HEBREW

## CONSONANTS

ayin    is rendered by '
aleph   is rendered by '
heth    is rendered by ch
sadhe   is rendered by s
tsayin  is rendered by ts

## VOWELS

Vocal *shewa* is rendered by ᵃ

Composite *shewa* is rendered by the appropriate vowel at the top of
the line. I have not attempted to distinguish between simple vocal
*shewa* and composite *shewa* with *pathach*.

I have normally marked a syllable long only where *matres lectionis*
occur; but I have not thought it necessary to mark a long 'a'
where *qamis* followed by a *He* occurs at the end of a word.

# TEXTS AND VERSIONS

The Hebrew Bible: *Biblia Hebraica*, ed. R. Kittel (4 e., Stuttgart 1949).

The Greek New Testament: K. Aland, M. Black, B. M. Metzger, and A. Wikgren, ed., *The Greek New Testament* (New York, etc. 1969).

The Septuagint: ed. A. Rahlfs (4 e., Stuttgart 1949).

Biblia Sacra juxta Vulgatae: ed. A. C. Fillion (Paris 1887).

English Bible: Revised Standard Version (London 1959).

Quotations from Philo are taken from *Philo Opera Omnia*, ed. L. Cohn and P. Wendland (Berlin 1897+).

# 1

# THE CONQUEST OF
# THE POWERS

The aim of this study is to show that fresh light on the meaning of Col. 2.14–15 can be found by examining a certain passage in the Targum of Palestine. A link is thereby found with Gal. 3.10–14: in both passages Christ's death on the cross is understood in the same way.

Several scholars have seen a close link between Galatians 3 and Colossians. Von Soden, for example, sees a link between Gal. 3.13 and Col. 2.14–15, saying that the 'curse' of Galatians means the same as the 'bond' of Colossians and the 'condemnation' of Rom. 8.1.[1] And Lindars (*New Testament Apologetic* (London 1961), p. 234) writes: 'The same thought [sc. that Christ bore our curse] is expressed in very different terms in Colossians 2.14.' The point is not that the Law is evil, according to Paul, nor that it was invented by evil angels, but that it has been made the instrument of death by the power of sin. We can even bring evidence to show that Paul thought of the power that thus misused the Law in terms of the devil, and so find a transition to the ideas behind the Colossians passage.

In 2 Cor. 11.2–3 Paul makes a passing reference to the Eden story:

> I feel a divine jealousy for you, for I betrothed you to Christ to present you as a pure bride to her one husband. But I am afraid that as the serpent deceived Eve by his cunning, your thoughts will be led astray from a sincere and pure devotion to Christ.

The words 'as the serpent deceived Eve' are in the Greek ὡς ὁ ὄφις ἐξηπάτησεν Εὖαν. The reference is, of course, to the Fall, and we note that Paul identifies the serpent with the devil. This is made plain in 11.14 where he says 'even Satan disguises himself as an angel of light'. I have argued elsewhere that this shows an acquaintance with the midrash now contained in the *Vita Adae et Evae*, in which the devil transforms himself into an angel of light in order to seduce Eve.[2] In Rom. 7.11 Paul uses the same language in a more general sense:

> For sin, finding opportunity in the commandment, deceived me and by it killed me.
>
> (διὰ τῆς ἐντολῆς ἐξηπάτησέν με καὶ δι' αὐτῆς ἀπέκτεινεν)

The reference to Gen. 3.13 is plain, though not quite as specific as in 2 Cor. 11.2–3. The important thing to note is that here sin performs the function which the serpent-devil performs in 2 Cor. 11, and that this is essentially the same event as is referred to in Rom. 5.12:

> Therefore as sin came into the world through one man and death through sin . . .,

except that here the event is extended so as to cover the arrival of the Law as well. Paul has used his own experience as a paradigm for that of mankind. The powers of evil are here using the Law (he calls it ἐντολή in the text, but associates it with νόμος in the next verse) as an instrument of destruction: the means by which the powers of evil kill is the Law. So the notion of evil powers using the Torah is not confined to Colossians. It is there in the background in Romans. The gap between the atonement doctrine of the two Epistles is not as great as has often been suggested.

Nearly all editors give cross references from Rom. 7.11 to 2 Cor. 11.1–3, 1 Tim. 2.14, and Gen 3.13. Michel also compares Heb. 3.13: 'that none of you may be hardened by the deceitfulness of sin'. Several scholars note the identity of sin and the devil here (e.g. Lipsius and Sanday and Headlam). Dodd writes: 'The description of the fall into sin in verses 9–11 reads like an allegorical interpretation of the Fall of Adam in Genesis.'[3] And Caird writes: 'It is remarkable how, in one passage after another in Paul's epistles, the law duplicates those functions which we have seen elsewhere attributed to Satan.'[4] Leenhardt suggests that the Law was really part of God's goodness. 'Instead of receiving the law as a sign of God's goodness, man takes exception to the word of God as to an arbitrary fiat.' This hardly hits off Paul's meaning: the Torah as such was not the word of God in the way Paul understands it. Paul does not portray man here as the rebel against God, but as the helpless victim of the moral predicament. S-B quote a midrash that the voice which uttered the Torah on Sinai went forth in two forms: it killed all who did not receive it and gave life to the Israelites because they did receive it. We may therefore proceed to examine Col. 2.14–15 in the assurance that the thought expressed there is continuous with the thought of the Galatians passage.

It is an exceptionally obscure and difficult couple of verses, so we must quote it in both Greek and English:

> ... ἐξαλείψας τὸ καθ' ἡμῶν χειρόγραφον τοῖς δόγμασιν ὃ ἦν
> ὑπεναντίον ἡμῖν, καὶ αὐτὸ ἦρκεν ἐκ τοῦ μέσου προσηλώσας αὐτὸ
> v. 15  τῷ σταυρῷ· ἀπεκδυσάμενος τὰς ἀρχὰς καὶ τὰς ἐξουσίας ἐδειγ-
> μάτισεν ἐν παρρησίᾳ, θριαμβεύσας αὐτοὺς ἐν αὐτῷ.

> ... having cancelled the bond which stood against us with
> its legal demands; this he set aside, nailing it to the cross.
> v. 15  He disarmed the principalities and powers, and made a
> public example of them, triumphing over them in him.

It will clarify matters if we begin by setting out the four main questions which this passage seems to pose. It will enable us the better to classify the various solutions which have been put forward by scholars.

1. Who is the subject of the long sentence, beginning in verse 13 with the verb συνεζωοποίησεν and carrying through at least to the end of verse 14? It may be taken for granted that the subject of ἀπεκδυσάμενος is the same as the subject of ἦρκεν.

2. What does ἀπεκδυσάμενος mean, and what is its object?

3. Does ἐδειγμάτισεν imply exemplary punishment?

4. Does ἐν αὐτῷ in verse 15 refer to Christ or to the cross?

We may add the note that those who answer Question 1 by saying 'God the Father' will answer Question 4 by saying 'Christ'.

Next we must make a suggestion which if it is correct points in the direction of certain solutions to these questions and away from others. This is the suggestion that behind Col. 2.14–15 lies the LXX of Num. 25.1–5. As it is not a very well-known passage, it should be quoted in full:

v. 1  While Israel dwelt in Shittim the people began to play the harlot with the daughters of Moab. These invited the
v. 2  people to the sacrifices of their gods, and the people ate, and bowed down to their gods. So Israel yoked himself to Baal
v. 3  of Peor. And the anger of the Lord was kindled against Israel; and the Lord said to Moses, 'Take all the chiefs of
v. 4  the people, and hang them in the sun before the Lord, that the fierce anger of the Lord may turn away from Israel.
v. 5  And Moses said to the judges of Israel: 'Every one of you slay his men who have yoked themselves to Baal of Peor.

The LXX does not differ greatly from the MT. As far as concerns our inquiry the interesting points are first, its rendering of 'chiefs of the people' in verse 4: ἀρχηγοὺς τοῦ λαοῦ; it does not render 'judges' in verse 5 with κριταί, its usual word for the Hebrew shoph^atim, but with φυλαῖς 'the tribes of Israel'. This means that the only rulers referred to in the passage as found in the LXX are the guilty leaders of Israel. Secondly, we may note that the LXX renders 'hang them up' in the same verse with παραδειγμάτισον. This forms the most obvious link with our Colossians passage, in view of ἐδειγμάτισεν in Col. 2.15. The Hebrew verb thus translated, hōqa' is from a root YQ'. In the Qal it can mean 'sprain, dislocate' (it is used of Jacob's thigh in Gen. 32.25), but in the Hiph'il, as here, it means 'expose'. The LXX uses παραδειγματίζω again in Jer. 13.22 for Hebrew chāmas ('suffer violence') apparently in the sense 'be put to open shame'. So also in Ezek. 28.17 for the Hebrew verb R'H (RSV 'to feast their eyes on you'). It is used in the LXX of Dan. 2.5 to mean 'you shall be punished in an exemplary fashion', where Theodotion translates 'you shall be for destruction' (there is no corresponding Aramaic). The noun παραδειγματισμός occurs twice in 3 Maccabees: in 4.11 it means 'a gazing stock' and in 7.14 'put them to death with ignominy'. Symmachus uses the noun in Ps. 31 (30). 21, perhaps for the vox nihili rukh^asē which may represent r^akhilē 'slander'. The idea of exemplary punishment is therefore definitely included in the meaning of this word. παραδειγματίζω is used only once in the New Testament, Heb. 6.6, but there very significantly: apostates 'crucify the

Son of God on their own account and hold him up to contempt'. Schlier quotes δειγμsατίζω from the *Acts of Peter and Paul* as meaning 'put to open shame'. He thinks that in Col. 2.15 it has the meaning 'bring to light' not in the sense of a proclamation but in that Christ manifested before the universe who was stronger. He says that παραδειγματίζω is often used in secular Greek for 'make an example of, punish'. The passage in Hebrews could really be looked on as a link between Num. 25.4 and Col. 2.15 since the word in Hebrews is identical with the word used in the LXX of Numbers and with the sense of the word used in Colossians.[5] δειγματίζω is not used in the LXX, but occurs in one other place in the New Testament, Matt. 1.19: Joseph does not want to 'make a public example' of his wife.[6]

With this clue to guide us, we find, as so often happens, a whole series of details that fall in with Paul's interpretation. It is the rulers who are publicly punished in this way, and it is the rulers who are the objects of ἐδειγμάτισεν in Col. 2.15 (ἀρχὰς καὶ ἐξουσίας). If we read on a little in Numbers, we find that in the next incident, the story of Phinehas' zeal, both Zimri and Cozbi, slain as an atonement by Phinehas (the LXX uses the word ἐξιλάσατο in Num. 25.13), are connected with the rulers. The LXX makes Zimri himself a ruler, and Cozbi is the daughter of a ruler of the Midianites (ἄρχων in each case; see Num. 25.14–15). Paul would presumably take the passage as a type of Christ's victory over the hostile powers. If so, Moses is here a type of Christ, unusual with Paul but not unparalleled. The hanging up of the rulers, or exposing them, is an act of atonement whereby God's wrath is averted in Numbers. Paul never speaks of Christ's death averting the wrath of God, it is true, but the general parallel of an act of atonement stands.

Another point that would appeal to Paul is that the rulers are condemned for idolatry. This element in the incident is strongly emphasized in the rabbinic midrash on the passage. In one passage in the Talmud a vivid account of the idolatry at Baal Peor is given, in the course of which one of the harlots says to an Israelite youth: 'I will not leave thee e'er thou hast denied the Torah of Moses thy teacher.'[7] Now in Gal. 4.8 Paul identifies the powers to which his converts were formerly subject as 'beings that by nature are no gods'. This in itself suggests that they had claimed divine honours; they seem to be

identical with τὰ στοιχεῖα τοῦ κόσμου in Gal. 4.3, a phrase
which links Galatians with Colossians. We shall be arguing
presently that this phrase must refer to the elemental powers.
Philo refers to this incident in three places: he connects the
idolatry perhaps with the mystery cults, for he says that the
revellers at Baal Peor were 'initiated into pagan rites' (τελου-
μένους τὰς μυθικὰς τελετάς).[8] He has, of course, an allegorical
interpretation as well, supported by an absurd etymology.

The Targum of Palestine on Num. 25.1–5 is of particular
interest for our purpose. Apparently this Targum sometimes
contains older material than does the Targum of Onkelos. The
Targum of Palestine paraphrases as follows:[9]

> And the people of the house of Israel joined themselves to Baala-
> Peor, like the nail in the wood, which is not separated but by
> breaking up the wood. And the anger of the Lord was kindled
> against Israel. And the Lord said to Moseh, Take all the chiefs
> of the people, and appoint them for judges, and let them give
> judgement to put to death the people who have gone astray after
> Peor, and hang them before the word of the Lord upon the wood
> over against the morning sun, and at the departure of the sun take
> them down and bury them, and turn away the strong anger of the
> Lord against Israel.

This passage certainly shows a tendency to link this incident
with Deut. 21.23, since it brings in both the mention of the
wood on which the criminals are to be hung and the emphasis
on the need to bury them at sunset. Deut. 21.23 is the verse
quoted in Gal. 3.13, so that this Targum suggests a link between
the Galatians passage and the Colossians passage. It is very
tempting indeed to think that Paul actually knew of this Targum, or the tradition that lay behind it, and that this explains
in part at least why he writes about Christ (for so we interpret
him) nailing the bond to the cross. The act of redemption reversed the act of trespass at Baal Peor. If this is too speculative,
at least the Targum provides clear evidence that Num. 25.1–5
and Deut. 21.23 were connected in rabbinic tradition, and
therefore confirms our suggestions that Paul had Num. 25.1–5
in mind when he wrote this passage in Colossians.

When the Targum goes on to the next incident, Phinehas'
act of expiation, it provides a remarkable piece of *Haggada*
elaborating the scripture narrative. Phinehas is represented as

transfixing his two victims with his lance and bearing them aloft: 'When he bare them aloft, the lintel was uplifted for him until he had gone forth. He carried them through the whole camp, six miles, without fatigue. He held them up by his right arm, in sight of their kindred, who had no power to hurt him. The lance was made strong, so as not to be broken with the load. The iron transpierced them, but was not withdrawn. An angel came and made bare their corpses in sight of the people' (Etheridge, pp. 434–5). Here surely is a remarkable example of both ἐδειγμάτισεν ἐν παρρησίᾳ and θριαμβεύσας αὐτοὺς ἐν αὐτῷ. It is not at all far-fetched to suggest that Paul was acquainted with the tradition enshrined in this passage, and had it in mind as he wrote Col. 2.14–15.

If therefore we are right in connecting Num. 25.1–5 with Col. 2.14–15, a number of controversial points would seem to have received at least a provisional solution. It is Christ who is the subject of at least verses 14 and 15, for it is he who through the process of crucifixion has won the victory over the rulers. ἀπεκδυσάμενος must be given some meaning consonant with Christ conquering the rulers, though we must not (at this stage at least) be dogmatic as to how, precisely, the crucifixion brought this about. ἐδειγμάτισεν must have the sense of exemplary punishment, as in the RSV translation, and not merely of proclamation. P. Vallisoleto (see n. 22 below) points out that the Syriac, Armenian, and Gothic versions all translate with a word meaning 'put to shame', though he does not himself adopt this meaning. And ἐν αὐτῷ must mean 'in the cross' not 'in Christ'.

But we have still to examine that strange phrase τὰ στοιχεῖα τοῦ κόσμου used in Gal. 4.3,9 and Col. 2.8,20. The great majority of modern editors seem to accept the conclusion that this phrase must mean 'hostile powers regarded as capable of determining human destiny by astral influence'. Exceptions to this can be found, of course: Kurze in an article published in 1921 challenged anyone to produce an example in Paul's day of στοιχεῖον meaning a spirit free from matter;[10] and much more recently in an extensive and weighty work Bandstra has rejected the usual modern interpretation.[11] Nobody has as yet taken up Kurze's challenge and Bandstra questions whether in Paul's day the word could mean 'astral spirit', though it certainly could mean 'heavenly body'. On the other hand, Kurze's second contention, that evidence of angel worship among the Jews is later than Paul's day, must be regarded as rendered doubtful by the evidence of the Qumran documents. The sectaries, though they did not worship angels, showed an interest in angels which later rabbinic tradition regarded as unhealthy, witness the rabbinic ban on speculations about Ezekiel's chariot vision. Bandstra thinks that the στοιχεῖα τοῦ κόσμου are 'the ineffectual precepts of the law, human philosophy'. But he agrees that in Col. 2.14–16 Paul does describe the angelic powers as conquered by Christ.

Despite Bandstra's objections, it seems impossible to resist the conclusion that by τὰ στοιχεῖα τοῦ κόσμου Paul did mean elemental powers. As long ago as 1896 Hincks pointed out that the author of Hebrews could describe angels as 'flames of fire' (quoting Ps. 104.4).[12] But fire was one of the elements (στοιχεῖα). It was not therefore a big step from an angel made of one of the elements to an angel (fallen) identified by a term for 'element'. Hatch found a reference in a Syriac book written early in the third century A.D. where the word corresponding to τὰ στοιχεῖα means 'the elemental powers' identified with οἱ ἄρχοντες.[13] And Macgregor cites a papyrus in which the moon-goddess is described as στοιχεῖον ἄφθαρτον.[14] He is quite sure that Paul represents these powers as having crucified Christ.

Commentators on Colossians must of course attempt to answer the question: Who is the subject of these two verses? It is indeed a most perplexing question because no one could deny that God the Father must be the subject of συνεζωοποίησεν in verse 13; no other subject is indicated right to the end of verse 15: but could Paul really have meant that the Father wiped away the bond, took it out of the way, nailed it to the cross, stripped himself of the powers (or spoiled the powers), made a public example of them, and triumphed over them in Christ? Put crudely like that it seems sheer patripassionism. However, a number of editors have bravely accepted this conclusion: obviously this is how the RSV text takes it, though the margin with its alternative translation of ἐν αὐτῷ as 'in it' suggests either that the translators were willing to contemplate a thoroughgoing patripassionism or that Christ might be the subject of verse 15. Von Soden and apparently Abbott[15] also follow this interpretation. Lohmeyer is emphatically on this side. But he has an interpretation peculiar to himself, as he sees the whole passage as an enthronement: the cross is not a battlefield but a throne-room; so ἐδειγμάτισεν must be taken as referring to the proclamation of an enthronement.[16] Dibelius follows the same interpretation as far as the question of the subject is concerned:[17] it is God who is the subject of ἀπεκδυσά-μενος, which he translates 'spoiled'. But he does not follow Lohmeyer's translation of ἐδειγμάτισεν, rendering it '*hat er zum Spott gemacht*'.

Many editors however agree that there must be a change of subject in the middle of this passage. The obvious point to make the change is at ἐξαλείψας, though Lightfoot postpones it till ἦρκεν.[18] He connects δόγματα with δογματίζεσθε of Col. 2.20, takes ἀπεκδυσάμενος as 'having stripped off and put away the powers of evil', and translates ἐδειγμάτισεν as 'displayed as victor'. Moule gives a very honest and judicious account of the difficulties and concludes: 'Perhaps we must acknowledge an illogical transition from one [subject] to the other in the course of this sentence.'[19] He translates: 'Divesting himself of the rulers and authorities, he boldly displayed them.' Robinson argues strongly for 'the flesh' to be understood as the object of ἀπεκδυσάμενος and for taking ἀρχάς and ἐξουσίας as the object of ἐδειγμάτισεν only: 'The dying Jesus, like a king, divests himself of that flesh, the tool and medium of their power, and thereby exposes them to ridicule for their pyrrhic victory.'[20]

A strong argument in Robinson's favour is the occurrence of ἀπέκδυσις τοῦ σώματος τῆς σαρκός in Col. 2.11 and ἀπεκδυσά-μενοι τὸν παλαιὸν ἄνθρωπον in 3.9. On the other hand, the tenor of the whole passage seems to demand that the powers should be the object of Christ's victory on the cross. It may be best therefore to take ἀπεκδυσάμενος as meaning 'throwing off the powers', with the words 'by means of throwing off the flesh' understood. Paul does not clearly differentiate between sin and flesh which sin has gained control of. Christ threw off in one mighty cast the flesh, sin, death, the devil, and all the hostile powers. Several editors (Lightfoot, Moule) have suggested the influence here of the vision of the High-Priest Joshua in Zech. 3.1–10. In favour of this is the coincidence of names: New Testament writers are perfectly capable of seeing a connection here. It must also be admitted that the action is similar: Joshua is stripped of his soiled garments. But there is a remarkable absence of verbal connections: 'Remove the filthy garments' in Zech. 3.4 is translated ἀφέλετε in the LXX. ἀπεκδύω and ἀποδύω do not occur in the LXX at all: ἐκδύω does, but not in this passage; and there is no evidence that other versions used the word or a cognate here. Also Joshua in this vision is too passive to be a satisfactory type of Christ: this could not be called Joshua's victory.

A brief article written more than sixty years ago seems to me to throw some useful light on the meaning of ἀπεκδυσάμενος. Rutherford suggests a link with Ps. 40.²¹ He quotes verse 12:

For evils have encompassed me without number;
my iniquities have overtaken me, till I cannot see.

The LXX translates 'evils' with a neuter plural κακά, but in verse 14 the evils have turned into people. Verses 14 and 15 contain a plea that all the psalmist's enemies should be put to shame. There are no verbal echoes here, but we know that Ps. 40 was considered messianic by some New Testament writers (cf. Heb. 10.5–10). Paul was perfectly capable of regarding this part of Ps. 40 as the Messiah's plea that his enemies should be put to shame, a plea vindicated in the cross and resurrection.

It is worth while pointing to the testimony of Ephesians about this difficult passage. In the parallel passage to Col. 2.13–15 it is quite plain that the author of Ephesians regards Christ as the subject of verses 14–15, and the object of this action is 'the enmity' (see Eph. 2.14–16). This looks more like the powers than the flesh, if we must choose between them. We regard the author of Ephesians as Paul's disciple, but his testimony must be given due weight. He is at least as likely to know what Paul meant as we are.

In the central problem connected with this passage, the question of the subject of verses 13–15, perhaps it might be allowable to propose a compromise solution: Paul throughout is thinking in terms of God-in-Christ. Later on we shall be suggesting that there are other passages in Paul where this is probably the right solution. Strictly speaking no doubt we must say that in verse 13 God the Father is the subject, and in verses 14–15 Christ. But the transition is possible for Paul precisely because he believed that throughout the redemptive events it was God in Christ who was acting. Larsson seems to have this in mind when he writes of this passage: 'Gott handelt in Christus und durch ihn.'[22] Kennedy well compares 1 Cor. 15.24, where it is Christ who is described as 'destroying every rule and every authority and every power' (πᾶσαν ἀρχὴν καὶ πᾶσαν ἐξουσίαν καὶ πᾶσαν δύναμιν).[23] This refers to the parousia, of course, but the process is inaugurated by the cross and resurrection. Finally in this context we might mention Megas' interesting article:[24] he rejects the notion that the χειρόγραφον of verse 14 is a description of a victory, like a τίτλος borne in a Roman triumph; nor is it like the placard on the cross naming the victim's crime: it is the bond symbolizing mankind's slavery to the powers. Christ has nailed it to the cross and thereby annulled it. Christ, he says, conquered the powers on the cross and nailed to it their chief weapon.

This brings us to the last point that must be made here, the connection between Christ's victory and the Law. There seems little doubt that there is a connection in the Colossians passage between the overthrow of the powers and the annulment of the power of the Law. This conclusion depends on interpreting the word δόγμασιν in 2.14 as a reference to the prescriptions of the Law. As far as I know, only Lohmeyer among modern editors rejects this conclusion. He argues that elsewhere in the New Testament the word is only used of the decrees of pagan powers. Is is true that both Philo and Josephus use the word for the detailed precepts of the Torah, but this, says Lohmeyer, is only because they are writing for Greeks. We cannot help suspecting, however, that Lohmeyer is unduly influenced by his 'enthronement' theory, and Eph. 2.15, which paraphrases with τὸν νόμον τῶν ἐντολῶν ἐν δόγμασιν, is a strong argument against Lohmeyer's view. It is indeed true that in the back of Paul's mind was probably the thought that what corresponded among the Gentiles to the Torah as a paralysing force was the direct influence of the powers operating through pagan deities. Larsson quotes Percy as maintaining that the δόγματα correspond in the realm of cosmological forces *vis à vis* the Gentiles to the Torah *vis à vis* the Jews,[25] but Larsson himself thinks that we cannot make out so neat a scheme in the Pauline Epistles. The powers had made use of the Torah as their instrument; if Paul had ever clearly expounded the question, no doubt he would have done so in terms of his discussion in Rom. 2 of the relation of the Gentiles to Law: the Gentiles' moral code, normally supported by the sanction of the divinities they worshipped, would be the instrument whereby the powers ruled them.

Into the question of whether Paul regards the evil powers as reconciled as well as defeated, we do not propose to enter. C. K. Barrett[26] and G. B. Caird (op. cit., p. 28) hold very firmly that they are reconciled, on the basis of such passages as Col. 1.16 and 20 and Eph. 3.10. The powers, they say, have been created, conquered, and reconciled (or are being reconciled). On the other hand, in Eph. 6.12 Christians are still wrestling against hostile powers; and it is difficult to make sense of the thought that death will be reconciled, if death is to be treated as a hostile power. The type of Num. 25.1–5 would rather point in the direction of the powers being abolished. But if this view is taken a distinction must be made between the powers and 'things on earth or in heaven'.

Thus we have in fact in this obscure passage a magnificent exposition of the central paradox of Christianity. God in Christ has laid himself open to the utmost that all hostile powers could do to him. He has been born into our history and accepted all the constraints and limitations which that implied. In one sense therefore it was the powers who crucified Christ (1 Cor. 2.8). But the paradox lies in the fact that in the deepest sense of all it was God in Christ who conquered the powers, crucified them, put them to death. What looked like the victory of evil was in fact the great victory of God in Christ over the devil, of light over darkness, of life over death. We may well quote John Donne:

> One short sleep past, we wake eternally,
> And death shall be no more, death, thou shalt die.[27]

# 2

# THE REPROACH
# AND VINDICATION OF
# THE MESSIAH

I

C. K. Barrett writes on p. 122 of his commentary on Romans:[1] 'The "messianic affliction" was probably the starting point of Paul's understanding of the cross, as it had been for Christians before him.' This indicates that our theme was not invented or discovered by Paul. C. H. Dodd seems to make the same assumption, when he points out that the citation of Ps. 69.9 by both Paul and John shows that the application of this text to Jesus probably antedates both these writers.[2] Grässer has pointed out quite recently that in the Epistle to the Hebrews all the details of Jesus' sufferings can be paralleled in the Psalms. But he is careful to add that this is no proof that they were invented by the early Christians.[3] We hope to bring plenty of evidence to confirm the view that the reproach of the Messiah was not 'discovered' by Paul as we look at Paul's treatment of the reproach theme. But it is important to realize that the early Christians did not invent the theme of the reproach of the Messiah. It seems to have been already there in the tradition of Judaism. What the first Christians did was to expand it and give it historical and theological content.

We can find this theme in the Midrash on the Psalms. This Midrash in its present form, of course, comes from a time far later than that of the New Testament; but the very fact that, even after a long period of anti-Christian polemic, the Midrash

contains this theme despite its apparent confirmation of Christian claims, suggests powerfully that it was an ancient and deeply
rooted tradition in the rabbinic exegesis of the Psalms. Thus one
rabbi says of Ps. 16.4 ('Those who choose another god multiply
their sorrows') that suffering is divided into three portions, one
received by the Patriarchs and all generations of men; one
received by the generation that lived under Hadrian; and one
to be received by the Messiah.[4] Ps. 89.50–1 ('the insults . . .
with which they mock the footsteps of thine anointed') is of
course interpreted to mean that the Messiah will be reviled.[5]
And Ps. 90.15 ('Make us glad as many days as thou hast
afflicted us') is explained in terms of 'as in the days of our
afflicted one', i.e. as in the days of the Messiah.[6]

Much nearer contemporary evidence is provided by the
*Hodayoth* of the Qumran Community. In Column iv, 10–11, the
author of the Hymns writes of 'the preachers of lies and seers of
deceit' as follows: 'They have withheld the draught of knowledge from the thirsty ones and for their thirst they make them
drink vinegar, so that they may gaze upon their error, etc.'[7]
The reference to vinegar comes from Ps. 69.21, one of the
reproach psalms. Indeed the citation comes from a passage
which is full of reproach:

> Thou knowest my reproach,
>     and my shame and my dishonour . . .
> Insults have broken my heart,
>     so that I am in despair (Ps. 69.19–20).

Unless this is a purely literary echo, which we have no right to
assume, the author of the *Hodayoth* is implying that the Qumran
Sect is the messianic community, to which messianic prophecies
can be applied. In this respect he differs from the early Christians, who only apply reproach passages to the Church if they are
already understood as applying *par excellence* to Christ (this is of
course the point of Rom. 15.3f). Indeed it seems clear that in
*Hodayoth* iv the psalm reference does not apply to the author,
leader (we must assume) of the community where he wrote,
since he has not been led astray by the false brothers. But the
messianic reference seems plain enough.

In order to explain why we are concerned with most of the
passages which we examine in this chapter, we have set out

below the connections between the two 'reproach' Psalms, 68
and 89, and the New Testament:

| | |
|---|---|
| Hebrews 13.11 | Psalm 69.7 |
| John 2.17 | 69.9a |
| Romans 15.3 | 69.9b |
| Romans 11.9 | 69.22–3 |
| Acts 1.20a | 69.25 |
| Romans 8.19–20 | 89.47 |
| Hebrews 11.26 | 89.50–1 |

We begin with Rom. 15.3. I have already given some attention to this citation in *Jesus Christ in the Old Testament*, pp. 153–5.
What I said there in effect was that Paul regards this verse from
the Psalms as an utterance of the pre-existent Messiah; that it
is not torn from its context and arbitrarily applied, but understood very much as a part of its context, even though that understanding is very different from what we today would regard as
correct; and that the verse is also quoted in the Fourth Gospel.
Consequently, we need not spend much time on the direct
consideration of Rom. 15.3, but, after reviewing what the
commentators have made of it, we will pass on to a consideration of the catena of citations in Rom. 3.

Rom. 15.3 runs as follows:

For Christ did not please himself; but, as it is written, 'The
reproaches of those who reproached thee fell upon me'.

οἱ ὀνειδισμοὶ τῶν ὀνειδιζόντων σε ἐπέπεσαν ἐπ' ἐμέ.

Paul exactly reproduces the LXX of Ps. 68.10 (69.9 in RSV
and 69.10 in MT). It is interesting to observe that we have
here in Rom. 15.3 an instance of the *deus absconditus* theme
which we find elsewhere in Paul, notably in 1 Cor. 2.6–10.
Those who insulted Christ were in fact insulting God, though
they did not recognize it. In the days of his flesh as in the time
of his glory, faith is necessary in order to recognize the Messiah.

Hans Windisch refers to Rom. 15.3 as a passage where Paul
cites the example of Jesus, but offers no word from the Lord,
only a quotation from the Psalms arbitrarily applied to Jesus,
and followed up by a list of *testimonia* about the salvation of the
heathen.[8] It is not, however, arbitrary in the sense that there is
no rationale behind it, or that the quotation is torn from its

context, as we shall be seeing. Lagrange denies that verse 3 is the proof for verse 1.[9] This is hardly the point: verse 3 is the proof of how Christ behaved, and the behaviour is the incentive for Christians. C. H. Dodd in his commentary on Romans suggests that 'Paul starts from the accepted position that the Psalm refers to Christ'. We would wish to make this more specific and say that the pre-existent Christ was believed to have uttered this verse of the psalm. Karl Barth has coined a phrase which hits it off nicely: '[Christ] passes through the Old Testament as the great Sufferer.'[10] C. K. Barrett's comment is also apt: 'The use of scripture at this point is significant. It means that the example of Christ is more than an example; it belongs to the pattern of revelation.' But it is Michel[11] who devotes most attention to the significance of the psalm quotation here: he thinks the psalm must have had a special significance in the early Church as the 'Leidenspsalm Jesu'; he emphasizes that σε must apply to God and not to one's neighbour, and he thinks that Paul sees in this psalm a prophecy of the words and work of Jesus, even 'a description of his way'. He adds that it is an open question whether the citation is understood as a direct word of Jesus or not. Lindars complains that the psalm quotation here does not really suit Paul's purpose.[12] This is, I believe, an impression which we gain if attention is confined to Ps. 69.10b. Once we look at the citation in a wider context we see how entirely suitable it must have been in Paul's eyes.

The passage Rom. 15.1–4 shows us how Paul regards the reproach of the Messiah. The reproach was described beforehand in Scripture by the pre-existent Christ who spoke through David in order to instruct and encourage us who live in the messianic age. We must now examine the catena of citations in Rom. 3.1–20, where we shall find that the reproach of the Messiah is also to be traced.

The catena in Rom. 3.10–20 is preceded by a few verses in the course of which Paul quotes Ps. 51. As this psalm according to my exegesis sets the note for the catena that follows, it may be as well to give first a paraphrase of Rom. 3.1–4; then to attempt to justify this interpretation, and only after that to proceed to examine the catena. I suggest therefore than the argument of Rom. 3.1–4 runs as follows:

'For the Jew circumcision does mark his privilege, that of being the trustee of God's oracles, those oracles from which God's whole character and future plan could have been learned. It is true that many Jews failed to understand this, but this does not discredit the faithfulness of God (τὴν πίστιν τοῦ Θεοῦ) who has carried out the promises contained in the oracles. On the contrary, God-in-Christ has proved right against the whole world, as is demonstrated in the cross and resurrection of Christ, and as was foretold in the oracles. When God was judged in Christ on the cross, he prevailed.'

Paul might think of the actual mechanism of Ps. 51.4 somewhat like this: the prophet David, inspired to express in this psalm his penitence for his adultery with Bathsheba and murder of Uriah, is moved by the Holy Spirit to speak also for all men to God and his Son about the judgement and victory of the cross and resurrection. That this is how Paul understands this verse from Ps. 51 is by no means self-evident, and we must produce the evidence.

We should first observe that immediately before the citation in Rom. 3.4 comes another reference to the Psalms. Paul writes:

What if some were unfaithful? Does their faithlessness nullify the faithfulness of God? By no means! Let God be true, though every man be false.

The Greek of the last sentence is

γινέσθω δὲ ὁ Θεὸς ἀληθής, πᾶς δὲ ἄνθρωπος ψεύστης.

This is an echo of Ps. 116.11, which RSV renders:

I said in my consternation,
'Men are all a vain hope'.

This is very unlike Paul's words but the LXX (115.2) runs:

ἐγὼ εἶπα ἐν τῇ ἐκστάσει μου
Πᾶς ἄνθρωπος ψεύστης.

This is no passing echo of Paul's for he quotes the previous verse of this psalm also in a very significant passage in 2 Cor. 4.13: Ἐπίστευσα, διὸ ἐλάλησα, 'I believed, and so I spoke'. There also the LXX is far from the meaning of the Hebrew. But the point is that there Paul in all probability takes the verse from Ps. 116 as an utterance of the Messiah, an utterance of faith in God's salvation.[13] In the context of the psalm the humiliation of the psalmist so emotionally expressed would be taken as referring to the passion. This interpretation fits well into the context of Rom. 3.1–4. What shows up all men as liars is the cross of Christ. The echo of Ps. 116 prepares for the more explicit reference to God's victorious judgement that follows.

Paul then quotes Ps. 51.4 (MT 51.6; LXX 50.6):

> That thou mayest be justified in thy words,
> and prevail when thou art judged.

The Greek is

> ὅπως ἂν δικαιωθῇς ἐν τοῖς λόγοις σου
> καὶ νικήσεις ἐν τῷ κρίνεσθαί σε.

Paul exactly reproduces the LXX. The LXX translator seems to have misunderstood the meaning of the infinitive construct *b*ª*shophteka* and taken it as passive 'when thou art judged' instead of active. The RSV quite correctly translates the MT as:

> so that thou art justified in thy sentence
> and blameless in thy judgement.

The νικήσεις of the LXX seems to be based on the Aramaic meaning of Z K H, 'conquer', whereas in Hebrew it means 'be clear' (*sic* S-B). The quotation is very purposefully introduced: it is adduced as proof of the statement: 'Let God be true though every man be false'. The wider context in Romans is one in which all men, Jews and Gentiles equally, are reduced to the same level under the judgement of God and therefore in need of his mercy. The echo of Ps. 116 has pointed to the cross, and some objective event, some world crisis, is needed in order to prove God right over against all men. Only the cross and resurrection can do this. If so, we must expect the indictment which follows in the catena of 3.10–20 to present the same feature, a reference to the judgement of the cross. One might see a connection between the λόγοι of the citation and the λόγια ('oracles') of 3.2. God has been vindicated in his words, because the prophetic oracles have been fulfilled in the life, death and resurrection of Christ. This is how Sanday and Headlam[14] take it: 'St Paul applies it [the citation] as if the Most High himself were put upon trial and declared guiltless in respect of the promises which he has fulfilled.' Michel and Leenhardt[15] also take τοῖς λόγοις as referring to τὰ λόγια. This implies that Paul understands the two quotations as uttered by different speakers: 'I said in my haste,[16] All men are liars!' is uttered by the pre-existent Messiah to God. The two lines from Ps. 51 are uttered by the prophet David to God concerning the cross and resurrection of Christ, in which God was vindicated.

The rabbinic commentators all interpret the verse in terms of God's vindication: S-B quote one rabbi to the effect that David says to God: 'I did it [his adultery with Bathsheba] so that thou mayest be proved right,' and then cites Gen. 8.21, 'the imagination of man's heart is evil from his youth'. In another passage the theory is put forward that every man after death has to sign a document in which all his deeds are recorded. He also says to God, 'You have judged me well.' All this is done in order to fulfil the words of Ps. 51.4.[17] The Midrash on the Psalms has the parable of a man who comes to a doctor with a broken leg: the doctor exclaims at the extent of the break, and the man says: 'It is all done for your benefit.' The greater the cure, the greater the fee. So David says he sinned for God's sake, so that all men might see the extent of God's mercy to the penitent. This text is then linked with Isa. 55.3–4, where there is first a reference to God's steadfast love for David, then Israel (or the servant) is given for a witness to the peoples. Thus David is a witness to God's mercy (Midrash 1, 472–3). This interpretation is particularly interesting, as it joins the vindication of God with a hint of the fulfilment of his promises. But it must be said that on the whole the rabbis seem to be doing with the text very much what Paul thinks he is doing with it, letting the wickedness of man show the justice of God (Rom. 3.5). Lagrange actually translates ὅπως δικαιωθῇς as 'that you may be recognized as just'.

This interpretation of Paul's use of Ps. 51 is confirmed by Lyonnet in an excellent article on the use of the *Miserere* here.[18] The psalm is used here, he says, in order to show that God is constant to his promises, while it is man who is false. The meaning of 'righteousness' and cognate words throughout this passage must be regarded as salvific not retributive. He points out that the LXX translation has helped out Paul's meaning, for it translates the MT *b^adobhr^aka*, 'in thy speaking', as plural 'in thy words'.[19] He points to verse 14 of the psalm:

> Deliver me from bloodguiltiness, O God,
>     thou God of my salvation,
> and my tongue will sing aloud of thy deliverance.

LXX is

ῥῦσαί με ἐξ αἱμάτων, ὁ Θεὸς ὁ Θεὸς τῆς σωτηρίας μου·
ἀγαλλιάσεται ἡ γλῶσσά μου τὴν δικαιοσύνην σου,

words which Paul would interpret of God's saving righteousness in Christ. Lyonnet makes the admirable observation that in the Bible God's righteousness is shown not in contrast to his mercy, but by means of it. This interpretation of Paul's use of the two psalm quotations cannot, it is true, be demonstratively proved, but it explains why Paul seems to give them so much emphasis and it fits in with everything else we know about Paul's theology.

The section Rom. 3.5–9 gives us the transition from this general condemnation of all men implied in Ps. 51.4 to the specific condemnation of the Jews which is contained in the catena. In fact Paul changes the persons about whom he is speaking with bewildering speed, no matter what interpretation we take of the section. I suggest the following:

v. 4   'all men are liars', uttered by the Messiah about the whole of humanity. The one exception, of course, is the Messiah himself. After all, even if this verse is taken as referring only to the psalmist, he excepts himself from this general judgement.

v. 5   'our wickedness'; the wickedness of all men.

v. 7   'my falsehood'; the speaker is an imaginary objector, very probably a Jew, but it must apply to all men.

v. 8   'As some people slanderously charge us with saying'; 'us' must refer to Paul and his companions in the mission.

v. 9   'Are we Jews any better off?' I think this is the right translation of that disputed word προεχόμεθα. Paul. having shown the general condemnation of mankind, is now about to use the catena to show the equal condemna- of the Jews. This does not rule out the possibility, as we shall be seeing, that the elemental powers may be con- demned also. But Paul would regard them as having used the Torah and its official guardians as their instrument.

Various suggestions have been made as to how this catena is structured, of which Leenhardt gives a useful number of examples. He says that A. Feuillet has suggested a scheme whereby the catena is intended to cover the whole human frame, throat, tongue, lips, mouth, feet. But if the catena is aimed at Jews as against Gentiles, this would seem to have little point. Others see a threefold scheme: (*a*) corruption in relation to God (verses 10–12); (*b*) corruption in the human personality itself (verses 13–14); (*c*) corruption in human relations (verses 15–17). But this does not work out neatly, since verse 13ab would be more appropriate in section (*c*); and anyway the citation in verse 18 is about relation to God. Michel has a similar division: sin against God, sin against fellow man, sin against themselves. None of these schemata is quite convincing, however. Equally diverse are the views as to the origin of the catena: Leenhardt thinks it is a sort of psalm in use among the Pauline communities. C. K. Barrett suggests that Paul drew it from an already existing *florilegium*. It is not very clear what general use such a *florilegium* would have in the early Christian community, though we can see its specific use in Romans. Michel, on the contrary, insists that this catena was collected by Paul and adapted to his theme, and not taken from a *florilegium*—a view to which we incline in view of the exposition we give of it below.[20] He describes it in his commentary as 'eine feierliche Klage-Liturgie', and calls it an early Christian psalm which shows traces of careful composition. He entirely agrees that the aim of the catena is to indict the Jews. Most significant of all is his comment: 'The end-time is a decisive element in the compilation.'

We may now proceed to comment on the elements in the catena, which we find to be seven in all. Is this a significant number, indicating perfection?

10   'None is righteous, no, not one;'

This does not correspond exactly to anything from the Psalms, and should probably be regarded as a title, or perhaps a statement of the theme. This is borne out by Paul's use of δίκαιος. He uses it among existing persons only of God and (as we shall be arguing) of the Messiah. In 1.17 we will be applying ὁ δίκαιος to Christ. In 3.26 it is God who is δίκαιος; in 5.7: 'Why, one will hardly die for a righteous man' implies, of course, that there are no righteous. In 5.19 it is applied to Christ as contrasted with Adam. Thus we reach the conclusion that only one could say: 'None is righteous', and that was the Righteous One himself. We may expect the catena to be uttered by the Messiah. Michel takes this phrase as the title of the catena and verse 18 as the conclusion or result. Calvin quite appropriately describes the phrase in verse 10 as a 'summa'.

Now follow the seven citations:

1. οὐκ ἔστιν ὁ συνίων,
   οὐκ ἔστιν ὁ ἐκζητῶν τὸν Θεόν.
   πάντες ἐξέκλιναν, ἅμα ἠχρειώθησαν·
   οὐκ ἔστιν ποιῶν χρηστότητα
   οὐκ ἔστιν ἕως ἑνός.

   'no one understands, no one seeks for God.
   All have turned aside, together they have gone wrong;
   no one does good, not even one.'

Paul has here followed the LXX of Ps. 13.2b–3c pretty closely (MT Ps. 14.2b–3c). Commentators quote Ps. 53 also, but this is only a doublet of Ps. 14, and may be excluded from consideration. He leaves out the introductory words: 'God looked down from heaven to see', as being irrelevant to this purpose. It is possible that Paul echoes verse 7 of this psalm in 11.26: 'O that deliverance for Israel would come out of Zion!' but it is more likely that he had in mind Isa. 59.20–1. The main relevance of this citation is to state the theme: the Messiah, and he alone, can make so general an indictment. The Midrash on the doublet, Ps. 53, is interesting. It takes the last two lines of the citation in the sense: 'There is none that doeth good, no, not the one', and 'the one' is Abraham, on the basis of Ezek. 33.24 (Midrash I, 486). It intends to show that these words of condemnation do not apply to Abraham. If Paul knew of some such exegesis, perhaps he would find it easier to apply it to the Righteous One, the Messiah.

2. τάφος ἀνεῳγμένος ὁ λάρυγξ αὐτῶν
   ταῖς γλώσσαις αὐτῶν ἐδολιοῦσαν.

'Their throat is an open grave,
they use their tongues to deceive.'

Paul here exactly reproduces the LXX of Ps. 5.10cd. The psalm is the cry of an innocent sufferer for help against his enemies, and as such would fit in very well to the situation of Christ in his passion. Note especially verses 9 and 12–13, which we may translate from the LXX as follows:

9a   Lord, lead me in thy righteousness *(δικαιοσύνη)* because of mine enemies . . .
12a  And let all rejoice who hope on thee . . .
13a  because thou hast blessed the righteous *(δίκαιον)*.

This might be regarded as a reference to the Messiah's vindication in the resurrection. Could it be, perhaps, that Paul thought of the 'open grave' as a reference to death, that grave from which the Messiah was to rise? If so, the enemies are probably to be regarded as the elemental powers as well as the actual individuals who were immediately responsible for putting the Messiah to death. At any rate it is surely along some such lines as these that we are to seek for an understanding of Paul's Scripture citations here.

3.   ἰὸς ἀσπίδων ὑπὸ τὰ χείλη αὐτῶν
     'The venom of asps is under their lips.'

Paul exactly reproduces the LXX of Ps. 140.3b (LXX 139.4b). This psalm is very similar to the last, a plea for help from oppressors. It ends with the same expectation of deliverance, see LXX verses 13–14.

13a  I know that the Lord will perform the judgement of the poor man . . .
14a  But the righteous (οἱ δίκαιοι) shall praise thy name.

This would speak to Paul of the vindication of Christ. Indeed we can observe in these psalms the same feature as can be noted in the 'reproach' psalms, 22, 69 ,and 89; the cry of complaint ends on a note of praise. Paul is not therefore in these psalms giving a general condemnation of mankind, but is showing us the Messiah pronouncing the condemnation of those who have sought his destruction.

4. ὧν τὸ στόμα ἀρᾶς καὶ πικρίας γέμει

'Their mouth is full of curses and bitterness.'

This is a quotation from Ps. 9.28 in the LXX, 10.7 in the MT. This is because the LXX divides Pss. 9 and 10 differently from the MT. The LXX gives thirty-nine verses to Ps. 9 and seven verses to Ps. 10, whereas the MT gives twenty-one verses to Ps. 9 and eighteen verses to Ps. 10. The RSV follows the MT, except that it does not count the psalm title of Psalm 9 as a verse. Paul follows the LXX fairly accurately, but the LXX translation of the MT is curious. The Hebrew has three words to describe the contents of the wicked man's mouth, 'ālāh, mirmōth, and tōk, which the RSV translates as 'cursing, deceit, and oppression' respectively. LXX has reasonably rendered 'ālāh with ἀρά, but for mirmōth it has πικρία and for tōk it has δόλος. It would have been more accurate if it had reversed the last two. This psalm, like the two previously quoted, expresses the cry of the innocent sufferer for relief from oppression. But there are two features in it which might well have appealed to Paul. The first is the title. It must be remembered that in the LXX the citation belongs to Ps. 9, so the title of Ps. 9 could be significant. It runs 'To the choirmaster: according to *Mūth-labben*. A Psalm of David'. The LXX renders the first phrase as usual with εἰς τὸ τέλος. The second phrase is mysterious, as nobody knows what it means. The Hebrew is 'almūth labben. Koehler-Baumgartner describe this as 'an unexplained technical note'.[21] The LXX renders with ὑπὲρ τῶν κρυφίων τοῦ υἱοῦ 'concerning hidden things of the son', deriving it from the Hebrew verb 'L M 'to be concealed' and ben 'a son'.[22] It is difficult not to suspect that Paul would find in this title the promise of mysterious truths about the Son to be found in this psalm, and that this would predispose him to understand it as the utterance of the Messiah: 'the prophet David has inserted this note in order to warn us that important truths about the Son are hidden in this psalm'. The Midrash on the Psalms (1, 131f) provides the most extensive commentary on this mysterious psalm-title, offering a whole series of alternative solutions, and thereby showing, of course, how popular a subject of discussion it was among the rabbis. Our argument requires that Paul would have read this psalm in Greek only, both because only the LXX translation of the title would seem to point to Christian mysteries, and because only in the LXX does the verse he quotes belong to Ps. 9. So we may confine ourselves to those rabbinic speculations which seem closest to the LXX interpretation. We may mention three:

(a)   'faults hidden from a son', so it refers to Israel's unwilling sins. These are forgiven on the Day of Atonement. We may observe that this is virtually the same translation as that offered by the LXX.

(b)   'hidden for the son': God hid the day of comfort from David.

(c)   'concerning death for the son'; the son is Israel: it signifies the death Israel must die if he sins, but repentance will deliver him. If Paul had known this interpretation, it would certainly have appealed to him.

The other feature of this psalm worthy of note is the element of vindication in it. The LXX of 9.5a can be rendered:

Because thou hast brought about my judgement and my right.

and verse 14b has:

thou who liftest me up (ὁ ὑψῶν με) from the gates of death,

in which Paul would certainly see a reference to the resurrection of the Messiah. Altogether, therefore, this short psalm quotation must have provided Paul with a great deal of theological reflection.

5.   ὀξεῖς οἱ πόδες αὐτῶν ἐκχέαι αἷμα
      σύντριμμα καὶ ταλαιπωρία ἐν ταῖς ὁδοῖς αὐτῶν,
      καὶ ὁδὸν εἰρήνης οὐκ ἔγνωσαν

'Their feet are swift to shed blood,
in their paths are ruin and misery
and the way of peace they do not know.'

This is a quotation made up of phrases from Isa. 59.7–8 though not exactly reproducing it. We know that Paul was interested in this chapter of Isaiah, since he quotes 59.20 in Rom. 11.26. The chapter contains a very grim and realistic description of Israel's sinful condition, culminating in a confession of sin in the first person plural. Then comes a description of how God remedied this situation:

> v. 17   He put on righteousness as a breastplate,
>           and a helmet of salvation upon his head.

The description ends with the promise that God will come as a redeemer (verse 20, quoted by Paul in Rom. 11.26), and the prospect of a covenant in virtue of which God gives Israel his spirit. The whole chapter would be regarded by Paul as a description of God's saving action in Christ. The words he quotes come from that part of it which describes the darkness just before the dawn, and that is, after all, exactly what Paul is doing in this part of Rom. 3. His catena is meant to represent the darkness, so that the light of God's salvation may be seen all the clearer..

6.   οὐκ ἔστιν φόβος Θεοῦ ἀπέναντι τῶν ὀφθαλμῶν αὐτῶν
      'There is no fear of God before their eyes.'

Paul quotes Ps. 36.2b (MT); 35.2b (LXX); 36.1b (RSV). Paul differs from the LXX only in writing 'their eyes' for LXX 'his eyes', a point wherein the LXX is more faithful to the MT. We may guess that Paul puts in the plural because he still has the last citation in mind, and anyway is applying these verses to the Jews as a whole. Here too we find the plea of the sufferer for deliverance from oppression. Verses 10 and 11 are worth translating from the LXX:

> For with thee is the well of life,
>     and in thy light shall we see light.
> Extend thy mercy to those who know thee
>     and thy righteousness (δικαιοσύνη) to those who are upright
>     of heart.

Paul would see here a reference to the resurrection and to God's vindication of the Messiah.

Before examining the seventh citation, which leads us on to a consideration of the second chapter of Galatians, we might perhaps review the first six. In all of the passages from which these citations come we may legitimately discern three features: they describe the darkness before the dawn; they imply the existence of the Righteous One; and they refer to God's vindication of the Righteous One. They do therefore fit into Paul's theological scheme as unfolded in Romans.

Lagrange[23] remarks of this catena that Paul does not employ these words as a prophetic witness, but as a witness which agrees with what he wants to prove. He cites Theodore of Mopsuestia in confirmation of this view. We can only suggest that the ancient Father and the modern Dominican seem equally unwilling to take Paul's interpretation of Scripture seriously. Nygren's[24] comment on the catena is worth quoting: 'To him who stands against God salvation does not come from his vindication before God. It roots in the fact that he is condemned as wrong. God lets him become a liar and a sinner.' It is surprising, however, that Nygren does not relate this to the cross, as, we have argued. Paul does in this catena.

7.  οὐ δικαιωθήσεται πᾶσα σὰρξ ἐνώπιον αὐτοῦ·

For no human being will be justified in his sight.

This is from Ps. 143.2b (and so MT), LXX 142.2b. The LXX is a fair rendering of the Hebrew, but Paul has πᾶσα σάρξ for the more accurate LXX πᾶς ζῶν 'every living being'. It is a plea for rescue from an enemy, one who, following the LXX translation of verse 3c, has 'made me sit in dark places like those who have been long dead', and in verse 6 the LXX runs:

I have stretched forth my hands unto thee.

Then in verse 10 comes the confident hope:

thy good spirit will lead me in the upright land.

Here is plenty of scope for finding reference to the death and resurrection of Christ, even perhaps the actual crucifixion in the phrase 'I have stretched forth my hands'. This line from Ps. 143 is also quoted in the *Hodayoth* xvi. 11:

For I know that no man beside thee can be just.[25]

The citation occurs in the context of a very fine confession of complete reliance on God rather than on one's own achievement. But it is not related to the cosmic action of God, as Paul's citation is, and it seems to apply only to a spiritual élite. Nor does it accompany a rejection of the works of the Law. Quite the reverse, in fact.

More significant for our purpose is the fact that Ps. 143.2b is also cited by Paul in Gal. 2.16 in almost identical terms. A careful study of the whole passage Gal. 2.11–21 reveals in fact a remarkable parallelism with Rom. 3.1–20. In the Galatians passage Paul's theme is that in the Christian dispensation Jews and Gentiles are on the same footing. We may note the phrase ἐξ ἐθνῶν ἁμαρτωλοί ('Gentile sinners') in Gal. 2.15. This confirms our conclusion that Rom. 3 is aimed at Jews, not at all men. Everyone in Paul's milieu agreed that unconverted Gentiles were sinners; he did not need to prove it. Then in Gal. 2.16 Paul explains how he understands Ps. 143.2; it is not a general statement that man is unworthy before God, but makes the specific point that the Law cannot justify man before God. Possibly Paul found this truth hinted at in the psalm itself. It begins thus in the LXX:

> Lord, hear my prayer,
>     give ear to my request in thy truth (ἀλήθεια),
>     hear me in thy righteousness (δικαιοσύνη);
>     and do not enter into judgement with thy servant.

In Gal. 2.14 Paul refers to 'the truth of the gospel', and of course his whole argument is about the nature of God's righteousness. He goes on in Gal. 2.17 to say:

> But if, in our endeavour to be justified in Christ, we ourselves were found to be sinners, is Christ then an agent of sin? Certainly not.

This is quite like Rom. 3.5–6: 'But if our wickedness serves to show the justice of God, what shall we say? That God is unjust to inflict wrath on us? (I speak in a human way.) By no means! For then how could God judge the world?' In each case Paul is contemplating a state of affairs in which God could be accused of being responsible for sin, and he strongly repudiates the suggestion. The argument in Gal. 2.17 seems to be:

'If we trust in Christ and not in the Torah for justification, and then are found scrupulously adhering to the *Halakha* which forbids Jews and Gentiles to eat together, we are sinners. Sinners according to the Law, because we have rejected the Torah as a way of life in the past and are therefore condemned by it, having anyway broken the *Halakha*. But we are also sinners in

Christ, because we show by our actions that we no longer trust in him, so we have fallen back into the realm of sin, wrath, and Law. But Christ cannot be blamed for this.'

Thus we might find an equation between 'is Christ then an agent of sin?' in Gal. 2.17 and 'do not enter into judgement with thy servant' of Ps. 143.2. Christ is not an agent of sin because he has in fact removed us from the sphere of judgement altogether. He, and we in him, have died to the Law; we have been crucified with Christ. If Christians use this as a mere excuse for antinomianism, Christ is not to be blamed for that. Christ is not a διάκονος ἁμαρτίας but a δοῦλος ἀληθείας.

It seems therefore that Gal. 2.11–21 is a fair description of the situation which Paul is describing in Rom. 3.1–20: dying to the Torah in order to be crucified with Christ. Since the cross is at the very centre of the passage in Galatians, it is not unreasonable to look for it in the corresponding passage in Romans. And Gal. 2.21 admirably sums up the significance of the catena in Rom. 3.10–20.

> if justification were through the law, then Christ died to no purpose.

In the catena Paul seems to document this assertion: 'The inspired prophet David reveals that righteousness is not by the Law, and that Christ's death, far from being purposeless, was atoning and justifying.' We can even trace a similarity of context: both passages lead on (*a*) to a consideration of the significance of Abraham, and (*b*) to a positive setting forth of the atoning efficacy of Christ's death. But these two elements are not in the same order in both Epistles, a matter which we shall be examining more closely later.

2

We now look at three passages in that section of Romans which is often described as remarkable for its freedom from scriptural citations as compared with the rest of the Epistle, 5.1—8.36. As we shall be seeing, Paul does not in fact abandon his reliance on Scripture in this section, though he does not have occasion to cite it explicitly.

The first passage is Rom. 6.7:

> ὁ γὰρ ἀποθανὼν δεδικαίωται ἀπὸ τῆς ἁμαρτίας
>
> For he who has died is freed from sin.

Diezinger in a very carefully worked out article has claimed that Paul is here echoing Ps. 88.5 (RSV; it is 88.6 in MT and 87.5 in LXX).[26] In order to appreciate his argument, we must look at the LXX context, with some care. Ps. 87.5 in the LXX runs:

> προσελογίσθην μετὰ τῶν καταβαινόντων εἰς λάκκον,
> ἐγενήθην ὡς ἄνθρωπος ἀβοήθητος ἐν νεκροῖς ἐλεύθερος,

which we may render:

> I was reckoned with those who go down to the pit,
> I became like a man without help, free among the dead.

The first line is a good rendering of the Hebrew. The second line is rather a telescoping of the sense. The RSV correctly renders it:

> I am a man who has no strength,
> like one forsaken among the dead.

But the word translated 'forsaken', *chophshi*, can mean a freedman or a freeman. Diezinger points out that Rom. 6.1–11 is all about dying and being free. The rabbis, he says, interpreted this verse to mean that the man who has died is no longer obliged to obey the Law, and S-B cite evidence to the same effect. Diezinger suggests that the προσελογίσθην of the LXX of Ps. 87.5 is echoed in the λογίζεσθε of Rom. 6.11. Symmachus, he points out, actually reads ἐλογίσθην here. He thinks that the earliest Christians applied these verses of the psalm to Christian baptism, in which the candidates 'went down' into the water, and experienced sacramental death and resurrection; though he believes that ἐν νεκροῖς ἐλεύθερος was originally understood by Christians of Christ, and taken as the equivalent of ἐκ νεκρῶν ἐγερθείς. The LXX ἀβοήθητος might have been taken as meaning 'without the help of the works of the Law' which Christians had renounced; and he even ranges as far afield as Rom. 8.33, where Paul (as we shall see) cites Isa. 50.8. The next verse in Isaiah begins κύριος βοηθεῖ μοι 'the Lord helps me', so that, argues Diezinger, Paul thought of Christians as 'helped by God and not by the Law'.

This does seem a suggestion worth considering. But if so, we must understand the psalm as Paul would have understood it, that is as being primarily an utterance of the Messiah and only applied to Christians as being ἐν Χριστῷ. If we do this, we find that it would hold great significance for Paul. He certainly might have understood it of Christ's death; there are plenty of references which he would find indicative of that, besides the passage to which Diezinger refers. There is, for example, the next verse, which runs in the LXX (87.6a):

> like wounded men cast away, sleeping in the grave,

and verse 7:

> they placed me in the lowest pit,
> in dark places and in the shadow of death

(Diezinger does in fact claim that verse 7a is relevant).
See also verse 10c:

> I have stretched out my hands to thee,

which might be taken as indicating the crucifixion, and verse 16:

> I am poor and in troubles from my youth,
> having been exalted (ὑψωθείς) I was humilated
> and without resource.[27]

This would give the special sense of ὑψόω meaning 'to exalt by means of death' which is a feature of the Fourth Gospel. In fact the Hebrew verb translated ὑψωθείς here is the same as that translated by ὑψωθήσεται in Isa. 52.13. We might suggest also that Paul would find a hint of the resurrection in Ps. 87.14b (LXX):

> and early shall my prayer come before thee.

The Midrash on the Psalms tells us that Rabbi Helbo took the phrase 'free among the dead' to refer to the generation that perished in the flood (Midrash II, 80). This suggests a remarkable parallel with a passage in 1 Peter. In 1 Pet. 3.18f the author describes baptism as an 'antitype' (meaning reality, not 'type') to the ark in the time of the flood. He also makes an obscure reference to Christ preaching to the spirits in prison, which many scholars think refers to Christ's activity among the dead during the period of his own sojourn among the dead, before his resurrection. Then in 4.1 he writes:

> Since therefore Christ suffered in the flesh, arm yourselves with the same thought, for whoever has suffered in the flesh has ceased from sin.

This last phrase ὁ παθὼν σαρκὶ πέπαυται ἀπὸ ἁμαρτίας is reminiscent of Rom. 6.7, and is referred to by Sanday and Headlam. But if we can link the two passages up by means of Ps. 88 and if we can imagine that both Paul and the author of 1 Peter knew the traditional interpretation found in the Midrash on the Psalms, we have found a piece of very early Christian midrash connected with Christ's 'descent into hell'. In Rom. 10.7 we have another such midrash. We begin to see that some themes which have hitherto been relegated definitely to the later New Testament period must now be regarded as being as early as Paul at least. Moreover the link with 1 Peter confirms my suggestion that Ps. 88 was seen by Paul as uttered by the Messiah, since it is in connection with Christ's death that the author of 1 Peter says that death frees from sin. Schoeps sees the connection between Rom. 6.7 and Ps. 88, but does not pursue it.[28] C. K. Barrett pertinently quotes Ecclus. 26.29:

> a tradesman will not be declared innocent of sin
>
> οὐ δικαιωθήσεται κάπηλος ἀπὸ ἁμαρτίας.

On balance, it seems very likely that Diezinger is right in seeing a reference to Ps. 88 in Rom. 6.7. It only goes to show how saturated Paul was in the Scriptures, even when he seems to be far from intending actually to expound any scriptural passage.

We now move to Rom. 8.19–21.

> For the creation waits with eager longing for the revealing of the sons of God; for the creation was subjected to futility not of its own will but by the will of him who subjected it in hope; because the creation itself will be set free from its bondage to decay and obtain the glorious liberty of the children of God.

It will be sufficient if we give the Greek of verses 19–20:

ἡ γὰρ ἀποκαραδοκία τῆς κτίσεως τὴν ἀποκάλυψιν τῶν υἱῶν τοῦ Θεοῦ ἀπεκδέχεται τῇ γὰρ ματαιότητι ἡ κτίσις ὑπετάγη, οὐχ ἑκοῦσα, ἀλλὰ διὰ τὸν ὑποτάξαντα ἐπ᾽ ἐλπίδι.

I suggest that this passage is in fact a sort of Christian midrash on Ps. 89.46–8. In particular, Ps. 89.47 seems to be behind Rom. 8.19–20 (it is Ps. 88.47–9 in the LXX and Ps. 89.47-9 in the MT). This is the English of 89.46–8:

> How long, O Lord? Wilt thou hide thyself for ever?
> How long will thy wrath burn like fire?
> Remember, O Lord, what the measure of life is,
> for what vanity thou hast created all the sons of men!
> What man can live and never see death?
> Who can deliver his soul from the power of Sheol?

But the LXX is by no means as faithful to the Hebrew as this: 88.48 runs:

> μνήσθητι τίς μου ἡ ὑπόστασις·
> μὴ γὰρ ματαίως ἔκτισας πάντας τοὺς υἱοὺς τῶν ἀνθρώπων;

This we may translate:

> Remember what is my hope;
> surely thou hast not created all the sons of men for vanity?

In fact the MT is obscure in the first line here. It has *zᵃchor 'ᵃni meh cheledh*, which is literally 'remember I what *cheled*'. But the RSV has followed Buhl in reading *Adonai* for *'ᵃni*, giving the sense 'Remember, Lord'. The word *cheled* is a rare one. It means 'that which continues'. Buhl suggests that the original word may have been *chādel* 'transient' giving the reading *meh chādel 'ᵃni* 'how transient am I!'

But the LXX must have read *cheled* for ὑπόστασις gives exactly the opposite sense to 'transient'.[29] On the other hand, it is very likely indeed that by the word ὑπόστασις the LXX translator meant 'hope, source of confidence', for this is how he uses ὑπόστασις in other contexts; for example, to translate the Hebrew *tiqvah* 'hope' in Ruth 1.12 and Ezek. 19.5; and in Ps. 39.7 (LXX 38.8; MT 39.8) it translates *tōcheleth* 'expectation'. This last passage is of particular interest, for it is very like Ps. 89.47:

> And now, Lord, for what do I wait?
> My hope is in thee.

LXX

καὶ νῦν τίς μοι ἡ ὑπομονή; οὐχὶ ὁ Κύριος;
καὶ ἡ ὑπόστασίς μου παρά σοί ἐστιν.

It is even possible that Paul's Greek translation of Ps. 89.47
may have read ἀποκαραδοκία or καραδοκία, for Aquila is quite
fond of these, or cognate, words to translate words in Hebrew
meaning 'hope, wait, expect'. In Ps. 39.7, for example, Aquila
has καραδοκία where the LXX has ὑπόστασις. Aquila translates the same Hebrew word *tōcheleth* with καραδοκία in Prov.
10.28.[30] Compare also Pss. 37.7 and 130.5 ,where he has used
ἀποκαραδοκεῖν and καραδοκεῖν respectively for Hebrew words
meaning 'wait or hope'. But as there is no direct link between
*cheled* and ἀποκαραδοκία, this must remain a speculation. It is
very interesting to note that the Vulgate agrees with the LXX
in both Ps. 89.47 (Vg. 88.48) and Ps. 39.7 (Vg. 38.8), reading
in the first '*memorare quae mea substantia*' and in the second '*et
substantia mea apud te est*'.

However, quite apart from a possible verbal connection
between ἀποκαραδοκία and Ps. 89, Paul would find even in the
LXX very much the pattern of meaning which he reproduces in
Rom. 8.18–25. One must attempt to read the LXX of Ps. 89 with
his eyes, and then one can see how nearly it fits into the thought
sequence of this passage in Romans. In Ps. 89.38–45 we have a
vivid account of the sufferings of the Messiah (verse 39 LXX),
including his reproach (ὄνειδος, verse 42 LXX); we suggest on
p. 49 below that Paul may even have found a reference to the
curse in verse 41 (LXX). In Rom. 8.18 Paul refers to the sufferings of the present time. Then in verse 47 (LXX) begins the
appeal, which lasts until the second last verse of the psalm 'How
long, O Lord?'. This is 'the creation waiting with eager long-
ing' of Rom. 8.19 (ἡ ἀποκαραδοκία τῆς κτίσεως). Then in verse 48
(LXX) of the psalm comes a reference to hope, and the psalmist
asks whether God has made (ἔκτισας) all men for vanity
(ματαίως)? This corresponds very closely to Rom. 8.20 'the
creation was subjected to futility' (τῇ γὰρ ματαιότητι ἡ κτίσις
ὑπετάγη). Verse 49 (LXX) in the psalm refers directly to the
transience and mortality of all human beings:

What man can live and never see death?

And in Rom. 8.21 the creation is to be 'set free from its bondage to decay'. One wonders whether Paul had not in mind the line in the LXX

ῥύσεται τὴν ψυχὴν αὐτοῦ ἐκ χειρὸς ᾅδου;

Will he free his life from the hand of Hades?

Finally, Paul would see in the next two verses a reference to the vicarious suffering of the Messiah, the atoning reproach which the Messiah's faithful servants are to share also.

Shortly afterwards Paul turns for a moment from the reproach of the Messiah to the vindication of the Messiah, and writes in 8.33–4:

τίς ἐγκαλέσει κατὰ ἐκλεκτῶν Θεοῦ; Θεὸς ὁ δικαιῶν· τίς ὁ κατακρινῶν;
Χριστὸς ['Ιησοῦς] ὁ ἀποθανών, μᾶλλον δὲ ἐγερθείς.

Who shall bring any charge against God's elect? It is God who justifies; who is to condemn? Is it Christ Jesus who died, yes, who was raised from the dead . . .?

This is an echo of Isa. 50.8:

v. 8    He who vindicates me is near
        Who will contend with me?
            Let us stand up together.
        Who is my adversary?
            Let him come near to me.
v. 9    Behold the Lord God helps me;
            who will declare me guilty?

The LXX of the first two lines of Isa. 50.8 is:

ὅτι ἐγγίζει ὁ δικαιώσας με·
τίς ὁ κρινόμενός μοι;

The Targum on Isaiah tends to interpret this utterance of the servant (which begins with 50.4) in terms of the prophets, rendering 50.5, as 'The Lord Elohim hath sent me to prophesy'; and the Midrash on the Psalms identifies the servant here with Israel: possession of the Torah enables Israel to give testimony against all the nations.[31] But Paul undoubtedly understands this passage as one in which the Messiah expresses his confidence in God's coming vindication of himself through the resurrection. Indeed, if we read this song from 50.4 onwards, we can see it as a passage which links the two themes of this chapter. We find both the reproach of the Messiah and his justification by God. And we find here in Paul's comment on it exactly the same emphasis on the resurrection of Christ constituting his vindication as can be found in Rom. 4.25:

Christ Jesus who died, yes who was raised from the dead.[32]

Paul next gives a list of afflictions which are unable to separate us from the love of Christ, and he concludes it with the words:

As it is written,
 'For thy sake we are being killed all the day long;
 we are regarded as sheep to be slaughtered.'

Paul's Greek does not differ from that of the LXX, and the LXX is an adequate rendering of the Hebrew. The quotation is from Ps. 44.22 (MT 44.23; LXX 43.23). Like the psalms in the catena in Rom. 3, it is a cry for relief from oppression. It is mostly in the first person plural but does pass over into the first person singular in verses 15–16. Paul must have thought of it as the cry of the messianic community, crystallizing at times into the cry of the Messiah. The reproach of the Messiah is certainly to be found in it. We might translate verses 16 and 17 from the LXX as follows:

All the day long my rebuke is before me,
 and the shame of my face has covered me,
 from the voice of the slanderer (ὀνειδίζοντος) and taunter,[33]
 from before the enemy and persecutor.

This is quite reminiscent of Rom. 15.3 and other reproach passages. We may ask ourselves, however: Why did Paul choose verse 23 particularly to quote? He wants an example of the ultimate affliction, death; and this verse according to his view shows us that Christ is with us even in death, for we are only enduring the messianic sufferings which he inaugurated. When we study the rest of the psalm, other points of connection between it and Rom. 8 spring to light. In the first place, Christ intercedes for his Church in this psalm, and in Rom. 8.34 he is represented as doing just this. Next, this psalm speaks of our affliction (θλῖψις, verse 25 LXX) and θλῖψις is the very first item in the list of our dangers in Rom. 8.35. The third item in this list is διωγμός 'persecution', and this is found in the psalm, where in verse 17 the psalmist refers to 'the enemy and the persecutor' (ἐκδιώκοντος). Another of the afflictions, 'nakedness' (γυμνότης), might be found in verse 11b (LXX) of the psalm:

> those who hate us have plundered us for themselves.

It is even possible that the previous verse to that which Paul quotes, verse 22b LXX, may have been in Paul's mind when he wrote Rom. 8.26–7. There he says that the Spirit (like Christ, even perhaps *as* Christ) intercedes for us, and he adds:

> For he who searches the hearts of men knows what is the mind of the Spirit.

The verse in the psalm perhaps referred to runs:

> For he [sc. God] knows the secrets of the heart.

Thus we could well imagine that for Paul Ps. 44 would be rather like John 17, a prayer in which the Messiah prays for his own, knowing well that his prayer would be answered in the deliverance which was to be given by God in and through him.

It may seem surprising that Paul quotes a psalm which is apparently devoid of any suggestion of victory in a passage which ends with so splendid an assertion of our victory in Christ. But the rabbis may help us to explain this. In the Midrash on the Psalms (1, 447–8) the comment on the last two verses of the psalm suggests a note of victory. They run thus:

> For our soul is bowed down to the dust;
> our body cleaves to the ground.
> Rise up, come to our help!
> Deliver us for the sake of thy steadfast love!

According to Rabbi Isaac,

> the Holy one, blessed be He, said to Abraham *I will make thy seed as the dust of the earth* (Gen. 13–16); and he continued, *Arise, walk through the land in the length of it and the breadth of it, for unto thee will I give it.* Therefore Scripture, after saying *Our soul is bowed down to the dust,* continues with the words *Arise for our help, and redeem us for thy mercy's sake,* that is, 'If we have good works, redeem us; but if we do not have good works, redeem us for thy name's sake', as is said, *redeem us for thy mercy's sake.*

This suggests that the rabbis found in the last verse of the psalm a promise of deliverance: Israel was in the dust, but the dust means the land that belongs to them, the land of promise.

Another comment points in another direction. Rabbi Berechiah said: 'When the kingdom [of Israel] is so far fallen that it is become like dust, look, as from a watch-tower, for deliverance. The Holy One, blessed be He, said to Israel "Make your good works blossom like the lily, and I shall redeem you forthwith!"' Now this is a reference to the title of the next psalm, Ps. 45. The rabbi interprets the Hebrew of the title as meaning 'For him who gives victory because of lilies'. 'For him who gives victory' is one of the rabbinic interpretations of the phrase *lam^anatseach* normally translated εἰς τὸ τέλος by LXX and 'To the choirmaster' by RSV. We cannot, of course, assume that Paul found the meaning of 'victory' in this phrase, but we may draw the conclusion that in rabbinic exegesis the last verse of one psalm could be illuminated by the title of the next; and in the LXX the title of Ps. 45 (LXX 44.1) contains the phrase ᾠδὴ ὑπὲρ τοῦ ἀγαπητοῦ, 'an ode on behalf of the beloved'.[34] Now Ps. 45 is in fact a triumphant hymn addressed to the king's son on his marriage day. Paul might therefore very well have found his note of victory in the next psalm to that which he quotes. This psalm is cited in Heb. 1.8 as addressed by the Father to the Son. In Rom. 8.32 Paul refers to the Father who did not spare his own Son. So Ps. 44, which seems to us rather incongruous in the triumphant context in which Paul quotes it, probably seemed to Paul a psalm which, for all its grim description of the reproach of the Messiah and of those who belong to the Messiah, leads on to a description of the Son's glorious triumph.[35]

A comparison with 2 Cor. 4.7–15 is interesting. There the suffering, precarious life of Paul and his companions is closely associated with the dying and rising of Jesus Christ. There also is a reference to a psalm regarded by Paul as messianic; and there also the passage ends in a note of triumph, probably suggested by the psalm itself. (See Ps. 116.16f.) The comparison confirms the suggestion that, in quoting Ps. 44, Paul has in mind the sufferings of the Messiah, reproduced in the sufferings of Christians, and that in Rom. 8 Christ is regarded not only as the saviour but also as the sufferer. C. K. Barrett considers that the sufferings of Christians, foretold in Ps. 44, 'formed part of the messianic affliction'.

# 3

We have undertaken in this study to examine the reproach and vindication of the Messiah according to Paul. We have seen plenty of evidence of his reproach, and also of his vindication, or justification. We have now to consider a special feature of his vindication. He was justified, we suggest, by faith. Paul, we maintain, envisaged the Messiah as having lived by faith.

The phrase 'the faith of the Messiah' is a question-begging one, and indeed runs the risk of bringing its user into the company of scholars whose conclusions have not been widely accepted as far as concerns this topic. A few scholars have attempted in the course of the last eighty years to show that πίστις 'Ιησοῦ Χριστοῦ and cognate phrases in the New Testament bear the same meaning as πίστις 'Αβραάμ bears in Rom. 4.12, 16, that is, that they mean Jesus Christ's own personal faith. But these scholars have all, I believe, attempted to prove too much. Thus G. Kittel in 1906, following a lead originally given by Haussleiter in 1896, argued that because πίστις 'Ιησοῦ Χριστοῦ means Jesus Christ's own faith, Paul does not expect Christians to believe in Jesus Christ, but 'according to Jesus Christ'.[36] This involved too much special pleading to be convincing. In fact the claim that πίστις 'Ιησοῦ Χριστοῦ means Jesus Christ's own faith does not imply the conclusion that Paul does not wish Christians to believe in Christ. On the contrary, we can only believe in Christ because he has been the pioneer in faith himself. Karl Barth seems to incline towards identifying 'the faith of Christ' with 'the faithfulness of God', in his commentary on Romans, for he writes: 'Whether we say "of the faithfulness of God" or "of the faith of men" both are the same.'[37] This interpretation has been taken up and emphasized by T. F. Torrance.[38] He strongly underlines the Hebraic background to Paul's thought, thereby giving πίστις the meaning 'faithfulness' rather than 'faith'. He describes Jesus Christ as 'the incarnate faithfulness of God' and writes 'the πίστις 'Ιησοῦ Χριστοῦ does not refer only either to the faithfulness of Christ and the answering faithfulness of man, but is essentially a polarized expression denoting the faithfulness of Christ as its main ingredient but also the answering faithfulness of man'. This looks very much like an attempt to have it both ways.

The latest attempt to vindicate this point of view is also the longest, a book by P. Vallotton in which he seeks to identify πίστις Ἰησοῦ Χριστοῦ and πίστις Θεοῦ.³⁹ He has no hesitation in speaking of God's faith, and develops the phrase to mean God's faith in man. God showed his faith in man by entrusting his Son to us. But if so, it may be argued, God's faith was betrayed, for man put his Son to death. It is difficult to see how 'the faith of God' can have any meaning except in an analogous sense as reflected in the faith of Jesus Christ. Indeed faith is an inseparable element in our human condition and can only be predicated of God incarnate. Equally precarious is Vallotton's attempt to define 'the faith of Jesus Christ' as faith in the saving power of his own work.

The attempt to argue directly about the meaning of πίστις Ἰησοῦ Χριστοῦ in the New Testament will not be made in this work: we shall simply begin from an exposition of various passages in Paul's Epistles, and try to show that the faith of the Messiah is in fact implied in them, if their full significance is explored. The conclusion certainly is that when Paul writes of 'the faith of Jesus Christ' he means both Christ's personal faith during his historical existence and our faith in him—and that the latter is based on the former. But no attempt will be made to draw any general conclusion about faith as described in the New Testament.

No man, Paul believed, can be justified by works, not even the Messiah. But the Messiah was justified, as we have seen, therefore he must have been justified by faith. And this, we maintain, is exactly the meaning of Rom. 1.17.

Anyone who attempts to expound Rom. 1.17 must first declare his attitude towards what might not unfairly be called the fashionable translation of the key quotation from Hab. 2.4, and this is what we propose to do. But first we must set out the text:⁴⁰

δικαιοσύνη γὰρ Θεοῦ ἐν αὐτῷ ἀποκαλύπτεται ἐκ πίστεως εἰς πίστιν, καθὼς γέγραπται, Ὁ δὲ δίκαιος ἐκ πίστεως ζήσεται.

For in it [sc. the gospel] the righteousness of God is revealed through faith for faith; as it is written, 'He who through faith is righteous shall live'.

It will be apparent at once what the fashionable translation is, since it has actually gained the text of the RSV. Leenhardt in his commentary gives a useful list of those who have adopted it: Beza, Lietzmann, Lagrange, Gaugler, Nygren. The last actually asserts that it is the only possible one! To this list we may add the names of Kirk, C. K. Barrett, J. A. Sanders, and A. Feuillet.[41] It may well be that the real originator of this translation is Calvin, who comments: 'But we do not live before God except by righteousness (*iustitia*): it therefore follows that our righteousness also lies in faith.'[42] The translation we are considering could well follow from this. But, whatever its source, this translation must be rejected. The inspiration behind it is no doubt partly theological: those who, like some Lutheran theologians, are very suspicious of any importation of sanctification into justification welcome the opportunity of getting rid of the idea that we can live by anything, even faith. This is perhaps why Nygren devotes so much space in his commentary to emphasizing this translation and no other. But it has now some Catholic champions, notably A. Feuillet, referred to above. Both Nygren and Feuillet also base their advocacy of this translation on the schema according to which they think the Epistle is laid out. Feuillet argues that πίστις is never found in Paul in connection with words for living, and suggests that Rom. 1.17—5.11 deals with righteousness and faith, and Rom. 5.12—8.39 with life and death. These arguments do not seem in themselves very convincing, especially as used to defend what must be admitted, other things being equal, to be a rather unlikely translation. Most of those who reject this translation do so on the common-sense grounds that if Paul had understood the verse in this sense, he could have written:

$$\text{ὁ δὲ ἐκ πίστεως δίκαιος ζήσεται.}$$

This is the argument of Sanday and Headlam, of Leenhardt, and of Michel. Ellis adds the consideration that the translation in question, at least as expounded by Nygren, assumes that there are two sorts of righteousness, faith-righteousness and law-righteousness. But in fact, writes Ellis, in Paul's theology there is no such thing as law-righteousness.[43] But an even more formidable objection can be brought: it must be remembered that Paul also quotes this text from Habakkuk in Gal. 3.11. At that point he fortifies it with Lev. 18.5: 'He who does them shall live by them', referring of course to the precepts of the law. But this directly implies a contrast between living by the law and living by faith, a contrast which, we shall be maintaining, is essential to Paul's argument in Gal. 3. If therefore Paul means by the text when cited in Galatians that the righteous has the way of faith to live by, it can hardly be argued that he means something else when he cites it in Romans. Barth has an interpretation which seems equally far from Paul's mind: the righteous 'shall live of the faithfulness of God'. This is not the same thing as faith as a way of life, which is what Paul means here.

We may therefore confidently reject the 'fashionable' translation and retain the more usual one, 'the righteous shall live by faith'. But 'the righteous' is ambiguous: Does it mean all the righteous or one particular individual? My contention is that according to Paul's interpretation it means one particular individual, the Messiah, and that the phrase should properly be translated, here and in Gal. 3.11:

the Righteous One shall live by faith.

This, as I hope to show, is in very good accord with Paul's main argument in Gal. 3.1–20. But it is also a sense which arises easily from the LXX translation. This is how Hab. 2.3–4 appears in the LXX:

v. 3    διότι ἔτι ὅρασις εἰς καιρὸν
        καὶ ἀνατελεῖ εἰς πέρας καὶ οὐκ εἰς κενόν·
        ἐὰν ὑστερήσῃ ὑπομεῖνον αὐτόν,
        ὅτι ἐρχόμενος ἥξει καὶ οὐ μὴ χρονίσῃ.

v. 4    ἐὰν ὑποστείληται, οὐκ εὐδοκεῖ ἡ ψυχή μου ἐν αὐτῷ·
        ὁ δὲ δίκαιος ἐκ πίστεώς μου ζήσεται.

Because the vision still awaits its time,
    and will rise to its fulfilment and not be in vain;
If he delays, wait for him,
    because a Coming One will arrive and will not linger,
    if he draws back, my soul will have no pleasure in him;
    but the Righteous One shall live by my faith.

It is in fact a very eschatological passage. The LXX, by translating the Hebrew of verse 3d as ἐρχόμενος, instead of making it apply to the vision, has imported the idea of a coming one and therefore given a messianic tone to the whole passage. This point is underlined by T. W. Manson, who comments: 'The

LXX interpretation of Habakkuk 2.3b–4 is through and through messianic.'[44] But he concludes that Paul uses the text in Romans and Galatians 'as a prophecy about Christians rather than the Christ'. This does not seem to me to follow at all. It is true that Paul interprets it of Christians, but only, I maintain, because it was first true of Christ. Schrenk makes the good point that Paul means by ὁ δίκαιος here 'he who is justified by faith', and we have shown good reason to believe that according to Paul the Messiah was to be justified by faith.[45] C. H. Dodd remarks apropos this passage: '[Paul's] argument would be much more effective with his Jewish Christian antagonists if it was already common ground between them that when the Coming One should come ὁ δίκαιος ἐκ πίστεως ζήσεται.'[46] This does put the passage in its true eschatological setting; but it would be an even more effective argument if Paul maintains that the Coming One also is to live by faith. It is interesting in this context to note that in the Mekilta this text is cited in the course of an encomium on faith in the form: 'But the righteous shall live by his faith'.[47] In the context it means 'shall live in the world to come', which is a slight indication that the text had an eschatological overtone in rabbinic Judaism.

This interpretation implies that Paul could understand ὁ δίκαιος as a description of the Messiah. This is not quite the same thing as saying that he regarded it as a title of the Messiah, but it is worth looking at the evidence that 'the Righteous One' could be used as a messianic title. Schrenk in the article just referred to points out that Jer. 23.5–6; 33.15 was applied to the Messiah by the rabbis. Here the phrase is 'a righteous branch' and the Targum actually translates it with the word Messiah.[48] The LXX has ἀνατολὴν δικαίαν; and it is worth observing that the verb ἀνατελεῖ occurs in the LXX of Hab. 2.3b. H. Dechent has provided the completest list of the occurrence of this title:[49] there are two clear examples of its use in the New Testament, Acts 7.52; 22.14; and a few places where it may very well be used as a title, e.g. Matt. 10.41: εἰς ὄνομα δικαίου, where the Marcan parallel has εἰς ὄνομά μου. There are also 1 Pet. 3.18 and 1 John 2.1. He notes the LXX translation of Isa. 53.10e referred to above. And he shows that 'the Righteous One' was certainly a title for the Messiah in the Book of Enoch, as in Enoch 38.2:

> When the Righteous One shall appear before the eyes of the righteous . . .

He does not mention Rom. 1.17, but he certainly seems to have produced enough evidence to suggest that this is a perfectly possible interpretation for Paul.

Hab. 2.4 is of course a passage which the Qumran sectaries regarded as important. A very good exposition of their treatment of the text is given by Lindars;[50] the subject is also discussed by Sanders.[51] Lindars says that the Qumran commentator had two points to make: (*a*) the just man will live by his faithfulness in observing the Torah correctly; (*b*) he will have faith in the interpretation of the Torah given by the Teacher of Righteousness.[52] This is just about as far from Paul's interpretation of the text as it could be. Sanders points out that both Paul and the sectaries 'believed that Habakkuk was addressing himself primarily to that moment in history which Qumran and the Church each believed it bore witness to'.

The rabbis regarded this text as a summary of the Torah: Moses, David, and various prophets each reduced the number of the commandments in the Torah, till Habakkuk (following Amos' example) reduced them to one: 'have faith'.[53] Of the 'fashionable' interpretation there is no trace in the rabbis. S-B quote an interesting comment by Rabbi Isaac b. Marion (*c.* A.D. 280), who says the sentence means: 'The Righteous One, blessed be he, lives by his handiwork.' The interpretation depends on a pun,[54] but is relevant for our purpose because it shows that 'the Righteous One' could be identified with God.

The author of Hebrews also quotes this text in Heb. 10.35–9. He is exhorting his readers to greater confidence and faith:

> Therefore do not throw away your confidence, which has a great reward. For you have need of endurance, so that you may do the will of God and receive what is promised.
> 'For yet a little while,
> and the coming one shall come and shall not tarry;
> but my righteous one shall live by his faith,
> and if he shrinks back,
> my soul has no pleasure in him.'
> But we are not of those who shrink back and are destroyed, but of those who have faith and keep their souls.

We observe that those who follow 'my righteous one' are

described as (literally) 'being of faith', like Paul's οἱ ἐκ πίστεως. The author of Hebrews follows the same text as Paul, except that he reads 'my righteous one'. This may well have been in his Greek text of Habakkuk, since it is read by one LXX manuscript.[55] Lindars (op. cit., p. 231) suggests that he has deliberately transferred the pronoun in order to emphasize the importance of individual faith. But it might just as well have been in order to underline the messianic significance of ὁ δίκαιος. It seems quite possible that the author of Hebrews also understood this text as a messianic prophecy. This is Vallotton's conclusion (op. cit., p. 67). The fact that the author quotes the line about 'the coming one' and inserts the definite article (absent from the LXX) makes this more likely. If so, he might perhaps have seen the line about 'shrinking back' as a prophecy of Gethsemane: the Messiah was tempted to shrink back, but resisted the temptation and went boldly on to accept the experience of death and vindication. We are to follow his example.

It cannot be taken as proved that Hab. 2.4 is regarded by Paul as a prophecy of the Messiah, but it is at least a reasonable suggestion and one that fits in with what else we know of Paul's approach. With this in mind we go on to examine Gal. 3.

This section and the next must take the form of a commentary on Gal. 3.1–20. The general line of my exposition of this passage has already been set out in print.[56] I maintain that Christ as the seed who inherits the promise must be thought of as inheriting it by faith; that there is therefore a contrast throughout the passage between faith as a way of life and the Torah as a way of life; and that the Torah put Christ under a curse and slew him because he lived by faith and not by law. But a detailed exposition should bring out in a much more explicit way Paul's use of Scripture.

Gal. 3.4–6 runs as follows:

> Did you experience so many things in vain?—if it really is in vain. Does he who supplies the Spirit to you and works miracles among you do so by works of the law, or by hearing with faith? Thus Abraham 'believed God, and it was reckoned to him as righteousness'.

The giving of the Spirit here is described as ἐξ ἀκοῆς πίστεως, and then in verse 6 follows the reference to Abraham's faith, in Gen. 15.6. We shall be studying Abraham's faith more closely in the next chapter, but here it is worth while asking whether Abraham may not have received the Spirit according to Paul. Luther in his commentary on Galatians claims that Abraham by believing was born of the Holy Ghost.[57] Such an idea is by no means beyond the range of Paul's thought.

Then follows the first blessing of Abraham, cited from Gen. 12.3. But it is introduced by two remarkable words: 'the scripture, *foreseeing* (προιδοῦσα) that God would justify the Gentiles by faith, *preached the gospel beforehand* (προευηγγελίσατο) to Abraham'. J. B. Lightfoot compares the rabbinic formula for introducing scriptural quotations: 'What has the Scripture seen ?'[58] Schlier rightly rejects the suggestion made by Sieffert: 'Every promise was an evangelium before the evangelium.'[59] This is to blunt the force of προευηγγελίσατο. It was essentially the same gospel; the era of faith and grace was present with Abraham, though not in its fullness. Paul quotes the promise as:

$$ἐνευλογηθήσονται ἔν σοι πάντα τὰ ἔθνη.$$

In you shall all the nations be blessed.

The LXX has πᾶσαι αἱ φυλαὶ τῆς γῆς 'all the tribes of the earth', more faithfully reproducing the MT. Lightfoot thinks that Paul is conflating Gen. 12.3 with Gen. 18.18. Certainly Paul's form of the quotation favours the interpretation he puts on it, for it specifically mentions the Gentiles over against the Jews, whereas the phrase in both MT and LXX merely indicates the whole world without discrimination. If the context of this blessing in 12.3 is to be taken literally, Abraham's faith is shown in his setting out from Haran, not in his believing God's promise about his seed. This is in line with Heb. 11.8 where Abraham's faith is shown in his setting out, not knowing where he was going. It is Sarah who in Heb. 11.11 shows faith over the birth of a son. (Unless the punctuation of the latest Bible Societies' Greek Testament is followed, which makes Abraham the one to show faith over the birth of a son.) But of course Paul does show later on in Gal. 3 and in Rom. 4 that Abraham's faith was also concerned with the promise about his posterity.

Then, in verses 10–12, Paul draws a contrast between two ways of life, the way of the Law, which is of works, and the way of faith. The first is proved by a citation of Deut. 27.26, supported by Lev. 18.5; and the second is proved by the citation of Hab. 2.4 which we have already examined. Paul's version of Deut. 27.26 is less faithful to the MT than is that of the LXX, since the LXX renders τοῖς λόγοις τοῦ νόμου 'the words of the law' for Paul's τοῖς γεγραμμένοις ἐν τῷ βιβλίῳ τοῦ νόμου 'all things written in the book of the law'. Thus Paul emphasizes rather more literal adherence to written rules: but the difference may be unintentional. The word ἐμμένει used by both the LXX and Paul to translate the Hebrew *yāqîm* is strange. It has the effect of making the meaning more suitable for Paul's purpose. The MT context is of a renewal of the covenant, a solemn affirmation of the Law at an historical moment. The LXX and Paul make it into a more general statement: anyone who fails to keep the Law automatically incurs a curse. The meaning of ἐμμένει is 'abide in, remain constant to'. Lagrange quotes Deissmann for the opinion that Paul is here unconsciously using a legal formula attested in papyri;[60] but there is no need for this hypothesis, since Paul took the word from the LXX. The Palestinian Targum adds a gloss to the effect that these words were spoken on Sinai, repeated in the tabernacle, and uttered again on the plains of Moab.[61] Several rabbis maintained that the event referred to in Deut. 27.26 was one of the occasions on which the whole Torah was repeated. Others said that general laws were proclaimed on Sinai, and more particular laws in the tabernacle and on the plains of Moab.[62] If we look at the context in Deuteronomy we see that it is a liturgical one: a miscellaneous set of laws ends in the summary: 'Cursed be he who does not confirm the words of this law by doing them. And all the people shall say, Amen'. So Paul gives us every indication that he regards the Torah as a whole as a way of life.

The quotation from Lev. 18.5 is made precisely in order to show that it is a question of two ways of life: either one lives by faith, or by the Law. The Messiah must have done one or the other. It is interesting that the Targum on Lev. 18.5 paraphrases thus: 'And you shall keep my statutes and the order of my judgements, which if a man do he shall live in them, in the life of eternity, and his portion shall be with the just' (Etheridge, op. cit., p. 201). Thus the Targum has added an eternal dimension, which Paul would no doubt have approved.

Lohmeyer has an interesting article on the 'works of the law', in which he shows that they are in effect a way of life.[63] In the Jewish view, works are really man's life, and 'the Law is God's gift to his people', so works are therefore a God-given way of life. Luther, very profoundly, takes the citation of Lev. 18.5 as basically ironical: 'Live in them if you can!' Lindars puts the point well when he writes of Gal. 3.12: 'Paul has forced the words to bear this meaning in order to make a complete contrast with another manner of life, i.e. faith' (op. cit., p. 229). Bring is therefore off the mark when he writes: 'The words in the law about doing the law referred to the fulfilment to come in Christ.'[64] Christ is not τέλος τοῦ νόμου in the sense that he fulfils it in all its details. On the contrary, he fulfils its intention by refusing to live by it and by living by faith, as God always willed.

We are now able to approach the difficult verse Gal. 3.13 in the right light. Paul quotes Deut. 21.23 in the form ἐπικατάρατος πᾶς ὁ κρεμάμενος ἐπὶ ξύλου. 'Cursed be every one who hangs on a tree'. This is not a literal translation of the MT and does not exactly correspond to the LXX. The LXX has κεκατηραμένος ὑπὸ Θεοῦ πᾶς κρεμάμενος ἐπὶ ξύλου. The main difference from the LXX is that Paul omits ὑπὸ Θεοῦ 'by God' and substitutes an adjective for the participle of the LXX. The MT is literally 'for a hanged man is a curse of God'. It does not have the words 'on a tree' in this sentence, though they occur twice in verses 22–23a. The Vulgate supports the LXX with: *quia maledictus a Deo qui pendet in ligno*. As has been often pointed out by editors, the meaning of the sentence in Deuteronomy is that the dead body of a criminal hung on a piece of wood contaminates the ground. The victim is not cursed because he hangs on a tree, but hanging on a tree is a sign of his being cursed. Both Holzmeister and Hoad consider that the application of this text to Christ goes back beyond Paul.[65] Holzmeister very reasonably suggests that this was a text brought against Paul by Jewish opponents. Paul had to answer it. This is probably one reason for his using it; but we hope to show below that Paul may have had other reasons for believing that according to the scriptures the Messiah would be cursed. Hoad thinks that the occurrence of ἐπὶ τὸ ξύλον in 1 Pet. 2.24 shows that this text was in fairly common use in Christian polemic. Paul's omission of ὑπὸ Θεοῦ can hardly be accidental: to leave it out suits his sense too well for that. In fact, however, his use of ἐπικατάρατος instead of the LXX κεκατηραμένος slightly favours the omission of ὑπὸ Θεοῦ, since it is doubtful if ἐπικατάρατος ὑπὸ Θεοῦ would be possible Greek. I can find no instance in biblical or secular Greek of either κατάρατος or ἐπικατάρατος used with ὑπό. A more natural construction with these words would be ἐνώπιον, as found in 1 Sam. 26.19. The rabbis take the sentence as meaning 'because of a curse against God' and conclude that this is an account of what must be done to one who has cursed God,[66] but this is certainly not Paul's interpretation. Similarly the Targums show a desire to moralize the verse. Onkelos has 'for he was hanged because he had sinned before the Lord', and the Palestine Targum offers: 'for it is execrable before God to hang a man, but that his guilt gave occasion'. Schoeps points out that the word for 'hanged' in the MT of Deut. 21.23, *tālūy*, is ambiguous: it could be taken as either 'hanged' or 'exalted'.[67] In this respect it reminds us of the Johannine use of ὑψοῦν 'to lift up'. There are other occasional indications that Paul was aware of this double meaning. Vollmer suggests that Paul omitted Θεοῦ because he applied the phrase to Christ.[68]

But there is another passage in Scripture which Paul may have regarded as throwing light on Deut. 21.23: this is Ps. 89.40 (in MT 89.41 and in LXX 88.41):

> Thou hast breached all his walls;
> thou hast laid his strongholds in ruins.

The LXX for the second half of this verse offers:

> ἔθου τὰ ὀχυρώματα αὐτοῦ δειλίαν.

But Symmachus for the word δειλίαν ('cowardice') has κατάρα.[69] The Hebrew word thus so diversely translated is *maḥittah*, which means 'terror' or 'ruin'. The LXX in other places renders it by a considerable variety of words—τρόμος, ἀλλοτρίωσις, πτόησις. The Vulgate moves a little closer to Symmachus with '*posuisti firmamentum eius formidinem*'. Now we know that early Christians in general, and Paul in particular, were greatly interested in Ps. 89 and regarded it as providing much information about the Messiah. The very next verse contains a reference to the reproach of the Messiah, the theme we have already discussed. If Paul did read κατάρα in Ps. 89.40b, he would have found in the psalm much to confirm his christological assumptions. Verses 28–38 say that God will maintain his anointed if he abides by God's laws; verses 39–46 describe how he has become a reproach and a cause of shame; verses 47–52 constitute an appeal for vindication.

One other Scripture text comes into consideration at this point, Gen. 22.13. The ram which Abraham is to sacrifice instead of Isaac is 'caught in a thicket by his horns'. LXX renders 'caught' by κατεχόμενος but the Hexaplar version used the verb κρεμάννυμι 'hang'. If Paul had this reading, it might have appealed to him. As we shall be seeing in the next chapter, Paul did not use the 'binding of Isaac' very prominently in his typology, but the ram as a type of Christ would have fitted into his Christology better than Isaac as a type of Christ.

The suggestion that in Gal. 3.13 it was the curse of the Law that Christ underwent and not the curse of God is one which has been made by several editors. Lightfoot, for example, writes: 'He was in no sense κατάρατος ὑπὸ Θεοῦ and St Paul instinctively omits these words, which do not strictly apply.' Lightfoot thinks that Paul here is seeing Christ in the role of the scapegoat, a suggestion also taken up by Blunt.[70] But this word is not applied to the scapegoat in the LXX, and the Epistle to the Hebrews, which does use the typology of the Day of Atonement, is very careful not to identify the scapegoat as a type of Christ: Burton puts the point very clearly: 'The curse of the law was not therefore an actual curse in the sense that the man on whom it fell was accursed of God; it was the verdict of the law, of pure legalism.'[71] He goes on to say that Christ delivered us from the curse by bringing to an end the regime of the Law. Similarly Larsson says that Christ himself died to the Law.[72] This would seem to come very close to saying that therefore Christ lived by faith, but in fact no commentator draws this conclusion. Both Lipsius[73] and Schlier point out that the use of ἐξαγοράζω (Christ redeemed us) in verse 13 implies a ransom, and that the ransom was his death on the cross. Schlier emphasizes that we were in a state of slavery. On the other hand, Lietzmann seems to be going too far in a Calvinistic direction when he writes: 'Christ has taken upon himself the curse which lay upon all the people of the Law and thereby redeemed us all.'[74] The difference between the Jews and Christ was that the Jews incurred the curse because they could not keep the Law, but Christ because he would not make the Law his way of life. Benoit seems to be making the same mistake when he says that Christ incurs the curse due to those who 'are under the regime of the Law and only rely on it'.[75] Christ, it is true, was born under the Law (Gal. 4.4), but he did not rely on it. We would likewise judge Büchsel to be quite astray when he maintains that the curse was the curse of God, because the Law was God's revelation according to Paul.[76] He thus attributes a thoroughly penal doctrine of the atonement to Paul.

We have thus traced in Paul a whole theology of reproach: relying on much traditionally messianic material in the Scriptures, he holds that Jesus Christ as the Messiah incurred the reproach which the Messiah was destined to bear on behalf of both God and man. He was maltreated and put to death but in the resurrection he was vindicated or justified by God, who had never given his approval to those who opposed the Messiah. This justification was a justification by faith, because the Messiah was always destined to live by faith and actually did so. It was because of this that he was put to death by the Law, the Law no doubt being used as an instrument of the powers. This messianic doctrine of Paul has great significance both for what Paul thought about the historical Jesus and for his doctrine of the Church—for the first because it throws a little more light on how Paul estimated the significance of the historic life, and for the second because, if Christ was justified by faith, not only are Christians justified by faith in Christ, but they are also justified in Christ by Christ's faith.

# 3

# ABRAHAM
# THE JUSTIFIED SINNER

———————

It is with Abraham that Paul's account of salvation history really begins. This is not to suggest that the story of God's saving acts in Christ only first comes into consideration in Romans with chapter 4. We have already observed that in his catena of Scripture citations in chapter 3 Paul has quite consciously referred to the great saving act of God in the cross. But chapters 1–3, as commentators have often pointed out, are mainly concerned with the negative aspect of salvation; they show that God has concluded all men under sin by means of the cross. Only with chapter 4 do we approach the positive aspects of salvation, faith, justification, promise. After all, Paul is not setting out to write a history of salvation; from the very first he writes under the assumption that the great crisis of salvation has already appeared, and he never attempts to hide or modify this assumption for the purpose of unveiling it later with some notion of emphasizing it by means of contrast. Indeed this all-pervading presence of the saving God is essential to Paul's theology. He does give something resembling an account of salvation history in chapters 4–11 of Romans; but this can only be given because the saving God, God always active in Christ, has now supremely declared himself in Jesus. There is no suggestion in Paul that the revelation in Jesus Christ is something so absolutely new that it constitutes a break in our knowledge of God. On the contrary, as we shall be seeing, the God who made himself known to Abraham is the same God who has made himself known to Paul in Christ.

Paul then begins in Rom. 4 by underlining Abraham's faith in response to God's promise. In 4.3 he quotes Gen. 15.6b, a verse which follows a far-reaching promise from God about Abraham's posterity. It is worth noting that in Gen. 15.4, where the MT has 'the word of the Lord' the LXX has 'the voice of the Lord'. God speaks to Abraham audibly: perhaps Paul would find here a hint of the pre-existent Christ speaking. It is most interesting to observe the words which Paul uses to describe what is related in Gen. 15.6:

> And to one who does not work, but trusts him who justifies the ungodly, his faith is reckoned as righteousness (Rom. 4.5).

God, in making this promise to Abraham and then reckoning Abraham as righteous because of his faith, is described as 'justifying the ungodly' (τὸν ἀσεβῆ). The obvious conclusion would seem to be that, when Abraham received the promise and believed, he could be described as 'ungodly'. Paul proceeds to elaborate his meaning by means of a psalm citation which shows, I believe, that this is precisely what he had in mind. He tells us that David's words are intended to apply to 'the man to whom God reckons righteousness apart from works'. We are therefore ready to find in the psalm that follows a description of Abraham, an Abraham who was 'ungodly' when God's voice came to him, but who is reckoned righteous by God because of his faith.

We shall be examining the psalm citation in a moment; but first it is relevant to notice how closely Paul has tied it down in verses 9–10 to this occasion and this occasion only:

> Is this blessing pronounced only upon the circumcised, or also upon the uncircumcised? We say that faith was reckoned to Abraham as righteousness. How then was it reckoned to him? Was it before or after he had been circumcised? It was not after, but before he was circumcised.

This blessing, mentioned in Ps. 32, was intended to refer to Abraham, and to Abraham on this occasion, i.e. at the precise juncture when he had believed God's promise (as recorded in Gen. 15) but had not yet received circumcision (as recorded in Gen. 17). This is the clear implication of Paul's language. The fact that so few commentators have realized this is no doubt due to the difficulties which it involves us in when we try to think of the Psalms in this way. How could words uttered by David (assuming they were uttered by David) apply to a situation in Abraham's lifetime? But we are concerned at the moment not with justifying Paul's methods of exegesis, but with finding out what they were, and what they mean for Paul's thought.

Traditional Jewish exegesis of the Psalms had no difficulty whatever in attributing any given psalm to a character who lived long before, or long after, David's day. Thus in Wisd. 10.20–21, Ps. 8 is referred to the crossing of the Red Sea:

> they sang hymns, O Lord, to thy holy name,
> and praised with one accord thy defending hand,
> because wisdom opened the mouth of the dumb,
> and made the tongues of babes to speak clearly.

The same tradition is found in *Tractate Sotah* in the Talmud, p. 150 (ed. A. Cohen in BT, London 1936). The Midrash on the Psalms suggests that Ps. 26.5–6 was uttered by Abraham: 'I hate the company of evil-doers, and I will not sit with the wicked, etc.' (Midrash on the Psalms i, 486, on Ps. 53.4). Or again the Midrash says that Ps. 67.1 was spoken by Moses, who foresaw that the tribe of Levi (the Hasmoneans) would overthrow Greece: 'May God be gracious to us and bless us, and make his face to shine upon us' (i, 534). And the Midrash on Ps. 68.18 in its purely Jewish form regards the verse as addressed to Moses, interpreted in terms of 'thou hast gone up on high, thou hast received gifts for men', i.e. Moses has climbed Mount Sinai and received the Torah (i, 341).

Just as psalms can be attributed to people who lived long before the time of David even though David is regarded as actually uttering them, so David can be described as speaking of events in Israel's history which took place long after he was dead. The Midrash on the Psalms is particularly fond of applying psalm citations to the history of Esther: this is true of Ps. 22.1, though others thought it applied to the time of Hezekiah when he was besieged by Sennacherib (i, 293, 298). The reference to the distribution of the sufferer's garments in Ps. 22.18 is also referred to Esther. The people of Susa planned to distribute her garments in anticipation of her overthrow (i, 304). It is true that the interpretation of Ps. 22 in terms of Esther's

history may be a reaction to the Christian claim that it referred
to the passion of Jesus; but it illustrates how easily the rabbis
could place a psalm in the context of a period remote from
David's. Another example of this occurs in the Midrash on
Ps. 55.18–19: 'He will deliver my soul in safety from the battle
that I wage, etc.' This is interpreted as a prophecy of Daniel
in the lions' den and of the three holy children in the furnace
(I, 494). Similarly the whole of Ps. 64, which is a plea for
deliverance from treacherous enemies, is interpreted as a prayer
of David on behalf of Daniel (I, 526). On exactly the same lines,
Ps. 137, with its specific references to the Babylonian captivity,
constitutes no problem for the rabbis, for David foresaw the
destruction of both the first and the second Temple (II, 331).
The idea that certain chosen figures in Israel's history were
given a prophetic vision of the history of their people subsequent
to their day is, of course, a most familiar feature of Jewish
midrash: Abraham was granted a vision of his people's history
(Midrash I, 434–5, on Ps. 5). And the *Biblical Antiquities* of
Pseudo-Philo gives us some examples of this. Thus Moses is
shown the future history of Israel up to the sack of Jerusalem
by Titus.[1] And even Joshua on his death bed is granted a
certain knowledge of future history (*Bibl. Ant.* xxiv, 4).

We can now consider the citation of Ps. 32.1–2 in Rom. 4.7
with some confidence that we know what Paul made of it. Both
the Hebrew and the Greek of Ps. 32.1–2 can apply only to one
who has sinned and has been forgiven. They cannot apply to a
man who has no sin to be reckoned. The Hebrew of the first
two lines is literally:

> The blessedness of those who are forgiven-of-sin, concealed-of-
> iniquity!

As we look at the psalm as a whole, we can see how it might
apply to Abraham's situation as understood by Paul. The most
notable point of contact is the use of ἀσέβειαν in verse 5. The
LXX is literally:

> And thou hast forgiven the ungodliness of my sin.[2]

Paul does not use the word ἀσεβής and cognates often (assuming
as we do that he is not the author of the Pastoral Epistles), and
he may have used it here because ἀσεβεία occurs in the psalm
which he quotes. On the whole it is a word which might be

more appropriate to the Gentile sinner than to the Jew, who might better be described as ἄδικος or ἄνομος. Then Paul might find in verse 3 a reference to Abraham's age, very relevant in view of his believing God's promise of posterity:

> my body wasted away,

but the LXX has literally: 'my bones grew old'. In Rom. 4.19 Paul describes Abraham thus: 'He did not weaken in faith when he considered his own body, which was as good as dead, because he was about a hundred years old'. Then in verse 10 we find something very like faith described:

> steadfast love surrounds him who trusts in the Lord.

The LXX has 'him who hopes on the Lord', and we think of Paul's words about Abraham in Rom. 4.18: 'In hope he believed against hope.' Again in Ps. 32.7 the psalmist exclaims:

> Thou art a hiding place for me,
> thou preservest me from trouble,[3]
> thou dost encompass me with deliverance.

This is reminiscent of God's words in Gen. 15.1: 'Fear not, Abram, I am your shield'; perhaps Paul would think of the various occasions on which Abraham had already been delivered from potential enemies, Pharaoh in Gen. 12, and in Gen. 14 Amraphel and his allies. It is very probable that Paul also knew of the midrash about Abraham's rescue from the furnace in Ur. In the LXX verse 8 of the psalm runs:

> I will cause thee to understand and will instruct thee in this way in which thou shalt go.

This fits in very well with God's assurance to Abraham in Gen. 15.7:

> I am the Lord who brought you out from Ur of the Chaldeans, to give you this land to possess.

It is also worth remarking that there are one or two phrases in the psalm which would seem to Paul to underline the fact that God's promises here are made to all believers, not to the Jews only. Thus verse 6 runs in the LXX:

> Because of this every one that is godly shall offer prayer to thee in an acceptable time.

This might well be the 'day of salvation', to which Paul refers in 2 Cor. 6.2, itself a citation from Isaiah. And in verse 11 the righteous (LXX δίκαιοι) are urged to be glad in the Lord and rejoice. The word 'righteous' would, we know, mean to Paul those who are justified by faith, Gentiles and Jews alike. Finally it is just possible that in verses 7 and 11 of the psalm, where the LXX uses the words ἀγαλλίαμα[4] and ἀγαλλιᾶσθε to mean 'my joy' and 'rejoice', Paul would be reminded of Abraham's joy at the promise of the birth of a son. In Gen. 17.17 Abraham is represented as laughing when he hears this promise. It is true, of course, that in the original text Abraham's laughter is a sign of disbelief, but rabbinic exegesis had probably by this time established the tradition that it was a sign of joy at the news. One account explains the laughter in Gen. 17.17 thus: 'He laughed that he and Sarah, being old, should have children . . . Abraham did not *wonder*, but said thus: "When I was young and strong I had no children, and now, when I and Sarah are old, that we should have children must be a miracle from God, and I believe that God can do all things".'[5] It is very probable also that the author of the Fourth Gospel is referring to this text when he represents Jesus as saying: 'Your father Abraham rejoiced (ἠγαλλιάσατο) that he was to see my day' (John 8.56).

It is not unreasonable to conclude, therefore, that we may take Paul quite literally when he says that Ps. 32 applies to Abraham's situation in Gen. 15. He must have regarded the psalm as uttered originally by Abraham (except of course for verses 8 and 9 which are God's speech), despite the fact that it was actually recorded by David. Abraham in fact is represented by Paul as a justified sinner.

This account of Paul's understanding of Ps. 32 is defended by Wilckens in an able article, though he does not study the psalm in detail.[6] He calls Abraham 'the paradigm of the Christian believer', and he fully accepts that Abraham is regarded by Paul as a sinner in need of forgiveness (p. 112). Ps. 32, he adds in a footnote on p. 113, might seem to apply directly to David, but he insists that it cannot in this context be separated from Abraham. He even suggests that εὑρηκέναι in Rom. 4.1 (omitted by RSV) really means that Abraham 'found grace'[7] (p. 116). He has some very interesting observations to make about Paul's view of the Old Testament: it is part of a process, culminating in Christ, not a series of 'prefigurations' or 'examples'. Abraham's faith is the same as the faith of Christians (p. 127n).

This conclusion is echoed by Zimmerli when he writes that according to Paul Abraham's faith 'does not belong to the time characterized by the subsequent giving of the Law, but stands in the sphere of evangelical promise.'[8] Michel agrees that ἀσεβής applies to Abraham according to Paul. He suggests that Ps. 32, which rabbinic exegesis applied to Israel only, is applied by Paul to all men. This is true, as long as we realize that it was applied to all men through (or in) Abraham; Abraham is here a representative of unredeemed humanity. Cerfaux approximates to this conclusion: 'Abraham is the first of believers. He is the prelude to the system of Christian justification by his faith.'[9] He suggests that in Paul's view the citation from Ps. 32 envisages those who are not circumcised when it pronounces its blessing. We would only modify this by saying that the psalm envisages all the uncircumcised *in Abraham*. C. K. Barrett agrees that, according to Paul, Abraham was a Gentile when he was justified by faith.[10] Anitra Kolenkow has an interesting discussion of the question: 'Did Abraham believe in a God who justifies the ungodly?'[11] She links this passage with Abraham's intercession on behalf of the inhabitants of Sodom in Gen. 18, and cites rabbinic evidence to show that some rabbis understood Abraham to be interceding for the ungodly as well as for the righteous in that passage. In Gen. 18, she says, Abraham tried to justify the ungodly, and Paul represents him as believing in a God who does just this. She also refers to various rabbinic passages where Abraham appears as an intercessor for the Gentiles. The suggested link with Gen. 18 is interesting, but in Rom. 4 Paul does not seem to be thinking of Abraham as an intercessor at all, and certainly not as righteous because of his intercession. Abraham is a representative of the Gentiles, but a representative in being forgiven and justified. If Paul gave any consideration to the story of Abraham's intercession on behalf of Sodom, he is more likely to have thought of it as proving that in fact there are not any righteous. For a wholehearted defender of Abraham's position as a justified Christian we may turn to no less a theologian than Martin Luther himself: Abraham, he says, by believing is born of the Holy Ghost. And 'Abraham's

Christ is our Christ'.[12] Karl Barth has a comment on this passage in his edition of Romans which is worth quoting:

> What is true of Abraham is therefore true also of the anonymous figure portrayed in the 32nd Psalm. Both are witnesses of the Resurrection, and both live by it. As independent historical figures apart from Christ, they are incomprehensible. They are types of that life of his which is prolonged longitudinally throughout the whole extent of time.

We would have to inquire more exactly what Barth means by 'types' before we could be sure whether this view agrees with the approach we have adopted here. But Barth finely portrays Paul's fundamentally christocentric understanding of the Scriptures. Leenhardt agrees absolutely that ἀσεβής applies to Abraham. He was in the position of a proselyte before circumcision. 'At that moment' Abraham was one of the godless.' He adds that Jewish tradition thought of Abraham as a proselyte because he is called *ger* 'a stranger' in Genesis, which was the technical term for a proselyte. On the other hand, he does not admit that Ps. 32 applies to Abraham: there are two figures, he says, Abraham the 'ungodly' and David the sinner. But, we may reply, Paul goes out of his way to emphasize that the blessing in Ps. 32 was uttered over one who was not circumcised. This could not be said of David.

Sanday and Headlam specifically deny that ἀσεβής applies to Abraham, and say it is taken from the psalm which Paul proceeds to quote. Far from being a disproof of the word applying to Abraham, we would see it as constituting a strong presumption that Paul thought of Abraham as the man described in the psalm. Lagrange also would distinguish between Abraham and the figure in the psalm. Nygren asks the question: 'Where does Scripture say that Abraham was "ungodly"? But that question is quite unnecessary. For Paul clearly does not mean to say that Abraham was sinful in special degree.' It is certainly helpful to have the question posed so clearly, but Nygren's answer is hardly satisfactory: the only link between David's prophetic utterance and the condition of all men is Abraham. As to Nygren's argument that Scripture nowhere describes Abraham as 'ungodly', we must bear in mind that Paul was not limited to Scripture in what he believed could be known about Abraham.

He could, we know, make use of contemporary midrash. But precisely this question comes under discussion next.

One thing is quite clear: in describing Abraham as a justified sinner when he believed God's promise about his posterity, Paul was running directly contrary to contemporary rabbinic tradition. The Abraham to whom God spoke the promises was already a figure of tremendous spiritual stature in rabbinic Judaism. The Midrash on Ps. 32 makes this quite clear, even though it does not directly connect the psalm with Abraham. It interprets *Maskil* in the title of the psalm as meaning 'look up'. If the sinner looks up, he will receive forgiveness. Nebuchadnezzar 'Lifted up his eyes to heaven' after his seven years, and was restored: 'If even the wicked, who deserve extermination, but look up to heaven, the Holy One (blessed be He) forthwith gives them pardon—how much more and more pardon, therefore, to Israel, children of Abraham, of Isaac and of Jacob, if they look up to heaven!' (I, 402). There is also a striking contrast in the way in which the blessing pronounced in this psalm is interpreted: '*Blessed is the man unto whom the Lord imputeth not iniquity*—provided, to be sure, the man has done a good deed to offset the iniquity. *And in whose spirit there is no guile*—that is, he must be a man whose study of the Torah is not deceitful.' The same Midrash gives ample evidence for the rabbinic belief that Abraham knew and observed the entire Torah. See Midrash on Ps. 1.6 (I, 18); R. Simeon taught in the name of R. Johanan that the torch in Gen. 15.17 meant the Torah, which Abraham was allowed to see beforehand (I, 426). The same belief is attested much earlier in Ecclus. 44.20. Writing of Abraham, Ben Sira says:

> he kept the law of the Most High,
> and was taken into covenant with him.[13]

Even greater claims were made for him. God is represented as speaking thus in the Mekilta: 'The faith with which their father Abraham believed in me is deserving that I should divide the sea for them.'[14] Sometimes Abraham is presented in the guise of the Second Adam:

> Our father Abraham was worthy of being made in the beginning before Adam. But the Holy One (blessed be He) said: Should I in the beginning make Abraham, and should he become corrupt,

there will be no-one to come after him and restore order. Therefore in the beginning I shall make Adam, and should Adam
become corrupt, then Abraham will come to restore order.[15]
Similarly Abraham is described as the arbiter of Israel's destiny: he deliberately chose 'the yoke of the kingdoms' for
Israel: 'Abraham was silent and sat still all that day [the day of
the visit of the three angels] and the Holy One (blessed be He)
asked him: How long wilt thou sit still and be silent? Bring thy
melancholy to an end, and choose the yoke of the kingdoms for
thyself'.[16] The alternative was that all Israel should be 'enslaved in Gehenna'.

There is also, as we have already noted, quite an extensive
midrash about Abraham's adventures in Ur before he moved
to Haran, and thence to Canaan. The Talmud says that he
underwent ten trials, one of which was his having to leave
Haran. Another was a trial in a fiery furnace in Ur. It adds
that the good things which God wished to bestow on the generations between Noah and Abraham, but which their sin prevented him from bestowing, were given to Abraham.[17] Vermes
believes that the kernel of the midrash about the furnace is to be
found in Isa. 29.22: 'the Lord, who redeemed Abraham'. Some
event had to be found which crystallized this redemption.[18] The
Midrash on the Psalms says that Terah, Abraham's father, was
a star-gazer and that Abraham was cast into the furnace because he said that he belonged to the Holy One, and not to
idols (II, 230–1). The *Biblical Antiquities* of Pseudo-Philo has
still another version: Abraham was cast into the furnace because he refused to take part in the building of the Tower of
Babel.[19]

There is however some evidence that in rabbinic tradition
Abraham was regarded as having experienced a conversion.
Josephus says that, while still in Mesopotamia, Abraham was
converted to a new conception of God. He concluded from his
study of nature that there was only one God.[20] Vermes shows
that there was an early tradition that Abraham was an idol-
worshipper in the house of his father, but that he experienced a
conversion to monotheism.[21] Jubilees puts his conversion at the
age of fourteen, others at the age of three: Philo, in *De Abrahamo* 81–2, says that Abraham had been reared as an astrologer
and remained so for a long time. He associates the conversion

with the change of name from Abram to Abraham. Compare also *De Virtutibus* 211–16, where there is an encomium on Abraham, who left behind the traditional astrology of his home because of his desire to find a clear vision of God: 'Therefore he is said to have been the first to believe in God, since he was the first to possess an unwavering and firm comprehension that there is one highest cause, and that this cause presides over the universe and all that is in it' (my trans.). A much later tradition describes Abraham thus: 'Abraham was 75 years old when he departed from Haran, and God said to him: Thou art 75 years old, and must drag about the country like a penitent, for the sake of this [thy trying condition] shall a Redeemer of Israel come out of thee, that is, Queen Esther.'[22]

We ought now to be able to come to some conclusion as to why and how Paul could regard the Abraham of Gen. 15 as a justified sinner. We cannot say with certainty how much midrash about Abraham's life in Mesopotamia Paul knew, but it is safe to conclude that he would know the story of Abraham's trial in the furnace, and the tradition that he had experienced a conversion. This last element of the legend would certainly make it easier for Paul to regard him as a justified sinner, despite the heavy weight of orthodox opinion against this. If Philo could represent the conversion as taking place when his name was changed from Abram to Abraham, an incident related in Gen. 17, it would not be difficult for Paul to place the spiritual crisis in Gen. 15. But it would be a mistake to imagine that, when Paul represents Abraham as a justified sinner, he has some special sin or sins in mind, such as the sin of idolatry, for instance. Anyway ἀσεβής is hardly the right epithet for an idolater! It is much more likely that Paul thinks of Abraham as a sinner because he was a Gentile, and was still a Gentile when God justified him for his faith. There was no need for Paul to prove that unconverted Gentiles were sinners (see Gal. 2.15). Abraham was a sinner because he was a Gentile, and as a justified sinner he represents all Gentiles, and indeed all humanity, since circumcision does not avail as far as justification is concerned. Thus Abraham's justification fulfils exactly the function which is required at the point in Romans where it comes: he is the prototype of believing Christians, a sinner (whether from Judaism or from the Gentile world) justified by faith.

But justified by faith in whom? This is a question which must obtrude itself, if Abraham is the paradigm of believers and a justified sinner. It may be relevant to take a look at Philo on this subject first, since he was so nearly Paul's contemporary and does place Abraham's conversion at very nearly the same juncture as Paul does. What is more, Philo associates Abraham's conversion with faith. The very philosophical sort of faith which Philo describes in the passage already quoted from *De Virtutibus* is nevertheless faith in God. Obviously faith in God was a theme to which Philo had devoted a good deal of thought. We may conjecture that his concept of faith had been challenged by Greek rationalists, and that he had had to defend it. He regards faith as an alternative to relying on our own speculations; it is thus very much faith *in God* that matters for Philo. He brings together Gen. 15.6 and Num. 12.7 where Moses is described (in the LXX) as 'faithful in all God's house', and he comments: 'So the best course is to believe God, and not to believe obscure speculations and uncertain conjectures.'[23] In another passage he meets the objection that Abraham deserves no credit for having believed in God; anyone can do that, no matter how evil his character, since it is God who promised. Philo replies that on the contrary it is no easy matter for men to believe, surrounded as they are by a mortal environment, by the distractions of wealth, health, and of friends. To wake up from all this to belief in God is no small accomplishment.[24] A similar contrast between faith in God and faith in power, riches, beauty, etc. is found in *De Abrahamo* 262–8. This contrast itself shows us something of how Philo differs from Paul in his conception of faith: for Philo faith is essentially looking away from the world to God. He defines it neatly in *De Vita Mosis* 1, 280: 'Faith is, as the old saying goes, the manifestation of things not seen.'[25] This is more like what faith means in Hebrews and what hope means in Paul. This view of faith can very easily be accommodated to an essentially philosophical outlook on life. He passes from moral to metaphysical philosophy. Thus '[The soul] hanging upon and dependent on a good hope, and regarding as undoubted that things not present are already present because of the dependable character of him who promises, finds faith, that perfect good, to be the prize'.[26] In *De Mutatione Nominum* 187 Philo suggests that Abraham had to use faith because of our mortal nature: for so much of our life we are bound to be misled by our physical nature, that he is happy who can attain to faith in God at all. Thus faith is necessitated by the fallacious nature of sense experience, and it is easy to pass to a description of faith as a process of 'looking beyond and mentally transcending all physical and non-physical objects'.[27] It is very nearly the Platonic *theoria*. Thus though faith in Philo is always in danger of turning into a species of philosophical contemplation, it is connected with Abraham's conversion, it is very much faith in God, and it is a way of life over against other ways of life.

In trying to understand the meaning of Abraham's faith for Paul, it is helpful to keep a close eye on Galatians chapters 2–4, the parallel passage to this part of Romans. Both in Galatians (2.16; 3.2, 5, 10) and in Romans (3.20, 27, 28) Paul defines faith by contrasting it with ἔργα νόμου 'works of the law'. We have already referred to Lohmeyer's article on this phrase. His conclusion is that in Judaism 'works of the law' would mean a God-given way of life. This very much points up Paul's contention that those who are ἐκ πίστεως have their own contrasting way of life. In his treatment of Abraham's faith in Galatians, Paul is more specific about what we might almost call the Christian character of Abraham's faith. In Gal. 3.5 he reminds the Galatians that their experience of the Spirit and of supernatural powers was due, not to the works of the law, but to 'hearing with faith'. He then goes directly on to say in verse 6:

> Thus Abraham 'believed God and it was reckoned to him as righteousness'.

It is almost as if Luther was right when he said that Abraham by believing was born of the Holy Ghost (see above). In verse 7 Paul can pass straight from Abraham to Christians: all are ἐκ πίστεως, they follow the way of faith. And in the next verse Paul actually describes Scripture as preaching the gospel beforehand to Abraham, προευηγγελίσατο, a word that means 'preaching the gospel by anticipation' not 'preaching a preliminary gospel'. It is not a word coined by Paul, since it is used three times by Philo, always in the sense of 'announcing good news beforehand', never meaning 'proclaiming a different message of good news beforehand'.[28] It is therefore not satisfactory to say that the gospel Abraham heard was the promise of the birth of a son. He did receive this promise, but he received more as well, the news about the seed who was to come, the Messiah, and the accession of the Gentiles, not to mention the resurrection as well. It is noteworthy that in Galatians the promise which elicits Abraham's faith comes from Gen. 12.3, where Abraham responds by setting out from Haran. This is more like the treatment of Abraham's faith which we find in Heb. 11.8–12, where Abraham's faith is shown in setting out not knowing whither he was going, and it is Sarah who shows faith by believing the promise that she would bear a son. But the words of Gen. 12.3 are repeated in Gen. 18.18 where the promise of a son has been given, so we cannot press this point too much. The phrase in Gal. 3.7 οἱ ἐκ πίστεως is a very striking one. Paul uses it exactly in this sense only twice again, once immediately below in verse 9, and once in Rom. 4.16 τῷ ἐκ πίστεως 'Αβραάμ. One might ask, Why does Paul not use κατὰ πίστιν? Or even οἱ πιστεύοντες? The answer seems to be that he wants to give the sense of a lineage, a line of descent from (and including) Abraham. In Galatians at least, that line runs: Abraham—Christ—Christians. By analogy οἱ ἐξ ἔργων νόμου (see verse 10) must mean 'those whose lineage is by the line of works'. Moses—unbelieving Jews—contemporary Jews who reject the gospel (but one should put in a plea for Moses: it is very unlikely that according to Paul, he did not believe the gospel). We may note that you are a sinner (ἁμαρτωλός) if you are (*a*) a non-Christian Gentile (2.15) or (*b*) a Christian who has fallen back on the law (2.17). We may thus further qualify the two phrases οἱ ἐκ πίστεως and οἱ ἐξ ἔργων νόμου as meaning respectively 'those who have been justified by faith' and 'those who have (failed to be) justified by attempting to obey the law'. The notion of two contrasted ways of life stands out clearly: the way of faith began with Abraham, was supremely demonstrated in Jesus, and is continued in Christians in contemporary life. The way of the law was promulgated through Moses, has been continuously but unsuccessfully attempted by most Jews ever since, and is now the great obstacle to contemporary Jews becoming Christians. One is reminded of Hebrews' description of the lineage of faith in Heb. 11.13: κατὰ πίστιν; they died 'in faith' as they had lived 'in faith'. One must therefore reject Lietzmann's comment that Paul was more interested in showing that Abraham was χωρὶς ἔργων than that he was²⁹ ἐκ πίστεως; Paul's treatment of the subject in Galatians surely clears him of this charge. Leenhardt well points out that the rabbis emphasized Abraham's faith, but treated it as a good work, and he quotes the Mekilta: 'Abraham received possession of this world and of the world to come peculiarly by virtue of his faith by which he believed in God.' Paul is equally far from this conception.

Can we therefore conclude that according to Paul Abraham believed in Christ? Very nearly, if not exactly. There is no difference between the character of his faith and that of Christians. He, like us, was justified by faith; like us he is a justified sinner. There is ultimately only one in whom we or anyone else can be justified, and that is Christ. But it is God who justifies in Christ; so perhaps the right answer to the question posed at the head of this paragraph is: Abraham believed in God-in-Christ; he was justified by God-in-Christ, the pre-existent, pre-incarnate Christ, of course. Paul goes neither as far as Hebrews in one direction nor as far as John in the other. Hebrews is very careful to emphasize the preliminary, imperfect nature of the condition in which the heroes of Israel lived their lives. They did know Christ (I believe this can be shown by a careful study of Heb. 11), but they knew him in an incomplete mode. John on the other hand makes it clear for those who take his language in chapter 8 of his Gospel seriously that Abraham did know Christ; he rejoiced to encounter him; he believed in the pre-existent Son. In between these two stands Paul: the logic of his argument should lead him to say that Abraham was justified in the pre-existent Christ. He probably believed this consciously; but he does not find occasion to say it, perhaps because it would be rather too strong meat for his readers. But it is the assumption behind his theology.

# 4

## MOTIVES AND TECHNIQUE IN THE COMPOSITION OF ROMANS AND GALATIANS

————⋘⋙————

Now that we have considered what believing Abraham meant to Paul, it should be possible, by means of comparing the passages on Abraham in Romans with those in Galatians, to come to some conclusions as to how and why Paul uses his scriptural material. This will mean primarily a comparison of Galatians chapters 2 and 3 with Romans chapters 3 and 4, though we will have to draw on material also in Galatians chapter 4 and Romans chapter 5. We arrange the material under four columns: the first is a brief description of the contents. The second gives the reference in Romans, the third the reference in Galatians, and the fourth the chapter in Genesis which supplies the scriptural material. We follow the order in Romans, which, as we shall see, is not exactly the order in Galatians. We must then try to draw out the significance of this table:

| SUBJECT | ROMANS | GALATIANS | GENESIS |
|---|---|---|---|
| All equal under the cross | 3.1–20 | 2.15–21 | |
| The victory of God in Christ | 3.21–5 | 3.10–14 | |
| Only one God in Christ | 3.26–31 | 3.15–29 | |
| Abraham, man of faith | 4.1–10, 13–25 | 3.6–9 | 15 |
| The meaning of circumcision | 4.11–12 | 5.1–12 | 17 |
| Life in Christ | 5.1–12 | 4.1–7 | |

At first sight Rom. 3.1–20 and Gal. 2.15–21 may not seem to be treating the same subject; but a closer examination shows that both have the same basic theme: by the crucifixion of Christ God has brought all men into the same predicament. If we compare the last verse of each passage we shall see how they converge. In Gal. 2.21 Paul writes: 'if justification were through the law, then Christ died to no purpose' and in Rom. 3.20: 'For no human being will be justified in his sight through the works of the law, since through the law comes knowledge of sin.' If our suggestion in chapter 2 of this work is correct, Paul has had the cross in view all through his catena of scriptural quotations in Rom. 3.9-18. In each case Paul passes on from an exposition of the equality of all men under the cross (the negative or judgement aspect of God's salvation) to expound the positive side of God's action in Christ. I have called this theme 'God's victory in Christ', because I believe this is what Paul has chiefly in mind, despite the forensic or apparently expiatory language which he uses. Our reference in chapter 1 of this work to Col. 2.13-15 must serve to bring out the element of victory implicit here.

Paul follows this in each case with a reference to the unity of God. This may seem a little strange to us, but in fact it is touching on something which was absolutely fundamental to Paul's thought; the exclusiveness of contemporary orthodox Judaism, Paul believed, could only lead to one theological conclusion: the God of Israel was the God of the Jews only, and the Gentiles simply had no god at all. Their pretended gods were no-gods. In one sense Paul accepted this, see 1 Cor. 10.20; Gal. 4.8; Eph. 2.12.[1] But he did not accept that the God of Israel had no interest in, no deliberate relation towards, the rest of the world. Israel's God had always intended to make himself known to the whole world. It was the Torah that had hindered this, or rather the attitude towards the Torah which the Jews had mistakenly adopted. Thus when God fully and supremely declares himself in Christ, it must follow that the exclusiveness is abolished, the *Torah as a way of life* is abrogated, and the unity of God is seen as a unity safeguarded by God's action in Christ and imperilled by the Torah-centred religion of Judaism. In this respect Rom. 3.29-30 can help to explain the obscurities of Gal. 3.15-19, as several modern scholars have realized.

Paul has here altered his order in Romans from that of Galatians. In Galatians the description of Abraham's faith comes between the exposition of the negative and the positive aspects of the cross. We can see why this should suit his purpose in Galatians: in that Epistle he wants to bring out the faith of the Messiah. Abraham it was who first exhibited the way of faith, a way followed by the Messiah in his all-important act of redemption. But in Romans Abraham comes after the two aspects of the cross. We can only guess why this should be so: perhaps Paul was not so much concerned to stress the faith of the Messiah in Romans, though our study of chapter 1 of this work has shown that the theme occurs there, and I would maintain that τὸν ἐκ πίστεως 'Ιησοῦ in Rom. 3.26 means 'him who follows in Jesus' way of faith'. More likely therefore that the transposition in Romans is due to Paul's desire to give a fairly full account of salvation history, such as we do not find in Galatians. If he was intending that his Romans readers should have something like a continuous account of salvation history in the law and the prophets, it was certainly more appropriate that he should first clearly outline both the negative and the positive aspects of the great act of redemption in which that history culminated, and then pursue the history in order, beginning with Abraham.

The section on circumcision is, strictly speaking, out of order in both Epistles. In Romans it comes in the middle of the section on Abraham's faith, a very natural position. In Galatians it is on its own, much later in chapter 5. We can see the reason for this too: among the Galatians there were those who regarded circumcision as absolutely essential. Paul therefore had to give it a place of its own when he dealt with it, and he uses in Galatians the most trenchant and personal language about it. What is surprising is that in Galatians the argument about circumcision is not supported by an appeal to Abraham's case. It would, one might imagine, have been an effective argument with the Galatians. One can only assume that Paul had not thought of it when he wrote Galatians. In any case Paul, in an exposition of the relation of Christianity to the Torah, had to deal with the question of circumcision, which is what lies behind both these passages.

I have called the last theme 'life in Christ'. It comes in more appropriately in Galatians than in Romans, following on the section on the unity of God. There is nothing corresponding to this immediately in Romans; I have assigned Rom. 5.1–12 to this theme because it is the first section dealing with this after the great passage consisting of Romans chapters 3 and 4. It does not correspond very closely to Gal. 4.1–7; in fact a much later passage in Rom. 8.12–17, offers a closer parallel to Gal. 4.1–7 with its reference to the Spirit, to sonship, to 'Abba', and to our inheritance. However, Rom. 5.1–12 does have certain things in common with the Galatians passage, a reference to Christ's act of redemption for instance (Rom. 5.6–10; Gal. 4.4–5), and a mention of the Spirit in our hearts (Rom. 5.5; Gal. 4.6).

We may perhaps pause at this point to observe that Paul cannot possibly have been using *testimonia* when he wrote these passages. It is true that most scholars have now abandoned the view so forcibly expounded by Rendell Harris, that the New Testament writers did not for the most part compose their works with a bible open before them, relying rather on catenae of proof texts which had been diligently collected by the very earliest Christians. But the discovery of the Qumran documents has suggested to some people that the early Christians may have used Scripture as the Qumran sectaries used it. The *pesher* method does not necessarily lead to piecemeal interpretation and 'text-slinging', but one does gain the impression from a good deal of Qumran exegesis that they relied on proof texts to a considerable extent. Indeed catenae of texts have now turned up among the documents recovered. It is therefore satisfactory to be able to say with great confidence that this is not Paul's method of procedure here: he must have had the Book of Genesis open before him as he wrote. We shall be giving some thought presently to what this implies about his originality.

But next we must try to resolve three questions which seem to present themselves (there is a fourth, more important than all, but it is reserved for separate treatment). First, why has Paul omitted in Romans the references to the giving of the Torah, to the angels, and to the position of Moses, all of which we find in Gal. 3? It is not a satisfactory reply to say that in the meantime Paul had lost interest in Moses, or had ceased to be concerned with the elemental powers. If we may be allowed to assume that 2 Corinthians was written between Galatians and Romans, we find in the midrash in 2 Corinthians 3 a lively interest in Moses' relation to the Torah and to the dispensation of grace; and we have only to glance at Rom. 8.38–9 to realize that the hostile powers had by no means disappeared from Paul's thoughts. One reason is perhaps that in Romans Paul was not concerned, as far as we can judge, with a Judaizing element, and therefore he was not under as great an obligation to put Moses in proper perspective. Another reason may be that Paul did not know the Romans personally, and therefore could not speak with as great confidence about their pre-Christian condition as he could in the case of the Galatians. Slavery to the powers, or to the Torah, was no doubt a general condition of unredeemed humanity in Paul's view, but a specific reference to it would be more likely to make sense if Paul were writing to those whom he had himself converted.

A second most interesting question is this: Why did Paul omit the Hagar 'allegory' when writing to the Romans? In Gal. 3.6–9 Paul deals with Abraham's faith, the record of which occurs in Gen. 16. In Gal. 4.21–31 he gives us his explanation of the significance of Hagar, drawn from Gen. 16 and 21. In Gal. 5.1–12 we have the meaning of circumcision, the institution of which is described in Gen. 17. In Romans, on the other hand, Paul gives a description of Abraham which includes the significance of the time at which he was circumcised, ignoring the existence of Hagar altogether. And when he does revert to his commentary on salvation-history in Rom. 9.1f, he mentions the birth of Isaac with the merest passing allusion to Ishmael, who is not named at all ('the children of the flesh' in 9.8). Why this omission? We are reduced to guesswork, but it is not difficult to think of a plausible answer. The 'allegory' of Hagar and Sarah is obscure, so obscure that scholars are still divided as to its meaning in several details. Again, in Gal. 4.21–31 Paul is in effect arguing that the unbelieving Jews are really sons of Hagar, not of Sarah, something that runs so contrary to the plain intention of the author of Gen. 16 and 21 that Paul may well have found it useless as an argument to employ against Jews. Finally, one might suggest that in Paul's experience people were misled by the phrase in Gal. 4.24 ἅτινά ἐστιν ἀλληγορούμενα. It has certainly misled the majority of commentators ever since it was written, as we hope to show later on. Rather than attempt to explain what he meant by that phrase,

Paul may have decided to omit the piece altogether when writing to the Romans. This last suggestion depends, of course, on the assumption that when Paul wrote Romans he had a copy of Galatians accessible. But I do not regard this as a rash conjecture.

The third question is this: Why does Paul use a completely different figure to describe the positive aspect of Christ's work from that which he used in Galatians? He uses κατάρα and the figure of the victim hung on a tree in Galatians. In Romans he uses ἱλαστήριον and the figure of the sacrifice on the Day of Atonement. Both figures are equally bound up with the Hebrew Scriptures. Neither can be understood by those who know nothing of the Old Testament. One reason is undoubtedly the sheer fertility of Paul's mind. As has been often pointed out, he was no scholastic theologian, tied down to traditional formulas. He had all sorts of different ways of explaining the work of Christ, all connected integrally with the Scriptures, but differing widely in the actual terms employed. Again, in Galatians, as we have noted, Paul was at grips with the Torah. He had to show that Christ had dealt decisively with a way of life centred on the Torah. The figure of the curse-bearing victim on the tree suited this purpose better. In Romans he was perhaps more concerned with the universality of the redemption: he therefore employed a figure which would bring this out. The Day of Atonement was a general removal of sins for all Jews: it would best provide the framework for a far more general removal of sin for all men once and for all. In this connection it is relevant to say that I do not think that T. W. Manson's thesis has been shaken: he maintained that ἱλαστήριον in Rom. 3.25 refers to the 'mercy-seat' in the holy of holies in the Temple. The word προέθετο 'put forward' is used to contrast the publicity of Christ's death with the secrecy whereby the High Priest alone entered the holy of holies and beheld the mercy seat: 'by his blood' contrasts with the blood of the goat and the calf which were slaughtered in the Temple on the Day of Atonement.[2] We thus find Paul in entire agreement with the author to the Hebrews in that he does not identify Christ with the type of the scapegoat. The scapegoat's blood was not shed.

Paul used something very close to the 'curse' figure again in 2 Cor. 5.20–1, and we shall be encountering traces of the sacri-

ficial figure also when we come to examine Rom. 11.13f, with
its link passage in 1 Cor. 5.6f. So it cannot be said that either
figure is isolated or outmoded in Paul's thought. In Galatians
he used a figure which is more easily connected with Christ's
victory over the powers, a point which does not come up in
Romans chapters 3–4. The connection we have traced in
chapter 1 of this work between Gal. 3 and Col. 2 underlines
this. Indeed we may well find a resolution of our problem in
Colossians, for we can find evidence of both the figure of offering and the figure of victory over hostile powers there: see Col.
1.22 and 2.13–15. It would be profitless to attempt any further
to explain the variety of Paul's genius.

Reverting for a moment to a consideration of Romans only,
we can find in the figure of Abraham an extremely interesting
typology. We must use this word with great care, for it is sometimes used in a very imprecise sense. What we mean is that we
can trace a continuous line or process running from Abraham
through Christ to Christians. This applies not only to Abraham's faith, which we have already explored, but to other
features of the figure of Abraham in Romans as well. Several
scholars have pointed out that Paul sees a connection between
Abraham's belief in God's power to quicken Sarah's dead womb
and Christian belief in the resurrection of Christ and of Christians in Christ. See Karl Barth's exposition of this theme in
his commentary on Romans.[3] Cerfaux also notes this.[4]
Nygren observes the connection between Rom. 4.17 and
Christ's resurrection, and comments: 'Abraham's faith has
significance as an example and type.' This is unexception-
able, as long as it is realized that 'type' does not mean
'imperfect image' or 'shadow', but 'identical faith with
Christian faith saving only the incarnation', to use the convenient word of a post-biblical theology. Leenhardt also sees
this connection. One could thus draw up a series of parallels:

| ABRAHAM | CHRIST | CHRISTIANS |
|---|---|---|
| Believed in God who justifies. | Lived by faith. | Believe in God-in-Christ. |
| Believed that God could raise the dead. | Was raised from the dead. | Are raised in Christ and believe in the resurrection. |

| ABRAHAM | CHRIST | CHRISTIANS |
|---|---|---|
| Was justified by faith. | Was justified by faith. | Are justified in Christ by faith. |
| Gave glory to God (Rom. 4.20). | Was raised to God's glory (Rom. 6.4; 15.9; Phil. 2.11). | Give glory to God (Rom. 9.23; 15.7; 2 Cor. 4.15). |

In this scheme Christ is the centre, and in a sense he points both ways. Thus he is both the seed who receives the promise originally uttered to Abraham and the fulfilment of the promise wherein Christians are included. He is both the fulfilment of Abraham's hope in the resurrection, and the means by which Christians have been sacramentally, and will be eschatologically, raised from the dead. Abraham's hope of resurrection was not exhausted in the quickening of Sarah's womb. This is surely indicated by the phrase which Paul uses in Rom. 4.17 to describe the God in whom Abraham believed:

Θεοῦ τοῦ ζωοποιοῦντος τοὺς νεκροὺς καὶ καλοῦντος τὰ μὴ ὄντα ὡς ὄντα.

God who gives life to the dead and calls into existence the things that do not exist.

Paul uses ζωοποιοῦν frequently for God's power in raising both Christ and Christians. The latter half of the phrase reminds us of 1 Cor. 1.28:

καὶ τὰ ἀγενῆ τοῦ κόσμου καὶ τὰ ἐξουθενημένα ἐξελέξατο ὁ Θεός, τὰ μὴ ὄντα, ἵνα τὰ ὄντα καταργήσῃ.

God chose what is low and despised in the world, even things that are not, to bring to nothing things that are.

But this verse describes the whole process of the cross, resurrection, and calling of Christians. So we may safely conclude that, according to Paul, Abraham had some intelligence of these things himself.

How far Paul meant us to take this typology of Abraham, it is very difficult to say. He would not have intended to press it so far as to suggest that the historical life of Jesus Christ was merely an incident in the process; but he certainly did not regard Abraham as exhibiting a purely external or formal resemblance to a Christian believer. Abraham knew and believed in the same God as Christians know and believe in; and that

God is known in Christ. At the end of this book we must ask ourselves in all seriousness what part this typology placed in Paul's theology as a whole.

Two verses at the end of Rom. 4 give us a remarkable insight into what Paul believed about the purpose of the Scriptures and their relation to history. We propose to reproduce them here, and to put after them three other passages from the New Testament (two of which are also Pauline) by way of illumination:

(a) But the words, 'it was reckoned to him', were written not for his sake alone, but for ours also. It will be reckoned to us who believe in him that raised from the dead Jesus our Lord' (Rom. 4.23-4).

(b) For whatever was written in former days was written for our instruction, that by steadfastness and by the encouragement of the scriptures we might have hope (Rom. 15.4).

(c) Now these things happened to them as a warning (τυπικῶς), but they were written down for our instruction, upon whom the end of the ages has come (1 Cor. 10.11).

(d) The prophets who prophesied of the grace that was to be yours searched and inquired about this salvation; they inquired what person or time was indicated by the Spirit of Christ within them when predicting the sufferings of Christ and the subsequent glory. It was revealed to them that they were serving not themselves but you, in the things which have now been announced to you through the Holy Spirit sent from heaven (1 Pet. 1.10-12).

In the first passage we observe that the writing down of the story of Abraham's justification served two purposes: it was written for his sake and for our sake. Paul believed, of course, that the whole of Genesis was written by Moses, who lived at least four hundred years after Abraham's time, if we follow scriptural chronology. It is therefore not easy to see what exactly Abraham gained by Moses writing an account of him so much later. Perhaps the third passage gives us a clue: the story of Abraham was written down so that Abraham could be an *example* to Israel. But he is a *type* to us Christians: that is to say, he shows us that belief in a God who raises from the dead has always existed since Abraham's time. Better still, he shows us that the God who raised Jesus from the dead was still the same

God, and known to be the same God, even in Abraham's day. We can, however, understand why Paul wanted to maintain that in some sense the Scriptures were written for the benefit of the contemporaries of the writers. This affirmation safeguarded the historicity of the narratives: if he had given the impression that the sole purpose of the Scriptures was to record types for the benefit of Christians, there was a danger that the whole record of God's revelation of himself before 'the end of the ages' dawned was to be a show, a play, a 'prefiguration'. What Paul believed to be history would have degenerated into pageant.

The second passage almost gives this impression. But we must remember that here Paul speaks of what was *written* in olden times, not what was done. He has just quoted an utterance from the Psalms which he regards as a prophetic utterance of the pre-existent Christ through the lips of the prophet David. It could have had no significance for David's contemporaries; its sole purpose in Paul's eyes was to predict what would happen to the Messiah. Perhaps we might allow this much significance for David's contemporaries: they could have learned much about Christ from this and similar utterances. This is in fact a particularly clear example of Christ as the centre of prophecy, because the purpose of this verse having been written is not only that we should be instructed but also that we should have hope. It looks forward from Paul's time as well as backward to the historical Jesus and to the prophetic utterance through David.

The third passage applies neatly to each of the first two citations of the Scriptures. Paul here has been expounding the significance of some of the events in Israel's wilderness sojourn, and he sums up its meaning in this verse. We must distinguish between why these events happened and why they were recorded. They happened as a warning to Israel in the wilderness. We must firmly resist the temptation to which so many commentators have fallen, that is, to translate τυπικῶς as 'by way of types'. They were not types for Israel of old, and Paul does not at all mean to suggest that the reason why they happened was to serve as types for us. That would be to fall into the error which we outlined above.[5] They happened in their own right, but they were recorded for our benefit. Moses, we may imagine Paul saying, wrote down the record of the wilderness sojourn for the benefit of those who, he knew, would live in the end-time, so that they might recognize their Lord active in days of old and see the consequences of disobeying him.

The fourth passage I have added because, though not from Pauline tradition, it gives a remarkably clear reflection of essentially the same attitude towards the Scriptures. The author of 1 Peter says plainly that the prophets did not utter their predictions for the benefit of themselves, or (we may conjecture) of their contemporaries. They did not know immediately why they uttered them, but on investigation they found that it was for the benefit of those who should live in the end-time, Christians, in fact. We should not rashly conclude that according to this writer the events of Israel's history of old had no significance in themselves, that he has fallen into the error of regarding salvation history as a pageant. Like Paul in Rom. 15.3, he is thinking here only of prophetic utterance, not of events such as Abraham's justification or the experiences in the wilderness.[6] On the contrary, more than one passage later in this Epistle shows us that the author did regard events in scriptural history as having a significance of their own; see 1 Pet. 3.5–6, 19–21. Perhaps the only difference here from Paul's view is that the author of 1 Peter seems to regard the prophets as not knowing about the end-time, not knowing the gospel in fact; though they were able to inform themselves about it. Paul always gives us the impression that both Moses and the prophets had a very good idea of the gospel and the events of the end-time. This comment in Rom. 4.23–4 on the relevance of Abraham to Christians serves to bring out clearly Paul's conviction that the events of what we call the 'Old Testament' were by no means old and outmoded, but were part of the one revelation of God in Christ.

Before passing on to a consideration of the last question raised by Paul's treatment of Abraham, we may allow ourselves a brief consideration of another aspect of it which has been discussed by one or two scholars. C. H. Dodd has asked whether Paul's material on Abraham is original, or whether he received it from Christian tradition.[7] He points to Acts 3.25, where Gen. 12.3 is conflated with Gen. 22.18 as the promise given to Abraham. On the ground that Paul quotes Gen. 12.3 and 17.5, but not 22.18, he suggests that the two traditions are

independent: 'Since Paul and the author of Acts have conflated the passages differently, we cannot suppose that the one
borrowed from the other.' He therefore concludes that Christian interest in Abraham pre-dates Paul. Lindars, on the other
hand, thinks that Paul's material on Abraham is his own.[8]
Goppelt in a more recent article has pointed out that it was the
typology of Abraham rather than the apocalyptic history-
schema that enabled Paul to break with the Torah.[9] This
would suggest that the Abraham typology was Paul's own
contribution to Christian thought.

There are really two distinct points here: Was Paul's Abra-
ham material original? And, what function did it serve in the
development of his thought? We might almost say that the
first of these two questions hinges on our decision as to whether
Christianity was preached to the Gentiles before Paul or not.
If it was, the figure of Abraham would be of very great importance, for he might be useful as a justification for admitting
Gentiles to the Church. On the whole it seems likely that the
Gentile mission was not begun by Paul, so we may say that
Dodd is right so far in maintaining that Christians were taking
an interest in Abraham before Paul's conversion. But when
Dodd goes on to maintain that any particular text or texts in
Genesis formed a primitive *testimonium*, one begins to have
doubts. As we have seen, Paul's treatment of Genesis does not
at all give the impression of being based on *testimonia*. As for the
evidence of Acts, a conservative estimate would allow an inter-
val of thirty years between Romans and Acts, plenty of time for
Paul's midrash on Abraham to have been modified. Acts 3 cannot be said with confidence to be from a special source. And
Stephen's speech in Acts 7, which certainly does seem to be
from a special source, does not cite any of the texts quoted by
either Paul or Acts, though it has several citations of its own.
This suggests a general interest rather than specific *testimonia*.
We may also refer to our suggestion made above that the point
about Abraham's circumcision, which is peculiar to Romans in
Paul, was one which occurred to Paul between the writing of
Galatians and of Romans. Stephen mentions Abraham's circumcision (Acts 7.7–8), but does not make any anti-Torah
capital out of it. All this suggests a general interest in Abraham
among the first Christians who preached to the Gentiles, but

not a traditional catena of texts. Both Paul and the author of Stephen's speech in Acts 7 elaborate the subject, Paul's midrash being considerably larger and more basic in his scheme of things. The author of Hebrews gives us his own midrash in Heb. 11.8–19. Leenhardt's point, referred to above, that Abrahas was regarded in contemporary Judaism as a proselyte would point in this direction also.

Goppelt is certainly justified in claiming that the Abraham typology helped Paul to break with the Torah. As we shall be seeing later on in this work, there is a very big principle involved here. It was not just that Paul was able to argue that the call of Abraham, regarded by all Jews as the beginning of their history as a separate people, was made to a Gentile, and implied a way of faith rather than the way of the law. It was more than that: Paul regarded Abraham as in some sense the first Christian believer. The gospel dispensation began with Abraham, and Paul was thus able to establish an all-important chronological priority for it over the law. We shall be arguing later on that this meant for Paul not just a sort of anticipation of eschatology, but rather a claim that the God revealed in the historical Jesus had always been knowable as such. The Abraham typology enabled Paul not only to bypass the Torah, but also to claim, in principle at least, a universalism that had always been potentially accessible.

On p. 70 above we claimed that there was one important question still left out of consideration in connection with Paul's treatment of the figure of Abraham. Anyone who has any acquaintance with the rabbinic presentation of Abraham will have noticed one remarkable omission in what we have written so far: nothing has been said about the 'Aqedah, the binding of Isaac, or, as it is often called, the sacrifice of Isaac. The important question is, therefore, Why does Paul apparently omit altogether this prominent incident in Abraham's life?

Only at the end of the discussion can we attempt to answer this important question. We must first give some evidence to show the place which the 'Aqedah played in contemporary Jewish exegesis. Philo, it is interesting to note, connects the 'Aqedah with Abraham's faith, though of course the 'Aqedah itself is explained in purely philosophical terms.[10] Josephus represents Isaac as a willing victim. He is described as a dutiful son and very religious.[11] Abraham tells Isaac that he must be sacrificed in order to show obedience to God. And Josephus describes Isaac's response to this information thus: 'Isaac . . . received the words with pleasure . . . and hastened towards the altar and the slaughter.' The *Biblical Antiquities* of Pseudo-Philo, probably about contemporary with Josephus, give further particulars. It is suggested that the merit of Isaac's offering caused God to choose Israel.[12] We have the same willingness on the part of Isaac to be sacrificed as we encountered in Josephus. We are even given some insight into the reason why God made this apparently cruel demand of Abraham: the angels were jealous of God's favour shown towards Abraham, so God put him to the test in order to show that he obeyed God from love, not from hope of reward. The parallel with Job is obvious, and indeed the rabbis did not fail to draw it.[13] The Mekilta says that God divided the Red Sea because the merit of Abraham's sacrifice of Isaac won this for them.[14] In the Talmud we have a legend of a girl who fell into a deep pit and reappeared unharmed, saying that an old man leading a ram had come to her help. This is Abraham and the ram he offered.[15] Still later sources show us that there was much dispute as to the precise degree of merit to be apportioned between Abraham and Isaac:

> Rabbi B'chai asks: Who had the greater merit, Abraham, who was about to slay his own son with his own hands, or Isaac, who was willing to be slain? Some of the sages say: Abraham had the greater merit, for it is much easier for a man to allow himself to be slain, than for a father to slay his son with his own hands. But some of the sages say: the merit of Isaac was greater, because Abraham explicitly heard direct from God that he was to slaughter his son, whereas Isaac had no such divine communication, he having heard from Abraham only, and yet was ready to be slain. The Rabbi B'chai maintains, however, that the merit of Abraham was greater, for Isaac was in duty bound to obey his father's bidding.[16]

There was also a tendency to suggest that Isaac actually died, i.e. that the sacrifice was consummated and that Abraham saw him brought to life again: 'As soon as the knife touched Isaac's throat his soul departed out of him. When he heard the voice from the throne of glory, that Isaac should not be touched, his soul returned into his body and Abraham unbound him and pronounced the [following blessing]: "Blessed art thou, O Lord, who revivest the dead!"' (ibid., p. 125). This is of course one of the Eighteen Blessings. In the same source Abraham is represented as saying to God: 'Thou hast sworn, and I too will swear, that I will not go down from here till that thou hast promised me that thou wilt remember this [the binding of Isaac] as an atonement for the sins of my children, as if I actually had poured out the blood of my son, and as if his ashes were actually spread upon the altar.'

In view of this evidence, a number of scholars have argued that Paul actually took the idea of the atoning death of Christ from the '*Aqedah* soteriology of contemporary Judaism. Thus Schoeps argues that Rom. 3.25 implies this, claiming that ὃν προέθετο ὁ Θεὸς ἱλαστήριον corresponds to Gen. 22.8 LXX: ὁ Θεὸς ὄψεται αὐτῷ πρόβατον 'God will provide himself the lamb' (MT *yir'eh*). He gives interesting additional rabbinic evidence about the significance of the '*Aqedah*: the Midrash Rabba on Genesis compares Isaac carrying the wood to one who takes his cross on his shoulder. The earliest specific identification of Isaac bound on the altar with Christ is in the Epistle of Barnabas. But he claims that Rom. 8.32 τοῦ ἰδίου υἱοῦ οὐκ ἐφείσατο is an echo of Gen. 22.2, where the LXX translates 'your only son' with τὸν υἱόν σου τὸν ἀγαπητόν.[17] This argument is taken up and reinforced by Vermes.[18] He too brings more rabbinic evidence: in the Targum of Jerusalem Abraham is described as making something like a high priestly prayer over Isaac. He conjectures that this interpretation of the '*Aqedah* may have been suggested by Isa. 53. This idea had already been suggested by Euler, who sees certain verbal parallels.[19] There was even a midrash which said that Isaac shed some of his blood on Mount Moriah. Another tractate claims that through the merits of Isaac God will raise the dead. There was even a tendency to say that the Temple sacrifices were only memorials of Isaac's sacrifice. Vermes thinks the '*Aqedah* motif is present in the synoptic accounts of Jesus' baptism, and even suggests that Jesus saw himself as fulfilling the figure of the '*Aqedah*. The latest champion of this view is J. E. Wood, who adds little except the unlikely suggestion that κατὰ τὰς γραφάς in 1 Cor. 15.4 refers, among other passages, to Gen. 22.[20]

C. K. Barrett is not convinced by Schoeps' equation of

προέθετο in Rom. 3.25 with ὄψεται in the LXX of Gen. 22.8. He thinks it much more likely that in Rom. 3 Paul had the Day of Atonement in mind.[21] In his commentary on Romans he allows the remote possibility that Rom. 4.24 might have a reference to the '*Aqedah*, but the only passage in Paul, he maintains, which we can be sure carries such a reference is Rom. 8.32. Many years before, Michel had commented on the absence of reference to the '*Aqedah* in Romans, and suggested that Paul omits it because it might seem to make faith into a service.[22] This suggestion is reinforced by a comment of Doeve's: he points out that in Jas. 2.21–2 the '*Aqedah* is in fact treated as a good work:

> Was not our father Abraham justified by works, when he offered his son Isaac upon the altar?[23]

This is not to suggest, of course, that Paul was consciously writing against James. We would rather regard the Epistle of James as a later reflection of the sort of argument that might be drawn by a Jewish Christian from the '*Aqedah*. Lindars also concludes that Paul deliberately avoids elaborating the '*Aqedah* in a typological sense.[24]

It must be confessed that neither Schoeps nor Vermes seems to have come near to proving his case—Schoeps' equation of προέθετο with either ὄψεται of the LXX or *yir'eh* of the MT does not carry conviction. Vermes has ultimately to explain Paul's apparent silence on the subject by saying that the equation was too obvious for Paul to think it worth mentioning.[25] But the Exodus typology was even more obvious and this does not prevent Paul from being very explicit about it in Rom. 9. In fact, if one considers the order in which Paul comments on salvation-history in both Romans and Galatians, it is not too much to say that when one comes to the place where the '*Aqedah* might well be expected to appear, there is a deafening silence.

This is particularly obvious in Galatians: Paul actually deals with the affair of Hagar and Ishmael in Gal. 4.21–31. This affair is narrated in Gen. 16 and 21; Paul certainly had Gen. 21 in mind, for he quotes Gen. 21.10, 12. Now the next incident in Genesis is of course the '*Aqedah* and the rabbis connected the two stories closely. Satan is described as pointing out to God that Abraham did not offer even a turtle dove to God out of the great feast which he is described as giving in Gen. 21.8. God replies that Abraham would be willing to offer his very son to him. 'Very well,' says Satan, 'order him to do so.' R. Levi explained the phrase 'After these things' in Gen. 22.1 as 'after these words' (literally following the Hebrew), and said that these were the words which Ishmael addressed to Isaac at the time of the feast: 'I am greater than thou in good deeds, for thou wast circumcised at eight days (and therefore had no choice), but I at thirteen years.' Isaac replies: 'On account of one limb wouldest thou incense me? Were the Holy One (blessed be He) to say unto me, Sacrifice thyself before me, I would obey.' Straightway 'God tested Abraham'.[26] Here, if anywhere, was the place to refer to the '*Aqedah*. Paul cannot have been ignorant of the traditional connection. Similarly in Romans, if Paul had wanted to refer to it, the end of chapter 4 would have afforded an excellent opportunity. He uses in 4.25 what may be a quasi-credal formula of Christ:

> who was put to death for our trespasses and raised for our justification.

The phrase translated 'put to death' is $\pi\alpha\rho\epsilon\delta\delta\theta\eta$, the very word that Paul uses in Rom. 8.32, where there very probably is a reference to the '*Aqedah* (but only a reference, not an elaborated typology): 'He who did not spare his own Son, but *gave him up* for us all.' The treatment of the '*Aqedah* in Heb. 11.17–19 would also suggest that this is a suitable context for it, since the offering is connected with the resurrection. But in fact Paul gives us no hint of the '*Aqedah* in Rom. 4. We can only conclude that he omitted it deliberately.

One cannot help speculating as to why this was. Undoubtedly the reason already suggested by Michel and C. K. Barrett must be recognized as a most plausible one: it would look very like a meritorious work. It was treated so by the rabbis, the Epistle of James is well on the road towards this conclusion. Whether the stress is put on Abraham's merit or Isaac's merit, the result is equally damaging to Paul's argument. Indeed the story is particularly favourable to the rabbinic account of the relation of faith to works. As we have seen, the rabbis were by no means averse to underlining Abraham's faith; quite the contrary. They appreciated it as much as Paul did; but they wanted to treat it as meritorious, as a work in fact. This was no doubt because of their desire to centre devotion on the Torah, and law observance could not be made central without considerable emphasis on works and merit. From their point of view the *'Aqedah* was an admirable illustration of this: faith was indeed necessary, but a faith which is proved and justified by means of works. Abraham believes God, and then in the *'Aqedah* proceeds to justify his belief by means of this great work. We can well imagine that Paul would have met this argument more than once during his ministry. He decides therefore to leave the *'Aqedah* alone in his commentary on salvation-history.

But we can suggest other motives also: the *'Aqedah* had probably been used by Paul's time as a means of validating the Temple sacrifices. They were memorials of the sacrifice of Isaac. Again, suppose Paul had followed the obvious and tempting line of typology offered by the *'Aqedah,* he would have found himself in difficulties sooner or later. Abraham is the type of the Father offering his only Son. But Paul uses Abraham in Galatians and Romans as the type of the Christian believer, even possibly as the type of Christ, but not of the Father. It would be most confusing to use Abraham at one and the same time as a type of the Father and of the Son. We may add that the *'Aqedah* was not actually a sacrifice: Isaac was not in fact offered. The tendency in later rabbinic exegesis to suggest that he actually died and was restored to life, or that he actually shed his blood, underlines this fact. If Paul used the *'Aqedah* as an inspiration for his substitutionary doctrine of the atonement (as Schoeps suggests he did), it was a most unsatisfactory one, since the voluntary victim was not in fact offered. If a type of Christ is to be found in the *'Aqedah,* it should be the ram, not Isaac. In fact we have suggested on p. 50 above the remote possibility that this may have been in Paul's mind. We may also suggest that the *'Aqedah* lacks the element of victory over the hostile powers which Paul desired, in Galatians at least. This was quite explicit in the 'curse' figure, and is brought out later in Romans, but would seem to have no obvious connection with the *'Aqedah.*

Finally, a comparison with the treatment of the *'Aqedah* in Hebrews is instructive. The author of Hebrews does refer to the *'Aqedah* but he sees it primarily as a type of the resurrection. Heb. 11.17–19 runs:

By faith Abraham, when he was tested, offered up Isaac, and he who had received the promises was ready to offer up his only son, of whom it was said, 'Through Isaac shall your descendants be named.' He considered that God was able to raise men even from the dead; hence, figuratively speaking, he did receive him back.

As Lindars points out (op. cit., p. 226), this corresponds to Rom. 4.17, where Abraham shows his faith in God's power to raise the dead by believing the promise concerning the quickening of Sarah's womb. If Schoeps' arguments were correct, the New Testament writers should regard the '*Aqedah* as primarily a figure of the death of Christ, not of his resurrection. The fact that contemporary Judaism may have seen this latter significance in the '*Aqedah* is not strictly relevant. In fact, as Schoeps points out, the earliest Christians' interpretation of the '*Aqedah* in terms of Christ's death is found in the Epistle of Barnabas vII, 3.[27] It is a curiously involved reference, almost made *en passant*. The author of the Epistle wishes to prove that Christ fulfilled the type of both goats killed on the Day of Atonement. In order to do this, he argues that the high priests of the Jews treated him as they treated the goat slaughtered in the temple on that day, while the people fasted. It is not clear whence he drew the details of the ritual of which he makes so much, but he does want to present a picture of the people fasting while Jesus is offered. He writes:

> Whoever will not join in this fast shall be put to death, the Lord commanded, since he himself was destined to offer the vessel of his spirit as a sacrifice, in order that the type which occurred when Isaac was offered on the altar might be fulfilled.

One wonders whether perhaps the point of this comparison may not lie in the very fact that Isaac's sacrifice was not consummated: Christ offered 'the vessel of his spirit'; he does not say 'offered himself, or his body'. We think of 1 Pet. 3.18: $\theta\alpha\nu\alpha\tau\omega$-$\theta\epsilon\grave{\iota}\varsigma$ $\mu\grave{\epsilon}\nu$ $\sigma\alpha\rho\kappa\grave{\iota}$ $\zeta\omega\sigma\pi\sigma\iota\eta\theta\epsilon\grave{\iota}\varsigma$ $\delta\grave{\epsilon}$ $\pi\nu\epsilon\acute{\upsilon}\mu\alpha\tau\iota$. Christ was 'put to death in the flesh but made alive in the spirit'. Perhaps the author of the Epistle of Barnabas is suggesting that Christ is like Isaac because he was willing to offer his spirit to death, but the Father did not demand this. In other words, it is the resurrection of Christ that is typified by the '*Aqedah*. At any rate the implication here is that it was Isaac who offered the sacrifice. Isaac is the type of Christ. It is not at all suggested that Abraham is the type of the Father.

We may therefore safely conclude that the '*Aqedah* theme as an inspiration for the vicarious death of Christ is almost entirely absent from the New Testament. There is just an echo of it in Rom. 8.32, but it is not used as a theological argument at all. When the '*Aqedah* is referred to in a typological context by the author of Hebrews, it represents the resurrection of Christ, and not his atoning death. And even when the theme does appear in early Christian literature in explicit connection with the death of Christ, the full significance of the typology is not clear; and there are even some grounds for suspecting that the author of the Epistle to Barnabas also saw the resurrection, rather than the death, of Christ as being the feature in the new dispensation which is specially foreshadowed by the '*Aqedah*.

# 5

# BIRTH WITH PROMISE

------◆◆◆◆------

In this study we examine two examples of Paul's treatment of a birth accompanied by a promise, one in Romans and one in Galatians, and are enabled thereby to draw useful conclusions both about Paul's technique and his theology. Our first example occurs in Rom. 9.6–13, and we quote verse 10:

> when Rebecca had conceived children by one man, our forefather Isaac . . .
>
> ῾Ρεβέκκα ἐξ ἑνὸς κοίτην ἔχουσα, ᾿Ισαὰκ τοῦ πατρὸς ἡμῶν.

All editors and translators, almost without exception, render κοιτὴν ἔχουσα here as 'having conceived, or became pregnant, by one man', thereby suggesting that this promise is different from the promise referred to in verse 7 above, in that it was made after the conception of the promised child, not before it or at it. But does κοίτην ἔχουσα in fact mean 'having conceived'? The lexicographical evidence is against this. According to Liddell and Scott, it has three meanings in secular Greek: 'bed (marriage bed or sick bed), lair, quarters'; 'going to bed, lodging'; 'parcel of land, chest, case'. The fourth meaning is confined to biblical Greek: 'sexual connection', and they quote this text, translating it 'to become pregnant by a man'. But when we look at the other biblical examples, the sense 'to become pregnant' is not necessarily implied. In the LXX κοίτη has three senses: (i) 'a bed'; (ii) 'emission of semen', κοίτη σπέρματος; (iii) 'sexual intercourse'. The notion of conception or pregnancy is not necessarily implied. The NT evidence confirms this: Luke uses it of 'a bed' (Luke 11.7); Paul, besides this passage, uses it in 13.13 in the plural to mean 'debauchery', i.e. promiscuous intercourse; and Heb. 13.4 uses it of intercourse within marriage. We must therefore conclude that the strictly sexual meaning of κοίτην ἔχουσα was invented by the LXX translators. This is simply because the words used for sexual intercourse in the ritual passages of the Pentateuch in the MT are all connected with the root *shākhabh* 'to lie down'. It is interesting to note that the only meaning given to the word in *A Patristic Greek Lexicon* is 'union, intercourse; of soul with God';[1] thus the biblical sense of the word has been retained but spiritualized.[2]

We must therefore conclude that ἐξ ἑνὸς κοίτην ἔχουσα means 'having had intercourse with one man' not 'having conceived by one man'. Rabbinic confirmation for this can be cited. There was a very definite calculation about Isaac's age, which strongly emphasized the twenty years that elapsed between his marrying Rebecca and his begetting Jacob and Esau. R. Isaac even drew the conclusion that Isaac was barren and had to entreat the Lord for himself as well as for his wife.[3] Another comment on Gen. 16.4 bears out the same point: 'And he went in to Hagar and she conceived.' The comment runs: 'As soon as he came to her she *immediately* conceived. Hence Hagar said of Sarah that she must not have been really pious, for she had been with Abram for many years and did not conceive, whereas I [Hagar] conceived *from the first time*.'[4] The promise seems to be attached to the act of intercourse. Compare also *Biblical Antiquities*, where it is claimed that Rebecca was in the third year of her marriage to Isaac before she conceived.[5] It looks therefore as if the full meaning of ἐξ ἑνὸς κοίτην ἔχουσα is 'having had one experience of intercourse with one man'. The point is not the absurd one that she might have become pregnant from two men, nor that she might have had two husbands. The point of the phrase is clear; just as the children who were born as the result of a divine promise in patriarchal times were the true seed, in contrast to the children born without such a promise, so today children born in baptism are children born according to God's promise, and are regarded by God as Abraham's seed.

Paul does in effect spiritualize the meaning when he applies it by implication to the new dispensation: in patriarchal times it is intercourse blessed by the word of promise that produces the seed which is reckoned seed by God; in Christian times it is those who are reborn through the promise (in baptism) who

are reckoned seed. Paul is not thinking in terms of lineage at
all. He is not saying: 'The lineage that begins with a promise is
the one that counts.' He is saying something much more like
John 1.13: 'who were born, not of blood nor of the will of the
flesh nor of man, but of God'. This applies in some sense to
Isaac, Jacob, Christ, and all Christians.

Sanday and Headlam explain the phrase thus: it was used
'to emphasise the exactly similar birth of the two sons. The
mother's name proves that they have one mother, these words
show that the father too was the same. There are none of the
defective conditions which might be found in the case of Isaac
and Ishmael.' But if this is what Paul meant, he should have
emphasized that they were born from the same mother, which
is not what ἐξ ἑνὸς κοίτην ἔχουσα means. There is nothing surprising in twins being born of the same father. What Paul is
concerned to emphasize is that the act of intercourse which had
God's blessing produced the child of promise, even though it
also produced a child of rejection. S–B give an accurate account of the meaning of κοίτη in the LXX, but do not draw the
conclusion outlined above. Lagrange acutely points out that
one Old Latin version translates 'ex uno concubito', and comments: 'Augustine, misled by this text, emphasised this unique
union'. On the contrary, this is no doubt what Paul meant,
though 'ex uno concubito' will not do as a translation by itself.
C. K. Barrett translates 'when Rebecca conceived, through
intercourse with one man'. But she could hardly conceive
through intercourse with more than one. Michel follows exactly
the same line of interpretation as Barrett. Nygren makes the
same point as Sanday and Headlam, 'both had the same father
and mother'. But this is not what ἐξ ἑνὸς κοίτην ἔχουσα means.

R. P. C. Hanson, referring to this passage in Romans, has
touched on the question of Paul's understanding of the birth of
Christ. He writes: 'If we are to see any analogy here between
the birth of Isaac and the birth of Jesus (which is of course far
from certain) it would suggest that Paul did not know of the
Virgin Birth, because there is no doubt that he believed that
Abraham was the father of Isaac.'[6] It is of course perfectly true
to say that Paul shows no knowledge of the tradition that Jesus
was born of a virgin. But we may surely draw some reasonable
conclusions from this passage as to what he would have thought

of that tradition. Here we have the story of two births with promise, one of them foretold by an angel. Jesus' birth as narrated in both Matthew and Luke is exactly this. In each case, Paul obviously regards as essential the divine promise which accompanies the act of intercourse that leads to the conception of the child. On the other hand, there could be no question in these two instances of a virginal conception, since the σπέρμα is an essential feature of the divine plan. One might therefore reasonably conjecture that Paul would certainly have regarded Christ's conception as accompanied by a promise, but would not probably have found any difficulty in assigning the natural role to a human father. As far as birth-with-promise is concerned, Christ must be regarded as occupying a central position: he would be like Isaac or Jacob in that it was the divine promise accompanying his conception that effectively made him the heir of the original promise to Abraham. He would be like us Christians, in that his task was to transfer the promise to the heirs κατὰ πνεῦμα. It would consequently be reasonable to suggest that Pauline Christology can stand without a strict doctrine of a virgin birth for Christ. But, inasmuch as the element of birth-with-promise is a marked feature of the birth narratives in both Matthew and Luke, Paul would certainly have understood and sympathized with their aim. Perhaps there is a moral here to be drawn about the possibility of those who do and those who do not accept the historicity of the virgin birth of Christ living together in harmony in the Church.

G. A. Dannall, in an interesting article, has suggested that Paul may have known the tradition of the virgin birth of Jesus.[7] He draws a parallel between the formula in Rom. 1.3–4 and Luke 1.35. He certainly shows the elements which the two passages have in common, but in my opinion the formula 'birth-with-promise' adequately covers those elements. It is perfectly true to say that for Paul Jesus' birth can have been no ordinary one, but this does not necessarily involve the conclusion that he believed it to have been a birth from a virgin. What is important for Paul is the divine, creative promise accompanying the conception, and not (apparently) the way in which the conception and birth actually took place.

We now turn to another passage in Paul which deals with one who was born according to promise, Gal. 4.21—5.1. Paul here distinguishes Ishmael and Isaac as 'born according to the flesh' and 'the son of the free woman through promise' respectively. He might well be accused of special pleading, since Hagar also received a promise from an angel before the birth of her son in Gen. 16.10:

> I will so greatly multiply your descendants that they cannot be numbered for multitude.

Perhaps we must simply let the charge rest. But it may be that Paul would defend himself by saying that the promise which gives a son κατὰ πνεῦμα must be uttered before the son is born or thought of. Admittedly this does not on the surface appear to apply to Jacob, whom Paul does claim as a son κατὰ πνεῦμα in Rom. 9. But he might perhaps have read Gen. 25.21–3 in such a way as to imply that the promise was effective from the moment that Isaac prayed on behalf of Rebecca, even though it was uttered only after conception had taken place. However, it may well be that this inconsistency was one of the weaknesses in his argument in Gal. 4.21f which induced Paul to leave it out of Romans.

Having set out the scriptural characters whose significance he intends to expound, Paul adds the words ἅτινά ἐστιν ἀλληγορού-μενα. We refrain from translating this phrase; the RSV has rashly rendered: 'Now this is an allegory'. One can understand the temptation to offer some such translation; it looks very obvious. But, just as τύπος in Paul does not necessarily mean 'type', so we are not justified in assuming that ἀλληγορού-μενα means 'are an allegory'. It is a plural after all, which one would not guess from the RSV. One could write down half a dozen possible alternative translations, any of which might prove to be right; for example:

'these things are capable of being allegorized'—but need not be if one does not feel inclined.
'these things must be allegorized', for taken literally they are not very edifying.
'these things are now being treated allegorically' by me, Paul, for reasons of my own.
'these things are written allegorically'—deliberately by Moses?
'these things are enacted in an allegorical way'—if this means anything.

With so much to choose from, we must attempt to fix the meaning of the word in contemporary Greek literature. The word does not occur in the LXX. Liddell and Scott say that the verb in the active means 'to allegorize' and in the passive 'to be spoken allegorically', and this is the sense they give it here. They also offer a third sense 'to speak figuratively or metaphorically'. It is a fairly late word; the earliest example cited by Liddell and Scott is from the fourth century B.C. They give no examples earlier than the first century A.D. for the word in its meaning 'interpret allegorically'. Our main source of information must therefore be Philo. He uses the active verb quite frequently to mean 'interpret allegorically', to find a philosophical, moral, or spiritual meaning which is other than the literal meaning. The passive verb he uses five times, as follows:

*De Iosepho* 28   having told the story of Joseph up to Joseph's being sold as a slave, he says that he proposes to add τὰ ἐν ὑπονοίαις: this must mean 'the deeper sense', and he continues: σχέδον γὰρ πάντα ἢ τὰ πλεῖστα τῆς νομοθεσίας ἀλληγορεῖται 'nearly all, or at least the major part, of the legislation bears an allegorical meaning'. Philo cannot mean 'is capable of being interpreted allegorically'.[8]

*De Cherubim* 25   τὰ μὲν γὰρ Χερουβὶμ καθ' ἑνὰ τρόπον οὕτως ἀλληγορεῖται 'now this is one method of allegorizing the Cherubim'. This suggests that there may be others; but Philo is not consciously indulging his fancy. He believes no doubt that several meanings could be intended by the text.

*De Decalogo* 101   there is a problem caused by the fact that God is described as having created the world in six days, although he does not need any period of time in which to create. But this problem 'is resolved in another passage by means of the allegorical method'; μεμήνυται διὰ τῶν ἀλληγορηθέντων ἐν ἑτέροις. Philo speaks of this method much as modern scholars speak of the 'traditio-historical method'. It is a well-known, quasi-scientific technique.

*De Exsecrationibus* 158   Philo actually refers to, though he does not quote, Isa. 54.1, which Paul cites a few verses after the one with which we are concerned. Philo says that the prophet's reference to the barren women becoming prolific 'allegorically signifies the soul'; ἐπὶ ψυχῆς ἀλληγορεῖται.

*De Exsecrationibus* 124–5 he is referring to the promise given in Deut. 28.13 that if Israel is obedient they will be the head and not the tail, and he writes: ταῦτα δὲ ἀλληγορεῖται τροπικῶς ἐξενεχθέντα, 'this phrase, when taken in a non-literal sense, bears an allegorical meaning'.

We may conclude from this that in Philo the verb when used in the passive always means 'bears an allegorical sense' and never means 'may be understood allegorically'. Philo believed that the passages he allegorizes were intended by God to be understood in an allegorical sense, even though he would not perhaps always claim that he had hit the right meaning. We know that he often suggested two, three, or even more etymologies for the same name, and apparently regarded them all as equally valid.[9] So he probably considered that Scripture might be intended to have several meanings at the same time. The fact that he allegorizes a text does not necessarily imply that he does not accept its literal sense as well.

When we look beyond Philo, we get the same impression: ἀλληγορεῖσθαι means 'to be expressed symbolically' not merely 'to be understood symbolically'.[10] Thus Hippolytus says of a certain writer: τὰ πάθη τὰ κατὰ τὴν Αἴγυπτον, ἅτινα, φησίν, ἐστὶν τῆς κτίσεως ἀλληγορούμενα σύμβολα 'the sufferings in Egypt, which are, he claims, symbolic expressions for the creation'. Clement of Alexandria speaks of 'animals used in an allegorical sense by Isaiah': τὰ ζῷα τὰ διὰ Ἠσαΐου ἀλληγορούμενα. Two other illuminating passages should be quoted. Origen writes of this very 'allegory' in Gal. 4.21f: 'Anyone who cares to read the Letter to the Galatians can learn how the narrative of the marriages and the unions with concubines are treated allegorically': ὁ δὲ βουλόμενος λαβεῖν τὴν πρὸς Γαλάτας ἐπιστόλην εἴσεται τίνα τρόπον ἀλληγορεῖται τὰ κατὰ τοὺς γάμους καὶ τὰς μίξεις τῶν θεραπινίδων. Here certainly ἀλληγορεῖται means 'are *understood* allegorically'; but no doubt Origen, would have held that, since we have Paul's warrant for it, they must have been intended allegorically also. Finally, here is an admirable comment from Theodotus on this very passage:

the inspired apostle said that these things were to be understood allegorically, not that they were to be understood differently; for he does not reject the historical narrative but teaches what it is that is foreshadowed in the narrative.

ἀλληγορούμενα εἶπεν ὁ θεῖος ἀπόστολος, ἀντὶ τοῦ καὶ ἑτέρως νοούμενα. οὐ γὰρ τὴν ἱστορίαν ἀνεῖλεν, ἀλλὰ τὰ ἐν τῇ ἱστορίᾳ προτυπωθέντα διδάσκει.

We may therefore conclude that we are safe in giving the following as a provisional rendering of Paul's phrase in Gal. 4.24:

these things are intended to convey a deeper meaning.

But what is that meaning? Is it an allegory or a type? An allegory is an explanation of the text that replaces the literal sense and has a purely arbitrary connection with it. In an allegory each detail corresponds to some idea or person in the complex which it expresses. A type is a pattern or set of circumstances which reproduces beforehand that set of circumstances of which it is a type. In this passage, then, what corresponds to what? It really is extremely complicated, for there are two women, two sons, two covenants, two Jerusalems, two bodies of believers, and perhaps two mountains. Further, the woman who in the scriptural narrative is distinguished by the fact that she is not the mother of the Jews is in Paul's account significant because she is the mother of all unbelieving Jews (i.e. the vast majority of Jews). Perhaps a table would make this clear:

| | |
|---|---|
| Hagar [a slave] | Sarah [free] |
| Ishmael [persecutor] | Isaac [persecuted] |
| [born κατὰ σαρκά] | [born κατά πνεῦμα] |
| covenant on Sinai | [the new covenant] |
| contemporary Jerusalem | Jerusalem above |
| Sinai in Arabia | [heavenly Sion or ?heavenly Sinai] |
| children of Hagar | children of the free woman |
| [unbelieving Jews] | [Christians] |

I have put in square brackets those items which are not explicitly mentioned, but must be understood if the analogy is to hold.[11]

It does look as if Paul is here giving us typology rather than allegory: Paul does not use his material in order to give us in-

struction about ideas, but in order to tell us what has happened:
the promise was uttered, the law was imposed, the yoke of the
law was broken, etc. Thus we could add a second, much briefer,
table, which tells us what this long series of contrasts means. It
would run like this:

| | |
|---|---|
| Hagar the slave bears a son who persecutes the son of Sarah, the free woman. She and her son are cast out by divine command. | The unbelieving Jews, enslaved to the Torah, persecute believing Christians, who are free in Christ. The unbelieving Jews are rejected by God. |

This, we believe, is what Paul's 'allegory' is intended to convey,
and it shows that the 'allegory' is really an elaborate piece of
typology. But we must now comment on the passage in detail.

It is easy to see how Christians can be sons of Sarah κατὰ
πνεῦμα, but much less easy to see how unbelieving Jews can be
sons of Hagar κατὰ σαρκά. It would be much easier if Paul had
contented himself with saying that Christians are sons of Sarah
κατὰ πνεῦμα whereas unbelieving Jews are sons of Sarah κατὰ
σάρκα, very much as he says in Rom. 9.5 that the Messiah is
from the Jews κατὰ σάρκα. Indeed, the simpler implied contrast
in Romans is probably an indication that Paul himself realized
that he had been too elaborate in this piece of typology in Galatians. It is probably significant that Hagar is an Egyptian:
Egypt in Rev. 11.8 is the name given πνευματικῶς to the place
where the Lord was crucified. RSV there translates πνευματικῶς
as 'allegorically', no doubt rightly. S–B give examples of rabbinic sayings in which Egypt is taken as typical of all kingdoms
which persecuted Israel.[12] And W. L. Knox writes: 'The
association of Egypt with evil and the material is a standing
convention in Philo.'[13]

There is great uncertainty as to the exact meaning of the
first few words of verse 25: Schlier points out that it could be
taken in two senses:

(a) Hagar corresponds to the mountain Sinai in Arabia.
(b) The name 'Hagar' signifies mount Sinai in Arabia.

He prefers the latter, so does Klausner,[14] and Doeve goes so far
as to translate the phrase into Hebrew:[15] *Hāgār* is equated with
*Hāhār*, the 'mountain' and must indicate the mountain on
which the law-covenant was given. He remarks that this sort of

exegesis, in which similar roots are brought together, is well authenticated among the rabbis. We need not, however, follow Lipsius, who finds an example of *Notarikon* here, the scheme whereby the letters or syllables of a word can be made each to represent a word on their own. He would translate συστοιχεῖ in the same verse as 'has the same alphabetical value as'.[16] On the whole it looks as if Klausner and Schlier and Doeve are right, and we should assume that Paul means by the words τὸ δὲ Ἁγὰρ Σινᾶ ὄρος ἐστὶν ἐν τῇ Ἀραβίᾳ 'the name Hagar signifies mount Sinai in Arabia'. As all editors point out, this underlines the fact that Hagar is an alien, whose true place is outside the land of promise. The word συστοιχεῖν is a rare one, and an exact parallel for the sense 'corresponds to' cannot be quoted. Moulton and Milligan offer τὰ σύστοιχα τουτοῖς from Epicurus, 'kindred phenomena to these', which seems sufficiently close. We are now in deep waters, for Hagar corresponds to Mount Sinai, and Mount Sinai corresponds to contemporary Jerusalem. We must take δουλεύει γάρ of contemporary Jerusalem and not of Mount Sinai. There would be no sense in saying that Mount Sinai was enslaved with her children, whereas there is plenty of point in Paul applying it to contemporary Jerusalem. The slavery he speaks of is of course enslavement to the Torah. Only a completely anachronistic modern nationalism could see it as a reference to the political bondage of Judea under the Romans. We have no reason at all to think that Paul would regard this as bondage, and anyway, if he did, most of Paul's readers were in precisely the same condition, the very people whom he describes immediately after as being free.

Then in verse 26 comes the reference to ἡ ἄνω Ἰερουσαλήμ 'the Jerusalem above', a reference which sets one thinking about similar ideas in both Hebrews and the Apocalypse. Compare Heb. 12.22–4. Rev. 3.12 speaks of 'the new Jerusalem which comes down from God out of heaven'. In Rev. 21.2,10 the seer refers again to the 'new Jerusalem' and 'the holy city, Jerusalem'. All these four references are strongly eschatological; in all of them the new Jerusalem has not yet been gained. At first sight the same impression is given by Paul's language in Gal. 4; ἡ νῦν Ἰερουσαλήμ is contrasted with ἡ ἄνω Ἰερουσαλήμ, which suggests that 'the Jerusalem above' is not present but future. On the other hand, the heavenly Jerusalem is free, ac-

cording to Paul, and Christ has set us free, who are its children
(Gal. 5.1). So it looks as if Paul is here being consistent in his
eschatology: the consummation is not yet, but as Christians we
already live in the new age; cf. 1 Cor. 10.11; and indeed we
could well compare Heb. 6.5; Christians have already 'tasted
the powers of the age to come'.

We may therefore approach the citation from Isa. 54.1 in
verse 27 with the clear understanding that, according to Paul,
this is a prophetic word addressed to the Jewish–Gentile Church
of the future. It is free from the yoke of the law; it is the true
mother of all believers according to God's eternal purpose. The
prophetic utterance is quoted in order to prove that this Church
is to be 'our mother' (verse 26). The context is very significant:
it comes immediately after Isa. 53, and would therefore mean
to Paul that what is going to happen as a result of the atoning
work of the Messiah described in that chapter is the enlargement
of Israel to include the Gentiles:

> Rejoice, O barren one that dost not bear;
> break forth and shout, thou who art not in travail;
> for the desolate hath more children
> than she who hath a husband.

The significance of Isa. 54.3, only two verses later, would not be
lost on Paul:

> and your descendants will possess the nations.

He would of course interpret it in terms of the Gentiles entering
the Church, and not of the conquest of the nations by Israel.
The Targum interprets it as a promise that Israel will ultimately be more numerous than the Gentile nations, especially
Rome. There is also evidence that this text was a subject of
dispute between Christians and Jews in the second century.[17]
We may note the variant reading πάντων ἡμῶν for ἡμῶν in
verse 26, probably not original, but a correct gloss in the sense
that Paul means the Jerusalem above is mother of 'all us
Christians'.

Verses 28–9 introduce us to a feature which is not very common in the New Testament, the detection of the Holy Spirit's
activity in the pre-Christian dispensation. In verse 28 the Gala-
tian Christians are called 'like Isaac, children of promise'.
When unpacked, this phrase must mean: 'as Isaac was born

according to the promise uttered by the angel at the oaks of
Mamre, so you have been born again in baptism according to
the promise cited above from Isaiah'. Then in verse 29 Paul
describes Isaac as τὸν κατὰ πνεῦμα [γεννηθέντα] 'one born according to the Spirit'. The usage is very like πνευματικὸν βρῶμα
in 1 Cor. 10.3. It does not mean that Isaac is a spiritual heir as
contrasted with heirs of the body. It means 'one born according
to a promise uttered through the Holy Spirit', and it implies
that his birth foreshadowed a spiritual dispensation as contrasted with Ishmael, who was born without this sort of promise, and who therefore foreshadowed a legal dispensation. But
both dispensations were in some sense realized in the course of
pre-Christian history according to Paul. Of course Paul can
only use this language to the Galatians effectively because the
Galatians are not physical descendants of Abraham and can
only be called his sons and heirs in a non-literal sense. We might
compare Gal. 3.3: 'Having begun with the Spirit, are you now
ending with the flesh?' But this applies only to their present
state. Perhaps a better comparison is 3.14:

> that in Christ Jesus the blessing of Abraham might come upon the
> Gentiles, that we might receive the promise of the Spirit though
> faith.

Here Spirit and promise are connected: a promise must be the
work of the Spirit, for it implies faith. In the case of Abraham
and Isaac we find promise and faith, so the Spirit must be at
work there. This reading of the activity of the Spirit into
Israel's history, apart from his inspiring the prophets (a feature
not wholly absent here), is rare. One such place is the difficult
sentence in 2 Cor. 3.17: ὁ δὲ κύριος τὸ πνεῦμά ἐστιν, which we
do not venture to translate. It shows at least how little Paul regarded the Old Testament as 'old'.

Verse 29 also gives us one of the clearest examples in Paul's
writings of his acceptance of contemporary rabbinic exegesis.
He does not need to prove his point when he says that Ishmael
persecuted Isaac. The reference is to Gen. 21.9:

> Sarah saw the son of Hagar the Egyptian, whom she had borne to
> Abraham, playing with her son Isaac.[18]

On p. 83 above we have already given one instance of a rabbinic midrash in which Ishmael argues his claim against Isaac.

Plenty of other evidence in the same direction can be cited:
some of the rabbis saw what can only be called an eschatological significance in the feast which Abraham gave for Isaac's
weaning in Gen. 21.8. 'The Holy One (blessed be He) will make
a great banquet for the righteous on the day he manifests his
love to the seed of Isaac.' The connection with the weaning
depends on a play on words.[19] Another version of Ishmael's
mocking runs thus: 'Ishmael mocked at the feast Abraham had
made for Isaac and said: Why is the merriment so great? a
feast is made for Isaac more than for me! Yet I am the first-born
and will inherit a double share.'[20] Other traditions represent
Ishmael's persecution as taking a much more robust form than
mere scoffing. S-B quote one rabbi as arguing that the word
for 'playing' in Gen. 21.9 $m^a tsacheq$ must imply bloodshed, because in 2 Sam. 2.14 the word is used for the young warriors
'playing' before the two armies, and this involved bloodshed.
Then Prov. 26.18, with its description of the madman as throwing 'firebrands, arrows, and death', is brought in to show how
Ishmael did his 'playing'. In *Bereshith Rabba* it is said that Ishmael under pretext of making a joke shot at Isaac with arrows.[21]

Paul then proceeds to quote Sarah's utterance from Gen.
21.10 in the form

Cast out the slave and her son; for the son of the slave shall not inherit with the son of the free woman.

Paul departs from both MT and LXX in writing 'the son of the
free woman' for 'my son Isaac'. He has thus turned it into the
form of a divine command rather than the personal utterance
of Sarah. We shall be considering the significance of this presently. For the moment we must ask what is the precise nature
of the connection indicated by that word in Gal. 4.31:

*So*, brethren, we are not children of the slave but of the free
woman.

In some way Gen. 21.10 proves the truth of this statement.
Perhaps the argument runs like this:

In Gen. 21 it is made clear that the true lineage of Abraham
goes through children whose birth is by promise and not by
mere physical descent. The claim for mere physical descent is
invalidated by the fact that Ishmael, who had physical descent

but not eschatological promise, was disinherited. The true descendants are born by promise, live by faith, and are free from the Torah. On the principles of Pauline typology, this means that today God has disinherited unbelieving Jews (who have only physical descent), and accepts as his sons those who are born by promise, live by faith, and are free of the Torah. This is a state of affairs which God has always intended.

It would be quite unreasonable to expect that editors should not have attempted to take Paul at his word (or what seems to be his word) and concluded that in this passage we have an allegory. Both Luther and Calvin seem to think that this is an inevitable conclusion, but they excuse Paul on the grounds that his allegory was not essential to his argument, but was added to give 'beauty' (Luther's word) to his work. Calvin calls it 'pulchram ornamentionem', and adds a long protest against the use of allegory in order to avoid the literal sense. Paul does not do this here, he says. A number of editors do not clearly distinguish between allegory and type; thus Lightfoot suggests that Paul is using ἀλληγορεῖν here much as he uses τύπος in 1 Cor. 10.11; but we have already contended that in the 1 Corinthians passage τύπος does not mean 'type'. Lietzmann begins by calling the passage 'a new allegorical-rabbinical treatment of prophecy on behalf of the truth of Paul's proclamation of freedom'. But he then goes on to say that Ishmael and Isaac are types of Jew and Gentile. We may say: if types, not allegories. Büchsel, in the article ἀλληγορεῖν in *TWNT*, takes it for granted that Paul means 'allegory' and not 'type' here. It is not surprising that, starting from this failure to distinguish the one from the other, he concludes that there is little difference between Paul's interpretation and that of Philo. Schlier translates ἀλληγορεῖν as 'allegorisch reden', but concludes that what we have here is more a typological than an allegorical interpretation. He thinks αὗται γάρ εἰσιν δύο διαθῆκαι 'these women are two covenants' is just the same as ἡ δὲ πέτρα ἦν ὁ Χριστός 'and the Rock was Christ' in 1 Cor. 10.4. But in fact the two passages are not on all fours. In 1 Cor. 10 we have an instance of the real presence of Christ in Israel's history of old. The relation of the women to the covenants is typological. Paul did not mean 'that Rock typified Christ'. Lampe describes this passage as 'allegory'[22] and so does R. P. C. Hanson. He writes: 'The "similar situation" typology has been strained and distorted in an unconvincing but highly rabbinical fashion into an allegory; that is all.'[23] I would prefer to say that it is still typology, but there is a tendency to over-elaboration (witness the equation of Hagar with Sinai and Sinai with contemporary Jerusalem) which would verge into allegory if pursued further. But Paul did not pursue it further. On the contrary, he dropped it. Amsler gives a fair description of what Paul is doing here, but seems to think that this can be called 'using the allegorical method'. He writes: 'He proceeds by means of allegorical analogies in order to underline the relation that exists between two very precise historical situations, that of the two descendants of Abraham of old (to which the text bears witness), and that of the church and the synagogue today.'[24]

Other scholars clearly distinguish between allegory and type, and say that what we have here is type, not allegory. Two of the older scholars make this point: Lipsius paraphrases ἀλληγορούμενα as 'in Gleichniss oder Typus gesagt', and Vollmer maintains that, though Paul uses ἀλληγορούμενα, he does not really depart from typology since he goes on to base his argument on historical events.[25] Lagrange has an excellent comment. He rejects the translation 'can be understood as an allegory' and prefers 'they have been uttered in order to indicate something other than the literal sense'. He agrees that the word 'type' would be more accurate, and quotes Chrysostom: καταχρηστικῶς τὸν τύπον ἐκάλεσεν ἀλληγορίαν, which we may render: 'by an extension of meaning, he calls what is really a type by the name of allegory'. Similarly Goppelt says that though Paul calls it an allegory it is really typology and claims that we have here no arbitrary rabbinic speculation.[26] Michel agrees with Vollmer's judgement, saying: Paul thinks more in terms of typology than of allegory in the strict sense.[27] Ellis supports this view also.[28] The last editor we may quote is Bring, who describes these verses as 'a typological exegesis of a well known passage'. He says it is in a formal sense allegorical, but the presentation is typological rather than allegorical.

It is not surprising that several scholars have condemned Paul for the unconvincing and tendentious way in which he has treated Scripture here. Windisch accuses Paul of 'the crassest

Rabbinicism' and of 'turning a Yes into a No'.[29] But a distinguished Jewish scholar has denied that Paul is really being rabbinic here. Schoeps describes this passage as 'a midrash founded on hellenistic speculation', and accuses it of offending against the rabbinic principle that 'no passage of Scripture can abandon its original meaning'.[30] We must sympathize with Schoeps here, and admit that Paul is in fact going against the plain sense of Scripture. But he can surely be acquitted of the actual charge which Schoeps brings against him. Since Paul is not writing allegory here but typology, he is not suggesting that Gen. 21 must not be given its original meaning. Its original meaning is important for him since it expresses the original historical events which he needs in order to pin down his whole theological scheme. He is maintaining that, besides their historical significance at the time, they also bear a deeper, more ultimate meaning. This is typology, not allegory. Nor does it seem to add very much to the debate to describe this as an 'hellenistic' speculation. As far as the character of the passage as midrash is concerned, it is thoroughly rabbinic. Indeed the same conclusion seems to emerge from our study of this passage as from the study of the rest of Paul's works: his theology is not rabbinic but Christian, but his methods are entirely rabbinic.

We have referred already to the fact that in verse 30 Paul has slightly altered the scriptural text so as to make it an utterance in the third person. Instead of it being Sarah's demand, it is an utterance of ἡ γραφή: 'What does the scripture say?' No doubt this is partly in order to represent Sarah in a better light. Instead of it being the demand of a jealous wife, imperious, capricious, unjust by any reasonable moral standard, it becomes the solemn direction of the Holy Spirit, a means by which God carries out his long-term purposes. We can, of course, note this tendency to whitewash scriptural characters at work among the rabbis also. No doubt the midrash about Ishmael persecuting Isaac was in origin an attempt to justify Sarah's behaviour. But one may well doubt whether Paul was much worried about presenting Sarah in a good light. Tradition had already seen to that. For him Hagar and Ishmael were divinely ordained types. This in itself should surely suggest that they were not allegories; it was what happened to them that mattered, not any message which they symbolized. Their being cast out was not, therefore, in Paul's eyes, an ordinary event, it was part of salvation-history. Again, as he looked at the text of Gen. 21, Paul would see that Sarah's demand in 21.10 was immediately ratified by an utterance of God in verse 12. Sarah had certainly been the instrument of the Holy Spirit in uttering her demand.

If so, it may be asked, was Paul really any different from Philo, who made the scriptural characters signify anything he chose? Isaac represents wisdom, Ishmael sophistry, so Ishmael has to be driven out. Sarah represents perfect virtue, Hagar 'intermediate training' so Hagar is subordinate to Sarah, and so on.[31] It must be confessed that as far as ignoring the original intention with which the text of Scripture was written is concered, there is little to choose between Philo and Paul. But then one could convict a great deal of rabbinic interpretation also of ignoring, not the literal meaning of the text, but its original intention. And Paul, it can be confidently claimed, is dealing with matters that really are integral to Scripture: Law, promise, works, faith, are important themes in Scripture in a sense in which virtue, training, and sophistry are not. Paul never succeeds in getting away from the content of Scripture in the way in which Philo invariably does. He had no desire to do so, for, in the very deepest sense, he did understand what Scripture was about.

Our study of Gal. 4.21f has led us into some complicated by-ways; but it has been necessary, for we could not ignore a passage which is so obviously concerned with promise and fulfilment, with divine action and its long-term intentions. Paul, we may remark with considerable relief, nowhere else goes into such elaborate detail in his typological exposition of Scripture. But the very elaboration has thrown a useful light on his methods and his presuppositions of interpretation.

# 6

## CHRIST THE FIRST FRUITS
## CHRIST THE TREE

———◆◆◆◆◆———

In this study we confine ourselves to the study of twenty-three verses in Rom. 11; indeed the longest section in the chapter is formally confined to a study of one half-verse. The material is however bound together by one theme; it is all an attempt to answer the question: How has God's choice passed from Israel of old to the mixed Jewish–Gentile Church of Paul's day? In these twenty-three verses Paul uses three distinguishable figures to help out his meaning, and what he writes is based on his meditation on at least four quite separate passages from the Scriptures, so we have no shortage of matters to study. Perhaps nowhere so confidently may we claim to have found our way back to Paul's work-shop as he wrote this Epistle.

We notice first that in 11.11 and 14 Paul uses the word παρα-ζηλόω 'to make jealous'. This constitutes a direct link with Deut. 32.21. There can be no doubt about this at all, since Paul has already quoted that verse in Rom. 10.19. As Deut. 32 will prove to be of crucial importance in the verses we are studying, it may be as well to quote Deut. 32.21. in full from the LXX:

> αὐτοὶ παρεζήλωσάν με ἐπ᾽ οὐ θεῷ,
> παρώργισάν με ἐν τοῖς εἰδώλοις αὐτῶν·
> κἀγὼ παραζηλώσω αὐτοὺς ἐπ᾽ οὐκ ἔθνει,
> ἐπ᾽ ἔθνει ἀσυνέτῳ παροργιῶ αὐτούς.

This we may translate:

> They moved me to jealousy with a no-god,
> they have provoked me with their idols;
> so I will move them to jealousy with a no-people,
> with a foolish people I will provoke them.

The connection here with Deut. 32 is noted by Dinkler,[1] C. K. Barrett, and Munck.[2] The last emphasizes it still further in his later work[3] when he writes: 'It is natural that Moses' sharp indictment of Israel occupies Paul's thoughts.'
But in fact we can find another link with Deut. 32 in 11.11–15; it lies in Paul's use of πταίω, πίπτω, and παράπτωμα. In verse 11, where he writes

μὴ ἔπταισαν ἵνα πέσωσιν;
have they stumbled so as to fall?

he obviously distinguishes πταίω and πίπτω. πταίειν means being offended or disgusted at the message of a crucified Messiah who lived by faith.[4] πίπτειν presumably means to be rejected or rather to destine oneself for rejection and therefore for ultimate perdition. He then describes this whole event with the words τὸ παράπτωμα αὐτῶν, which RSV renders with 'their trespass'. But surely the context requires not 'their trespass' but 'their fall' or 'their stumbling' or 'their failure'? What Paul is concerned with here is not Israel's sin as such, but Israel's fall. They stumbled and fell from their place in God's favour, and the Gentiles (strictly the mixed Jewish–Gentile Christian Church) have taken their place. It is interesting to see how the English versions render παράπτωμα here: AV and RV offer 'fall' (RV margin 'trespass'); Moffatt offers 'lapse', Phillips 'failure', NEB 'because they offended'. The problem is that the context demands 'fall' whereas the lexicographical evidence is on the whole on the side of 'trespass'. This is the only meaning of παράπτωμα in the LXX. Also, everywhere else in the NT (including ten other instances in Paul plus one in Ephesians) it means 'sin' or 'trespass'. In secular Greek its original sense is 'a false step', which would suit well enough here. On the other hand, if we look at the very similar word παράπτωσις, we find a possible link with the meaning which the context requires here. Jer. 22.21ab runs:

I spoke to you in your prosperity,
but you said, 'I will not listen'.

This is rendered by the LXX with:

ἐλάλησα πρός σε ἐν τῇ παραπτώσει σου,
καὶ εἶπας, οὐκ ἀκούσομαι.

The word rendered 'prosperity' by RSV and παράπτωσις in LXX is *shalwah*. Now twice in Theodotion's version of Daniel the Aramaic equivalent of this word, *shālū* or *shᵃlēwa'* is rendered with παράπτωμα (Dan. 4.27; 9.24). Thus παράπτωμα can be used to describe a condition of culpable carelessness arising from prosperity. But this is precisely the condition of Israel described in Deut. 32.15–16:

> But Jeshurun waxed fat, and kicked;
>    you waxed fat, you grew thick, you became sleek;
> then he forsook God who made him,
>    and scoffed at the Rock of his salvation.
> They stirred him to jealousy with strange gods;
>    with abominable practices they provoked him to anger.

So we find here in Deut. 32 these two thoughts brought together, Israel's carelessness arising from prosperity or security, and God being provoked, a thought which leads on later in the Song to the description of God counter-provoking Israel. We may reasonably conclude that Paul had Deut. 32 in mind here, and even that he drew from it what we might call a 'theology of jealousy'. He found in it a clue to God's purpose with regard to Jews and Gentiles.

Since we are to devote considerable attention to Rom. 11.16a, we should quote it:

εἰ δὲ ἡ ἀπαρχὴ ἁγία, καὶ τὸ φύραμα

If the dough offered as first fruits is holy, so is the whole lump.

The question we are set to answer is: Who are indicated by the ἀπαρχή (first fruits) and the φύραμα (lump of dough) respectively? The answer which is to be put forward here is that Christ is the ἀπαρχή, and the φύραμα indicates all who are 'in Christ' at any time. The same solution must of course be given to the question of the meaning of verse 16b but that can wait till we discuss it. This is a solution which has been accepted by very few commentators. There are two other solutions, both of which have been supported by the authority of many scholars: we may call them (*a*) and (*b*).

(*a*) *The* ἀπαρχή *means Abraham or the patriarchs. The dough is therefore the Jews.*

This view is supported by Sanday and Headlam, who quote

verse 28, where Paul says that the Jews are 'beloved for the sake of their forefathers'. But there it is a question of calling, and no one can doubt that the patriarchs were called. Here it is a question of holiness: does Paul actually commit himself to the very rabbinic doctrine that the merit of the patriarchs is passed on to Israel down the ages? It seems very unlikely. Sanday and Headlam's view is supported by Lagrange, S-B, and Michel. The last two point out that Adam was called 'the first fruits of the world'. But no one, presumably, would suggest that he was holy. Dodd also takes this view, but adds that it is one which is hard to reconcile with Paul's previous denial that physical descent from Abraham gives any claim to God's blessing. Nygren also thinks that the ἀπαρχή, as well as the ῥίζα in verse 16b, means Abraham and the patriarchs, and here we must also put Schoeps,[5] and Munck,[6] though these two only apply it to the ῥίζα. Finally, Delling sides with this view, saying that the ἀπαρχή is the Jewish people as a whole, especially Abraham.[7] Karl Barth has in his commentary a modified version of this view. He writes: 'The parables of fulfilment and lump, of root and branch, must not be taken as referring to some immanent or organic continuity between the church and its primal origin or final end.' Paul, he adds, may be thinking of the patriarchs, but if so 'only as bearers of the eschatological possibility'. Difficult as this conception may be, it does witness to that uneasiness about this interpretation which C. H. Dodd expressed. It is indeed the inconsistency with Paul's thought on this subject elsewhere that is the main objection to this solution of the problem.

The other solution is:

(b) *The ἀπαρχή is the first converts among the Jews and the φύραμα is presumably any Jews who should be converted in the future.*

This view is put forward by Leenhardt; he does not apply it to the ῥίζα–κλάδοι figure as well, but draws a sharp distinction between the figure in verse 16a and that in verse 16b. Lietzmann also thinks that the ἀπαρχή is the Jewish Christians, but reverts to view (a) in interpreting the figure of the root and the branches. C. K. Barrett is also inclined to adopt this view, but he adds most significantly: 'It is not impossible that behind the Jewish Christian Paul sees the figure of Christ himself, whom he actually describes as the "first fruits" in 1 Cor. 15.20.' The great argument in favour of view (*b*) is the fact that Paul uses ἀπαρχή in Rom. 16.5; 1 Cor. 16.15 to describe first converts among the Jews. But it is worth pointing out that in the first of those passages Epaenetus is described as ἀπαρχὴ εἰς Χριστόν, 'the first convert . . . for Christ'. Perhaps it might have been better if the RSV had translated the phrase literally 'the first convert into Christ'. The great objection to view (*b*) is the difficulty of applying it to both figures in verse 16, and the unlikelihood that Paul changes the application of his figure in the middle of a sentence. We should not fail to note the solution of Gennadius, cited by Lietzmann, to the effect that the ἀπαρχή is Christ, the ῥίζα is Abraham, both φύραμα and κλάδοι are the Jewish people. The view defended below is actually espoused by Whiteley, though not argued in detail.[8]

It is relevant to look at Philo's use of ἀπαρχή. In one passage he is discussing the peculiar position of the Jewish people among the nations: they are like an orphan child, he says, but because of this they are the special objects of God's mercy; and then he writes: 'Consequently they have been marked off out of the whole human race as a sort of first fruits to the Creator and Father.'[9] In another passage he has an interpretation of φύραμα. He writes, 'If we must speak the truth, we are really that lump of dough ourselves, since many substances have been brought together and mixed together that we may be completed.'[10] It is interesting that Philo thinks of the whole Jewish race as an ἀπαρχή; we shall be arguing below that Paul could easily move from such an idea to the thought of Christ, the 'verus Israel', as the ἀπαρχή. The fact that Philo feels he has to allegorize the φύραμα is also significant. Both he and Paul feel obliged to find a deeper meaning for what was originally a purely cultic, or even magic, ordinance. Philo's comment on the φύραμα is made apropos Num. 15.19–20. The Talmud makes an interesting comment on the same passage: 'If anything that had been separated unto the Lord falls into non-sacred produce, etc., the former hallows the latter with its own sanctity and renders it similarly prohibited.'[11] Obviously Num. 15 lies behind Paul's figure, and to this we must now turn.

The phrase ἀπαρχὴ φυράματος ('the first fruits of the dough') comes from the LXX of Num. 15.20; it translates the Hebrew phrase *rē'shīth 'arisōthekhem*, which the RSV renders 'the first of your coarse meal'. The phrase should be looked at in its context, Num. 15.17–21:

> When you come into the land to which I bring you, and when you eat of the food of the land, you shall present an offering to the Lord. Of the first of your coarse meal you shall present a cake as an offering; as an offering from the threshing floor, so shall you present it. Of the first of your coarse meal you shall give to the Lord an offering throughout your generations.

It may be very significant that ἀπαρχή in this passage translates *rē'shīth*, the same word as is used in Gen. 1.1 for 'in *the beginning* God created the heavens and the earth', and which, translated as ἀρχή, plays such a significant part in the high Christology of Col. 1.15–20. It may also be important that this command is associated with the entry into the promised land. For Paul, being 'in Christ' was an anticipation of the consummation at the parousia, when all the elect would be in full possession of God's promises. Perhaps into this command to offer the ἀπαρχή when Israel reaches the promised land Paul would read a type of the offering of Christ, as the ἀπαρχή for Christians of the complete sanctification of all God's elect that was only to be consummated at the parousia. In this connection it is relevant to note the use of ἀπαρχή in the rest of Paul's writings. In 1 Cor. 15.20, 23 Christ is described in connection with the resurrection as 'the first fruits of those who have fallen asleep'; verse 23 expresses this even more clearly: 'Christ the first fruits, then at his coming those who belong to Christ (οἱ τοῦ Χριστοῦ)'. This would correspond quite closely to what we seem to have here: the ἀπαρχή Christ, is holy, and so therefore is the φύραμα, all who belong to him. We have already noted the usage in Rom. 16.5 and 1 Cor. 16.15. In Rom. 8.23 Christians are described as having 'the first fruits of the Spirit', meaning 'the first fruits consisting of the Spirit'. This is not so very far from saying that Christ is the first fruits, especially in view of the close association between Christ and the Spirit in Paul's thought. Finally, we note that in 2 Thess. 2.13 Paul describes the Thessalonians as, ἀπαρχὴ εἰς σωτηρίαν which we may translate as 'the first to experience salvation'. He is using it of first converts in the same sense as in Rom. 16.5 and 1 Cor. 16.15.[12] Thus we may claim that the thought of Christ as the ἀπαρχή is by no means inconsistent with the use of the word elsewhere in Paul's works, as long as we keep firmly before us the vital link which the theology of ἐν Χριστῷ gives between the ἀπαρχή and the φύραμα.

With this in mind, we turn to Num. 15 once again, and we immediately are struck by the significance which Paul would find in this chapter. In 15.14 we find instructions about presenting 'a pleasing odour to the Lord', ὀσμὴν εὐωδίας, a phrase which is actually used of Christ's self-offering in Eph. 5.2. The author of Ephesians was quite sufficiently close to Paul for this to be relevant evidence. The passage from which the phrase ἀπαρχὴ φυράματος comes is immediately followed (Num. 15.22f) by a series of prescriptions as to what to do 'if you err, and do not observe all these commandments which the Lord has spoken to Moses'. The author of this passage in Numbers is of course only giving the correct procedure for dealing with involuntary breaches of the Torah, but Paul might well see it as a reference to the interim period, between Moses and Christ, during which sin is made even more obvious and effective by means of the law. Finally we may well observe that Num. 15.14–15 emphasizes strongly that the home-born Israelite and the stranger who has become a proselyte must obey the same law, the same ordinance. Verse 16 runs in the LXX:

> νόμος εἷς ἔσται καὶ δικαίωμα ἓν ἔσται ὑμῖν
> καὶ τῷ προσηλύτῳ τῷ προσκειμένῳ ἐν ὑμῖν
>
> There shall be one *nomos* and one *dikaiōma* for you,
> and for the proselyte that is attached to you.

Would not Paul find here a prophecy of the accession of the Gentiles? It would speak to him of a time when there would be only one order for Jew and Gentile alike, an order in which in Christ Jew and Gentile would be able to observe not the detailed prescriptions of the law, but the law's righteous intention, τὸ δικαίωμα τοῦ νόμου, the very phrase Paul uses in Rom. 8.4: 'in order that the just requirement of the law might be fulfilled in us' (cf. also Rom. 5.16, 18). Have we not perhaps stumbled upon the very quarry from which Paul has taken his theological vocabulary?

In the light of Num. 15, we may now ask: What is the logical connection between Rom. 11.15 and 16? It seems to run something like this: 'Do not imagine that the Jews, by their temporary refusal of the Messiah, have lost their election. They are already called and chosen in Christ. By their eventual return they are only taking up the calling and consequent holiness which was theirs by God's promise and covenant from the first.' From this it would certainly follow that the ἀπαρχή is Christ. But if so, we seem to see before us the outlines of a remarkable quasi-eucharistic theology, not unlike that which we meet in 1 Cor. 10.1–11, since Christ is the ἄρτος the bread, for which the dough or the grain provides the materials. Let us recall Num. 15.20:

> Of the first of your coarse meal you shall present a cake as an offering.

But in the LXX the cake becomes a loaf:

> ἀπαρχὴν φυράματος ὑμῶν ἄρτον ἀφαίρεμα ἀφοριεῖτε αὐτό.

Inasmuch as this monstrously un-Greek sentence would mean anything to a non-Semite, it must be translated:

> the first fruits of your dough, the loaf, you shall separate it as a separation.

In fact the Targum of Jerusalem renders it in very much the same terms:

> Of the first of your dough you shall give a separation unto the Name of the Lord.[13]

We have thus here in Romans a sort of parallel to 1 Corinthians. In the Corinthian Epistle we have Christ as the ἄρτος and Christians as the φύραμα; also Christ associated with the cup of wine. Here we seem to have Christ as the ἄρτος, Christians (in the very widest sense) as φύραμα, and, if our argument below is valid, Christ as the olive tree. Admittedly the olive tree is not the vine, and oil is not wine. But then in the Old Testament sacraments referred to in 1 Cor. 10 manna is not exactly bread and water is not wine, but they could be seen as types. Paul's thought here is not explicitly worked out, but we are surely justified in finding in Romans a distinct parallel to the eucharistic theology which we meet in 1 Corinthians.

We must, therefore, if we are to explore Paul's figure in Rom.

11.16a thoroughly, examine those passages in 1 Corinthians where Christ is described as the loaf and Christians as the dough. We begin with 1 Cor. 5.6–8:

> Your boasting is not good. Do you not know that a little leaven leavens the whole lump? Cleanse out the old leaven, that you may be a new lump, as you really are unleavened. For Christ, our paschal lamb, has been sacrificed. Let us, therefore, celebrate the festival not with the old leaven, the leaven of malice and evil, but with the unleavened bread of sincerity and truth.

Here Christians are the φύραμα 'lump', and the connection is made between the φύραμα and the paschal lamb, a reference to Exod. 12 which we must presently explore. But for the moment we should consult those commentators on 1 Corinthians who attempt to define the relation between the Passover and Christ's sacrifice as implied in this passage. One influential school describes Paul as allegorizing the Passover. Thus Lietzmann sees a word-play on Exod. 12.19; 13.7. The argument, he says, runs as follows: 'Since you are as Christians the true ἄζυμοι, then the true Passover feast is introduced through the death of Christ, the true Passover lamb, that festival in which he continually lives.' Paul, he adds, 'allegorises the Passover feast and takes it as a type of Christianity'.[14] Our confidence in the accuracy of this explanation must be considerably shaken by Lietzmann's failure to distinguish between allegory and type. Woollcombe[15] and Allo[16] also describe this as an allegory of the Passover. Euler describes the relation much more carefully in the following words: 'Just as for the Israelites a new era broke in with the institution of the Passover offering, so also for Christians with the Passover offering of Christ.'[17] This is 'similar situation' relationship, i.e. typology. The author of a very recent commentary, C. K. Barrett, prefers to use the word 'analogy' to describe the relationship: 'The analogy with the Jewish Passover is not perfect, for in ordinary Jewish practice it would have been necessary to dispose of the leaven before the feast had taken place. In the Christian application, God has been beforehand in providing the lamb for the sacrifice.'[18]

Unless Paul could assume some acquaintance with Exod. 12 on the part of his readers, his reference would be quite meaningless. This chapter prescribes how the Israelites are to observe the Passover, and in it the Passover lamb and the unleavened bread are closely associated; see verse 8

> They shall eat the flesh [sc. of the lamb] that night, roasted; with unleavened bread and bitter herbs they shall eat it.

In verse 11 the lamb is apparently identified with the passover, and is simply described as πασχὰ Κυρίου:

> καὶ ἔδεσθε αὐτὸ μετὰ σπουδῆς· πασχά ἐστιν Κυρίου.

> And you shall eat it with haste. It is the pascha of the Lord.

Paul is not alone in seeing the Passover lamb as a type of Christ. The same thought appears in John 19.36:

> For these things took place that the scripture might be fulfilled, 'Not a bone of him shall be broken'.

This prohibition of breaking a bone in the lamb is found in Exod. 12.46 'and you shall not break a bone of it', a connection noted by Goudge.[19] Thus the passage from 1. Cor. 5.6–8 seen in the light of Exod. 12, has provided us with an essential link. In that passage the φύραμα means Christians, and the Paschal lamb is Christ regarded as an offering. We may therefore reasonably argue that in Rom. 11.16, since the ἀπαρχή is certainly an offering in view of Num. 15, and since the φύραμα is quite reasonably interpreted as all who are in Christ, the ἀπαρχή also indicates Christ. But with this passage from 1 Corinthians we are introduced to the thought of a feast connected with the Christian Passover. The offering is also, it seems, a communion. We turn therefore to 1 Cor. 10.14–22 for further light on this, and find the wheel has come full circle, since that passage points back to the Scripture passage with which we began this chapter, Deut. 32.

We must quote the whole passage from 1 Cor. 10, since it is a sort of midrash on Deut. 32.15–21:

> Therefore, my beloved, shun the worship of idols. I speak as to sensible men; judge for yourselves what I say. The cup of blessing which we bless, is it not a participation in the blood of Christ? The bread which we break, is it not a participation in the body of Christ? Because there is one bread, we who are many are one body, for we all partake of the one bread. Consider the practice of Israel: are not those who eat the sacrifices partners in the altar? What do I imply then? That food offered to idols is anything, or

that an idol is anything? No, I imply that what pagans sacrifice they offer to demons and not to God. I do not want you to be partners with demons. You cannot drink the cup of the Lord and the cup of demons. You cannot partake of the table of the Lord and the table of demons. Shall we provoke the Lord to jealousy? Are we stronger than he? (1 Cor. 10.14–22).

Robertson and Plummer see a link with Deut. 32, and point out that Κύριος throughout this passage in 1 Cor. 10 must mean Christ.[20] Allo writes: 'We are one because there is only one loaf.' This loaf, he says, is the heavenly bread, the body of Christ. In other words, Christ is identified with the loaf, and this in its turn with Christians, a very important point for the understanding of our passage in Romans. Héring suggests that 'those who eat the sacrifices' in verse 18 are primarily the priests and levites, but secondarily the people as a whole.[21] This is no doubt right, in which case we have by analogy a hint that in the new dispensation all Christians are now in the position the priests of old were in. We do not need to enter into the complicated debate as to what exactly Paul means by being 'partners with demons'. It is very well summed up by C. K. Barrett, who also rejects the distinction made by Robertson and Plummer between μετέχειν and κοινωνεῖν. We may certainly accept the conclusion, well argued by Jourdan, that whatever participation in the body and blood, and table, of Christ meant to Paul it did not mean actually eating and drinking Christ, since Paul does not suggest that those who attended heathen feasts actually ate and drank demons.[22] For our purpose the important features of this passage are the link with Deut. 32, the suggestion that Christians can be under the dominion of demons in the form of heathen gods, and the equation of τράπεζα (table) with θυσιαστήριον (altar). Editors on the whole have not paid much attention to the scriptural background to this passage. Conzelmann, for example, gives only one reference to Deut. 32.17, in a list of references, and one to Mal. 1.7,12, τράπεζα κυρίου. Barrett just mentions it, but maintains that the parallels from Israel of old are analogies not arguments. Our investigation of the related passages in 1 Corinthians and Romans, together with the pentateuchal sources that lie behind them, should make us hesitate before accepting this conclusion. We are in touch with a whole Pauline theology of Christ and the

Church, of Eucharist and offering. The content he drew from his Christian tradition, but the vocabulary comes from the Scriptures. The hint of the continuing power of heathen gods must remind us that the emphasis found in Colossians on Christ having conquered them is not necessarily a deutero-Pauline development.

We turn then to Deut. 32, a passage which we know that Paul studied carefully. There is evidence from the rabbinic tradition that this chapter was regarded as eschatological. Deut. 32.14, with its description of the rich delights which Israel had enjoyed, is interpreted as applying to the world to come.[23] Verses 13–16 would therefore be of great significance to Paul. It speaks of Israel being fed with 'oil out of the flinty rock', a phrase that would mean the prosaic petrol to us moderns, but would probably remind Paul of the giving of water from the rock to which he has just referred in 1 Cor. 10.4. It may also link up in his mind with the olive-tree metaphor which is soon to follow in Rom. 11. Then in verse 14 we read of

> the finest of the wheat—
> and of the blood of the grape you drank wine.

Here are both bread and wine[24] with a reference to blood, quite enough to point Paul to the Eucharist, which he is of course discussing in 1 Cor. 10.14–21. There follows in Deut. 32.17 the reference to no-gods which Paul actually quotes in 1 Cor. 10.20:

> They sacrificed to demons which were no gods,
> to gods they had never known.

And finally in verse 21 comes a reference to both the sorts of jealousy, God being provoked to jealousy by Israel's apostasy (echoed in 1 Cor. 10.22) and his responding by provoking Israel to jealousy by favouring another people, the theme of Rom. 11.11–14. It is therefore no exaggeration to say that 1 Cor. 10.14–21 is a Christian midrash on Deut. 32.17–21.

We must be careful to note how Paul uses this scriptural material. The Deuteronomy passage in Paul's interpretation gives an anticipation of the predicament of the Church in the new era, just as the narrative of the Exodus and the wilderness sojourn does in 1 Cor. 10.1–13. It can therefore be used as a warning to Christians not to fall into the same error. But it also acts in its own right as prophecy, a prophecy of the refusal of the Jews to accept the Messiah and of the accession of the Gentiles. Generally speaking, we may say that Paul uses the Deuteronomy passage paranetically in 1 Corinthians and prophetically in Romans. But we must not press the distinction. It is very doubtful whether Paul would have consciously recognized it. A third important point must be made: according to Paul, Christ is present in the Deuteronomy passage, warning, recording, promising. We may be sure that the 'real presence' of Christ is regarded by Paul as being just as recognizable in Deut. 32 as it is in the events in Israel's history to which he refers in 1 Cor. 10.1–13. But this presence was not, of course, incarnation. The presence under the old dispensation, though real, was less direct, less permanent, and less redemptive than in the era of the new covenant.

We may sum up our elaborate discussion of half a verse in Rom. 11 by saying that we have been studying what is in effect an important segment of Paul's theology. In 11.16 Christ, we claim, is the ἀπαρχή. It is he who has offered himself, so that the φύραμα, all who are in Christ from Abraham down to the latest convert to Christianity, is made holy and able to offer itself in him. There is a reference to what we may certainly call the sacraments enjoyed by Israel of old, wherein the pre-existent Christ as author of both food and drink was present to his people. Both Christian sacrifice and Christian Eucharist are unavoidably present here, though Paul is not emphasizing them in the Romans context. Indeed, when fully examined, Rom. 11.16a and its related passages fully bear out the contention that, according to Paul, the pre-existent Christ was present in Israel's history. When one sees how Paul can use the sacrificial offerings in the ritual of the Torah as types for Christ's offering of himself, one can understand the temptation under which a catholic theology of the Eucharist has always stood to conclude that in some sense Christians offer Christ in the Mass. But two considerations must give us pause here: first, the type in the old dispensation is not guaranteed as a perfect foreshadowing: it may be an imperfect type, as Adam was of Christ. And second, all Paul's use of scriptural figures here depends on the basic assumption that we (and all other devout worshippers of God from Abraham onwards) are in some sense in Christ. In fact, we are driven nearer and nearer to the conclusion (actually reached by the end of chapter 11) that whatever God does he does in Christ. Thus, since all our offering is made in Christ, we can never be sufficiently distant from him to offer him. The figure of the olive tree, as expounded below, drives this lesson home: Christ bears us and not vice versa. But at least we may claim to have found good reason to doubt the oft-repeated assertion that in the New Testament there is no connection between Eucharist and sacrifice.

Like Leenhardt, we are making a division between 11.16a and 16b. But, unlike Leenhardt, we do not regard the two figures as having different explanations:

καὶ εἰ ἡ ῥίζα ἁγία, καὶ οἱ κλάδοι

and if the root is holy, so are the branches.

Just as we interpreted the first fruits and the lump to mean Christ and those who are in Christ, so with the root and the branches. Perhaps the strongest argument in favour of this interpretation is the fact that in Paul's theology the only continuous lineage is one of faith, not physical descent, and the only continuous locus of faith is Christ. Where there is no purely human continuity, if there is to be continuity it must be provided by God, and that means provided by God-in-Christ.

It is surely significant that in the only other place, apart from this passage in Rom. 11, where Paul uses ῥίζα it means Christ. In Rom. 15.12 he quotes the famous messianic prophecy from Isa. 11.10:

'The root of Jesse shall come.'

The fact that it is not in Paul's own words but is part of a scriptural citation adds to its significance. In the context of Israel's history, 'the root' could hardly mean anything else to Paul but the Messiah, and Israel's history is certainly what he is expounding here. For Philo, however, as for many of Paul's editors, the root can only mean Abraham and his posterity Israel. He writes of Abraham thus: 'From him, as if from a root, that shoot sprang which philosophically examines and contemplates everything in the universe, whose name is Israel.'[25] But Philo's very language shows that he is aware that the words 'root' and 'shoot' come from Isa. 11.1-10. Even though Philo was probably not very much interested in the Messiah, he cannot eliminate language which is in fact messianic, and to the messianic overtones of 'root' in Judaism we must now turn our attention.

There are in fact two main passages in the Scriptures where 'the root' seems to have a messianic significance, Isa. 11.1–10 and 53.2. In the first passage, the two important verses are as follows:

> v. 1ab   καὶ ἐξελεύσεται ῥάβδος ἐκ τῆς ῥίζης Ἰεσσαί,
> καὶ ἄνθος ἐκ τῆς ῥίζης ἀναβήσεται . . .
>
> v. 10a   καὶ ἔσται ἐν τῇ ἡμέρᾳ ἐκείνῃ ἡ ῥίζα τοῦ Ἰεσσαὶ
> καὶ ὁ ἀνιστάμενος ἀρχεῖν ἐθνῶν.

The mistranslation of the LXX in 11.10 is an interesting question which we cannot pursue here. We will be content to note the Hebrew words translated by ῥίζα or similar nouns. In 11.1 ῥάβδος represents the Hebrew *chōter*. ῥίζα is used to render both *geza'* in 1a and *shōresh* in 1b. ἄνθος corresponds to the Hebrew *nētser*. In 11.10a ῥίζα translates *shōresh*. Thus, whereas in the first verse the 'root' is the stock that gives birth to the new shoot, in verse 10 it represents the new shoot itself. Obviously there is scope here for the 'root' being identified with the 'shoot'. The Targum is so convinced that this is a messianic reference that it dispenses with the language of metaphor altogether and renders:

> And a kin shall come forth from the sons of Jesse, and an Anointed one from his son's sons shall grow up.

Here the 'root' is the dynasty of David. But it continues the same method in verse 10:

> And it shall come to pass at that time, that the son of the son of Jesse, who is about to arise as a sign to the peoples, to him shall the kingdoms be subject.

The Targum has thus clearly identified the 'root' with the Messiah. Maurer points out that ῥίζα can mean both 'remainder' and 'beginning of a new growth', and suggests that ἡ ῥίζα τοῦ Ἰεσσαί was considered by the translators of the LXX to be a messianic title.[26] He quotes Ecclus. 47.22:

> he [sc. God] gave a remnant to Jacob,
> and to David a root of his stock;

the last phrase is translated by Ben Sira's grandson as ἐξ αὐτοῦ ῥίζαν.²⁷ Here then is another passage where the ῥίζα means the Messiah. Maurer takes the view, all the same, that in Rom. 11.16 ῥίζα means Abraham and the patriarchs.

The other place where 'the root' might have messianic overtones is Isa. 53.2ab

> For he grew up before him like a young plant,
> and like a root out of dry ground.

The LXX has a strange mistranslation here:

> ἀνηγγείλαμεν²⁸ ἐνάντιον αὐτοῦ ὡς παιδίον,
> ὡς ῥίζα ἐν γῇ διψώσῃ

> We proclaimed before him like a child,
> like a root in a thirsty ground.

The word translated by the LXX with παιδίον is *yōnēq*, which means 'a sucker, young plant'; and ῥίζα, as often, renders *shōresh*. In their original context these lines described the growth and upbringing of the servant; but there seems some reason to believe that the passage came to be looked on as messianic. The LXX mistranslation παιδίον could lead to its being associated with the very messianic passage Isa. 9.6:

> For to us a child is born.

The LXX (9.5) translates 'child' here with παιδίον. The Targum has transferred the description from the individual to the messianic community, a tendency which we meet in the Qumran documents. It offers

> And the righteous shall grow up before him even as budding shoots; and as a tree that sendeth forth its roots by streams of waters, so shall the holy generations increase in the land that was in need of him.

Euler points out that ῥίζα is the rendering for *shōresh* not only in the LXX, but also in Aquila, Symmachus, and Theodotion.²⁹ It is therefore extremely likely that this is what Paul's Greek version would have. At any rate Paul would find in this verse, in a chapter which we know he studied, another reference to the Messiah as 'the root'.

Whatever meaning we think Paul attached to ῥίζα in Rom. 11.16, it is very difficult to deny that he thought of it not merely as a root, from which in the past a stock sprang and thus produced branches which may exist at a much later time. He also thinks of it as continually existing, and indeed as continually nourishing the branches; see 11.17–18, where we read of the 'rich root' of the olive tree as supplying the branches and of the root as supporting the branches in Paul's own day.[30] This makes it very difficult to think of the root as meaning merely Abraham or merely the patriarchs. Completely in line with this is the description in Rev. 5.5 of Jesus as ἡ ῥίζα Δαυείδ 'the root of David' and in 22.16 as ἡ ῥίζα καὶ τὸ γένος Δαυείδ. This latter phrase shows that ῥίζα is to be understood in the sense of 'stock' (i.e. continuous organism) and not only of 'root' (i.e. one part of the whole plant). If, therefore, the 'root' figure must be thought of as applying to some organism through the ages, the *Hodayoth* references to this figure become relevant. *Hodayoth* vi.15 refers to a *nētser*, which Mansoor translates 'twig'. It is to grow into 'an everlasting planting'. This is a reference not only to the messianic 'shoot' of Isa. 11.1, but also to Isa. 60.21 'the shoot of my planting'.[31] Mansoor is quite sure that the 'everlasting planting' is the sect itself. In the ensuing hymn this plant is described as spreading all over the world, and it will bring judgement on the guilty, especially on those who had fallen away from the sect. In *Hodayoth* viii.1–12 we read of a budding 'sprout' that spreads out its branches, that is trampled on by men, and fed on by beasts. It is to be concealed in a sort of garden of Eden and protected by angels. It also seems to be tended by the author of the *Hodayoth* in his capacity as a gardener. Thus it seems very likely that in the Qumran documents the 'root', viewed as an organism growing in history, is the messianic community. It has a brilliant eschatological future, though it will no doubt have its share in the messianic woes. Paul's interpretation is perfectly comprehensible if we consider his circumstances and his faith. Not long before his time this 'root-plant' language to which the LXX (if not the author of Isa. 11.1–10 himself) had given a messianic complexion is used by the Qumran sectaries to describe the messianic community, existing for a considerable period of time, probably as much as two hundred years. They may even have traced a sort of 'apostolic succession' in the period between Moses and the original Teacher of Righteousness.[32] All Paul does is to add to this conception the belief that the Messiah has come in Jesus, and naturally 'the root' becomes the Messiah himself, and the branches those who are 'in Christ'. It seems the most natural explanation of Paul's meaning in Rom. 11.16f. Paul now proceeds to elaborate his figure of a tree with root and branches. Despite the fact that many versions (e.g. the text of the Greek New Testament in the 1966 edition of the Bible Societies and the RSV) begin a new paragraph with verse 17, we must not be misled into thinking that Paul is now introducing a new figure. All the evidence is against this, not least the fact that the words 'root' and 'branches' are still essential elements in his metaphor. What he does in verse 17 is to give us a new and surprising detail about this tree. It is an olive, not, as we might well have expected, a vine. Indeed we may well ask why Paul does not make his tree a vine. It is a most frequent image for Israel in the Scriptures; it would fit in well with the eucharistic passage which Paul's study of Deut. 32 inspired in 1 Cor. 10.14–21. Here also Deut. 32 is, as we have seen, in the background. Why not a vine?

The answer is that Paul has a quite different Scripture passage in mind as he elaborates his picture of the tree with its root and its branches, in order to explain how Israel has continued down the ages and into the messianic era. It is a passage from Jeremiah, one in which Israel is presented in vivid language not as a vine but as an olive. Jer. 11.16 runs as follows:

> The Lord once called you, 'A green olive tree, fair with goodly fruit'; but with the roar of a great tempest he will set fire to it, and its branches will be consumed.

The words are of course addressed by God through the prophet to Israel. The LXX translation has by no means rendered the Hebrew accurately. It offers:

> ἐλαίαν ὡραίαν εὔσκιον τῷ εἴδει ἐκάλεσεν Κύριος τὸ ὄνομά σου· εἰς φωνὴν περιτομῆς αὐτῆς ἀνήφθη πῦρ ἐπ’ αὐτήν, μεγάλη ἡ θλῖψις ἐπί σε, ἠχρεώθησαν οἱ κλάδοι αὐτῆς.

This gives the sense:

> The Lord had called thy name a beautiful olive tree, in appearance, affording good shade. At the voice of its circumcision fire was kindled on it; great is the affliction upon thee; its branches have been damaged.

We need not try to speculate as to why the first line of this verse
has been so loosely translated, but this mistranslation of the
phrase 'the roar of the great tempest' is important for our purpose. The LXX has quite mistakenly introduced the notion of
circumcision.[33] It has also introduced the word 'affliction'
(θλῦψις) into the text.[34] As we consider this passage, we can
easily see what Paul would make of it. In the first place, it gives
him the figure of a tree for Israel, which he needed. Again, in
the LXX its branches are not totally consumed, as in the
Hebrew, but 'damaged': ἠχρεώθησαν. This is not so far from
Paul's ἐξεκλάσθησαν in verse 19. He would certainly see a significance in the LXX's extraordinary rendering 'at the voice of
its circumcision fire was kindled upon it'. Indeed, if it is Israel
in Christ that he has in mind, it would make astonishingly good
sense to him: at the command of the circumcised in Israel,
Israel attempted to destroy herself, or else God kindled fire
upon her at the command of the circumcision, a reference to
the judgement of the cross. The word θλῦψις is introduced by
the LXX, and would speak to him of the messianic affliction,
inaugurated in Christ, continued or reproduced in the Church.
As we have noted above, the fact that the LXX (whether
deliberately or not) has turned a figure of total destruction into
one of partial destruction would suit Paul's purpose admirably.
Again, we must surely conclude that Paul has chosen this
figure himself. The very suggestion that it could have formed
part of a collection of *testimonia* is absurd. If so, he must have
read it in its context. But it is followed by one of those moving
protests on the part of Jeremiah, an intimate appeal to God for
vindication. Verse 19 runs:

> But I was like a gentle lamb
>   led to the slaughter.
> I did not know it was against me
>   they devised schemes, saying,
> 'Let us destroy the tree with its fruit,
>   let us cut him off from the land of the living,
>   that his name be remembered no more.'

Paul would read this as an utterance of the pre-existent Christ,
prophesying his death and vindication. As we have seen, Paul
certainly understood Christ as speaking in the utterances of the
innocent sufferer in the Psalms. This utterance falls exactly into

that pattern. Indeed we might claim that this verse is evidence that Paul meant by the olive tree not just Israel, but Israel in Christ. It is tempting to see a confirmation of this in the phrase 'let us cut off the tree with its fruit', but in fact this is not how the LXX translates this phrase.[35] However, apart from this point there is quite enough evidence to suggest how Paul understood this passage.

Several editors note the reference to Jeremiah, as for instance Sanday and Headlam, as well as Michel. Ellis notes that the rabbis applied the passage to Israel.[36] It is indeed interesting to notice what they made of it. In one passage in the Talmud Abraham is represented as standing in the ruins of the Temple at the time of its destruction by Titus. After pleading with God in vain, he says in despair: 'Perhaps, heaven forfend, there is no help for them.' Then came forth a heavenly voice and said 'The Lord called thy name a leafy olive tree, fair with goodly fruit; as the olive tree produces its best only at the very end, so Israel will flourish at the end of time.' Again R. Joshua b. Levi said: 'Why is Israel likened to an olive tree? To tell you that, as the olive tree loses not its leaves either in summer or winter, so shall Israel never be lost either in this world or in the world to come.' R. Johanan said: 'Why is Israel likened to an olive tree? To tell you that, just as the olive tree produces its oil only after pounding, so Israel returns to the right way only after suffering.'[37] This tradition of interpretation of the figure obviously suits Paul's meaning: it adheres to the LXX interpretation of seeing the figure as one of affliction, but not of complete destruction; it suggests that the passage is actually describing what will only be fulfilled in the end-time; and it emphasizes that ultimately all Israel will return to the right way, exactly what Paul says in 11.26. The only difference between Paul and the rabbis lies in the meaning of 'Israel'; Paul would have said it meant Christ and all who are in Christ.

One more point remains to be made: however one interprets Paul's figures of first fruits and dough, of root and branches, of the olive tree, when one comes to apply the figure to the accession of the Gentiles, as Paul does throughout verses 17–24, it is almost impossible if one is thinking in Pauline terms not to equate the tree with Christ. After all, the Gentiles have come to Christ, been grafted into Christ, live in Christ. Paul does not say that they have come to Israel, or even to the Church; he must have the thought of Christ in his mind all the time as he elaborates the figure. This can be demonstrated by two examples, one from antiquity and one from our own day. Clement of Alexandria, writing on the theme of the grafting in of the Gentiles, says, 'This process of grafting, initiated by the apostle, can be done upon the cultivated olive, Christ himself, that is to say, upon the tree consisting of those who believe in Christ.'[38] Clement assumes without question that in the deepest sense the olive tree must be Christ. The modern instance occurs in an article by P. E. Hughes.[39] He assumes without saying so that the root of the tree is Abraham; he quite rightly interprets Abraham's seed in Paul as meaning first Christ, and then those who are in Christ. Commenting on the olive tree figure he writes: 'The continual fruitfulness and well-being of the several branches depends upon a vital union with the trunk whereby they are enabled to partake of the "root and fatness of the tree" (Rom. 11.17).' Thus, without perhaps being aware of it, he has moved into the assumption that Christ is the olive tree through his application of the figure of the Gentiles. Finally, referring to Gal. 3.8, he writes: 'Thus the engrafting of the Gentiles was by no means a new purpose of God, but an age-old one implied even in the terms of his covenant with Abraham.' This seems to drive home the conclusion that, once you take the root and branches figure together with the olive-tree figure, you cannot avoid the conclusion that Christ is both the root and the tree; you cannot avoid reading Christ back into the history of Israel of old. This in fact is what Paul did.

We cannot conclude this chapter better than by quoting Karl Barth. It is true that in his famous commentary on Romans he sometimes seems to be more concerned to find his message in Paul than to elucidate Paul's message. But in the *Church Dogmatics* he gives us, in the course of elaborating his theology of the Church, a spendid commentary on Romans 9—11. He writes:

> But not all who are 'of Israel' are so in the way in which this is to be said of Jesus of Nazareth. Strictly speaking, he alone is Israel, and it is only in him, as his prophets, witnesses, forerunners, that others are as well, those who are specially elected in him, with him, and for his sake.

And again:

> All Israelites as such are the ancestors or at least the kinsmen of this seed who is the meaning and goal of the whole, the one thing common to all the members, the constituent ground of their right to exist as Israelites. This being the case, although in order of time he is the last Israelite, he can also be regarded and designated as the first, as the seed, and therefore as the root from which they have all come and grown . . . It is [only] when the illustration is understood in this way that we can understand the weighty and thrice repeated 'holy' ascribed [v. 16] both to the firstfruit and to the root.[40]

Except that Paul would have added that Christ was previous in time as well as coming in the fullness of time, I believe this truly represents his thought.[41]

# 7

## PAUL'S USE
## OF RABBINIC MATERIAL

Our aim in this study is to show how Paul uses traditional parenetic material drawn from his Jewish background. The word 'rabbinic' is strictly speaking anachronistic, but may be excused as indicating clearly enough material which has reached us today through the rabbinical medium of the Talmud.

We are concerned here with that part of the Epistle to the Romans which extends from 12.9 to 13.10. There are in fact five explicit scriptural references in it, only one of which presents any textual difficulties. We intend to suggest that in this section Paul may be using traditional rabbinic material for purposes of exhortation, since there is a passage in the Mishnah which presents certain interesting parallels to it. It is hardly necessary to add that Paul has thoroughly Christianized his material. There would seem at first glance to be no very clear parallel, since we do not intend to comment on any material in 13.1-7; all the resemblances we claim lie in the two sections 12.9-21 and 13.8-10. If the alleged parallel indicates a genuine use of rabbinic parenetic material by Paul, then the section 13.1-7 must be regarded as an after-thought, or even perhaps a later addition by another hand. This last suggestion has been made by J. Kallas.[1] At any rate his contention does seem to be correct that 12.21 leads on very smoothly to 13.8. But we need not commit ourselves to any dogmatic theory of interpolation. It will be enough if we point out the intrusive nature of 13.1-7. Paul must not be denied the right to emend his own work.

It will also be convenient to examine the one citation which entails textual difficulties before we look at the passage as a whole. This occurs in 12.17. Paul writes:

μηδενὶ κακὸν ἀντὶ κακοῦ ἀποδιδόντες·
προνοούμενοι καλὰ ἐνώπιον πάντων ἀνθρώπων·

Repay no one evil for evil, but take thought for what is noble in the sight of all.

The text is also quoted in 2 Cor. 8.20–1, thus;

στελλόμενοι τοῦτο, μή τις ἡμᾶς μωμήσηται ἐν τῇ ἁδρότητι ταύτῃ τῇ διακονουμένῃ ὑφ' ἡμῶν· προνοοῦμεν γὰρ καλὰ οὐ μόνον ἐνώπιον Κυρίου ἀλλὰ καὶ ἐνώπιον ἀνθρώπων.

We intend that no one should blame us about this liberal gift which we are administering, for we aim at what is honourable not only in the Lord's sight but also in the sight of men.

Paul has adapted the LXX text to his purpose without seriously altering its meaning. It is the text of Prov. 3.4 and runs:

καὶ προνόου καλὰ ἐνώπιον Κυρίου καὶ ἀνθρώπων,

which can be translated:

and take thought for what is noble in the sight of the Lord and of men.

In his Romans citation Paul has omitted the reference to God and inserted πάντων 'all'. In his citation in 2 Corinthians he has merely put God and men in apposition. The difficulty arises, however, when we compare the LXX (and Paul's text) with that of the MT. The Hebrew gives a distinctly different sense. For the purpose of clarification we will quote Prov. 3.3–4 from the RSV:

v. 3   Let not loyalty and faithfulness forsake you;
        bind them about your neck,
        write them on the tablet of your heart.
v. 4   So you will find favour and good repute
        in the sight of God and man.

The LXX has nothing corresponding to the phrase 'write them on the tablet of your heart', but goes straight from 'bind them about your neck' to 'you will find favour', thus

ἄφαψαι δὲ αὐτὰς ἐπὶ σῷ τραχήλῳ, καὶ εὑρήσεις χάριν.

Fix them firm on your neck, and you will find favour.

Then follows the line quoted above. The Vulgate follows the Hebrew closely, except in one respect:

> circumda eis gutturi tuo,
> et describe in tabulis cordis tui;
> et invenies gratiam et disciplinam bonam,
> coram Deo et hominibus.

> bind them about your neck
> and write them on the tablets of your heart;
> and you will find favour and good training,
> in the eyes of God and men.

In one very small detail the Vulgate is closer to the LXX than the MT. It translated the Hebrew word which is literally an imperative ('and find favour') as a future indicative, no doubt conveying the correct meaning.[2] We can now see quite clearly why it is that the LXX used προνόου. The word does not translate *maʿtsa'* ('find') but *sēkel* ('repute'). The LXX translator has mistaken the noun for a verb, and has rendered it as if it was in the imperative.[3]

But even so προνόου is not a very obvious word wherewith to translate the root SKL, even assuming that it is taken to be a verb and not a noun. Elsewhere in the LXX *sēkel* is rendered by some word meaning 'intelligence' or 'intelligent', e.g. Prov. 12.8 with συνετοῦ and Ecclus. 8.9 with σύνεσιν. But in Prov. 16.22 both LXX and Symmachus use ἔννοια, which is nearer the sense of προνόου. The verb προνοεῖν elsewhere in the LXX is used to translate the Hebrew verb *bīn* 'to understand'. In Job 17.15 it is used by Theodotion to translate *shūr*, a word meaning 'behold, regard' (LXX ὄψομαι). This has some significance in view of the parallel in the Mishnah.

In 2 Cor. 8 Paul uses this citation from Prov. 3.4 in a context of encouraging the giving of the Corinthian church. He has been accused (among many other things) of misappropriating funds; and he says that by sending the 'brother who is famous among all the churches for his preaching of the gospel' he is, in some way not very clear to us, avoiding any imputation of misappropriation. Not that Paul is in any way conscious of guilt in this respect, but he wishes to be guiltless in the eyes of men as well as in God's eyes—and hence the quotation. In Romans the context is more general: Christians are to avoid giving offence to non-Christians if at all possible, and the reference to being guiltless in God's eyes is not necessary, so is not made explicit. But the thought of Christian giving is not very far away. Paul goes on to quote from Proverbs an injunction to care for even one's enemy if he is in need. Rom. 13.8 warns Christians not to owe anything to anyone, and passes on to the great command as the true summary of our duty towards our neighbour. So the Proverbs text is also used here to reinforce teaching about how to manage our worldly goods. It seems likely that Paul used this text as a stand-by when he was giving advice to converts on this subject.

Michel's comment on Paul's use of this text is significant: 'Paul paraphrases our text in a Targum-like (*targumartig*) way, both in this context and in 2 Cor. 8.21'. This is a just remark, but it should not be understood to mean that Paul has wrested the Scripture quotation for his own individual purpose. The comparison with a Targum is most appropriate, since we find in the Talmud that this text can be used in very much the sense Paul gives to it. In the *Tractate Shekalim* careful instructions are given as to how the half-shekel tax is to be actually placed in the relevant chamber in the Temple, the aim being to avoid any suggestion of misappropriation.[4] 'For it is a man's duty to be free of blame before men as before God, as it is said *And be guiltless towards the Lord and towards Israel*; and again it says *Thou shalt find favour and good understanding in the sight of God and man.*' It thus turns out rather surprisingly that what appears at first sight to be Paul's exploitation of the Greek mistranslation for his own ends is in fact found in the rabbinic tradition itself, a tradition which presumably stems directly from the Hebrew. This is not the first time that this has happened. Compare, for example, the way in which Paul's treatment of Job. 41.11 in a context of the pre-existent Wisdom is confirmed in the Targum on Job.[5] Such evidence makes one wonder whether scholars in the past have not been too hasty when they accused Paul of twisting Scripture to his own ends. What seems to us a fantastic and far-fetched interpretation of some text often proves to be simply the generally accepted understanding of it in Paul's day. Paul the unscrupulous perverter of Scripture often turns out to be simply Paul the well-read rabbi.

We have thus brought Paul at this point within range of

rabbinic exegesis. His use of Prov. 3.4 is not necessarily peculiar to himself. We must now refer to the passage in the Mishnah which seems to afford us a parallel here. It is Mishnah 9 and 10, quoted in chapter II of *Tractate Aboth* in the Talmud.[6]

> He [R. Johanan] said unto them: Go forth and observe which is the good way unto which a man should cleave. R. Eliezer said: A good eye. R. Joshua said: A good associate. R. Jose said: A good neighbour. R. Simeon said: One who looks [ahead to see] what [consequences] shall be brought forth [by his actions]. R. Eleazer said: A good heart. Said he [R. Johanan] unto them: I prefer the words of Eleazar b. Arach to your words, for within the comprehensive character of his words are your words [included].

> He further said to them: Go forth and observe which is the evil way from which a man should remove himself far. R. Eliezer said: An evil eye. R. Joshua said: An evil associate. R. Jose said: An evil neighbour. R. Simeon said: One who borrows and repays not [it is all one] whether one borrows from man or one borrows from the All-Present—as it is said: *The wicked borrows and payeth not; but the righteous dealeth graciously and giveth.* R. Eleazer said: An evil heart. Said he [R. Johanan] unto them: I prefer the words of Eleazar b. Arach to your words, for within the comprehensive character of his words are your words [included].

> They [each] said three things. R. Eliezer said: Let the honour of thy friend be as dear to thee as thine own. And be not easily provoked to anger. And repent one day before thy death. And [he also said]: Warm thyself before the fire of the wise, and beware of their glowing coals that thou mayest not be singed, for their bite is the bite of a fox, and their sting is the sting of a scorpion, and their kiss is the kiss of a serpent, and all their words are like coals of fire.

We need not continue to reproduce the words of these rabbis. They seem to have been added to in any case, since when the three sayings of the five rabbis are ended, another junior contemporary of theirs, R. Tarfon, is brought in to add his sayings.

If we now consider Rom. 12.9–21 and 13.8–10 as one passage on the one hand, and compare it with these three paragraphs in the Mishnah on the other, we can perceive certain interesting parallels. We might set them out thus:

ROMANS 12–13                          MISHNA chapter 11

12.9  hate what is evil,              The good way unto which a man
      hold fast to what is good       should cleave ... the evil way
                                      from which a man should remove
                                      himself far

12.13 contribute to the needs of the  a good eye
      saints

The editor of *Aboth* says 'a good eye' means generosity, and
compares Prov. 22.9: 'He who has a bountiful eye will be
blessed, for he shares his bread with the poor.' Paul actually
quotes the verse immediately before this in the LXX in 2
Cor. 9.7, which is of course a passage with a strong emphasis on
the importance of giving.[7]

12.17 take thought for what is noble  one who looks ahead
      in the sight of all

12.18 live peaceably with all men     be not easily provoked to anger

12.19 never avenge yourselves

12.20 by so doing you will heap burn-  Warm thyself before the fire of the
      ing coals upon his head         wise. And beware of their glowing
                                       coals, that thou mayest not be
                                       singed

The parallel here is remarkable, but it must be confessed that
neither Paul nor the Mishnah makes very clear what the figure
of 'burning coals' is exactly intended to convey. S-B point out
that the text in Proverbs (25.22) draws the conclusion that if
you heap coals of fire on the enemy's head 'the Lord will reward you'. But this is not exactly Paul's meaning. They add
that the rabbis interpreted the text to mean that the enemy
would repent, or that you would make him your friend. They
show that some rabbis interpreted the text as meaning that one
should fight the evil inclination (the enemy) by studying the
Torah, supplying food and drink being understood in this
sense. They also quote the sentence from *Aboth* which we have
put opposite Rom. 12.20, but make no comment on it. Finally,
they quote another passage from the rabbis in which the text is
said to give us the figure of an oven. From the same place come
bread to feed us and coals of fire to destroy us. So God is the
source of both good and evil; he fed Israel with the manna but
destroyed Sodom with fire. Michel says the text is a difficult
one and is hardly likely to have meant very much to the

Christians in Rome; the general sense is that the opponent is to
be won over, brought to repentance. The latest commentator
on this text, Klassen, relies heavily on an Egyptian repentance
ritual (already noted by Michel) wherein carrying a tray of
burning coals on one's head was a sign of penitence.[8] He concludes that Paul's meaning is that you should adopt an active
aggressive attitude towards evil in order to overcome it with
love. Most editors are agreed as to the general sense of the
quotation in Paul's context: the enemy is to be won over, reconciled by active forgiveness and love. At first sight the *Aboth*
passage would seem to have very little to do with this. It seems
to be advice on how to treat the Sages who can show us this
good way. Israelstam inclines to interpret the passage in terms
of the Torah. The Torah is often compared to a fire. The commentators, he says, take the phrase about 'glowing coals' to
mean 'a warning against behaving towards the Sages in a
manner incompatible with the dignity which should be theirs
as exponents of the Torah'. 'The fire of the Torah', we are
told, 'is an ever potent one, even when the Sages are, as it were,
not aflame but only resembling glowing coals.' The fox's bite,
the scorpion's sting, and the serpent's hiss are all understood
in the same way, though he does offer an alternative explanation for the last figure which would make it a criticism of the
Sages rather than a warning against their power. And the
'coals of fire' at the end of the sentence is paraphrased thus:
'Their mere words, even if they seem unimportant, should be
heeded, as they, too, are aglow with the divine fire of the
Torah.'[9] This explanation, it must be conceded, seems to grow
more and more unconvincing as it goes on. In the first place, it
is by no means certain that 'the fire of the wise' refers exclusively to the Torah, and it is most unlikely that 'glowing coals'
or 'coals of fire' mean the Torah. We may be quite certain that
the rabbinic identification of the enemy as the evil inclination
is a later development, as is also the suggestion that feeding him
means stifling the evil inclination by studying the Torah. And
when it is suggested that the fox's bite, the scorpion's sting, and
the serpent's hiss refer to the deleterious effects experienced by
those who act towards the Sages 'in a manner incompatible
with the dignity which should be theirs', we cannot help feeling
that quite unsuitable language is being employed to express

this idea. The fox, the scorpion, and the serpent are not figures used in the Scriptures to express the awe and dignity of the divine revelation. On the contrary, they are much more often used to describe either the punishment suffered by those who have sinned, or the malice of the ungodly. Foxes in Scripture are symbols of ruin, e.g. Ps. 63.10; Lam. 5.18; Ezek. 13.4. Scorpions indicate difficulty, extreme discomfort, resistance, severity, e.g. 1 Kings 12.11; Ezek. 2.6. We may note especially Ecclus. 26.7, where taking hold of 'an evil wife' is 'like grasping a scorpion', and even more 39.30, where 'scorpions' are mentioned among the things created by God for vengeance.[10] We remember that Paul, just before citing the 'coals of fire'ʹ text, has cited 'Vengeance is mine' from Deut. 32.35. As for serpents, in Ps. 58.4; 140.3 the enemies of the psalmist are compared to serpents. Prov. 23.32 is even more relevant, for there the ultimate effect of alcoholism is to 'bite like a serpent'. None of this looks like the awesome effect of divine revelation on the disciple. Suppose, however, that the 'coals of fire' text is being used in *Aboth* in essentially the same sense as in Rom. 12.20, but is being viewed from the point of view of the recipient of the coals of fire, then we have an interpretation that makes excellent sense of the passage. We are to beware of the fire of the wise because their instruction may bring to us the pains of remorse, repentance, and conversion. It is thus not a warning against the painful effects of offending rabbinic dignity, but of the risk of being converted. In this sense the Torah could be legitimately brought into the explanation, at least if the text is used in a rabbinic context. But what is common, according to this interpretation, to both Paul and *Aboth* is the emphasis on the painfulness of conversion. The enemy is converted in Paul; the disciple is converted in *Aboth*. Michel points out that what Paul adds to the rabbinic precept not to repay evil with evil is the positive exhortation actively to overcome evil with good. And we may well feel justified in attributing this significant modification of the precept to Jesus himself. As many editors have pointed out, Rom. 12 and 13 is a passage in which a remarkable number of echoes of Jesus' teaching can be traced, and the explanation of the 'coals of fire' text in terms of overcoming evil with good is entirely in line with that 'radicalization of the Torah' which some modern scholars trace in Jesus' teaching.[11] At any rate this interpretation seems to make more sense of R. Eliezer's vivid string of metaphors and explains the remarkable parallel with Rom. 12.20.

| 13.8    Owe no one anything | one who borrows and repays not |

The ensuing reference in *Aboth* to borrowing from God shows that almsgiving is in mind here.

| 13.9    You shall love your neighbour as yourself | Let the honour of thy friend be as dear to thee as thine own |

Israelstam comments on this sentence in the *Aboth* 'on the principle of *Love thy neighbour as thyself*' (Lev. 19.18). So we are justified in suggesting that the same Scripture text lies behind both passages.

These seven points of resemblance between the two excerpts from Romans and *Aboth* respectively do not demonstrate a connection, but they suggest one. It is true that the order of the materials is different in each work, but there is enough here to suggest that behind each lies a common tradition. The tradition must originally have been connected with teaching about daily life, duties to one's neighbour, and particularly almsgiving. We have suggested that Paul's form of the tradition came through Jesus and that it was Jesus who imprinted on it what distinguishes it most from the purely rabbinic tradition of *Aboth*. If we are correct in seeing a connection here, then this passage is a very remarkable one from the point of view of our present work, since it shows us Paul using scriptural material, interpreted according to the rabbinic tradition of his day, not for typology or doctrine, but for exhortation or ethical teaching. At the same time, however, we must be careful not to claim that Paul is using scriptural material taken directly from his rabbinic repertoire without passing it through the sieve of his Christian belief. If we are right in tracing this treatment of the theme back to Jesus himself, Paul is not here writing as if he were not a Christian. He is in fact reproducing the teaching of the historical Jesus and this accounts for the link with rabbinic tradition.

D. Daube has already suggested, on the basis of Paul's use of participles as imperatives in this passage, that he is using an early Christian ethical code based on Jewish models.[12] This thesis has been elaborated and defended by C. H. Talbert in a recent article.[13] Talbert only deals with Rom. 12.9–21. He thinks that he can identify the original Semitic code by removing Hellenistic and editorial additions. He does refer to the passage in *Aboth* mentioned here, and points out the parallel between 'Go and see what is that good way' and 'Go and see what is that evil way' on the one hand and Rom. 12.9b on the other. He considers 12.9b and 20 are part of the redactional material and not part of the original code because they are quoted from the LXX and because of the use of the Pauline formula 'it is written'. We have studied Paul's methods enough to realize that the fact that a citation is given in LXX form is not proof that it has no rabbinic exegesis behind it; and Talbert has made no attempt to investigate the meaning of 12.20. Generally speaking, we may claim that the conclusions of both Daube and Talbert strengthen our case here for Paul's having used traditional rabbinic parenetic material. But we would not claim to be able to isolate exactly the original material lying behind this passage, as Talbert does. Indeed we would regard any such attempt as a precarious enterprise.

# 8

# PAUL'S INTERPRETATION
# OF SCRIPTURE

————◆◆◆◆————

In this study we consider four important issues that have been discussed by scholars concerning Paul's method of interpreting Scripture. But first we must spend some time in examining what Paul means by 'the old covenant' and 'the new covenant' in this context, a subject which, as we shall see, needs considerable clarification.

Perhaps in no other area of Paul's thought is it more difficult not to be misled by modern presuppositions than in this one. Not only is our approach to Scripture very different from that of any early Christian, because of the critical method which we employ. Even the traditional pre-critical attitude to Scripture is not the same as Paul's for the very reason that it is founded on a two-testament Bible. This is not true of Paul. He knew only one sacred book, what we call the Old Testament. The very use of this name separates us, and all Christian students of the Bible as far back as Tertullian at least, from Paul himself. It could not be the 'Old' Testament for him, as he knew no book called the New Testament.

In any case what we call the Old Testament was not old for Paul. On the contrary, it was full of prophecies, information, dialogue about the new order. In it Christ, the founder of the new order, was frequently to be heard speaking. In it Paul found records of the activity of Christ, an activity which indicated, for those who had faith, what was going to happen when the new order was to be inaugurated by the coming of Christ in the flesh. Certainly Paul is as far as possible from identifying the Scriptures with the Torah. He indeed might use νόμος occasionally as a convenient abbreviation meaning 'the Bible'. After all, he could hardly be expected to give it its full title every time he referred to it, 'the Law and the Prophets and the Writings'. But holding the view which he held about the place which the Torah had in God's plan, he could not possibly have regarded the Scriptures as a whole as old, out-dated, or Torah-centred. According to Paul, the Torah had never been intended by God as anything but a temporary expedient, whose main function was to bring men to a realization of their sin and their inability to obey God by means of obedience to the Torah.

From this it follows that in Paul's eyes the Scriptures, far from being identical with the Torah, were superior to it. Not in the sense that they were written first, for no doubt Paul held the view that the whole Pentateuch was written by Moses; but in the sense that they recorded a period before the Torah existed, a period in which many events of the greatest importance in salvation-history took place. Before anything was known of the Torah, God revealed his character and purpose to Abraham: justifying faith, the election of God, grace, the promise of eternal salvation, all these things were known, and recorded in the Scripture, hundreds of years before the Torah was given on Sinai. Not only so, but even when Moses comes to the period of the Sinai covenant his writings are full of intimations that the way of faith, and not the way of Torah-obedience, is God's way for man. We shall be considering presently how far Paul found a double meaning in Scripture, a literal and a spiritual, or an immediate and an eschatological. For the moment it is sufficient to emphasize that even those passages in the Torah which seem to us to commend strict Torah-observance as God's will would seem to Paul to be speaking frequently of the gospel of grace. As he read Deuteronomy, for instance, he found side by side with passages explicating and commending the Torah texts which spoke to him of faith and grace. This Book, which to us appears to be written in order to enjoin observance of the Torah on Israel, is also, we must remember, full of references to 'this word'. Paul would take these as references to 'the word of faith'. What looks to us like a uniform commendation of Torah-observance looked to him like a major treatise on the word of faith, the gospel, with occasional instructions about the Torah.

Consequently, it makes no sense at all to suggest that Paul

thought of the Scriptures as 'the Old Testament'. For Paul, the old testament means the covenant on Sinai, 'ordained by angels through an intermediary'. This covenant was indeed recorded in the Scriptures, but the same Scriptures indicated also that this covenant was neither God's first word nor his last word. What we call the Old Testament Paul regarded simply as the Bible, the book in which was recorded God's whole plan, purpose, and character. This plan was, of course, only fully carried out in Jesus Christ, but there is never any question in Paul of God's character or God's plan having been changed by the coming of Christ, since God had already, before Christ's coming in the flesh, recorded in the Scriptures what he was like and what he intended to do. A very great deal about Christ could therefore be learned from the Scriptures. Until Christ came in the flesh, it was indeed impossible for most men to learn about him. But in the days before his coming in the flesh it would have been possible for Israel at least to learn something about him; and the great leaders of Israel did know something of him. Abraham, Moses, David, Elijah, Isaiah, Hosea, Joel, these at least understood something of Christ, and most of them spoke of him. In fact Paul was in greater danger of suggesting that everything about Christ was already capable of being known in the Hebrew Scriptures than he was of regarding those Scriptures as outmoded. Paul had no intention whatever of attempting to write new Scriptures. There was not time for such an enterprise; it had never formed part of the eschatological programme. Above all, it was totally unnecessary. The new Israel, the Christian Church, already had their Scriptures: they were the same as those acknowledged by the old Israel. There might be a need for a certain amount of commentary—and that, to a large extent, is what Paul supplies in Romans and elsewhere.

It is truly extraordinary how far that familiar phrase 'the Old Testament' has mesmerized even the most alert scholars. It is very difficult to find a single editor who does not assume that when Paul uses the phrase ἡ παλαιὰ διαθήκη he means 'the Old Testament' in the sense of 'the Hebrew Bible' or at least 'the Pentateuch'. Since Paul uses this phrase only once in his extant writings, we must examine that passage in order to prove our point. He does however come very near to using it in his elaborate typological passage in Gal. 4.21f. He speaks of 'two covenants' in 4.24. But they immediately turn into women: 'One is from Mount Sinai, bearing children for slavery; she is Hagar.' She corresponds to 'the present Jerusalem'. This shows that, despite his using Hagar as a type, Paul does not think of an old covenant as having been made during Hagar's lifetime. There is only one old covenant, that made on Sinai.

We turn therefore to 2 Cor. 3.14, the passage where ἡ παλαιὰ διαθήκη is specifically mentioned. Owing to the confusion which the Christian use of 'the Old Testament' for the first half of the Bible has occasioned, it will be as well to quote most of two verses, 14 and 15:

ἄχρι γὰρ τῆς σήμερον ἡμέρας τὸ αὐτὸ κάλυμμα ἐπὶ τῇ ἀναγνώσει τῆς παλαιᾶς διαθήκης μένει μὴ ἀνακαλυπτόμενον ὅτι ἐν Χριστῷ καταργεῖ-ται· ἀλλ' ἕως σήμερον ἡνίκα ἂν ἀναγινώσκηται Μωϋσῆς κάλυμμα ἐπὶ τὴν καρδίαν αὐτῶν κεῖται.

We give the RSV translation, although we hope to show that at one important point it is misleading:

> for to this day, when they read the old covenant, that same veil remains uplifted, because only through Christ is it taken away. Yes, to this day, whenever Moses is read a veil lies over their minds.

This is a very obscure passage, and we wish to avoid discussion of those aspects of it which do not concern our purpose. We will therefore begin by making one point of cardinal importance: καταργεῖται in verse 14 cannot govern κάλυμμα. (This is a point made clearly by Feuillet in de Christ Sagesse de Dieu (Paris 1966), p. 118.) The verb means to 'abolish, render idle, hinder', but it cannot apply to a veil. In any case the correct verb for the taking away of a veil is supplied in this passage. It comes in verse 16:

> When a man turns to the Lord the veil is removed.

ἡνίκα δὲ ἐὰν ἐπιστρέψῃ πρὸς Κύριον, περιαιρεῖται τὸ κάλυμμα.

περιαιρεῖται is a translation of the Hebrew word sur in Exod. 34.34. If, therefore, καταργεῖται in verse 16 cannot refer to κάλυμμα, it must refer to τῆς παλαιᾶς διαθήκης and we must translate the verse (for the moment) thus:

> when they read the old covenant, that same veil remains uplifted, because only through Christ is the covenant abrogated.

This makes excellent sense. But we must in that case understand 'the old covenant' as meaning 'the covenant on Sinai', not 'the book called the Old Testament'. In any case, it is much easier to think of a covenant being 'abolished' or 'rendered null' than a book being abolished. It would be absurd to represent Paul as declaring that the only Scriptures which he acknowledged were abolished! We must, consequently, understand Μωϋσῆς in the next verse as being the wider category. It means the Pentateuch, in which the narrative of the giving of the old covenant on Sinai is to be found. Commentators who translate τῆς παλαιᾶς διαθήκης as 'the Old Testament' argue that Paul is using the wider term in verse 14 and the narrower ('Moses' = 'the Pentateuch') in verse 15. But there is no obligation to understand it this way. Paul can just as easily be understood as referring first to the narrative of the old covenant, than to that part of the Bible in which that narrative is found. It is true, of course, that according to the interpretation given here the phrase

ἐπὶ τῇ ἀναγνώσει τῆς παλαιᾶς διαθήκης

must then be taken to mean 'at the reading of the narrative of the old covenant'. But parallels can be found for this: cf. Mark 12.26:

οὐκ ἀνέγνωτε ἐν τῇ βίβλῳ Μωϋσέως ἐπὶ τοῦ βάτου . . .

have you not read in the book of Moses, in the passage about the bush . . .

And Luke 20.37:

Μωϋσῆς ἐμήνυσεν ἐπὶ τῆς βάτου . . .

Moses showed, in the passage about the bush . . .

We should note also that in 2 Cor. 3.3 the contrast is between stone tablets and hearts. This would point to the Sinai covenant, part of which at least was written on stone tablets, and not to the Hebrew Scriptures, or even to the Pentateuch alone. Thus there can be no excuse for equating ἡ παλαιὰ διαθήκη with the Hebrew Scriptures here.

A few, a very few, editors have realized this. Schmiedel, for example, translates the crucial phrase in verse 14:

in so far as it had not been disclosed that the old Covenant is outdated in Christ.[1]

But Plummer makes it clear that he takes τῆς παλαιᾶς διαθήκης as meaning the Pentateuch. He well compares Heb. 8.13, though this tells against his interpretation, since plainly there the old covenant means the Sinai legislation and the cult, not a book at all.² Strachan translates 'when the Old Testament is read aloud', which is further explained by the words 'the veil that hangs for the Jew over the sacred book'.³ Plainly, he assumed unconsciously that Paul thought of the Hebrew Scriptures as 'the Old Testament'. Lietzmann uses almost the same phrases in German. He does indeed take καταργεῖται with τῆς παλαιᾶς διαθήκης and not with κάλυμμα. But this leaves him with the thesis that Paul could describe the Hebrew Scriptures as *vergänglich*. One wonders whether Lietzmann ever consciously faced this conclusion. It looks at first sight as if Allo is going to side with Schmiedel and not commit himself to the conclusion that Paul believed the only Scriptures he knew to have been abrogated, for he paraphrases τῆς παλαιᾶς διαθήκης as 'l'alliance de Sinai'.⁴ But presently we find him writing 'the Old Testament which was inspired by God and also reflects the divine glory, has been reduced to nothing, abolished'. It is difficult to image a more glaring instance of interpreting Paul from the standpoint of a time when the canon of the New Testament was completed. Finally, we may refer to Héring, who does not commit himself to an interpretation of the phrase, but who arouses our suspicions by translating it: 'sur la lecture de l'Ancien Testament'.⁵

This point needs to be driven home, so we give below the translation of the phrase in 2 Cor. 3.14

ἐπὶ τῇ ἀναγνώσει τῆς παλαιᾶς διαθήκης

offered by eleven different English versions, cited in chronological order:

| | |
|---|---|
| King James Version | 'in the reading of the old testament' |
| RV | 'at the reading of the old covenant' (mg. 'or testament') |
| Weymouth | 'during the reading of the book of the ancient covenant'⁶ |
| Moffatt | 'when the Old Testament is read aloud'⁷ |
| Knox | 'the reading of the old law'⁸ |
| Phillips | 'when the Old Agreement is read to them'⁹ |

| RSV | 'when they read the old covenant' |
| NEB | 'when the lesson is read from the Old Covenant' |
| Jerusalem Bible | 'when the old covenant is being read'[10] |
| Today's English Version | 'as they read the books of the old covenant'[11] |
| Barclay | 'when they hear the lesson from the old covenant being read in the synagogue'[12] |

Of these versions, seven make it clear that they think τῆς παλαιᾶς διαθήκης means a book. On the whole the more literal the translation the more accurate. Those who paraphrase usually paraphrase wrongly. To this Phillips is a most honourable exception.[13] But it is surely significant that the most modern of these versions is both the wordiest and the least accurate.

One other interesting point remains to be made in this conection: in Galatians Paul writes quite freely of the covenant which God made with Abraham (see 3.15, 17; 4.24). He regards it as a proleptic one, only consummated in Christ. It is not, of course, ἡ παλαιὰ διαθήκη but is really part of the new covenant. But in Romans, when he is dealing with essentially the same material, he drops the covenant language. There are in fact only two references to διαθήκη in the Epistle, 9.4 and 11.27. The first occurs in a list of the privileges of the Jews in which valid and outdated elements are thrown together indiscriminately. The second is in a citation from the Scriptures, and plainly points forward to the end-time. We may ask, Why has Paul dropped in Romans the covenant-language used of Abraham in Galatians? We may suggest two reasons: first, it was confusing. Strictly speaking, it meant a new covenant with Abraham, an old covenant through Moses, a new covenant through Christ. Secondly, in rabbinic tradition the covenant with Abraham was very closely connected with the institution of circumcision in Gen. 17. Of course Paul in Galatians underlines the covenant of Gen. 15, made before the giving of circumcision; but experience in arguments with Jews perhaps taught him that it was very difficult to distinguish the two. So he decided in Romans to insist on only two covenants as far as Christians were concerned, the old one on Sinai and the new one of Golgotha.

We have examined 2 Cor. 3.14 in the light of what the commentators say about it. But we must now consider some more general comments made by scholars on the topic of Paul's whole approach to the Scriptures. Vollmer, in his extremely able pioneer book on the subject written as long ago as 1899, is obviously puzzled about the question: 'How can Paul claim the νόμος as authoritative, while he considered it to be outdated by God?'[14] He answers it, as Michel does thirty years later, by saying that Paul used the Law itself as a weapon against the Law.[15] This is only true if one is allowed almost to make a pun on that word νόμος, which admittedly Paul comes near to doing. The part of Scripture known as the Torah told Paul that the Torah given on Sinai was to be abrogated, and had never been intended as a way of life by God. Michel adds in the same work a very illuminating comment on Paul's understanding of covenant: Paul, he says, recognizes only two covenants, a free and a legal. Michel contrasts with this the treatment of the covenant on Sinai in the Epistle of Barnabas. The author says that there was only one covenant, that of Sinai, but the Jews misunderstood it in a literal sense; they should have perceived its spiritual meaning. Schoeps has some interesting remarks to make on this subject.[16] Paul, he says, had to prove that the real meaning of the Torah was something other than its literal observance. He adds: 'the abolition of the Law is for Paul part of his messianic teaching.' This is only true if taken in the very widest sense, i.e. in the sense that Paul finds messianic teaching throughout the Scriptures. Paul does not say: 'In the messianic age the Law will not apply.' He says 'the word is near you' (Rom. 10.8). Even before Christ's coming in the flesh, the Law had in a sense ceased to apply. Literal observance of the Law, according to Paul, was never God's intended way of life for Israel.

F. Hesse seems to pass too easily from Paul's interpretation to our modern interpretation when he says that in the Old Testament we really have another religion, and goes on to say: 'here we are facing the situation which Paul characterizes by speaking of the veil that hangs before the hearts of those who read the Old Testament without Christ.'[17] But can one so easily identify the difference between the Hebrew Scriptures as modern Christians understand them and as the Jews of old understood them, with the difference between the Hebrew Scriptures as Paul understood them and as contemporary Jews understood them? Has Hesse not omitted the all-important fact that for us there is, as there was not for Paul, a second volume called the New Testament? It could never have remotely occurred to Paul that the religion of 'the Scriptures' was different from his own. For him there was only one set of Scriptures and only one religion belonging to it.

Here we may mention together two scholars who seem to suggest that in some way Paul saw Christ revealed in the Torah, or through the actual Law-prescriptions. Bandstra writes: 'Whatever Paul may say about the effectiveness of the old covenant, this should not be interpreted as if Christ and his benefits were entirely absent in the old dispensation.'[18] What exactly does 'the old dispensation' mean here? According to Paul, God was known by faith as the God of grace from Abraham onwards. If by the 'old dispensation' is meant 'the legislation on Sinai', this statement is not accurate: Christ and his benefits are known before and beside the Sinaitic legislation, but not in it or by means of it. Similarly Bring writes that Paul does not deny the Old Testament. Properly understood, it confirms and clarifies his faith.[19] From Paul's point of view, Bring might as well have written that the Scriptures confirmed and clarified Paul's faith, a statement which is true but hardly original. Bring also says that all early Christians agreed that the Psalms and certain passages in the prophets pointed to Christ, but Paul added to this that the Law itself points to him. Here again we must distinguish: if by 'the Law' Bring means 'the Pentateuch', then this is obvious. Passages such as Deut. 32 and 33 were themselves of a prophetical nature and could easily be regarded as messianic. But if he means that in some sense legal prescriptions pointed to Christ, we can hardly agree. Except in very rare instances (we have suggested one on pp. 109f above), Paul does not try to find prophecies of Christ in strictly legal passages.

In Amsler we have a French scholar who takes more seriously Paul's interpretation of Scripture than do many of his German contemporaries, but who does not seem to have pursued his insights far enough.[20] 'For the apostle Paul,' he writes, 'a true hermeneutic of the Old Testament could only be an hermeneutic ἐν Χριστῷ ... that is, one founded on the event of the historic "coming of Jesus Christ".' This is well said, as long as it is understood that the ἐν Χριστῷ can be said in some sense directly of the 'Old Testament' period, not just proleptically. Similarly Amsler claims that quotations from the Scriptures in Paul are neither *florilegia* borrowed from Paul's rabbinic teachers, nor proofs in the sense which the Apologists wished to give to the word, but 'witnesses that will corroborate the apostolic *kerygma* with all the authority of the divine word'. Once again we must say that this is perfectly true, if it is added that the witness is to something present at the time of utterance as well as to something which was to be fulfilled only in the end-time. Amsler expresses this again later on thus: 'The scriptural testimony cited by the New Testament does not serve to establish faith by means of exegesis, but to illuminate it by allowing us to see, through the scriptural prophecy concerning history, the decisive theological dimension of the coming, the death and the resurrection of Jesus, an event which appeared so insignificant on the surface.'[21] This suggests that Paul never uses Scripture to prove that anything had been prophesied, but only to illuminate the significance of the event when it happened. This is hardly a fair account of the matter. Paul does use Scripture to prove that the events of the end-time had been foreknown and provided for in God's plan. For example, all the citations in Rom. 10 are quoted in order to prove that the events of Jesus' day had been known long beforehand to certain privileged people (Moses, Isaiah), and that God had taken every precaution in order to see that they should be foreknown.

We may now hope to have established Paul's general view of Scripture and to have shown up the misunderstanding which is created by the notion that Paul regarded anything in the Scriptures as being outdated but the actual Sinaitic covenant itself. In this connection we must look at a number of questions particularly related to Paul's use of Scripture. They are four in number: Paul's treatment of the words of Scripture; Paul's recognition of the presence of the pre-existent Christ in Israel's history; Paul's use of typology; and how far Paul can be described as making use of allegory. These are best subdivided as follows:

## Paul's treatment of the words of Scripture

Before the discovery of the Qumran documents, the complaint was frequently made that Paul altered the words of Scripture to suit his own purposes, not regarding them as sacrosanct or in-fallible. For example, Windisch, apropos Paul's treatment of Deut. 30.12–14 in Rom. 10.6–8, accuses Paul of 'correcting the text of Moses with a supremely arbitrary hand'.[22] Among less forthright commentators, the phrase 'a free retreatment of the text' is often used. The Qumran discoveries however should make us more cautious in levelling this charge at Paul. Some-times at least, what looks to us like a passage where Paul has altered the text of Scripture to suit his purpose turns out to be nothing of the sort. Paul is in fact quoting the translation of the Hebrew which he had before him. It happens to be different from the LXX. We could refer, for example, to five places in Romans where Paul's variation from the LXX is probably con-firmed either by a Hebrew tradition or by an alternative Greek translation.

Rom. 9.27:    Paul reads ὑπόλειμμα for LXX's κατάλειμμα but other LXX evidence suggests that ὑπόλειμμα was in Paul's text.[23]

Rom. 9.33:    λίθον προσκόμματος καὶ πέτραν σκανδάλου is vindi-cated against the LXX by both Greek and Hebrew sources.[24]

Rom. 10.7:    Paul's alteration of Deut. 30.13 is attested by one of the Targums.[25]

Rom. 11.35:   Paul's translation of Job 41.11 indicates a version which followed one interpretation of the Hebrew (see p. 291, n. 5).

Rom. 12.17:   Paul's application of Prov. 3.4 is found in the Tal-mud.

Neither in Rom. 10.7 nor in 12.17 can we defend Paul's render-ing as a correct translation of the Hebrew original; so those two passages raise in an acute form the question: How far was Paul prepared to go in altering the text to suit his exegesis? We may dismiss out of hand Windisch's accusation of sheer arbitrari-ness. In fact, as we have seen, the example which provoked this accusation now proves to be not a case of arbitrary alteration. Paul was appealing to an already established exegesis of the text. The same may surely be said of Prov. 3.4: though Paul's use of the text seems to be dependent on a mistranslation of the LXX, that use is found in the Talmud. Paul was therefore, we say with confidence, no innocent Septuagint worshipper, like Philo or Justin, who will blithely appeal to some purely Greek idiom in order to prove their point. He certainly did not feel himself bound to the literal meaning of the Hebrew text. But neither did the rabbis or the compilers of the Targums. The question is: How far did he venture to go from the actual words of the text? Ellis has given some answer to this question in an article in *NTS*.[26] He writes:

> Taken as a whole, the Pauline citations reflect in a substantial measure the *pesher* type moulding of the text which in some cases is determinative ... His [Paul's] idea of a quotation ... was rather a quotation exposition, a *midrash pesher* which drew from the text the meaning originally planted there by the Holy Spirit and expressed that meaning in the most appropriate words and phrases known to him.

This seems to suggest an undue measure of arbitrary alteration on Paul's part. Paul never consciously 'moulded' texts. When we do find him following this or that tradition of interpretation it usually proves to be an accepted tradition, not Paul's own invention. If the present work has shown anything, it has shown that Paul often regarded his Scripture citations as proofs. Proof texts that have been arbitrarily tampered with are ineffective as proofs.

Schmid also discusses very much the same point.[27] He gives several examples of scriptural texts which Paul has altered slightly in order to bring out the point he is making; e.g. 1. Cor 3.20:

> The Lord knows that the thoughts of the wise are futile,

where Paul has substituted 'the wise' for 'men' in the original. Schmid draws the conclusion that the *ipsissima verba* of Scripture were not sacrosanct for Paul. This seems a precarious conclusion. As Schmid himself points out, Paul sometimes argues from the *ipsissima verba* ('It does not say "and to offsprings", referring to many', Gal. 3.16). We could perhaps suggest that Paul is more careful about the verbal accuracy of his citation where he is using them for strict proof, as in Gal. 3. 1 Cor. 3.20 is hardly on a par with this. Schmid discusses one or two other passages, such as Rom. 10.6f and 10.18, with its apparently irrelevant citation of Ps. 19, and concludes that such examples make the use of the *sensus plenior* a difficult device. But in fact both Rom. 10.6f and Rom. 10.18, when examined against the background of the accepted exegesis of the day, prove to be very far from being bizarre and irrelevant uses of Scripture citation.[28] Paul uses the same licence of interpretation that contemporary rabbinic exegesis allowed itself, no more and no less. In many places where he seems to be altering the text of Scripture, he is in fact following either his own Greek version or an already existing tradition. Where he has changed the text himself, it is either because he is quoting from memory and therefore does not think the citation of great importance; or because he is referring to a text which is so well known that no one will imagine he is quoting it accurately, e.g. Rom. 12.17 with 2 Cor. 8.21; cf. also our discussion of 1 Cor. 9.9 below.

An excellent object lesson in Paul's treatment of the words of Scripture is found in his double citation of Isa. 40.13 in Rom. 11.34 and 1 Cor. 2.16. Here we see both Paul's flexibility and his fidelity to the text. He feels quite free to divide the two clauses of the LXX text, using one for one occasion (ὃς συμβιβάσει αὐτόν in 1 Cor. 2.16), and the other for the other (τίς σύμβουλος αὐτοῦ ἐγένετο in Rom. 11.34). But he does not alter the text. His fidelity is shown in the fact that he will not alter the LXX's νοῦν Κυρίου, although he must have known that the Hebrew had *rūach*, and πνεῦμα would have suited his argument better in 1 Cor. 2.

We ought perhaps to note a suggestion of Goppelt's about Paul's technique in citing Scripture, even if only to show how unfounded it is.[29] Goppelt suggests in a footnote that Paul refers to the Old Testament as 'Moses' or νόμος when he wishes to emphasize its character as mere letter. All our evidence to date goes against this; and when we look at the passages in question (only seven in all), we find that there is no support for the suggestion at all. Μωϋσῆς λέγει occurs in Rom. 9.15; 10.5; 10.19; 1 Cor. 9.9. In all but the third of these there is no particular emphasis on the letter at all; indeed in 1 Cor. 9.9 it is exactly the reverse! Rom. 10.5 might seem to give some colour to the suggestion:

> Moses writes that the man who practises the righteousness which is based on the law shall live by it.

In fact, however, the contrast is not between what Moses says and what Christ says; but between two ways of life, the way of Torah-obedience and the way of faith, both equally recorded by God. The three instances of ὁ νόμος λέγει are equally far from proving Goppelt's point, Rom. 7.7; 1 Cor. 14.21, 34. In Rom. 7.7 the law says 'You shall not covet', thereby showing us what sin is. But one of the Ten Commandments can hardly be regarded as a good example of the character of the Old Testament as mere letter! The two examples from 1 Cor. 14 are both places where Paul, far from casting any aspersion on the νόμος, highly approves of what it says. It is probable that any attempt to show that Paul's introductory formulas have anything to tell us as to how authoritative he considers the citation that follows will prove equally vain.

## How often does Paul recognize the activity of the pre-existent Christ in Israel's history?

This is a topic to which I devoted a whole chapter in a previous work.[30] It is relevant in this context only because it has a bearing on how Paul interpreted the Scriptures. That Paul sometimes recognized such activity few will deny in view of 1 Cor. 10.4: 'And the Rock was Christ'. In the chapter referred to just now, I also traced this belief in 2 Cor. 3 and Rom. 10. We may confine ourselves therefore to the question: Have our studies in the rest of Romans found any more instances of this belief? We may answer: not on the surface, but very probably it may be found implied in some places. We may point to 9.15, where the treatment of the famous theophany in Exod. 33 and 34, and the link which 'grace and truth' gives us with John's treatment of the same theme in John 1.14, makes one suspect that here Paul believed the pre-existent Son was the revealer of the Father's glory. Another place is 11.4, where perhaps the introduction of that word χρηματισμός, quite absent from the original, suggests that the voice that spoke to Elijah was, according to Paul, the voice of the Son. The whole question is brought into relief by 11.34–5, where, in a passage in which on the surface there is nothing but an ascription of praise to the Father, there can be little doubt that Paul finds a reference to the Son as the Father's counsellor and mediator of creation. W. L. Knox writes of this passage:[31] '[this citation] would naturally be useful as a proof-text, implying that God had a counsellor in creation, namely Wisdom.' If we once realize that, in any passage where Paul thinks of the Father as acting in Israel's history, he is actually thinking of God-in-Christ as the agent, we shall not be surprised to find the 'real presence' of the pre-existent Christ anywhere in Paul's exegesis of Scripture.

Here we may conveniently consider some interesting comments by C. K. Barrett on this question. He inclines to deny that there was any 'real presence' until the incarnation; he suggests that Abraham, for example, is thought of by Paul as belonging still to the age of the flesh, the age which is still under the rule of 'the elemental spirits of the universe'.[32] Thinking of both Abraham and Moses he writes: 'Neither of them experiences the victory over the powers of evil, which did not take place until, with the fulness of time, God sent forth his Son.' This seems too absolute a way of putting it. According to Paul, Abraham was a justified sinner, justified by faith; and Moses knew that God intended the way of faith for Israel, and not the way of the Torah. It is not therefore that Abraham and Moses could hope one day to stand where we stand, but that all Christians now 'stand where Moses stood'. Abraham and Moses had faith, and shared in the messianic age by anticipation. A little farther on Barrett writes:[33] 'Thus, for Paul though Jesus Christ is the divine intruder, his intrusion follows a pattern that could, in a sense and in some degree, have been predicted.' It is, one may be permitted to suggest, exactly this concept of Christ as a divine intruder that Paul wished to discard. In Paul's view, far from being a divine intruder, Christ had been present in Israel's previous history. How often he had been present, it is not easy to say. The author of the Fourth Gospel seems to suggest that all theophanies recorded in the Scriptures were really Christophanies. We cannot with confidence attribute this view to Paul. But when we note how often Paul finds Christ speaking in Scripture, when we concede (as we must) that on certain historic occasions in Israel's past Paul believed the Son to have been present, we must confess that merely to trace a predictable pattern in Scripture is not enough. The Son was there, could have been apprehended, and was believed in by some.

## Paul's use of typology

Amsler writes as follows about Paul's view of the events in Israel's history: 'They have not their value in themselves, but ... they are relative, secondary, because they bear the imprint of saving eschatological events.'[34] This is a view of Pauline typology quite often put forward by scholars, but it is not one which emerges from the passages we have examined in this work. On the contrary, the typological event is as real as the event which it typifies. And this is equally true of the person who is a type. Those sacraments of Israel in the wilderness described in 1 Cor. 10 are as events as real as any celebration of the Christian Eucharist. Christ was really present there, though not κατὰ σάρκα, if we may borrow a phrase used by Paul in a slightly different context. Abraham really repented, really believed, and was really justified by faith. When we study together 1 Cor. 10.11, Rom. 4.23, and Rom. 15.4, we must conclude that the events in Israel's history had full reality for those who took part in them, but were *recorded* for our benefit. They did not take place for our benefit, and Paul never says they did. Pursuing the theme through Paul's exposition of salvation-history, we must say that Isaac really was the seed born according to promise; and Pharoah was quite as real an example of obduracy overruled by God's providence in his day as were the Jews in Paul's day (Rom. 9.17–18). Indeed in some ways Pharoah was an even clearer example, since he died unrepentant, while Paul hoped that the Jews might yet repent in his day. In Rom. 9.27–9 we have the suggestion of a whole pattern of events; we might call it the remnant through the ages. This particular theme is resumed in 11.1–4. But it would be wrong to suggest that these events did not take place in their own right. The fact that they present a pattern which Paul believes has been reproduced and accentuated in the messianic era does not make them any less real or any less genuinely historical events. What the two sets of events have in common is God-in-Christ, that is to say, God manifested in his characteristic saving activity.

But we must distinguish between perfect types and others. Perfect types are Abraham as believer, Isaac as the promised seed, Pharoah as the sort of person who disobeys God and thereby

serves God's purpose. There are also people who seem to be
related to Christ as types, but whose relation is quite as much
one of dissimilarity as of resemblance. These are such figures as
Adam, Moses, and Jonah. Adam is in fact the only person in
the Pauline writings to whom the word τύπος is applied. In
Rom. 5.14 he is called τύπος τοῦ μέλλοντος, which presumably
means 'a type of him who is to come', though, in view of Paul's
argument, one is greatly tempted to translate it 'a warning for
the future', and discard the rather confusing word 'type' in
this context. At any rate, Adam seems to be most significant for
the points wherein he differs from Christ. He was in the image
of God, but lost it by the Fall. Christ is the image of God and
renewed it in us. Adam, one man, represents all men, and in
him all fell. Christ, one man, represents all men and in him all
are made alive. Adam wished to be as God, disobeyed and was
condemned. Christ was equal with God, did not regard this as
a privilege to be jealously guarded, obeyed God to the death
and was raised from the dead. Perhaps we can best describe
Adam as an imperfect type. The word which Hebrews uses for
this is ἀντίτυπος (Heb. 9.24); but in 1 Pet. 3.21 precisely the
same word is used to indicate the eschatological reality, so we
must resist the temptation to use the word 'anti-type' for
Adam.

Moses is also an imperfect type, in so far as he is a type of
Christ at all in Paul's writings. In fact Paul does not naturally
regard Moses as a type of Christ.[35] This is not a figure which fits
into his normal scheme of things. Moses is rather the mediator,
whose presence indicates the indirectness, and therefore the inferior nature, of the relationship between God and Israel
established by the Torah. In several places in the Pauline
Epistles where scholars have too easily claimed to see Moses as a
type of Christ, we can detect the 'real presence' of the pre-
existent Christ himself; and there can be no question of Moses
being a type of Christ while Christ is present. But undoubtedly
the implications of Paul's use of the Targum on Deut. 30.12–14
in Rom. 10.6f are that Moses going up Sinai and bringing down
the Torah is a type of Christ descending from heaven bringing
salvation for mankind.[36] The same implication is present in the
midrash on Ps. 68.18 in Eph. 4.8f. In both Rom. 10.6f and Eph.
4.8f Moses is certainly an imperfect type, for one could point to

a whole series of features in which what Christ did does not correspond to what Moses did (Moses had to go up Sinai first; what Moses brought was an impermanent and inadequate way of life, etc.). We may suggest, however, that in view of the parallel with Jonah found in Matt. 12.39–40, Paul did not himself originate the midrash on Deut. 30.12–14, but it formed part of his tradition. Amsler is therefore mistaken in claiming that in Paul's writings Moses and the Law offer a type for Christ and grace.[37] This sort of typology is native to the Epistle to the Hebrews, but not to Paul's Epistles. Another place where Moses appears as an imperfect type is Col. 2.14–15, for which Num. 25.1–5 provides the typology. The great difference between Moses and Christ here is that Moses punished the rulers by hanging them himself on a tree, whereas Christ overcame the powers by himself hanging on a tree.

A third example of imperfect type would be Jonah, implied though not mentioned in Rom. 10.7. The points at which he is defective as a type of Christ are obvious: he did not in fact die; his 'going down to the abyss' was not voluntary, etc. He was what he is called in Matthew's Gospel, a 'sign' but nothing more.

We must therefore distinguish these three classes of exegesis which Paul applies to Scripture, real presence, typology, and imperfect types. This raises a very interesting question, one that has often been answered without very much consideration of Paul's actual practice: How far is it true to say that Paul finds a double meaning in Scripture? At first sight it would seem obvious that he does, and so does every rabbi who treats any text in anything but the most straightforward and literal way. This does not imply, of course, that Paul finds a 'double meaning' in every text he quotes. If one were to begin, for example, with Rom. 1.17, it would not be true to say that Paul finds a double meaning in Hab. 2.4. Paul would say that the true meaning is simply this: the Righteous One, when he comes, will live by faith. What can we say of the catena in Rom. 3.10–18? Here we may perhaps distinguish: in so far as Paul believes any of these citations to have been uttered by David only, there is a double meaning, one for David's own day, and one for the messianic age. But many of them, we have suggested, are regarded as uttered by Christ. If so, there is only one meaning, that which is true of the messianic age, and therefore applies to the cross. Similarly there does not seem to be any need to posit a double meaning for Ps. 32.1–2 cited in Rom. 4.7–8: these words, according to Paul, apply to Abraham. They were written down, it is true, years later by the prophet David. This was done for our instruction; but this does not give them any extra, second significance. In just the same way, Paul would find in Ps. 44.22, which he quotes in Rom. 8.36, one meaning only, the Messiah's account of the afflictions of the messianic community.

Even when we are dealing with typology rather than prophecy, it is not always necessary to suppose that Paul sees two meanings in Scripture. In Rom. 9.17, for example, where God's words to Pharoah are cited from Exod. 9.16, the phrase 'double meaning' hardly seems a just description. We might say the words have an extended reference. Paul quotes them, not only in order to show how God dealt with Pharoah, but also how he deals with unbelieving Israel in Paul's day. Nevertheless Paul does not suggest that Exod. 9.16 really applies to the Jews of his own day. It seems probable that we should not see a double meaning in the citation of Hos. 2.23; 1.10 in Rom. 9.25–6 either. Paul probably means to indicate that these words apply to the remnant in the last days and to nothing else. It is, however, tempting to follow the lead of many scholars and see a reference here to Northern Israel. If so, then we do have a double meaning here: the words apply primarily to the situation in Hosea's day, and secondarily to the remnant in Paul's day. The double application can be made because the situation is similar in both epochs.

The test case here comes in the exposition of Deut. 30.12–14 in Rom. 10.6f. It does not seem that Paul could possibly allow the possibility of a double meaning here: once grant that when Moses uttered it, or when it is viewed κατὰ σάρκα, or from any viewpoint at all, Deut. 30.12–14 was intended to encourage observance of the Torah, and Paul's whole case has collapsed. He must insist that the passage is a great witness to the righteousness which is by faith, and that the language about going up and going down referred to Christ. What then of the typology of Moses and Jonah which we have just been discussing? Paul would have said that Moses and Jonah were there to afford a contrast. They are denied by implication in the text in order to show the true salvation-event. The same approach must be carried through when we come to Rom. 10.15–16: there is only one gospel, though it could in some sense be known during Israel's earlier history. This is certainly true of the citations from Deut. 32 and Isa. 65 in Rom. 10.19–21; but it does not seem so easy to apply to Ps. 19.4, cited in Rom. 10.18. The difficulty here is not that the psalm quotation seems to have no connection with the gospel at all. We have already shown that rabbinic interpretation of the psalm made it apply to all sorts of things to which it would on the surface appear to have no reference at all. Nor does the difficulty consist in the fact that there might seem to be a necessary reference to some event in David's day. Paul would not find that a necessary conclusion at all. The difficulty is rather that it is very tempting to see a reference to the universal promulgation of the Torah. But we must remember that for Paul the Torah was not in fact something which God originally intended all the nations to possess. It had a much more limited function in God's plan. Hence it seems likely that he quotes Ps. 19 in order to claim for the gospel what contemporary rabbinic thought claimed for the Torah. Here then is not a double sense, but one sense claimed instead of another. Of all the other Scripture citations in Romans, it seems probable that they fall either into the category 'prophetic information about Christ', e.g. Rom. 11.34–5; or that of 'prophetic utterance by Christ', e.g. 15.9f. They are not, strictly speaking, scriptural texts which bear a double meaning.

What of the two important texts in Gal. 3.13 and 4.21f? Must we not fall back on a theory of double meanings here at least? As far as concerns the citation of Deut. 21.23 in Gal. 3.13, Paul seems to be either applying a general principle found in the Law to the one (supremely important) example of Christ's crucifixion; or he sees it as a direct prophecy of Christ. In view of the light which our study of Col. 2.14–15 and Num. 25.1–5 has thrown on the question, it seems more likely that the latter is true. In neither event do we find a double meaning in the text.

At first sight it seems a hopeless enterprise to maintain that there is no double meaning in the 'allegory' of Gal. 4.21f. We have two wives, two covenants, two mountains, two cities, etc.

Must there not be two meanings also? If so, where do we find these two meanings? Paul does not deny the literal truth of the facts about Abraham's two wives, and their respective sons. The typology comes in the events of the conception of the two sons, their birth, education, and careers, together with the divine promises that accompany these events. If it is typology, and not allegory, then there does not seem to be room for a double meaning for any given verse of Scripture. Perhaps it would be more true to say that the events have a double significance, though even here it is doubtful if there is more than an extended significance. Paul apparently argues like this: 'It was the free woman's son who received the promise: from this I conclude that we Christians are the true descendants of Sarah, not the Jews who are in bondage to the Torah.' This is not a double meaning in the common Philonic sense, i.e. the deeper meaning has a much closer connection with the literal meaning than is usual in Philo; and Paul certainly does not mean to deny the literal meaning. It would be just perhaps to summarize Paul's view thus: 'These events are to be understood as having a deeper significance than the literal sense, valid though that certainly is.' The element of eschatology in Paul prevented him from cutting loose altogether from the original meaning: where Philo says so often 'it does not have this literal significance, but rather that moral or psychological meaning', Paul says 'as at that time . . . so it is now' (Gal. 4.29). There is therefore in the 'allegory' of Galatians a double sense implied, but it is kept strictly within bounds by means of typology.

Michel seems to be saying much the same thing when he remarks that the difference between Paul and Philo lay in Paul's emphasis on salvation-history, a subject which did not interest Philo.[38] He adds that Paul does not as Philo does distinguish between the literal sense and the real meaning. We must add, however, that Paul does not waste any time on speculating as to what the text meant during its veiled period. It has only one meaning for him, and even that meaning could have been understood by some during the period when it was veiled. Michel is not really fair to Paul when he says elsewhere[39] that Paul, in common with all New Testament writers, paid no attention to the historical context in which his citations occurred. It is quite true, of course, that he had no conception of

our insistence on establishing the historical situation in which
the texts were written. But this does not mean that Paul was in-
different to history. He had his own historical schema, and very
often the historical setting is important for Paul. Examples of
this are Rom. 9.15, the theophany to Moses, and Rom. 11.3f,
Elijah's experience on Mount Horeb. In the first God's revelation of his character of mercy is all the more significant as having been made at a point of great importance in the story of
Moses' part in the wilderness sojourn. In the second, there can
be no doubt about the importance of an historical context which
Paul himself indicates so clearly. We may equally vindicate
Paul from Windisch's charge (already referred to) of arbitrary
interpretation. It seems arbitrary to us, till we have examined
Paul's assumptions and the assumptions of contemporary
exegesis. When we do this, we find that there was nothing
arbitrary about it. Paul had his own Christian presuppositions;
he combined these with the accepted methods, and sometimes
with the accepted exegetical conclusions, of his own day. This
is not an arbitrary procedure, no matter how different the
results it produces may be from what we would produce using
our methods today. Schoeps, writing from the standpoint of a
modern orthodox Jew, is better placed to understand what Paul
was doing. Schoeps agrees in fact very largely with Michel's
conclusions when he says that the difference between Paul's
typology and that of Philo is that Paul directed his typology
towards τὰ ἔσχατα, the end events.[40]

James Wood, in his book on the interpretation of the Bible
written ten years ago, shows very little understanding of Paul's
approach to Scripture. He suggests, for example, apropos the
catena in Rom. 3.10–18, that 'Paul was not basing the truth of
his argument solely on the words he quotes, even although he
precedes them with the formula "as it is written"'.[41] We have
seen how inadequate this is as an explanation of Paul's citations.
One might well ask: If it is not for proof, why does Paul quote
Scripture here? Again, in considering Paul's citation of Exod.
33.19 in Rom. 9.15 Wood accuses Paul of taking it out of its
context: what was originally meant as an assurance of the certainty of the divine grace is used by Paul to prove God's freedom
in his choice of those who are to be blessed. A closer examination of this passage would surely show that this is not what Paul

has in mind, and that the context in which the citation comes has importance for Paul. Wood's final remark is equally unfortunate: 'It must be remembered that typology was not as common in the New Testament as at a later date among the Fathers.' If this is meant to suggest that typology as an approach to Scripture is relatively unimportant in the New Testament, we must dissent. We may guess that the only reason why we have not more typology in the New Testament is because we have not got more exegesis of the Scriptures.

Baumgärtel has an interesting theory that the use of typology in the New Testament is very closely connected with παρά-κλησις, 'exhortation'.[42] It is never used gratuitously, he says, but only to establish some point of παράκλησις. Now it is certainly true that typology is often found in a context of παράκλησις; the obvious example is 1 Cor. 10.1–11. But to say it cannot occur otherwise is certainly not true of Paul. It cannot be claimed that Romans chapters 9–11 come in the category of παράκλησις, but these chapters are replete with typology.

Fitzmeyer offers us an interesting parallel with Qumran here:[43] he classifies texts quoted from the Scriptures in Qumran documents into four categories: (a) literary or historical—the text is cited in the same sense as intended by the original writer; (b) modernization—a text originally applying to contemporary events is vague enough to be applied to something else; (c) accommodation—a text has to be twisted or manipulated in order to yield the sense required by the Qumran writer; (d) eschatological—a text looks forward to the future and the Qumran writers say it is yet to be fulfilled in the end-time. Into category (b) he would put, among others, Rom. 15.3 and 1 Cor. 10.5–7. This is fair enough, but in both these instances there is one essential difference from Qumran, the presence of the pre-existent Christ, prophesying in the first passage, active in the second. There is nothing corresponding to this in Qumran exegesis. Müller makes one point of interest to us in an article written quite recently.[44] He points out that Paul sees salvation-history as centred on Christ and extending into the past as well as into the future towards the Parousia. It was indeed this way of looking at things that enabled Paul to interpret Scripture as he did.

## *Did Paul ever use allegory?*

By 'allegory' in this context we mean either interpreting a text in a sense which completely ignores its original meaning, or in a sense whose connection with its original meaning is purely arbitrary. Before asking the question about Paul, we may begin by observing that allegorical interpretation in this sense is certainly found in the Qumran documents. Two good examples can be quoted from what Vermes calls 'The Damascus Document' (called 'The Zadokite Document' by R. H. Charles). In DR vi we have a comment on the text of Num. 21.18:

> the well which the princes dug,
> which the nobles of the people delved,
> with the sceptre and with their staves.

The comment runs thus:

> The Well is the Law, and those who dug it were the converts of Israel who went out of the land of Judah to sojourn in the land of Damascus. God called them all *princes* because they sought him, and their renown was disputed by no man. The *Stave* [*sic*] is the Interpreter of the Law of whom Isaiah said *He makes a tool for his work* [Isa. 54.16]; and the *nobles of the people* are those who come to dig the *Well* with the *staves* with which the *Stave* [*sic*] ordained that they should walk in all the age of wickedness.[45]

This certainly seems to deserve the name of allegorical interpretation, and is much further from the original meaning of the text than is what we are accustomed to in Paul. It is more like Philo's technique. There is no obvious connection between a staff and the interpreter of the Law, despite the attempt to bridge the gap by means of Isa. 54.16. A process of digging a well with staves has been allegorized into a process of studying the Law by means of special methods. A similar allegorical treatment of Amos 5.26–7 follows in C.D. vii, too complicated to be explained here; what the author of the document believes to be a reference to a tabernacle (rendered 'Sakkuth' in RSV) is explained as meaning the books of the Law; and the name of the star-god Kaiwan is interpreted as meaning the books of the prophets.[46] Once again the style of interpretation is much closer to Philo than to Paul, as far as distance from the literal meaning of the text is concerned.

Next we may point out that the rabbis also used allegorical interpretations of Scripture. We have already encountered one: the rabbis interpreted heaping coals of fire on an enemy's head by feeding him as stifling the evil inclination by means of study of the Torah (see p. 131 above). But several others could be quoted from the Midrash on the Psalms. Thus, in the very passage which the Qumran document treated in Num. 21.18, we find the 'staves' interpreted as meaning the Torah,[47] and in another passage we find an even fuller allegorical interpretation of this verse: the well is the Torah; and the names that occur in the ensuing verses are all allegorized so as to provide a description of a man studying the Torah and of the blessings that result from it. Again, the Midrash on Ps. 27 interprets 2 Sam. 5.24 'the sound of marching in the tops of the balsam trees' to mean that when Israel is in distress God is also in distress (the link is the fact that the trees are regarded as thorny shrubs and thorns mean distress). This would certainly seem to qualify as allegorical interpretation. Another similar interpretation occurs in the Midrash on Ps. 37, where 'tamarisk tree' in Gen. 21.33 is allegorized to mean 'food and drink'. So also in Ps. 42.1 the 'hart' is interpreted as meaning God. We could also point to an allegorical treatment of Abraham's vision of God at the covenant in Gen. 15 which we find in Pseudo-Philo's *Biblical Antiquities*,[48] so that Abraham is represented as being shown both heaven and hell. Another clear example occurs in *Tractate Gittin*, where an allegorical interpretation is given of Gen. 27.22 'The voice is Jacob's voice, but the hands are the hands of Esau': '"the voice" here refers to [the cry caused by] the Emperor Hadrian, who killed in Alexandria of Egypt sixty myriads on sixty myriads, twice as many as went forth from Egypt . . . "The hands are the hands of Esau": this refers to the government of Rome, which has destroyed our house and burnt our Temple and driven us out of our land.'[49] This is interpreting the text in a sense much farther from the original than anything which Paul attempted. Thus allegory, in the sense of an interpretation of a text which seems to have only an arbitrary connection with its literal meaning, is well known in contemporary Jewish exegesis.

As far as Paul is concerned, there are really only two places where he might seem to be using allegory, as opposed to typology. The first we have dealt with. We came to the conclusion that in Gal. 4.21f Paul was in fact using typology, not allegory; but that his typology becomes so complicated and uncontrolled that it is beginning to verge into allegory. The connection, for example, between the two women and the two mountains depends on the slender etymological link whereby Hagar could be taken to mean 'the mountain'. As in the example quoted from the Midrash on the Psalms (1, 81), etymologies of names easily lead on to fanciful allegorizing. It was, of course, a favourite technique with that master of allegories, Philo.

The other passage in Paul is 1 Cor. 9.9, and this we must now examine in detail; 1 Cor. 9.8–10 runs as follows:

Μὴ κατὰ ἄνθρωπον ταῦτα λαλῶ, ἢ καὶ ὁ νόμος ταῦτα οὐ λέγει; ἐν γὰρ τῷ Μωϋσέως νόμῳ γέγραπται, Οὐ κημώσεις βοῦν ἀλοῶντα. μὴ τῶν βοῶν μέλει τῷ Θεῷ; ἢ δι' ἡμᾶς πάντως λέγει; δι' ἡμᾶς γὰρ ἐγράφη, ὅτι ὀφείλει ἐπ' ἐλπίδι ὁ ἀροτριῶν ἀροτριᾶν, καὶ ὁ ἀλοῶν ἐπ' ἐλπίδι τοῦ μετέχειν·

Do I say this on human authority? Does not the law say the same? For it is written in the law of Moses, 'You shall not muzzle an ox when it is treading out the grain.' Is it for oxen that God is concerned? Does he not speak entirely for our sake? It was written for our sake, because the ploughman should plough in hope and the thresher thresh in hope of a share in the crop.

It has often been claimed that Paul is here deliberately setting aside the literal meaning of the text in favour of another which has none but an arbitrary connection with it. If so, that would certainly be an instance of allegory. We must however examine the background to this text before we come to any conclusions.

We should note in the first place that Paul's figure of the threshing ox here is only one of a constellation of figures which he uses to illustrate his point. In verse 7 he also uses the figure of the soldier on campaign, of the vinedresser, and of the herdsman. In verse 10 he adds to this the figure of ploughman and of the man who does his own threshing. What is distinctive about the figure of the threshing ox is that it carries the authority of Scripture. As far as this richness of figures carries us in the way of evidence, it is some slight indication that Paul does not mean to exclude the literal meaning of the Scripture citation. After all, all the other figures are used as analogies, which are only valid if they are understood literally in the first place. But this does not in itself carry us very far.

Paul quotes Deut. 25.4, which the LXX renders with

οὐ φιμώσεις βοῦν ἀλοῶντα.

The Hebrew is literally: 'Thou shalt not muzzle the ox in his threshing',[50] a point which was of some significance to the rabbis, as we shall be seeing. The difference between κημώσεις and φιμώσεις appears to be the difference between the more specific and the more general; κημόω is to muzzle an animal, more particularly a horse. φιμόω is to gag anything or anyone, often used, as in Matt. 22.12, 34; Mark 1.25; 4.39; Luke 4.35, of putting someone to silence. Moulton and Milligan suggest that φιμόω may have been a more colloquial word.[51] It seems likely that Paul's Greek version had κημώσεις, and that it is neither a mistake of memory on Paul's part, nor the effort of a later scribe to smarten up Paul's Greek: the nouns κῆμος and φίμος can be used interchangeably in translation Greek. In Prov. 26.3 Symmachus uses φίμος where Aquila uses κῆμος for the Hebrew *metheg* a bridle.[52] One might guess therefore that the verbs were interchangeable also in translation Greek.

The older editors tend to attempt to vindicate Paul from the charge of dismissing the literal meaning. Thus Robertson and Plummer say that Paul does not mean that God has no care for oxen, but that there is also a higher meaning, relating to the support of the ministry. They point out quite rightly that much hinges on how we translate that word πάντως ('entirely' in RSV). It could mean 'doubtless', in which case Paul is merely claiming that the second meaning must be understood as well as the first. Or it could mean 'entirely', in which case the literal meaning is excluded. They point out that the difference is neatly expressed in the Vulgate's translation 'utique' as contrasted with that of Beza 'omnino'. They prefer the Vulgate. Similarly Evans says: 'God does care for the oxen, but of course he cares also for the human labourers.'[53] Goudge appears to try to have it both ways; of course Paul does not deny that God cares for the oxen, but he does seem to say here that this particular passage refers not to oxen but to human labourers. Lipsius is driven to the desperate remedy suggested by Bois of inserting an οὐ before the πάντως.[54] Lietzmann suggests that Paul here is echoing the same sentiment as Philo (which we examine below) that God cannot be concerned in his legislation with mundane details. On the other hand, Allo maintains that Paul could not possibly have intended to rule out the literal meaning. Héring, however, seems to think this quite possible. He describes it as an instance of the law of Moses being interpreted spiritually: according to Paul this text really has the preachers of the gospel in mind. The two latest editors have no doubt at all that Paul does exclude the literal meaning. C. K. Barrett writes: 'The only interpretation that is not forced is that in the Old Testament law God has in mind not oxen, but Christian preachers and their needs.' He adds that of course Paul realized God did care for oxen, but 'it was a quite different truth that he [Paul] found in the Old Testament and expressed here'.[55] Finally, Conzelmann thinks that Paul follows the Hellenistic–Jewish principle that God's legislation is concerned only with the loftiest matters and that therefore the detailed legislation must be allegorized.

Perhaps if we turn to the rabbinic background of the quotation from Deut. 25.4, we may be able to make up our minds on this problem. Its position in the book is very significant. It comes just after a command limiting to forty the number of stripes that may be imposed on a criminal and just before the command to the brother to raise up seed on his deceased brother's widow. When we turn to the Targum of Palestine, we find that already this context is beginning to influence the interpretation of the command in 25.4:

> You shall not muzzle the ox in the time of his treading out; nor the wife of the [deceased] brother, who would be mated with one smitten with an ulcer, and who is poorly related [or 'who hath nothing of his own'], shalt thou tie up with him.[56]

The effect of this conflating of the two commands is to extend the meaning of the prohibition of muzzling the ox; it may be applied to levirate marriage also. We find exactly the same phenomenon several times in the Talmud; by the principle of proximity of texts, the prohibition to muzzle the threshing ox is applied to various circumstances connected with the levirate law. See *Tractate Menahoth* 1, 346; *Tractate Makkoth* 94, 108;

*Tractate Yebamoth* 10; *Tractate Pesahim* 194. It shows incidentally how very familiar and influential was this prohibition in Deut. 25.4. In *Tractate Makkoth* 160 we have a good example of this prohibition influencing the preceding command: because the instruction about flogging is followed by the prohibition about the threshing ox, the conclusion is drawn that the strap with which the flogging is inflicted must be made of calf hide. In *Tractate Me'ilah* 47 the Hebrew 'his threshing' is taken to mean 'the owner's threshing', and the conclusion is drawn that the prohibition does not apply to an ox threshing on Temple property, since that is not the owner's threshing, an indication of how the prohibition could in certain circumstances be robbed of its force.[57]

Even more interesting are the places where the prohibition is applied analogically to other situations concerned with persons, not animals. S-B give one very clear example from *Tractate Baba Mezi'a*: if a man is working for someone else, he may eat of what falls loose at his feet from the material he is working on; e.g. a vine-dresser may eat the grapes that fall at his feet. An equally relevant example occurs in *Tractate Gittin*: a situation is envisaged in which the wife of one of the *'am hā'ārets* is grinding corn in her own house. She eats some of the ears that fall to the ground. This is technically stealing from her husband; but she might plead Deut. 25.4 in extenuation; and it is implied that she would be justified.[58] All this evidence goes to show that Deut. 25.4 was a very familiar text with the rabbis, one which was extensively used as a sort of norm for the elucidation of other texts; it was very freely applied in an analogical sense, though no rabbi suggests that the literal meaning can be ignored.

We should perhaps glance at the passages which have been cited in order to show that Paul regards the literal meaning of the text as unworthy of God's notice. There is really only one such passage in Philo: *De Specialibus Legibus* 1, 26: 'For you will find all this elaborate detail indicates indirectly (αἰνιττομένην) the improvement of your morals. For the Law is not concerned with irrational creatures, but with those who possess mind and reason.'[59] An equally clear example of the same sentiment occurs in the Letter of Aristeas 144: 'You must not take the reductionist view (μὴ γὰρ εἰς καταπεπτωκότα λόγον ἔλθῃς), as if

Moses in his legislation gave particular attention to flies and weasels and that sort of thing. But all this is set out with righteousness in view, for the sake of chaste study (ἐπίσκεψιν) and correction of character.'⁶⁰ Philo does refer to Deut. 25.4 in *De Virtutibus* 146; but he simply says that these prescriptions about the ox and other animals are a mark of the Law's humanity. It does not, however, seem at all likely that Paul's comment in 1 Cor. 9.9–10 is motivated by a desire to avoid associating the sacred law with too mundane details. Paul had no particular reason for rationalizing or philosophizing the detailed prescriptions of the Torah, as had both Philo and the author of the Letter of Aristeas. The last thing he would have dreamt of saying is that the Torah is primarily concerned with correction of character. Those who suggest that Philo's reasons for explaining away the detailed prescriptions of the Law could ever be the same as Paul's have surely mistaken the genre of literature which Paul was writing.

The Deuteronomy citation also appears in 1 Tim. 5.18, which we should give in its context, quoting verses 17 and 18:

οἱ καλῶς προεστῶτες πρεσβύτεροι διπλῆς τιμῆς ἀξιούσθωσαν, μάλιστα οἱ κοπιῶντες ἐν λόγῳ καὶ διδασκαλίᾳ· λέγει γὰρ ἡ γραφή, Βοῦν ἀλοῶντα οὐ φιμώσεις· καί, "Αξιος ὁ ἐργάτης τοῦ μισθοῦ αὐτοῦ.

Let the elders who rule well be considered worthy of double honour, especially those who labour in preaching and teaching; for the scripture says, 'You shall not muzzle an ox when it is treading out the grain', and 'The labourer deserves his wages' . . .

We note that the text follows the LXX with φιμώσεις. This is hardly an argument in favour of φιμώσεις in 1 Cor. 9.9, since we need not assume that the author of the Pastorals had the text of 1 Corinthians in front of him. We take the view that 1 Timothy is not by Paul, but belongs to a period at least a generation later. It seems very likely that διπλῆς. τιμῆς in verse 17 means not 'double honour' but 'double honorarium', i.e. τιμή refers to a definite sum of money. There is plenty of evidence for this meaning in the LXX; and Moulton and Milligan give examples of τιμή meaning 'price'; the cognate τίμημα can mean 'payment'. Liddell and Scott give many examples of τιμή meaning 'reward, present'. It hardly seems likely that clergy would be receiving regular stipends as early as the end of the first century;

but they might very well be receiving an honorarium. If τιμῆς here is to be taken merely as 'honour', the Deuteronomy quotation is singularly lacking in point. Both it and the ensuing dominical precept must refer to actual money, or at least support, in this context. Thus, by the time of the Pastoral Epistles Deut. 25.4 had become the stock text for justifying the giving of money or gifts in kind to clergy and the question of the literal sense, or of whether God cared for oxen or not, no longer arose. One might say that the author of the Pastorals has coarsened the use of this text; or perhaps merely that he is primarily interested in its practical application in the life of the Church. The allegorical meaning has now completely ousted the literal.

We should be able to come now to some conclusion about our original question: Does Paul use allegory in 1 Cor. 9.9? We may answer with some confidence: not consciously. It was, as we have seen, a very familiar text used by the rabbis in a variety of contexts. The analogical use of it would be more familiar to Paul than the literal. Paul does not mean that God is uninterested in animals, or that the divine legislation is not concerned with mundane details. It is not, probably, a text which Paul has studied. He quotes it only *en passant*, in the context of a whole series of figures drawn from various aspects of life. But he has not reached the stage where the literal meaning has disappeared, as had happened a generation later. Formally, therefore, it is an example of allegory, but we may acquit Paul of deliberately designing an allegorical use of the text. Paul only approaches the confines of allegory when he allows his typology to become too complicated; or when he is referring to a well-known text without reflecting very much on its exegetical implications.

Before we end our chapter on Paul's interpretation of Scripture, we must underline once more what we have had occasion to notice more than once already: often, when Paul gives us the impression that he is offering free theological speculation, he is in fact writing a midrash on Scripture. The significance of this must be examined in the next chapter, but here it is important to emphasize the fact. If we look back over the material we have dealt with in these studies we can point to at least nine places where we have detected this feature. We should notice that none of these passages is one where Paul is ostensibly expounding Scripture, as in the famous midrash on Deut. 30.12–14 in Rom. 10.6f, for example. They are all passages in which Paul either does not quote Scripture at all, or merely seems to be echoing it *en passant*, or referring to it by way of illustration. They are as follows:

Paul is writing a midrash

| | |
|---|---|
| Gal. 3.18–20 | on Deut. 33.2–5 |
| Col. 2.14–15 | on Num. 25.1–5 |
| Rom. 6.7 | on Ps. 88.5–6 |
| Rom. 8.19–21 | on Ps. 89.46–8 |
| Rom. 8.33–4 | on Isa. 50.7–9 |
| Rom. 8.34–9 | on Ps. 44 |
| 1. Cor. 5.6–8 | on Num. 15.20–6 |
| 1 Cor. 10.14–21 | on Deut. 32.17–21 |
| Rom. 11.17–24 | on Jer. 11.16–19 |

To this one might add that in Rom. 10.19 and 11.11–12 Paul gives us a sort of midrash on the 'jealousy' motif based on Deut. 32.16–17, 21. And again, if one were to include Pauline passages not examined in the present work but only referred to, one could add two more examples of midrash:

| | |
|---|---|
| 2 Cor. 4.13–15 | on Ps. 116.8–19 |
| 2 Cor. 5.19—6.2 | on Isa. 49.1–8 |

No doubt if one were to examine the rest of the Pauline writings carefully, other examples of this sort of unostentatious midrash would come to light. We need not imagine that in such passages Paul is intentionally commenting on Scripture, or even that he expects his readers to recognize his scriptural allusions. The important point is that the inspiration for such passages is Scripture. He wrote them in the form he did because he had been meditating on Scripture. It should surely convince us once for all of the principle with which we began: for Paul what we call the Old Testament was the living and active word of God. Large sections of what many commentators regard as Paul's cosmological speculations in Rom. 8 turn out to be based on his study of Scripture. Whatever we today may think about Paul's theology, we may be sure that Paul himself as he wrote Rom. 8

was not under the impression that he was offering a speculative theology at all. He thought that he was being faithful to the basic intention of Scripture. How far he was so, and to what extent he was influenced in his understanding of Scripture by non-scriptural factors, are questions which we must consider among others in the last chapters of this book. But we may claim at least to have established that Paul believed himself to be what we today would call a biblical theologian. The fact that Ps. 44, for example, played for him rather the part that John 17 plays for us, or that Deut. 32.17–21 played the part that 1 Cor. 11.17–34 plays for us (to make it a little more complicated), is something which we must accept if we are to understand how he interpreted his Bible. We are not today in his position in relation to Scripture, and no Christian has been since the emergence of the canon of the New Testament. Only if we begin by trying to place ourselves in his position have we any hope of finding common ground with him on the question of the interpretation of Scripture.

# 9

## PAUL'S TECHNIQUE
## OF INTERPRETATION

———◆◆◆◆———

In this chapter we continue the theme of the last. But whereas in the last chapter we were considering the general significance of Paul's interpretation of Scripture, in this one we shall be mainly concerned with details of his technique. For convenience' sake we divide our material under six headings.

### 1. Did Paul have a different approach to the various divisions of Scripture?

Several scholars have suggested that Paul on occasion likes to support an argument by quotations from the three divisions of Scripture, the Torah, the Prophets, and the Writings, and have pointed to such passages as Rom. 10.18–21; 15.9–12. There may be something in this. On the other hand, the first of the passages hardly presents a clear case of this triple citation, since the quotation from the Writings (Ps. 19.4 in Rom. 10.18) really belongs to a separate step in Paul's argument. Again, when we look at such passages we do not find that Paul's arguments are any more strained than appears in other places where there is no such triple citation; nor do we ever get the impression that Paul is raking through the three divisions of Scripture in order to find proof texts from each. It is true that sometimes Paul is hard put to it to find a text which exactly proves his argument: for example, Gen. 25.23 quoted in Rom. 9.12 is not really a promise in the sense in which Paul's argument strictly requires it to be. But one cannot point to any passage where one can say with confidence: here Paul has given a citation from each division of Scripture in order to strengthen his argument. We may conclude therefore, that if Paul found himself able to draw what appeared to him relevant and cogent texts to prove his point from all three divisions of Scripture, he was no doubt gratified; but that we never find him going out of his way to do so.

There is however one Book in Scripture to which Paul may justly be described as having a special relationship, and that is the Book of Psalms. This is not to suggest that his use of this Book is unique in the New Testament, which is very far from being the case, but that his interpretation of the Psalms enabled him to use the Book in a more flexible way than any other Book in the Scriptures. His approach to the Psalms enabled Paul, so to speak, to move around in time more freely than he can do with any other book, more freely even than he can do with the prophets, who can speak contemporaneously or predictively, but not retrospectively; and more freely also than with the Torah. The rabbis were prepared (*a*) to locate a psalm in any period of Israel's history from Abraham to their own day; (*b*) to accept a triple meaning for any given verse in the Psalms, applying it to David, to Israel, and to the world-to-come. Compare the following quotation from the Midrash on the Psalms 1, 338:

> Our masters taught: In the Book of Psalms all the Psalms which David composed apply either to himself or to all Israel. Each Psalm that speaks in the singular applies to David's own person, and each Psalm that speaks in the plural applies to all Israel. Whenever *For the leader; with string music* is used it introduces a Psalm which applies to the age-to-come.

See also 1, 230: R. Yudan taught in the name of R. Judah: 'All that David said in his Book of Psalms applies to himself, to all Israel, and to all the ages.' This liberty Paul inherited and elaborated, in the sense that, reading 'the age of the Messiah' for 'the world-to-come', he discovered in the Psalms all sorts of information about the Messiah and his age, very often supplied by the (pre-existent) Messiah himself. We have already argued in chapter 3 above that he represents Ps. 32 as applying to Abraham. Ps. 19 he may well take as having a double reference to Sinai and to the gospel. Above all, it is in the Psalms that the suffering, rejected, and triumphant Son speaks. His use of the

Psalter thus enabled Paul to be supremely christocentric in his exegesis of Scripture—we might say even cross-centred; see, for instance, his catena in Rom. 3.10–18. Of course this christocentric approach is not confined to the Psalter; the pre-existent Messiah speaks in the prophets as well, especially in Isaiah, and even in the Torah; we think of such places as Rom. 10.6, 19; 15.10. In the catena in Rom. 3 he can pass easily from Psalter to Isaiah and back without any conscious break. One could construct the major part of Paul's Christology from his Psalm quotations alone. They tell him about the Messiah's sufferings, e.g. Rom. 8.36; 15.3; about his descent into hell: Rom. 6.7; about his resurrection and ascension: Eph. 4.7 (*exceptis excipiendis*); about God's dealing with man at the fall: Rom. 8.20; about the Lord's Supper perhaps in 11.9; certainly about the spread of the gospel in 10.18. They are the vehicle by which the Messiah is to praise God in the Church (Rom. 15.8); they foretell the accession of the Gentiles (Rom. 15.11); they tell us about the Messiah's faith, as well as his death and resurrection (Ps. 116 cited in 2 Cor. 4.13); they show how the ministers of Christ are to reproduce the life of Christ in their own lives (Ps. 117.18 LXX, referred to in 2 Cor. 6.9).[1] The Psalms were intimately connected with Paul's doctrine of justification by faith (Ps. 143.2 cited in Gal. 2.16 and Rom. 3.20). Indeed, if one had to point to any single Book in the Scriptures on which Paul relied more than on any other, one would have to point to the Psalter. This is a distinction, it must be added, which Paul himself would not have understood at all. For him, all the Scriptures were equally the work or vehicle of the Holy Spirit. This preference for the Psalms is one of the most important respects in which Paul as exegete of Scripture is utterly different from Philo.

We are now in a position to indicate those parts of the Scriptures on which Paul relied most heavily for his basic teaching and this is something which mere statistics of frequency of citation would not necessarily tell us. We can rank the various Books from this point of view as follows:

1. Psalms and Isaiah
2. Genesis
3. The rest of the Pentateuch

4. The other prophets, such as Jeremiah, Hosea, Joel, Habakkuk
5. A miscellaneous list, including some historical books, Job,
   Proverbs, and in the apocrypha Wisdom

There are two names remarkable by their absence from the list,
Ezekiel and Daniel. We find only two specific quotations from
Ezekiel in Paul: he quotes Ezek. 13.10 in 1 Thess. 5.3, and he
may be echoing Ezek. 37.27, in 2 Cor. 6.16, the strange Qum-
ran-like fragment. Neither of these passages has much significance for his theology. Similarly his sole specific quotation of
Daniel is his citation of Dan. 11.37 in his account of the 'man of
sin' in 2 Thess. 2.4. One can only say that the special themes
found in these two books did not particularly fit into Paul's
theology. Though Paul has his own equivalent of the Son of
Man Christology, he makes no use of the title; and anything in
Ezekiel that would specially appeal to Paul (such as Ezekiel's
emphasis on God's free grace and on Israel's lack of merit) was
also in Jeremiah, where Paul found other material (such as the
figure of the olive tree in Jer. 11) of which he could make good
use.

Thus we answer the question at the head of this sub-section
by saying that Paul was not interested in one part of Scripture
rather than another because of any views he might be supposed
to have held about the authority or inspiration of that part. The
reason why he cites some parts of Scripture rather than others is
because of their contents. He was interested in certain topics;
salvation-history; messianic allusions in the Psalms; references
to the pre-existent divine Wisdom; messianic and evangelical
passages in the prophets; Christian ethics, closely related to
doctrine, which he found in Proverbs, and so on. When we look
at the parts of Scripture which meant most to him, we see perhaps the very sharpest difference between Paul and all contemporary non-Christian interpreters of the Scriptures. Philo's interests are totally different (he hardly quotes any but Torah
texts); those of Qumran are by no means the same; an exposition of Habakkuk or Nahum such as we find among the Qumran writings would look very different in the hands of Paul.
And when we compare his interests with those of orthodox
rabbinic Judaism, we see a great difference also. We miss in

Paul some of the most constant features in rabbinic exegesis, such as the exposition of the rules of the Law (*Halakah* proper); their obsession with the vindication of Israel; their reference of the Psalms to events in David's own life; their interest in Esther; their surprisingly frequent reference to the Song of Songs. Above all, of course, we miss their Torah-centric approach. These differences are easily explained in terms of the various theologies which lay behind the four traditions we have been comparing. Paul's scriptural exegesis is christocentric because he is a Christian.

## 2. Does Paul use Scripture for anything but proof?

Before we answer this question, we must make two qualifications. First, we are thinking here not of scriptural allusions or echoes, or writing which is based on a scriptural meditation, such as Rom. 8.18f; but of deliberate quotation of Scripture, whether introduced by a formula or not. Secondly, by 'proof' we do not mean formal proof introduced as part of an argument. We mean rather: Does Paul use Scripture in any other way but theologically, as a source and authority for his doctrine? Thus, for example, Paul's citation of Isa. 49.8 in 2 Cor. 6.2 does not ostensibly prove anything, for Paul at that point is not arguing in that sort of mode. But it is an essential text for explaining what Paul believed about the nature of the Son's vindication. So the scriptural citation in 2 Cor. 6.2 would qualify as 'proof' in the sense intended here.

We must answer our original question with a firm Yes. There are passages where Paul is quoting Scripture in a strictly non-theological way. We can point to just a few examples in Romans; there is the citation of Isa. 52.5 in 2.24, which seems to be purely illustrative. There are the two citations of the Book of Proverbs in 12.17, 20 (cf. also 2 Cor. 8.21). But, as we have shown in chapter 7 above, the citation in 12.20 is by no means unrelated to Christ. There is his citation of Deut. 17.7 in 1 Cor. 5.13 (though we would have to ask whether there was not in fact a genuine theological context for this in the assumption that the Church is the inheritor of Israel's duties). And there is the ecclesiastical legal text (Deut. 19.15) quoted in 2 Cor. 13.1:

'Any charge must be sustained by the evidence of two or three witnesses.' This is certainly not used theologically. But Paul is being perfectly consistent here: he is dealing with a situation in which the level of grace and faith can no longer be maintained. The offender has outraged Paul's attempt to treat him in Christian terms; by Paul's own principles, nothing remains but the level of Law (though this does not mean the offender is beyond redemption); so a legal text quoted as a legal text is perfectly appropriate.

On the whole, it is remarkable how little Paul uses Scripture for anything but proof. We have frequently had occasion in studying Romans to protest against the assumption of scholars that Paul is using Scripture illustratively rather than theologically. And we cannot help suspecting that if one were to examine the rest of Paul's writings one would find that many scriptural quotations which seem to be merely illustrative are really deeply theological. There are however two citations in 2 Cor. 8 and 9, connected with the same underlying theme, which are introduced with the formula καθὼς γέγραπται and constitute fairly full citations of Scripture; these merit our attention, since, if they are purely illustrative or 'accommodatory', they demand considerable modification of our conclusion that Paul only rarely uses Scripture in this way.

The first of these passages is 2 Cor. 8.15:

> ὁ τὸ πολὺ οὐκ ἐπλεόνασεν,
> καὶ ὁ τὸ ὀλίγον οὐκ ἠλαττόνησεν.

He who gathered much had nothing over, and he who gathered little had no lack.

Paul is quoting Exod. 16.18; he differs very little from the LXX, which in its turn adequately represents the MT. RSV translates it with virtually the same words as it uses to translate the citation in 2 Cor. 8.15. The Targums hardly elaborate. The Palestinian Targum slightly expands by translating:

> Nothing remained over from the supply of him who had collected a lot; and he who had collected a little had no lack in his supply.[2]

The passage is from the description of the giving of the manna in the wilderness. The picture is of what R. P. C. Hanson felicitously calls the 'thermostatic' way in which the supply of the manna was supernaturally controlled, so that everybody got what he needed, no more and no less, independently of how much or how little he had collected.[3] Paul, however, uses it in the context of his endeavours to persuade the Corinthians to contribute generously to his fund for poor Christians in Judea. He argues on his well-known principle of complementarity: the material wealth of the Corinthian Christians should supply the material poverty of the Judean Christians; and the Judean Christians make up for it by their spiritual wealth, which they bestow on the Corinthians by sending them Paul and his fellow-missionaries.[4] The ultimate end is equality: as in the case of the manna, all end by having what they need.

Philo refers to this passage once.[5] This is his comment: 'The divine Word distributes equally to all who will use it the heavenly nourishment of the soul (which is in fact wisdom). This Moses calls "manna". Equality is deliberately intended. Moses bears witness to this when he says . . .' Here follows the text. We note with interest that the giver of the manna is the divine Word. Paul's corresponding figure is of course the pre-existent Christ—not that we can assume any direct connection between Philo and Paul. Then, Philo's allegorizing of the manna as wisdom enables him to avoid the suggestion which editors have found in the text that some Israelites were greedy and some careless in their collecting of the manna. Wisdom is something of which you cannot have too much, and we can hardly picture anyone deliberately restricting his acquisition of wisdom. Thus Philo's treatment could be said to have prepared the way for Paul's in the sense that it transfers the whole incident into the sphere of spiritual transactions, and that it whitewashes the Israelites and represents the affair as a matter of God giving rather than of Israel procuring.

Editors on the whole tend to be rather critical of Paul for his use of this text. Schmiedel cautiously remarks that it is either a proof or a casual (*zutreffende*) analogy. Plummer points out quite reasonably that equality is all the two situations have in common: the equality of the Israelites is obligatory; that of the Christians is voluntary. As we shall see, however, that is not the point Paul is making. Lietzmann is more censorious: what matters to Paul, he says, is only the sound of the words (*Wortlaut*), not the context of the utterance. Strachan echoes this complaint, saying that the connection is 'largely verbal', adding: 'in God's scheme of things, typified in the manna story, it does not pay to be selfish', and C. S. C. Williams also notes the 'slight verbal connection'.[6] Calvin takes a rather wider view; he links the text with 'man shall not live by bread alone'. The manna in the wilderness, he says, corresponds to our daily bread. He then draws economic lessons for the Church of his own day. Allo makes the point that Plummer made: the incident in Exodus shows us God's intention. J. J. O'Rourke, in direct contradiction to Lietzmann, writes: 'By citing a portion of a passage, Paul intends his hearers to remember the context in which it comes.'[7]

It is only when we turn to R. P. C. Hanson's small commentary on the Epistle that we find an editor who is prepared to take Paul's citation seriously and to interpret it in the light of what we know of Paul's theology as a whole. He writes as follows: 'The phenomenon, St Paul implies, was a foretaste or prophecy of the self-adjusting love of Christ in his members, which supplies the needs of each without deficiency or embarrassment.' Here surely lies the true explanation of Paul's use of this text. He is not drawing moral lessons from the Scriptures in order to reprove the selfishness of the Corinthian Christians. He is doing exactly what he does in 1 Cor. 10.1–11; he is showing that God in Christ acted with Israel of old in essentially the same way as he acts among Christians in Paul's own day. We must not forget that, when we come to read 2 Corinthians, we already know something about Paul's belief concerning the manna incident. The manna was spiritual food and it was given by Christ. Hence Paul is not trying to suggest that those in Israel of old who collected more than they needed were selfish, any more than Philo is suggesting that you can collect too much wisdom. He is, as R. P. C. Hanson says, viewing the manna incident as a type, a type of God's self-giving in grace. Of course this self-giving is to be reproduced in the Christian communities, and in this sense Paul is drawing moral lessons from the Scriptures. But he does it through Christ, not directly; and therefore this passage does classify as a proof text in the sense we have outlined above.

The truth is that the collection for Christians in Judea was an enterprise which held for Paul a great theological significance.

If we consider the language he uses about it, we shall see that the generosity which he demands from his converts is constantly associated by him with the generosity displayed by God-in-Christ. At the very beginning of chapter 8 Paul uses, about the giving of the churches in Macedonia, language which we also find him using of God's self-giving in Christ; περισσεία ('abundance'), πτωχεία ('poverty'), ἐπερίσσευσεν ('abounded'), πλοῦτος ('wealth'). This whole operation is described in 8.1 as 'the grace (χάριν) of God which has been shown in the churches of Macedonia'. In 8.9 he writes:

> For you know the grace (χάριν) of our Lord Jesus Christ, that though he was rich (πλούσιος ὤν), yet for your sake he became poor (ἐπτώχευσεν), so that by his poverty you might become rich (πλουτήσητε).

In between these two verses we have verse 7, where Paul urges the Corinthians to 'excel (περισσεύητε) in this work also' and 'work' here translates χάριτι. It is unnecessary to elaborate the theme of 'wealth' (πλοῦτος) in connection with God-in-Christ (cf. Rom. 11.33); but it is worth noting how often Paul uses the verb 'to abound or excel' (περισσεύειν) of God and of his work in Christ. See Rom. 3.7; 5.15; 1 Cor. 14.12; 15.58; 2 Cor. 1.5; 4.15; 9.8. It is just possible that Paul takes the word from his Greek version of the Scriptures. Aquila translates Deut. 30.9 'The Lord your God will make you abundantly prosperous' with περισσεύειν.[8] So we have in fact lighted on one more example of Pauline typology in this passage, and are not justified in classifying it as mere scriptural adornment.

We now turn to the second passage, 2 Cor. 9.6–9. Here we have a series of texts from Proverbs, followed by a full quotation from the Psalms. Paul is dealing with essentially the same subject as in the previous chapter, Christian giving. In 9.6 he may be echoing Prov. 11.24. He writes:

> ὁ σπείρων φειδομένως φειδομένως καὶ θερίσει,
> καὶ ὁ σπείρων ἐπ᾽ εὐλογίας ἐπ᾽ εὐλογίαις καὶ θερίσει.

he who sows sparingly will also reap sparingly,
and he who sows bountifully will also reap bountifully.

Prov. 11.24 runs in the RSV:

> One man gives freely, yet grows all the richer;
> another withholds what he should give, and only suffers want.[9]

This is not very close to Paul's words. Nor is the LXX much closer:

εἰσὶν οἱ τὰ ἴδια σπείροντες πλείονα ποιοῦσιν,
εἰσὶν καὶ οἱ συνάγοντες ἐλλατονοῦνται.

There are those who scatter freely their own and make it more; and there are those who, gathering in, are diminished.

The LXX συνάγοντες is not a very accurate translation of the Hebrew *chōsek*; but both Aquila and Symmachus use the verb φείδεσθαι instead, 'to spare'. This it is that suggests a link with 2 Cor. 9.6. Rabbi Hillel the Elder is reported as saying: 'If thou seest a generation which is eager for the knowledge of the Torah, spread it abroad, as it says, " *There is that scattereth and yet increaseth* ".'[10] This may have some significance for Paul's interpretation, as we shall see.

Paul follows with an equally puzzling though more explicit reference in verse 7:

ἱλαρὸν γὰρ δότην ἀγαπᾷ ὁ Θεός

for God loves a cheerful giver.

This is certainly a reference to the LXX of Prov. 22.8c:

ἄνδρα ἱλαρὸν καὶ δότην εὐλογεῖ ὁ Θεός

God blesses a man who is cheerful and a giver.

The difficulty is that there is nothing in the MT to correspond to this line and the next one. It is not easy to guess how these two lines have crept into the text of the LXX. The line we have quoted might have been originally an alternative version of the MT 22.9a, which RSV renders:

He who has a bountiful eye will be blessed.[11]

It is even possible that Paul's sentence in 9.6 was originally a rendering of the Hebrew of Prov. 22.9a and 8a:

He who has a bountiful eye will be blessed.
He who sows injustice will reap calamity,

especially as the LXX of 8a is

ὁ σπείρων φαῦλα θερίσει κακά

He who sows foully will reap evil,

which is nearer to 2 Cor. 9.6.[12] We know that Prov. 22.9a was used by the rabbis to encourage generous giving. There was an opinion among the rabbis based on this verse that the Torah was originally given only to Moses and his seed, but that Moses in his generosity shared it with all Israel.[13] But the suggestion was strongly opposed. The LXX renders this line rather inaccurately with:

ὁ ἐλεῶν πτωχὸν αὐτὸς διατραφήσεται

he who pities the poor will himself be supported,

but this is very much the sentiment expressed by Paul in 2 Cor. 9.6b, 8, 10. All we can conclude with confidence is that we are here in touch with a number of 'giving' texts from Proverbs habitually used by Paul to encourage generosity among his converts and probably inherited from his rabbinic tradition. The question of whether they are used merely for exhortation must wait until we have examined the Psalms quotation which follows in verse 9.

The citation is of Ps. 112.9, and runs thus:

Ἐσκόρπισεν, ἔδωκεν τοῖς πένησιν,
ἡ δικαιοσύνη αὐτοῦ μένει εἰς τὸν αἰῶνα

He scatters abroad, he gives to the poor;
his righteousness endures for ever.

Paul agrees almost verbatim with the LXX, which is a fair translation of the MT. The Midrash on the Psalms attributes this psalm to Abraham, because it is alphabetical, going from *'aleph* to *tau* and Abraham kept the Torah from *'aleph* to *tau*. Thus they interpret 'his seed' in Ps. 112.2 as referring to Isaac, very much indeed as Paul might.[14] Perhaps this gives us a clue to how Paul understood the psalm. As we read it in the LXX, we cannot fail to notice several phrases that link up with Paul's 'theology of giving': there is δόξα and πλοῦτος in verse 3. Verse 4 runs in the LXX (Ps. 111.4, of course):

ἐξανέτειλεν ἐν σκότει φῶς τοῖς εὐθέσιν
ἐλεήμων καὶ οἰκτίρμων καὶ δίκαιος

a light has risen in darkness for the upright,
merciful and pitiful and righteous.

The last three adjectives are very much those which Paul applies to God or (as we have argued) to the Christ; see Rom. 1.17;

9.15. Paul might interpret the light rising of either the appearance of the Messiah in the flesh or of his resurrection. In the verse which he actually quotes, it is very difficult to reconcile with Paul's theology any view except that the 'righteousness which remains for ever' is Christ's righteousness in Christians, rather than an 'alms-righteousness' of their own. We can hardly envisage Paul as preaching in Galatians and Romans a doctrine of justification in Christ, and in 2 Corinthians a doctrine of justification by alms-giving. The last line of verse 9 which Paul does not quote, runs in the LXX:

τὸ κέρας αὐτοῦ ὑψωθήσεται ἐν δόξῃ

His horn shall be exalted in glory.

Paul might apply this also to Christ's resurrection. We cannot be as confident about the christocentric reference of this Psalm citation as we can about the citation in 8.15; but on the whole, knowing what we do about Paul's methods of scriptural exegesis, it seems likely that he sees Ps. 112 as applying first to Christ, and secondarily to Christians in Christ. If he knew the tradition that attributed the authorship of the psalm to Abraham, that would help him to see it that way, for he would understand the psalm as uttered by Abraham, with a reference (in verse 2) to his seed, which is Christ; but intended prophetically of the Messiah. Strachan's comment on 2 Cor. 9.8 is very appropriate here: '"God is able to make every kind of grace abound in you." Christianity did not begin as a social movement, but originated in the Person of Jesus Christ.' And as we read 2 Cor. 8 and 9, we see how very much everything that is done is done in us by God in Christ, so that we are never left with the idea that the Corinthians' giving could be something which originated in themselves. It is the gift of God. This is implied in almost every word of 9.6–10. And the chapter ends with two verses in which Paul reverts to the great theme of 'the surpassing grace of God in you'. The 'inexpressible gift' of verse 15 is not only the gift of Christ. It also means the gift of what Christ can do in the Corinthians.

We conclude, therefore, by repeating that Paul does occasionally use Scripture in a non-theological way; but that his whole mind is so deeply permeated by his theology of 'in Christ' that frequently citations which appear on the surface to be simple moral exhortation taken from the Scriptures and applied directly to Christians prove on closer examination to have a deeply christocentric meaning.[15]

Before we leave this topic, however, we should attempt to defend Paul from a charge which has been brought against him by very weighty authority, the charge that he was primarily interested in the predictive element in Scripture. This is of course a view which goes to the opposite extreme from those who suggest that Paul uses Scripture only as illustration. This view charges him with using it mainly as an Old Moore's Almanack. The most eminent champion of this view is Bultmann. He maintains that New Testament writers as a whole regard the Old Testament as primarily a corpus of predictions. They are really only interested in the prophetic aspect of Scripture, understood in the strictest sense of the word 'prophetic'. He also accuses them of extensive allegorizing, though he makes no attempt to distinguish allegory from typology.[16] His view is summed up in the following sentence:

> In reality this method of finding prophecy—whether with or without allegorizing—abandons the text of the Old Testament to the mercy of arbitrary choice, and the grotesque examples in the apostolic fathers are simply the consequence of the method of the New Testament authors.[17]

James Barr has more recently emphasized the importance of the predictive element in Scripture for the writers of the New Testament.[18]

But Bultmann's conclusions about this emphasis on prediction are not justified, as can be seen when we look at the examples he quotes. In fact Paul is not greatly interested in the predictive element in the Scriptures as such, at least not in the sense in which Bultmann means it. Thus of Rom. 15.3–4 he says that, according to Paul 'we can learn from Scripture that what happened in Christ corresponds to prophecy'.[19] To whose prophecy? David's? It seems unlikely. What Paul is interested in showing is that we can learn from the utterance of the pre-existent Christ something about the meaning of his sufferings on earth. It is true that the predictive element enters into it, but that is not the main point for Paul. The main point is that the Scriptures can give us information about Christ. He does not emphasize the predictive element as such. Similarly Bultmann maintains that in Rom. 10.4f Paul interprets Deuteronomy as 'a prophecy of justification by faith'. But it was not a prophecy but a statement of justification of faith that Paul found in Deut. 30. There was no need to prophesy about it, for it was already possible, and in the case of some (e.g. Abraham) actual. The same distortion of perspective occurs when Bultmann describes Paul in 1 Cor. 10.1–11 as seeing in the narrative of the wilderness sojourn 'a prophecy of the Christian sacraments'.[20] Paul is careful to distinguish the various elements in this situation: the events of the wilderness sojourn happened to the Israelites of old as warnings ($\tau\upsilon\pi\iota\kappa\hat{\omega}s$ 1 Cor. 10.11), and therefore happened in their own right. They were written for our admonition. Nowhere does Paul write in the vein of 'look how wonderfully prophecy is fulfilled in our Christian sacraments'. Bultmann is misled because he throws everything into the end-time, and has no idea of the real presence of the pre-existent Son in Israel's history. Thus Bultmann's objection to Paul's citation of Ps. 19 in Rom. 10.18 is really aimed at the wrong target. The words of the psalm, he says, are not a prophecy at all. Paul in fact does not say they are. They are a statement about the range of the gospel message, in Paul's view, and we must be prepared to accept the conclusion that when they were uttered in the era before Christ they were already in a sense true. Certainly Paul does not quote them for their predictive value. He quotes them in order to show that the Jews of old had no excuse if they did not realize the full extent of the message of God's redemption. Naturally to criticize Bultmann's conclusions about the New Testament exegesis of Scripture is not *ipso facto* to justify that exegesis. We must agree with Bultmann that we today cannot adopt that exegesis ourselves. But we must not bring against Paul at least charges of which he is innocent. We have only to compare his methods with those of Qumran to realize how far he was from regarding Scripture as purely predictive.[21]

## 3. Can we guess how Paul would have interpreted those parts of Scripture on which he does not comment?

This may be a rash question. Why should we indulge in useless speculation about matters for which the evidence does not exist? But in fact we have been doing something like this throughout this work: and unless we are to characterize Paul's exegesis of Scripture as completely capricious and unpredictable, there must be certain lines discernible which would enable us to make a reasonable conjecture about how he would interpret those large areas of Scripture that he leaves unmentioned. Indeed our ability to make reasonable conjectures about this question is an index of our success in divining Paul's mind on the subject of Scripture. In any case, we are not the first to ask this question. James Barr has asked it about New Testament writers as a group.[22] His guess is that, if we had more New Testament exegesis of Scripture, we would find more use of allegory.

A scholar who has made a similar attempt is Diezinger whom we have already quoted on p. 30 above.[23] He claims that Lam. 3.53-5 is a passage which would have made a strong appeal to Paul, and even goes so far as to suggest that Paul may have compared it with Ps. 88.6, because of the link provided by the word in the LXX λάκκος, 'pit'. Without necessarily accepting his suggestion, we may well agree that this is the right way to tackle the question: we proceed from those passages which we can be confident Paul did study to those which are sufficiently like them to suggest how they would have appeared to Paul.

We can in fact outline a rough method which would enable us to judge how Paul might interpret almost any passage of Scripture. In the first place, there were certain themes, often characterized by key words, that attracted him because he found in them a link with the redemption which God had effected in Christ: χριστός, δικαιοσύνη, δικαίωμα, σώζειν, ῥύεσθαι, wherever these words appeared in a theological context, Paul would probably find references to Christ. δοῦλος in the Psalms, or in Isaiah, particularly if the servant was undergoing suffering or appealing for salvation; this would be claimed by Paul as a messianic reference. He was also alert for references to the gospel: λόγος Θεοῦ or ῥῆμα, the word εὐαγγελίζειν, these would attract him. We know how he would interpret this sort of language. But this is very obvious; we have done little more than indicate the sort of passages in which any Jew of a missionary turn of mind would be interested. It was no doubt because there are traces in the LXX of this universalist or missionary element that Paul was so often able to quote the LXX in a Christian sense.

We still have to ask: What would Paul have made of those parts of Scripture which do not exhibit these characteristics? It is no use replying that he would have passed them by, or rejected them. He believed no doubt with all devout Jews that the whole of Scripture was valuable and that no part could be 'written off'. What, for example, about the many ritual instructions in the Pentateuch? We have had some examples of these in chapter 6 of this work; on the basis of this we can say that Paul, where it seemed to him appropriate, saw ritual instructions in terms of typology (perhaps imperfect typology, as clearly exemplified in Hebrews). Where this did not seem reasonable, he would no doubt have said that it was part of the mechanism of the Law. The intention of God in giving the Torah on Sinai was to reduce the Jews to despair of their own efforts; this required a great many detailed instructions to effect. But there are some indications that Paul saw a certain limited value in Torah-observance for Jews; compare his remarks on circumcision in Rom. 2.25; 4.11. Thus he might have accepted some ritual prescriptions under this heading. Another element in Scripture which might seem to present difficulties to Paul is the frequent reference to God's wrath, or the cursing of enemies in the Psalms. Paul had his own very profound concept of the wrath of God, which does not involve the presentation of God as personally angry with men. Presumably therefore he interpreted references to the wrath of God in the Scriptures in this light. We have frequently had occasion to ask ourselves what did Paul make of this or that psalm, and quite often the psalm in question has contained either violent denunciations of enemies or confession of personal sin. If Paul imagined such psalms as uttered by Christ, what would he make of such utterances? Denunciations of enemies he would understand as the enemies whom Christ overcame in his cross and resurrection, the στοιχεῖα τοῦ κόσμου. Confession of sin he would perhaps have understood as a sort of vicarious penitence. Christ, who has assumed sin-prone human nature, can be said to confess our sins and to acknowledge God's judgement on that nature, while at the same time experiencing God's vindication as the sinless servant.

Finally, there are the various genres of literature in the Scriptures of some of which (e.g. Ecclesiastes, Daniel, Song of Songs) Paul makes little or no use. In as far as he encountered in them the themes which appealed to him, they present no problem; and the obscure citation of Job in Rom. 11.35 shows that he could on occasion find justification by faith in what appears to us to be the most unlikely passages. But even where there is a dearth of such themes, we can make some generalizations about how Paul would have understood such Books. The historical Books would not themselves seem to require much explanation. He accepted them as did all orthodox Jews, as straightforward history. Sometimes no doubt he would have found typology there, as in our examples of Num. 25 quoted on p. 4 above. Since all history in Israel was written in a more or less prophetic tradition, there were always references to the covenant or the people of God that would have had a christocentric significance for Paul. We would suggest that James Barr is mistaken in suggesting that, had we more New Testament exegesis, we would have more allegory. It is much more likely that we would have more typology. Indeed, we might have more attempts to identify the real presence of Christ in Israel's history, a field which the historical Books certainly make available from time to time. When we try to guess what is going on behind the scenes in Acts 7 and in Hebrews, for example, we may be forgiven for guessing that these authors would have found many more Christophanies in the Scriptures had they had more scope for exegesis. As for the Wisdom literature as such, we have several clues to help us to imagine how Paul interprets it. Where opportunity allows, he finds Christ as the pre-existent Wisdom of God. But this accounts for only a small fraction of the Wisdom literature. For the rest, he accepts the prudential ethics, but accepts them in Christ. His approach to Proverbs, for example, is most probably through Christ; and where possible he sees the descriptions of how the righteous or God-fearing man behaves as fulfilled primarily in Christ and secondarily in Christians. The traditional use of such Books as Proverbs which he had inherited from his rabbinic training was not repudiated by Paul the Christian, but was reorientated to Christ as its centre.

What then shall we say to Bultmann's accusation that 'the

grotesque examples [of allegory] in the apostolic fathers are simply the consequence of the method of the New Testament authors'? In one sense, he is right. Very often the way in which the apostolic fathers deal with a text is a good guide to the way in which Paul would deal with it. In particular, the propensity of the apostolic fathers (Epistle of Barnabas, Melito, Justin) to find Christ active in Israel's history is a fair indication of how we should interpret much New Testament exegesis, Paul's included. There is no absolute break between Paul's exegesis and that of the earliest non-canonical Christian writers. They were carrying on the same tradition. But they did not always have the insight or profundity of a Paul or a John; thus Barnabas' interpretation of the Sinai covenant is, as we have seen, not that of Paul. Barnabas is anxious not to have to restrict something so important as the first promulgation of the Torah purely to the Jews as far as its validity is concerned. Paul knows better. Again it is very doubtful whether Rahab's red cord in the story of the spies would have seemed significant to Paul as it does to Clement,[24] where it indicates that there will be redemption through the blood of Christ for all who believe. But it must be admitted that these are differences of taste and proportion rather than of principle. Where Bultmann does go wrong is in his failure to distinguish between typology and allegory. We are not justified in saying that Paul's typology was verging towards allegory. On the contrary, when it did verge in this direction he had the discernment to correct it, as we can see if we compare Galatians with Romans. In as far as the apostolic fathers indulge in allegory rather than typology, they are being unfaithful to Paul's tradition of scriptural exegesis.

Above all, Bultmann is mistaken in describing the New Testament exegesis of Scripture as 'arbitrary'. We are really impinging here on the subject of the final chapters, but it is relevant here to assert that Paul, however strange his methods of exegesis may seem to us today, had a profound respect for the text of Scripture. He never consciously attempts to alter it; he never even offers a paraphrase of it. We can therefore be more confident about how Paul would interpret any given passage of Scripture than we can be, for example, about Philo. Indeed Philo offers us an instructive parallel here. For all his belief in the full inspiration of God which seized Moses when he spoke or wrote, Philo can be far freer in his treatment of the text of Scripture than Paul would ever dream of being. Philo can paraphrase freely. Compare, as a good example, the rendering by Philo of Exod. 33.18. It occurs in a passage where Philo is describing Moses' request to God to be allowed to see him. He paraphrases the whole passage from 33.13 onwards, and when he comes to 33.18 'I pray thee, show me thy glory',[25] he renders as follows: 'As a result of thy guidance I am convinced that I could never have the strength to receive the clear vision of thy appearance. But I implore that at least I may behold the glory that surrounds thee.'[26] By means of his paraphrase Philo has ended by more or less inverting the sense of the original since presumably Moses in asking to see God's glory meant that he wanted a vision of God himself, and not of his angel or of some inferior manifestation. Such a paraphrase would be quite alien to Paul's method. Of that we may be confident.

## 4. How far, in Paul's view, were the prophetic writers of Scripture conscious of the full significance of what they were uttering?

This is no academic question, for it brings up the whole matter of Paul's understanding of the inspiration of the Scriptures. I have already discussed this question from some aspects in *Studies in the Pastoral Epistles*.[27] I there compared, among other passages, 2 Tim. 3.14–17 with 1 Pet. 1.10–12. I concluded that in the Pastoral Epistles (as also in 2 Peter) what I called the Philonic view of inspiration prevailed, i.e. that those who wrote Scripture were the unconscious mouthpieces of the Holy Spirit, whereas in 1 Peter the prophets were regarded as taking a keen interest in what the Holy Spirit was uttering through them. I also pointed out that we know what the Qumran sectaries believed on this point, since we have in the Commentary on Habakkuk a passage which runs as follows: 'And God told Habakkuk to write these things that were to come upon the last generation, but the consummation of the period he did not make known to him.' In the words of F. F. Bruce, the *rāz* or mystery was revealed to the prophets, but not its *pesher* or interpretation. I did not however draw any definite conclusions about Paul's views on this point.

We can point to rabbinic evidence here. In the *Biblical Anti-quities* for example, an apocryphal character called Cenez utters prophecy on his deathbed: 'The holy spirit that dwelt in Cenez leapt upon him and took away from him his bodily sense, and he began to prophesy.'[28] When he comes to himself, he is not aware of what he has been saying. Here then, in what is presumably a purely Hebrew setting, is a distinctly Greek doctrine of inspiration. In the Midrash on the Psalms, the Sons of Korah, who are certainly regarded as prophets, are represented as saying apropos the psalm-title to Ps. 46 'According to Alamoth' (which is here interpreted as 'hidden things'): 'The things we saw are hidden, and we did not understand what we saw.'[29] This would seem to be in line with 1 Peter and Qumran: they saw the mystery but not its interpretation. An even clearer distinction is made apropos Ps. 90: 'R. Eleazar taught us in the name of R. Jose ben Zimra: None of the prophets, as they uttered their prophecies, knew that they were prophesying, except Moses and Isaiah, who did know.'[30] This might indicate a 'Greek' doctrine of inspiration: the prophets were unconscious media of divine utterance; or it might, presumably, be a much more modern view: the prophets thought they were uttering God's word to their own generation. Only in the perspective of history can we know that their words carried a deeper meaning. But the former meaning seems the more likely.

Scholars have often suggested that Paul has a less mechanical doctrine of inspiration than some of those outlined above (I have discussed the views of some of these scholars in the chapter of *Studies in the Pastoral Epistles* already referred to). Vollmer, for instance, suggests that Paul shows more interest in the various authors of Scripture than does the author of the Epistle to the Hebrews.[31] Michel changed his mind about this; in his earlier book he claimed that Paul shows interest in the personality of Isaiah, but in his commentary on Romans he abandons this view.[32] J. D. Smart maintains that, because Paul reads Scripture ἐν πνεύματι, he has a less rabbinic and therefore less mechanical view of the nature of inspiration than had the rabbis.[33] This seems to be importing nineteenth-century views of scriptural exegesis into Paul's theology. It is quite true that Paul wished Scripture to be understood 'in the Spirit', but this does not at all mean that he had a view of the method of inspiration different from that which he received in the tradition in which he was educated. Reading the Scripture in the Spirit did not mean making greater allowance for the personalities of the authors or for the circumstances in which they wrote. It meant reading them with christocentric presuppositions.

Amsler had an interesting discussion on this point, for at the end of his book he devotes some pages to defending the typological exegesis of the Old Testament, maintaining that 'the proper task of typological interpretation is to consider the event not in its exact historicity but in its theological significance'.[34] He goes on to attempt an answer to Fohrer's objection that, if we suggest that the writers of the Old Testament were not fully conscious of their meaning, we empty the Old Testament of all significance. He answers in effect that the meaning was implicit, but had to be unpacked or revealed by the events of the New Testament. It would be fascinating to attempt a comparison of this view of the relation of the two Testaments with Newman's view of the development of doctrine; but it would, unfortunately, be quite irrelevant to our theme.

When we turn to Paul, we do not find any indications that in his view the biblical writers were unconscious of the meaning of what they were saying. It is true that when Paul, for example, writes in Rom. 10.20 'Then Isaiah is so bold as to say', he is not showing an interest in the prophet's psychological state as he uttered the prophecy. This is shown by the fact that the words uttered by the prophet in Isa. 65.1 are not the prophet's own comment but are the utterance of God. Paul would certainly not have considered that Isaiah had any choice as to whether he would utter God's words or not. So the boldness belongs to God and not to the prophet. But it does not follow from this that Paul regarded Isaiah as an unconscious medium of divine communication. We must remember that the rabbis regarded certain biblical characters, such as Abraham and Moses, as very well informed about the future of Israel. It seems from Paul's language very likely indeed that Paul thought of the writers of Scripture as having full information about what they were saying, and indeed on occasion as knowing about the messianic era. After all, if our argument is correct, in Paul's view all the Jews of old could have known a great deal about Christ. It is true that their hearts were hardened, but there were some certainly who did know.

We think, for instance, of the difficult midrash in 2 Cor. 3. There Moses puts on the veil so that the children of Israel should not know the true significance of the presence in the tabernacle. This means that Moses did know it, and even that Moses recognized the pre-existent Christ in the *Sh<sup>a</sup>kinah* whom he encountered in the tabernacle. Again, in Rom. 10.16 Isaiah is quoted as saying: 'Lord, who has believed what he has heard from us?' Paul certainly here envisages Isaiah as speaking with God (probably with the pre-existent Christ) about what he himself has been uttering. And certainly what he has been saying in this context can hardly be anything but Isaiah's account of the suffering servant. If Isaiah can speak about the reception which his words received, it is most unlikely that Paul regards him as ignorant of the full significance of those words. It is worth remarking that when the author of the Fourth Gospel cites these words from Isaiah in John 12.38, he certainly regards Isaiah as being fully informed about their import, for Isaiah is immediately told about the divinely decreed hardening of Israel's heart. A similar passage occurs in Rom. 11.1–8. There the prophet complains to God (or possibly to the pre-existent Christ) that he alone is faithful and is answered by the assurance that there is a remnant who have not bowed the knee to Baal. Shortly afterwards Paul quotes a passage from Deuteronomy to show that God has blinded the eyes of the Jews. It seems very likely that, in Paul's opinion, the faithful interpreters of God's will knew all about the remnant and the blinding. Another example is Hosea in Rom. 9.25f. Paul knew of course about Hosea's children and about his being commanded by God to marry Gomer. While it is possible to envisage a prophet uttering words the meaning of which he did not understand, it is more difficult to imagine him performing actions under divine possession the meaning of which he did not understand, particularly if those actions entailed marrying a woman and begetting children by her. This example of Hosea is helpful, because it suggests that Paul did not adopt the view which we encountered in the Midrash on the Psalms that Moses and Isaiah knew all about the meaning of their prophecies, but that the other writers did not. It seems likely that, in Paul's view, all the inspired writers knew the full prophetic significance of what they wrote.

In this respect we may claim that Paul differs from the rabbis, and also from some of the later writers in the New Testament. He does not seem to have been influenced by what I have called the 'Greek' doctrine of inspiration according to which the authors of the Scriptures were what we would today call automatic writers. They knew the full significance of what they wrote. But this does not of course mean in any way that Paul held a modern doctrine of inspiration. He was as fully convinced as any rabbi that the writers of Scripture were supernaturally endowed with knowledge of future events. They were in fact in some sense Christians before Christ.

## 5. Did Paul use 'testimonia'?

Since James Rendel Harris published in 1917 his theory that the writers of the New Testament depended very largely for their scriptural material on books of *testimonia*, the question has diminished in importance. It is now generally recognized that Rendel Harris overstated his case, and the great majority of scholars would accept C. H. Dodd's verdict: 'The composition of "testimony-books" was the result, not the presupposition of the work of early Christian biblical scholars.'[35] Even the discovery of *florilegia* of messianic or other texts among the Qumran documents has not caused a revival of Rendel Harris' theory of testimony-books.

It is still, however, a perfectly reasonable theory to maintain that Paul does make use of scriptural texts which were already conflated, either by himself or by somebody else, for apologetic purposes. We must distinguish two quite separate propositions here: (*a*) Paul inherited from those who were Christians before him an interest in certain parts of Scripture, and even probably certain conflations of Scripture texts which Christian apologists had used before him; (*b*) Paul made use of a regular set of linked texts, which formed the basis of Christian apologetic in his day. Everybody, presumably, would accept proposition (*a*); about (*b*) there would be far more doubt. C. H. Dodd, for example, though he indicates those passages of Scripture in which the early Christians were most interested, does not

suggest that there was any systematic arrangement used by
Paul or by anyone else. Michel maintains firmly that Paul did
not use any previously existing *florilegium*, and that any collection of texts he may have used would not have with him the
same status as Scripture as a whole.[36] Paul had no substitute
for the Bible. Doeve likewise explicitly rejects the *testimonia* suggestion on the grounds that the rabbis never lifted texts out of
their context and preserved them, so to speak, on cardboard.[37]
He insists that the rabbis always regarded the context, and that
this applies to Paul also.

W. Windfuhr, in a brief article written forty-five years ago,
finds traces of rabbinic methods of connecting texts which might
appear to run counter to Doeve's contention. He describes two
such methods: one is 'chain-exposition' (*Kettenerklärung*), in
which the successive elements in a text are illustrated from
other parts of Scripture; and the other is 'stringing pearls'
(*Perlenaufreihen*) whereby one text is associated with others
which have an identical or similar content. He would see an
example of the first type in Rom. 10.6f, and of the second in
Rom. 4.1–12, where Gen. 15.6 is associated with Ps. 32.1–3.[38]
Neither of these examples is very convincing: in Rom. 10 the
texts which Paul cites seem to be connected primarily by the
exigencies of his argument rather than by any set scheme; and
the example in Rom. 4 is too brief to prove anything very much.
We may however heartily agree with Windfuhr when he maintains that Paul often cites a group of texts in order by means of
the group to prove his point, rather than citing them as isolated
proofs.

It will be helpful at this point to review the places in Romans
where it seems possible that Paul is relying on a conflation of
texts, whether made by others or by himself. They prove to be at
most five in number. The first is Rom. 3.10–18, what we have
called the catena. It seems very probable that this is a list which
Paul had to hand. He did not compose it specially for the Letter
to the Romans. But it does not look like a *testimonia*-list composed by some Christian apologist for general use. Michel's
opinion, that Paul himself composed it for his own purposes,
seems more likely. And our study of the texts that compose the
catena in their settings serves to confirm this conclusion. Next
comes 9.33. Here we must acknowledge a conflation of two

texts from Isaiah. In view of the appearance of these texts elsewhere in the New Testament (including Rom. 9.33), as well
as their use in the Qumran literature, it is very likely that Paul
was not the author of this conflation; he received it from his
(Christian) tradition. Perhaps the same can be said for 11.8, our
third example, where a text from Deuteronomy and one from
Isaiah have been conflated, especially as the divinely intended
blindness of the Jews must have been a leading theme in early
Christian apologetic.[39] The fourth passage is 11.26–7, where it
seems probable on the whole that it is Paul himself who has
conflated two passages from Isaiah. The two citations do not
seem to be linked by any particular key-word, but they do fit
Paul's theology very well. The last example, 11.34–5, is much
more doubtful. The text from Isaiah and the text from Job may
have been combined before the Christian era. See Wisd. 11.20–
22, where it is possible that the author is meditating on the two
Scripture passages Isa. 40.12, 15 and Job. 41.11. On the other
hand, it cannot be claimed that these two texts, either
separately or combined, would have been of much use to a
Christian apologist. Whether, therefore, Paul originally combined them, or whether they were already combined by someone else when Paul used them, they constitute no evidence that
Paul used *testimonia*. Our conclusion on this question must therefore be that, though Paul had no hesitation in using texts which
had already been used or conflated by Christian apologists
before him, this does not suggest in any way that he did not
make the texts his own, or that he relied extensively for scriptural proof on existing sets of proof texts. In the great majority
of instances we may be sure that Paul did his own Bible-study
and found his Scripture proofs by reading Scripture for himself.

There is, however, implicit in the view that Paul used *testimonia* a suggestion which has received more support from
scholars. This is the suggestion that Paul in using Scripture ignores the context from which he takes the texts.[40] If any such
suggestion is still entertained by the reader of this work, it must
be admitted that it has been written in vain, since the constant
tenor of our argument has been that we cannot understand
Paul's interpretation of Scripture unless we examine the context from which his citations are taken. But there is a refinement

of this suggestion which may well occupy us for a moment. Michel claims that Paul, and indeed all writers of the New Testament, ignore the *historical* context from which their citations come.[41] Similar to this is James Barr's statement that the writers of the New Testament, though they may have considered the context from which their citations were taken, did not necessarily understand the context as a whole.[42] If by this is meant that the writers of the New Testament did not have our conception of the importance of discovering the contemporary meaning of scriptural texts, we must of course agree. And we have already noted that in his use of the Psalms Paul does not reproduce the rabbis' interest in their context (or presumed context) in David's life. But it is not true to say that Paul had no interest in the historical context of his Scripture quotations. In some instances at least, the historical situation is of vital interest, because it constitutes the point of the argument, e.g. his locating of Gen. 15.6 and Ps. 32 before the circumcision of Abraham. Indeed in this instance Paul is being, from our point of view, too much, not too little concerned with the historical context, for he argues that Ps. 32 was in fact uttered originally in one particular historical context, whereas we would probably be inclined to conclude that its historical origin was not so easy to determine, and of less importance if we could determine it. It is also possible that Paul may see a certain significance in Moses' words in Deut. 30 just because they were uttered in the plains of Moab. See Rom. 10.5–8. The Qumran sectaries saw great importance in the historical context in which the Book of Deuteronomy claims to be set. Paul may have thought that Moses' utterances in this Book were more likely to give a final verdict on the true significance of the Torah just because they occurred not long before his death. We could also point to his citation from Hosea in Rom. 9.25–6. We are not justified in concluding that he regarded these words as uttered in a void, or that he paid no attention to the actual historical situation of Hosea. Elijah is another example: no devout Israelite could read the words quoted by Paul in Rom. 11.3f without recollecting the famous experience of the prophet on Mount Horeb; and we may be quite confident that Paul has this in mind as he quotes the words. Indeed, when we read such passages as Rom. 10.6f; 10.19; 15.10, we may well suspect that

Paul valued these texts partly because of the historical situation in which they were uttered. They showed, he believed, that at the very period when the Torah was being promulgated, God was also indicating that his real will was for Israel to pursue another way of life, the way of faith. Thus the accusation that Paul ignores the historical context from which his citations are taken has proved only partially true. In other passages the historical context is of importance to him. What has made this charge plausible as a general conclusion is that Paul's notion of the course of Israel's history is at so many points different from ours, so that we do not always find it easy to recognize when that history is significant for him.

It is convenient at this point to mention a recent unpublished dissertation by H. Ulonska, a pupil of Professor H. Conzelmann, which bears on this subject.[43] He deals with the Old Testament citations and allusions in Paul's letters. His general thesis is that they are not to be understood as proofs, but more as parenesis and illustration (see pp. 78 and 193). He denies, for example, that Paul 'christianizes' the Old Testament; in Rom. 4 all he is doing is showing that sonship does not necessarily involve circumcision (pp. 50–1). Ulonska denies that Paul really draws his theology from the Old Testament; and suggests that he uses it mainly as ammunition against individual opponents, thereby reverting to a view of Adolf Harnack's. Of Rom. 15.3 he says that Paul is not thinking about the psalm context at all, but simply applying an example taken from the Old Testament to the situation of the 'weak' and 'strong' Christians in Rome. He does not, however, examine Ps. 69 from which Paul quotes there in any detail, or he could hardly have passed so hasty a judgement. Indeed his whole work suffers from a lack of detailed examination of the citations which Paul makes. Only because the citations are not studied in their context is it possible, we may suggest, to come to conclusions so different from those which we have reached in this work. Indeed, had Ulonska realized how large a subject he was dealing with, he would probably never have attempted to encompass it in so relatively small a thesis. His work is, however, favourably quoted by Conzelmann in his *Outline of the Theology of the New Testament* and therefore deserves mention.

## 6. Did Paul read the Scriptures in Hebrew?

The answer to this question is not as obvious as may appear at first sight. We might be tempted to answer out of hand with a Yes. How could Paul have been so well acquainted with contemporary exegesis, with both midrash and *Haggadah*, if he did not know Hebrew? But we can point to at least two works earlier than Paul's whose authors show some considerable acquaintance with midrash and *Haggadah* though we may be very confident that they were not able to read Hebrew. These are the Book of Wisdom and Philo's works. It seems most unlikely that the author of the Book of Wisdom could read the Scriptures in Hebrew; but he is certainly acquainted with traditional exegesis and midrash. See, for example, Wisd. 10.20-1, where the author quotes Ps. 8 in connection with the crossing of the Red Sea. Exactly the same tradition is found centuries later in the Talmud.[44] Similarly, there is very good evidence indeed that Philo's knowledge of Hebrew was absolutely minimal, certainly not enough to enable him to read the Scriptures in the original.[45] But he does show some knowledge of midrash. Thus a knowledge of midrash and traditional exegesis does not in itself prove a competent knowledge of Hebrew. In Paul's day it could have been acquired through Greek. On the other hand, the two examples cited are both from Alexandria. This was a very special sort of area as far as Jewish culture was concerned; it is difficult to point to anywhere else of which it can be said that at that period an effort was made to combine Jewish religion with Greek thought. And we have no reason at all to connect Paul with Alexandria. If we accept as history Luke's statement that Paul studied under Gamaliel, then the question is settled. He must have studied in Jerusalem and known Hebrew. (See Acts 22.3.) According to the *Jewish Encyclopedia*,[46] Gamaliel I lived 'in the second third of the first century A.D.' and was a grandson of Hillel. All the references to him in the Talmud represent him as an expert in Torah-observance rather than in exposition of the Scriptures. There is one incident narrated of him which suggests the most interesting speculations: 'I remember R. Gamaliel was standing on a high eminence on the Temple Mount, when the Book of Job in a Targum Version was brought before him, whereupon he said to the builder, "Bury it under the bricks".' H. Freedman explains that this was because of its possible heretical tendencies. Below we note that a Targum of Job in fragments has been found at Qumran. Perhaps this may be why R. Gamaliel objected to it so much. One cannot help wondering whether a former pupil of his, Paul of Tarsus, may not have paid too much attention to such books and hence set his teacher against them! Chronologically Paul could have studied under Gamaliel.[47]

But even if we do not accept Luke's statement, it is possible to bring evidence that Paul could read his Bible in Hebrew. One can point to two passages where this seems an almost unavoidable conclusion. The first is 1 Cor. 2.16. It is very hard indeed to resist the conclusion that Paul knew the MT had *rūach*, even though he is faithful to his Greek version in writing νοῦν. The passage immediately preceding the citation is all about the πνεῦμα τοῦ Θεοῦ, and it would have suited Paul's purpose admirably if he could have concluded his argument with a quotation that ran 'Who knew the spirit of the Lord?' Paul is aware, we suggest, that the Hebrew had 'spirit' but remains faithful to the LXX 'mind'. The other place is Gal. 3.13. Though we have examined this passage already, we have not so far considered its bearing on the question of Paul's knowledge of Hebrew. The point is this: the MT of Deut. 21.23 is literally 'a hanged man is a curse of God'.[48] Paul obediently follows his Greek version in writing ἐπικατάρατος instead of what would be a literal translation, κατάρα. But he describes Christ not as ἐπικατάρατος but as γενόμενος κατάρα. This suggests very strongly that he was acquainted with the Hebrew.[49]

At the same time it must be said that Paul shows no signs of frequently consulting the Hebrew. Vollmer's judgement still stands: 'He himself lived in and with the Greek text.'[50] Michel only modifies this by saying that, though Paul was certainly competent to consult the Hebrew text, 'he lived and worked only with the Greek Bible'.[51] Since Vollmer's day, and since the publication of Michel's *Paulus und seine Bibel*, the discovery of the Qumran documents has thrown a flood of light on the Greek versions used by the various authors of the New Testament, and, among other things, has made it clear that to ask whether any given author 'followed the LXX' or not is an oversimplification. As we have seen, Paul's Greek text is sometimes

closer to Aquila, Symmachus, or Theodotion than it is to
our LXX. At the same time it has become equally clear that
many of the LXX divergencies from our MT are not the result
of the vagaries of our LXX translators, but reflect an actual
Hebrew original. To quote a recent review by an expert on the
LXX: 'It is now becoming increasingly clear, however, thanks
to certain of the Qumran finds ... that Septuagint texts that
are at variance with the MT are in fact based on variant
Hebrew texts, which the translators faithfully reproduced in
Greek form.'[52] Many of these translations have been noted as
we have gone through Romans. It may be worth while, however, to mention a few others, apart from those which Paul
actually reproduces. We note first Num. 25.4, where the LXX's
παραδειγμάτισον 'make a public example of', though not a correct translation of the Hebrew, is supported by the Targum of
Palestine. In Isa. 59.20 the Targum is on the side of the LXX in
the rendering 'those who turn others from transgression' rather
than the intransitive 'those who turn from transgression'. In
Deut. 32.43 all three Targums agree with the LXX (and Paul)
against the MT in rendering 'Praise [God], Gentiles'. Finally,
we may point to Isa. 11.10, where the Targum appears to support the LXX in reading into the MT text the sense of 'rise up'.
What this comes to is a warning that, when Paul follows his
Greek version against our Hebrew version, he is not necessarily
slavishly preferring the Greek to the original, nor is he necessarily preferring the Greek because it suits better his ideas of
prediction. These considerations take a good deal of the edge
off Bultmann's accusation that the writers of the New Testament frequently claim as a prophecy fulfilled a text which
depends on the LXX translation for its character as a fulfilment.[53]

It does seem, however, that Paul had a certain respect for the
Greek version. Our two examples from 1 Cor. 2.16 and Gal.
3.13 would seem to indicate this anyway. Perhaps it was simply
because he wished to quote from a version which his readers
possessed. It is true that Ulonska questions both whether Paul's
readers were well acquainted with the LXX, and whether Paul
was able to carry a Septuagint round with him on his travels.[54]
But a simple consideration of Paul's actual use of Scripture in
Romans alone would seem to answer both these questions.

Even if Paul used Scripture only as illustration and not as proof
(which of course we deny), his frequent scriptural references
can hardly be dismissed as mere pyrotechnics; he really believed the Romans would appreciate his references (quite apart
from the fact that he says in Rom. 7.1 that they 'know the
law'). Also, if the evidence produced in this work has any weight
at all, Paul was constantly engaged in deep and prolonged
study of the Scriptures. He must have had with him a Greek
translation of the Torah, the Prophets, and the Writings.

There is some doubt as to the nature of Paul's Greek version
of the Book of Job. Paul's version seems to vary very considerably from our LXX and in some ways to be closer to the Hebrew. Vollmer even suggested that in Paul's day there was no
accepted Greek version of Job. It seems, however, that Philo
quotes Job in Greek.[55] Michel also assumes in his commentary
that there was an LXX version of Job in existence in Paul's
day, for he notes that Paul's version is quite different.[56] Fragments of a Targum on Job have now been found at Qumran,[57]
and it seems likely that, if an Aramaic version had been made
by Paul's time, an official Greek one might also have been
completed.

A further indication that Paul must have known Hebrew
would exist if we could prove that he was acquainted with the
Targums. Positive proof of this we can hardly expect. Ellis
thinks that Paul may sometimes be reflecting a Targum.[58] The
question is not: 'Do we find in Paul material which we also find
in the Targums?' We certainly do. The question is rather:
'Did this material reach him via the Targums?' On the whole
it seems likely that it did. The evidence of the Targum of Jerusalem on Deut. 30.12–14 and of the Targum of Palestine[59] on
Num. 25.1–5 would seem to suggest that Paul's knowledge of
the midrash contained in those two passages in the Targums
came to him through the Targums rather than through the
general exegetical training he had received. But we cannot be
positive on this point.

Thus Paul appears as a well-educated rabbi who had during
his period of training studied the Scriptures in Hebrew, and
who could refer to them in Hebrew when he needed to and
when opportunity offered. But he was normally quite content
to use them in his Greek version. Without going to the extremes

of Septuagint-worship which we meet in Philo and later in Justin, he had apparently no doubts about the adequacy of his version. We might perhaps compare the position of a veteran missionary of a previous generation, who had had an excellent training in Hebrew and Greek in his youth, and can still consult both Hebrew Bible and Greek New Testament if required to, but who normally uses his English version, and normally regards a comparison between that and the vernacular in which he works as sufficient.

# 10

# PAUL AS EXEGETE AND
# THEOLOGIAN

————◆•••◆————

Our task in this chapter is to compare Paul as an exegete of Scripture with his contemporary workers in the same field but belonging to another tradition. Now that we have explored his principles and technique of biblical interpretation we ought to be in a good position to make this comparison. Then we have to attempt to judge the extent to which he drew on the Scriptures for this theology, and how far we must describe him as indebted directly to extraneous sources. After this we will at length be free to face the last great question posed by this work, the question of the justification of Paul's interpretation of Scripture.

It is not surprising that ever since the emergence of modern biblical studies, scholars have from time to time made comparisons between Paul and other contemporary interpreters of the Hebrew Scriptures. But only fairly recently have we had sufficient material to justify a comparison. The most obvious reason for this is the discovery of the Qumran documents. But it could also be said with justice that only within the last fifty years have the materials been easily available for studying the rabbinic tradition; and equally recent is the entry of Jewish scholars into this field, a development which has so greatly illuminated our understanding of rabbinic Judaism. We begin by noting some of the remarks which scholars have made about the comparison between Paul and his contemporaries. Not by any means all of them will be from after 1950, so we must make allowances for their ignorance of the Qumran tradition.

We can point then to three contemporary traditions of

exegesis, Philo's, that of Qumran, and that of orthodox Judaism which developed after Paul's day into what we call rabbinic Judaism. Lietzmann as early as 1911 describes Paul's treatment of the desert sojourn in 1 Cor. 10.1–11 as 'the Haggadic method'.[1] This implies a comparison with rabbinic method and puts Paul's work here into a certain category, that of *Haggadah*. We shall attempt to show presently that this is an inappropriate description of what Paul is doing in 1 Cor. 10; but it may serve as an introduction to our topic. In 1931 Marmorstein, in an article called 'Paulus und die Rabbinen', made a very interesting comparison between Paul's treatment of Adam in Rom. 5.13–21 and rabbinic treatment of the same subject.[2] He takes it for granted that Paul's methods of interpretation and those of contemporary Judaism are the same, but he points out a difference of theological assumptions. The rabbis, he says, did not hold that all men necessarily sinned after Adam. Some believed that Moses was sinless. And secondly, the rabbis maintained that between Adam and Moses the Torah was known and obeyed by some (notably Abraham). These conclusions, as far as concerns the comparison we are making here at any rate, agree very much with our own: there was no difference in method between Paul and contemporary Judaism. The difference consisted in their respective theological assumptions.

Michel, in an article published in 1933, helps us further to define these assumptions when he says that what distinguishes Paul from Judaism is not his doctrine of God, but his doctrine of the act of God.[3] This is a subtle but important distinction. Can you share with another religious tradition the same doctrine of God if you believe that God has acted decisively and finally in his Son, and the other tradition does not? One would be inclined to answer 'yes' to this question when one reads the critique which modern Jewish scholars make of Christianity. What they object to is not the theoretical possibility that God could have acted in his Messiah, but the historical claim that he did. Their other objections tend to concentrate on what they conceive to be Paul's doctrine of the atonement and are not immediately relevant to what we are discussing here. It might perhaps be suggested that here is the dividing line between Judaism and Islam, for Islamic theology can never admit that God could become incarnate. For Judaism the possibility may not be ruled out. But properly speaking a Jew, and not a Christian, should be heard on this point.

One of the most distinguished of modern Jewish scholars who have attempted a not wholly unsympathetic critique of Christianity is Klausner. He describes Christianity in general terms as a compromise between Judaism and paganism, whereas Philo attempted a compromise between Judaism and Hellenism.[4] But he was writing in 1944, and the discovery of the Qumran documents has since put a question mark against the conception of a relatively pure Judaism in the first century A.D. unadulterated by extraneous elements, a conception with which Klausner seems to be working throughout his book. He says, quite correctly of course, that the writers of the New Testament had to justify their rejection of the Torah and their retention of the Jewish Scriptures as inspired, and that they did this by borrowing allegory from Philo. This is, of course, grossly inaccurate as far as concerns Paul. We have only observed two examples of allegory proper in Paul's writings, and one of those (Gal. 4.21f) is not intended as allegory. It is largely untrue of the rest of the New Testament as well. There are examples of allegory in the Fourth Gospel, for instance, but they are rare.[5] Typology is much more characteristic. It is quite true to say that typology was one of the instruments by which early Christians freed themselves from literal Torah-observance; but no one could maintain that Paul or anyone else borrowed typology from Philo. When he comes to detailed examination of Paul, however, Klausner is much fairer. He writes, for example, 'It would be difficult to find more characteristically Talmudic expositions of Scripture than those in the Epistles of Paul' and of 2 Cor. 3 he says: 'This interpretation is typically Midrashic in its form, and is changed from a Jewish to a Christian interpretation only by its deliberately altered content.'[6] So that when Klausner sets himself to examine Paul's exegesis in detail he is a witness on the side of the view we defend here: Paul's methods were rabbinic.

This conclusion is extended to the whole of the New Testament by Doeve: 'In my opinion, then, we must conclude that there is no essential difference between rabbinic and New Testament use of Scripture.'[7] On the other hand, when he comes to apply technical terms to Paul as exegete, he uses language which might mislead. For example, he calls Paul 'an accomplished haggadist'.[8] If this means that Paul himself invents narrative *Haggadah*, we must decisively disagree; but we discuss the question at length presently. His distinction between *Halakah* and *Haggadah* is interesting, because it pretty well coincides with the first definition offered by Wright which we also discuss below. Doeve writes: 'The former [*Halakah*] is precept for conduct; it gives norms; the latter edifies, comforts, admonishes; it lacks the normative character of Halakah.'[9] We shall be concluding presently that such a clear-cut distinction is not one which is appropriate in classifying the scriptural exegesis of the New Testament writers.

Lastly in this context we must note Amsler's judgement. He admits that Paul uses the technique of rabbinic exegesis, but he claims that, whereas this led the rabbis to the height of fantasy, in Paul it served 'a conception of Scripture which was markedly coherent as the document of the divine promise'.[10] This judgement is really impinging upon the subject of our last chapter, since Amsler seems to be agreeing with Baumgärtel's theory that it is the concept of promise (*Verheissung*) that provides the uniting theme both for the Old Testament as a whole and between the two Testaments. But what concerns us here is his claim that Paul's presuppositions in interpreting Scripture (not his technique) enabled him to avoid the heights of fantasy reached by the rabbis. It is a truism among the older commentators that rabbinic exegesis is fantastic compared with that of the New Testament, but it is surprising to find such a judgement here. It may be suggested that the older scholars only failed to find New Testament exegesis equally fantastic because they did not understand it, or were not willing to admit that it was exegesis and not mere illustration. Judged by our modern standards, it seems pretty fantastic to claim, as Paul I believe does, that Abraham uttered Ps. 32; or that Ps. 88.5 refers to Christ's descending into Hades; or that Num. 25.1–5 is a foreshadowing of Christ's victory on the cross. So far therefore as remoteness from our modern methods of interpretation is concerned, there seems little to choose in point of fantasy between Paul's exegesis and that of the rabbis. We must remember also that we have in the Talmud, in the Midrashes and Targums, much more rabbinic exegesis, extending over a much longer period of time. Perhaps if we had more New Testament exegesis we would find it even more fantastic. We can however point to one respect in which rabbinic exegesis was bound to be more complicated and fantastic than Paul's: a great deal of rabbinic exegesis is *Halakah*; that is to say its purpose is to apply the Torah to the moral direction of everyday life. Since (we believe) the Torah was never envisaged by its authors as giving directions for every conceivable moral situation, and since the historic and social predicament of rabbinic Judaism was inevitably different from that in which the Torah was composed,[11] the effort to deduce from it detailed directions for everyday conduct inevitably involved complicated, elaborate, sometimes fantastic, and very often quite unconvincing exegesis. Christians avoided this, not because their technique of exegesis was different, but because they did not accept the Torah as normative for life.

We turn now to our own attempt to view Paul as an exegete against the background of his contemporary exegetes. The comparison with Philo should be simple. Despite the tendency of some scholars to portray Paul as a sort of Christian version of Philo, the difference is very great indeed. Paul has nothing like Philo's indiscriminate use of allegory. Paul is far more faithful to the concept of salvation-history than is Philo. Paul's eschatology and messianic doctrine alone differentiate him sharply from Philo. We may say without hesitation that Paul is closer to rabbinic Judaism in almost every respect than is Philo. The one point of resemblance between the two over against rabbinic Judaism is that both of them were, consciously or unconsciously, anxious to avoid the full application and literal understanding of the Torah in everyday life.

Before we turn to our comparison with Qumran and rabbinic Judaism we must have some discussion about the use of technical terms. Throughout this work so far we have used the word midrash, without defining it, to refer to a number of passages in Paul's writings, and have even suggested that a fair proportion of what has hitherto been regarded as Paul's free theological speculation is in fact midrash on Scripture. It is probably accurate to say that we have used midrash so far to mean 'written meditation on the significance of a passage of Scripture with a view to bringing out its full meaning'. We must however

examine the meaning of midrash more closely if we are to defend this definition. In so doing we are greatly aided by A. G.
Wright's most able work *Midrash: the Literary Genre* already referred to in the last chapter. Wright's book is specifically written in order to arrive at a satisfactory definition of midrash,
since the word has been used with great inexactitude of late by
some scholars. Wright begins by giving a definition of midrash
in rabbinic Judaism.[12] In this context, he says, midrash means
the interpretation of the Bible, especially of legal texts in the
Torah. Within this area are two sub-areas: *Halakah* and *Haggadah*. *Halakah* is the assembling of legal statements from the
midrash without their proof texts. *Haggadah* is any non-legal
Bible interpretation. It was only later, he claims, that the term
*Haggadah* became restricted to narrative, especially legendary
narrative. This definition reminds us of that of Doeve referred
to on p. 204 above. Now if we are to apply these terms thus defined to Paul, we must conclude that he wrote only *Haggadah*,
since he is never concerned to assemble legal texts, and he is not
interested in the application of the Torah to everyday life. But
in fact in the rest of his book Wright does not follow this strict
definition. He prefers instead to define midrash generally as
'any drawing out of the sense of Scripture', a definition which
is sufficiently close to ours given above for us to be able to
accept it unreservedly.[13] He then sub-divides this large area
into three sections: exegetical midrash, homiletic midrash, and
narrative midrash.[14] The technique of midrash he describes
simply thus: 'one begins with a text of Scripture and proceeds
to comment on it in some way'.

This triple division of midrash is one which suits our approach
to Paul as an exegete very well. We can say that, following this
definition, Paul gives us plenty of Christian midrash. But he
only gives us examples of the first two categories, exegesis and
homily; never of the third, narrative. Most of Paul's midrash is
directly exegetic: he cites the text and proceeds to draw out its
implications. But sometimes he is homiletic, especially in those
places, such as Rom. 8.19f, where he does not specifically quote
a text, but echoes it and lets himself be guided by it. Another
example of homiletic midrash is Rom. 6.7. When we say that
we never find narrative midrash in Paul, we mean that we
never detect him composing, inventing, imagining, or elaborat-

ing narrative additions to the text of Scripture himself. He does of course use already existing narrative midrash; we can point to many instances of this: 1 Cor. 10.1–11, the moving rock; 2 Cor. 11.3–14, the seduction of Eve by the serpent; Gal. 4.29, Ishmael persecuting Isaac; and so on. But he never gives us reason to suspect that he is himself embroidering the biblical narrative. He uses only what came to him by tradition. This is why we demur at Doeve's description of Paul as 'an accomplished haggadist' (see p. 204 above).[15] In so far as the word 'haggadist' conveys any meaning, it would seem to indicate 'one who writes *Haggadah*' (or narrative midrash in Wright's sense of the term). But we never find Paul himself writing narrative midrash. He only uses that of others. He is in this respect a sober and restrained exegete. Indeed we can say as much for all the writers of the New Testament. We are never led to think that they are themselves inventing *Haggadah*, a narrative midrash. This consideration should give us pause if we are ever tempted to do what some synoptic scholars have done, and apply to the stories of Jesus in the Synoptic Gospels the word '*Haggadah*'. Quite apart from the fact that the Synoptic Gospels could not without serious distortion be described as meditations on Scripture, we have no reason to believe that any writer of the New Testament himself manufactured *Haggadah*. It may be indeed that *Haggadah* is not the sort of thing that anyone can be detected in the act of inventing. Perhaps it just grows, or accrues, or appears ready made. Perhaps it is like the peduncles in Teilhard de Chardin's *Phenomenon of Man*; we can never hope to see it in the process of emerging. But the solid fact remains that Paul does not write *Haggadah* in the sense of himself inventing narrative about the Scriptures.

When we attempt to compare Paul as an exegete with the Qumran sectaries, we find ourselves apparently faced with another variety of midrash called *midrash pesher*. This is a technical term coined by modern scholars to describe the exegetical method of the Qumran sect. The word *pesher* signifies 'meaning', and especially in the commentaries on scriptural books which have been recovered from Qumran, the word '*pishro*' ('its meaning') is the regular link between each item in the text commented on and the interpretation given by the commentator. But Wright objects to this new technical term.[16] The *pesher* method of exegesis, he says, is just one possible way of carrying out exegetical midrash, and to turn it into a distinct genus of midrash is only to confuse matters. We will be well advised to follow Wright in this rejection of the phrase '*midrash pesher*'. This is all the more sensible in view of the fact that if we were to accept the new category '*midrash pesher*' we would have to say that Paul employs both exegetical midrash and *midrash pesher* quite indiscriminately, passing from one to the other without noticing it. For example, in Rom. 10.6–8, his thrice-repeated phrase τοῦτ' ἔστιν could very well be a loose rendering of *pishro*; here is *midrash pesher* if anywhere. But there is obviously no real difference between this sort of exegesis and the exegesis which precedes or follows it. The Qumran sectaries used the *pesher* formula because so much of their exegesis consisted in the point-by-point identification of features in the scriptural text with features in their contemporary scene. In other words, what distinguishes their midrash is not its method, or its subject-matter, but its conclusions.

Widening our scope a little, we might well say that as far as technique is concerned there is no fundamental difference in the matter of exegesis between Qumran, Paul, and the rabbis. They are all using *pesher*, in the sense that they all make identifications between persons and events mentioned in Scripture and persons and events mentioned in their own day. Consider, for example, how often in rabbinic exegesis Edom means Rome, or how often the sack of the Temple by Titus is identified as a fulfilment of Scripture. The unfortunate fact that there is as yet no agreement among scholars as to what were the actual contemporary events with which the Qumran sectaries identified their scriptural prophecies does not in the least prove that they did not identify them with contemporary persons and events. The differences between the three, Qumran, Paul, and the rabbis, lies entirely in the different theologies which lie behind the respective traditions. The Qumran sectaries believed that they were living in the penultimate age, the age before the *eschaton*. They felt obliged to wait, obeying the Torah according to the original 'Teacher of Righteousness', until the eschatological war began. Paul, on the other hand, held that Jews and Gentiles alike should rejoice in the salvation already achieved by the Messiah. The rabbis concluded that Israel must go on obeying the Torah according to the tradition of the Pharisees until the coming of the true Messiah. Their various theologies meant that they were interested in rather different areas of Scripture; but it cannot be said that either the sectaries or Paul invented a new method of expounding Scripture. As far as Paul is concerned, his originality consisted not in his technique but in his theology.

One question remains: Does Paul ever employ *Halakah*? Not, of course, in the strict sense of the word. The Christian attitude towards the Torah was such that full-blown rabbinic *Halakah* was out of the question. No writer in the New Testament is so much on the side of Judaism as to try to apply the Torah of Moses to the problems of everyday conduct, least of all with the subtlety and legalistic detail which is so familiar in the Mishna and Talmud. But may there not be occasions when Paul is using a sort of Christian *Halakah* in order to resolve problems of conduct? We would first have to establish what it is that he uses instead of the Torah. The only possible candidate for this is the tradition he possessed of the 'words of the Lord'. We do find him doing this in some places, e.g. 1 Cor. 14.37. But it was most probably not a written tradition and therefore hardly amenable to *Halakah*. Another possible place is one we have already explored, Rom. 12.9—13.10, where we have suggested that Paul is in fact expounding a scriptural text, but expounding it in the light of the way in which he knew Jesus had understood it. If this is *Halakah*, it is very different from the rabbinic *Halakah*, so different in fact that there does not seem to be much point in using the same word for both. The same judgement applies to the instances we have traced of Paul using texts from Proverbs and the Psalms in connection with Christian giving. The line of exposition passes through Christ, and thereby passes out of the sphere of Torah altogether. The sort of purpose that rabbinic *Halakah* was intended to serve simply did not coincide with the needs of the early Christian community.

We now turn to a consideration of Paul as theologian. But we are not concerned here to compare Paul as a theologian with contemporary theologians of other traditions (a task not relevant to our inquiry); rather to inquire how far our study has enabled us to trace the sources of his theology. Now that we have surveyed the method and rationale of his interpretation of Scripture, does it throw any light on the origin of his theology?

Of course the question of the sources of Paul's thought is one which has been actively debated by scholars for more than a century. But it has not very often been asked in the context of his interpretation of Scripture; and it may afford a relatively new approach to the question to do so. Feuillet, it is true, does deal with this subject to some extent in his important work *Le Christ, Sagesse de Dieu*. For example, he suggests that Paul found in the Book of Wisdom some inspiration for his practice of tracing the activity of the pre-existent Christ in Israel's history,[17] and also for his doctrine of the Christian's life 'in Christ'. Both these suggestions seem well founded. One could easily imagine how the language which the author uses about his communion with Wisdom would seem to Paul most appropriate to describe his own experience of communion with Christ. One thinks of 6.16:

> she goes about seeking those worthy of her,
> and she graciously appears to them in their paths,
> and meets them in every thought.

Raymond E. Brown in a series of articles has drawn attention to the undoubted links which exist between Paul's concept of 'mystery' and both the Wisdom literature of the canon and the Qumran literature.[18] We may be sure that a Wisdom motif lies behind the citations in Rom. 11.33–6; so that a picture begins to emerge perhaps of Paul's theological development. The primitive kerygma which he received on his conversion would certainly include the assertion that everything which happened to Jesus was according to the Scriptures (1 Cor. 15.3–4). This causes Paul to search the Scriptures for traces of Christ's activity there. How diligently he searched them we have constantly been able to demonstrate in the preceding chapters. He finds in the Scriptures, besides the patently messianic prophecies, and the references to Israel as the suffering servant, hints of a distinguishable hypostasis within the godhead. The figure of Wisdom is perhaps the point where this hypostasis is more easily perceived, but Paul would perceive it elsewhere also. He would find it in the σύμβουλος, the Counsellor with whom the Messiah is easily identified. He would find it in the νοῦς Κυρίου, and there would be no difficulty for Paul in the fact that the

Hebrew said *rūach*, for he would not have worked out our later theology wherein the persons of the Trinity are clearly distinguished from each other. This in turn leads on to a process of detecting the activity of this pre-existent Being in Israel's history, and so ultimately no doubt to the conclusion that the name Κύριος (which Paul knew of course to be a rendering of the unutterable Tetragrammaton) could signify this pre-existent Son rather than the Father.[19] The end term of this process as far as Paul is concerned is found in Colossians where the identification of Christ with the creative Wisdom is explicit and where we have a Christology theologically as advanced as that of the Fourth Gospel.

All the elements we have mentioned here are important; the suffering servant figure, for example, is vitally important because it enabled Paul to interpret so much of the Psalms in a christological sense. Indeed one of the conclusions of our study must surely be to put a question mark against the assumption so widely held by New Testament scholars that the identification of Jesus with the suffering servant first meets us only in Luke and 1 Peter, and that it did not form part of the very earliest preaching. Paul, we must insist, looks on Jesus as the suffering servant, both of the Psalms and of Isaiah (he would not have seen any point in distinguishing them as sources). Whether this can tell us anything about Jesus' own attitude to the tradition of the suffering servant is another question. But the possibility that it formed part of his understanding of his mission cannot be lightly set aside.

If this is anything like a correct picture of the development of Paul's theology, one important conclusion seems to emerge: in all the elements of that theology which we have considered so far, there is not one that comes to Paul from any tradition of thought extraneous to the Judaism of his day. But this is a conclusion which is denied by the most eminent living scholar of the New Testament, Rudolf Bultmann. Bultmann holds that Paul at several points in his theological scheme borrows directly from two non-Jewish sources, from what he calls Gnosticism, and from the Hellenistic mystery religions. He says, for instance, in his *Theology of the New Testament* that these were the two sources from which Paul took materials,[20] and is equally explicit about the materials he took from each. Thus he says that

Paul describes Jesus' death 'in analogy with the death of a divinity in the mystery religions'. But Paul simultaneously interprets 'Christ's death in the categories of the Gnostic myth, regarding his death as unified with his incarnation and resurrection or exaltation'.[21] Bultmann cites as evidence of this the hymn in Phil. 2.1–11. Two pages later Bultmann specifically denies that Paul confined himself to the categories of Jewish cultic and juristic thinking. On the contrary, he deliberately borrowed from these extraneous sources. In another work, Bultmann says that Paul made use of the Gnostic myth of the archetypal man,[22] and adds a page later that the distinction between the ψυχικός ('natural man') and the πνευματικός ('spiritual man') is Gnostic. Again 'Paul is using mythological concepts derived from Gnosticism when he states that the Old Testament law does not come from God, but was given by angelic powers'. Bultmann sees in 1 Cor. 2.8f a Gnostic concept of the mysterious divine Wisdom which the rulers of the world failed to recognize.[23] And he concludes that 'Christian sacramental theology differs little from that of Gnosticism, if at all'.[24]

As far as concerns the claim that Paul borrowed from Gnosticism, we encounter an historical difficulty, well expressed by R. McL. Wilson in a recent work.[25] Our evidence for Gnosticism as a distinctive scheme of thought, he says, all derives from a time well after that of Paul. Hence Wilson refuses to talk of 'Gnosticism' during the period when the New Testament was being written. He prefers to use the word Gnosis for that period, and to reserve the term Gnosticism for the time at the beginning of the second century when a system emerges. This means that Bultmann's picture of Paul borrowing from an existing body of thought will hardly do. Wilson describes what happened thus: 'Paul, for example, can accept the contemporary *Weltanschauung* of his time but he rejects the Gnostic interpretation of it.'[26] This is perhaps a statement of the case from which Bultmann himself would not dissent. What is very difficult to believe is that Paul could have deliberately borrowed from any source extraneous to Judaism. The relevance of our evidence about his use of the Scriptures is perhaps that it can often suggest an alternative source for his ideas, and, other things being equal, it is much more likely that the Judaistic source is the right one, if it can be shown to exist. Thus the language describing the

Christian dying with Christ, rising with him, suffering with him triumphing with him, could very well have come from Paul's interpretation of the Psalms. We have seen how Paul certainly finds in the Psalms the description of the Son's sufferings, death, and resurrection. It is a truism to say that in the Psalms the subject varies remarkably between the first person singular and the plural; and we have found many places in Paul's writings where what he believed to be true of Christ is applied by him to Christians; compare, for instance, Rom. 8.19f; 8.36; 15.3; 1 Cor. 4.9–13; 2 Cor. 4.14–15; 5.18—6.2; 6.9; 9.9. Indeed this is the great principle lying behind his doctrine of ἐν Χριστῷ. But in one of the passages to which Bultmann appeals for confirmation of his theory, Phil. 2.1–11, Paul concludes this hymn with the exposition in christological terms of a passage from Scripture, Isa. 45.21–3. This is a passage that would hold great significance for Paul, especially as it appears in the LXX. The last sentence of verse 21 runs thus:

δίκαιος καὶ σωτὴρ οὐκ ἔστιν παρὲξ ἐμοῦ.

There is none righteous and a saviour but I.

Paul would know of course that the name 'Jesus' means 'saviour', and we have already suggested that he regarded Christ as the 'Righteous One' *par excellence*. Similarly in the LXX of Isa. 45.25 we read:

ἀπὸ Κυρίου δικαιωθήσονται καὶ ἐν τῷ Θεῷ ἐνδοξασθήσονται πᾶν τὸ σπέρμα τῶν υἱῶν Ἰσραήλ.

From the Lord will be justified, and in God will be glorified, the whole seed of the sons of Israel.

Here is the Pauline theology of redemption by the Father through the Son in one sentence. It may well be, therefore, that this midrash on Isaiah is Paul's original contribution to the hymn, and that those scholars are right who see in this passage not the adoption by Paul of a Gnostic myth, but rather the Christianization of a hymn whose cosmology is not that of Paul, very much as he adapts to his own use the rather different Christology of the early formula in Rom. 1.3–4. This would correspond far more to Wilson's conclusion that Paul accepted 'the contemporary *Weltanschauung* of his time' than to Bultmann's suggestion of wholesale borrowing.

In two other passages where Bultmann finds Gnostic borrowings, our study may perhaps suggest a different interpretation. The first is Gal. 3.19–20, where Bultmann claims that the concept of the Law as not coming from God but from hostile angelic powers is a Gnostic feature. But the notion of the law as 'mediated by angels' (διαταγεὶς δι᾽ ἀγγέλων) is already there in rabbinic tradition, and can easily be inferred from Deut. 33.1–5. Anyway Paul does not deny that the Torah came from God; only that it came directly from God. It is quite possible that in Paul's view the elemental powers had made the law an instrument of the slavery they imposed, but this was not God's purpose. God had his own purpose for the Torah; that is why Paul can call it 'holy', and 'spiritual' (Rom. 7.12,14). The second passage is 1 Cor. 2.6–8f, where Paul speaks in a very allusive way of 'a secret and hidden wisdom of God . . . None of the rulers of this age understood this; for if they had, they would not have crucified the Lord of glory.' This certainly sounds Gnostic; there is evidence later for a Gnostic myth of the hidden redeemer. We must remember Raymond Brown's conclusions, however, about the Semitic provenance of the conception of the hidden Wisdom of God. We need not go outside Judaism in order to find a source for such language. And there is also here in all probability a scriptural inspiration. I have pointed out elsewhere that behind this passage there lies in all likelihood a meditation on Ps. 24.[27] Especially in the LXX version, this psalm can be understood as a dialogue between the redeemer returning to heaven and the powers whom he has vanquished, now for the first time recognizing him for whom he really is. Of course this does not dispose of the question as to the origin of the concept of the hidden redeemer; but it does suggest very strongly that, wherever Paul drew the concept from, it was from a Jewish and not a pagan source.

Another allegedly Gnostic theme which Bultmann finds in Paul is the myth of 'the redeemed redeemer'. Our conclusions in chapters 2 and 3 of this work might seem at first sight to confirm this suggestion: we have argued that Paul regards Christ as having himself undergone the experience of living by faith, justification by faith, and salvation. But this very evidence points away from Gnosticism as the probable origin of this theme: in the first place it is proved and demonstrated in Paul's

eyes by citations from the Psalms and Isaiah in which Israel as
the suffering servant is identified with Christ. And secondly it
implies that Christ lived a real human life on earth, since living
by faith, appealing to God for succour, and undergoing the experience of salvation from (ultimate) death by God are all un-
deniably human experience. A theme, therefore, which is
proved by extensive quotations from Scripture, and which
demands that the redeemer should have had a fully human experience of life, seems to point away from Gnosticism rather
than towards it. At least it does not suggest that Paul himself
found this theme outside Judaism. We leave a consideration of
Bultmann's suggestion as to the origin of Paul's sacramental
doctrine for discussion a little later.

This is not to imply that Paul was not influenced by contemporary ideas: we have just admitted that he does have the
concept of the hidden redeemer; and there can be no doubt that
he does think of Christ as having overcome the hostile elemental
powers, τὰ στοιχεῖα τοῦ κόσμου, on the cross. But it does make a
considerable difference whether we regard these ideas as coming
to Paul because they were already incorporated in one tradition
of Judaism, or because he deliberately borrowed from a non-
Jewish philosophy. In the former case, Paul was in much the
same position as any member of the Qumran community, a
community which was impeccably Hebrew, but which was also
very much open to oriental and even Hellenistic influences. In
the latter case, Paul is a conscious syncretist, deliberately building up a system from both Jewish and pagan elements. The
evidence on the whole does seem to favour the first hypothesis:
Paul was no deliberate syncretist. Based on the Jewish apprehension of the God of Israel, his system did admit of various influences from inside Judaism, a Judaism which was a much
more variegated thing than Bultmann's hypothesis would seem
to allow.[28] In this respect indeed Paul compares very favourably
with Philo. Compared with Paul, Philo is a thoroughgoing syncretist, incorporating all sorts of elements from Greek moral
and metaphysical philosophy into his Jewish religion. Paul, we
may say, though he was sensitive to the currents of thought of
his day, did not allow his fundamental theological insights to be
determined by such elements of contemporary belief as he
accepted.

Cerfaux takes a very similar position to that outlined above: he doubts, for example, whether the oriental myth of the archetypal man has influenced Paul directly and thinks that all can be explained in terms of Paul's study of Scripture and his knowledge of traditional rabbinic exegesis.[29] Cullmann likewise believes that Paul rejected the Philonic doctrine of the two Adams, an earthly and a heavenly, and that he identified the heavenly Adam with the Christ who was to come.[30] G. Delling, in a useful article written ten years ago, suggests that the pre-existence doctrine was to be found at least implicitly in the Christian tradition before Paul received it, and that it came from Judaistic, and not Hellenistic, Christianity.[31] He criticizes Bultmann on the same grounds as Wilson does, that is, for drawing his evidence for pre-Pauline Gnosticism from sources which long post-date Paul's day. And he strongly agrees with Cullmann against Bultmann that the use of the term $Κύριος$ for Christ comes from Aramaic, and not Hellenistic Christianity. It is remarkable how much of what W. L. Knox wrote on the subject of the origin of Pauline theology is still valid today. It is true that his theory of the origin of the Wisdom concept in Judaism (that it was elaborated in conscious opposition to the cult of Isis) would not be accepted by many today;[32] but he has much to say of value about the provenance of Paul's thought. Thus he points out that the rabbis were quite ready to identify the gods of the nations with the rebellious angels; and had no difficulty in regarding the Gentiles as being thereby under the influence of astral powers. Of Gal. 3.19, however, he writes: 'The Torah itself was not the work of the elements; the angels who delivered it on Mt Sinai were the righteous angels who serve God, not the rebels who rule the world.'[33] In the light of a judgement such as this, Paul appears not as the deliberate syncretist of Bultmann's imagination, but as a rabbi who was open to the various influences of thought that we now know did mould the beliefs of his Jewish contemporaries.

May we conclude, then, that Paul took his theology entire from Scripture? Diverse answers have been given to this question. Ellis goes so far as to say, 'Paul's theology stems primarily from the Pentateuch.'[34] But Feuillet writes: 'It would be completely false to imagine that St Paul has taken his Christology from the Old Testament.'[35] Both statements may well be true.

What Ellis means no doubt is that many of Paul's theological terms come from the Pentateuch (e.g. σπέρμα, ἱλαστήριον, διαθήκη, ἀπαρχή) and so does his concept of salvation-history. On the other hand, Paul's Christology comes primarily from the historical figure of Jesus Christ and from the impression he made on his disciples, as well as from Paul's own experience of communion with Christ in the Church. But we have found that very often a passage in Paul that seems to be free theological construction is in fact founded on Scripture. We have even suggested that some of his most familiar phrases such as ἀποκαραδοκία τῆς κτίσεως ('expectation of the creation'), and δικαίωμα τοῦ νόμου ('the just requirement of the law') are drawn from Scripture. Paul, as we have suggested, found in the Psalms a great enlargement of the basic concept of the suffering Messiah, which he received from Christian tradition. And it must be added in justice to Ellis that many passages in the Pentateuch itself which seem to us to have little connection with Christology do in fact seem to inspire Paul. In particular we would mention Exod. 33 and 34 ('the God of mercy'); and also Deut. 32 and 33, the two Songs where early Christians found much messianic material.

To complete our picture of the sources of Paul's theology as far as they are revealed to us as a result of our study, we should give some consideration to the question of how much Paul received from the Christian tradition in which he was instructed after his conversion. This is, of course something of a speculative question, since our evidence for answering it is scanty and debatable; but it is a reasonable question to ask, and one on which our study might be expected to throw some light. By way of clearing the way, we must briefly indicate the point Paul had reached when he came to receive instruction, assuming that he was instructed and that it took place after his conversion, during those 'three years in Arabia'. See Gal. 1.15–18. We assume that at that point he had had the following experiences:

(a) a rabbinic training in Jerusalem, in which very probably R. Gamaliel I had a part. The sharp distinction made by Bultmann between Palestinian Judaism and Hellenistic or Diaspora Judaism does not seem justifiable. Nothing that we have discovered about Paul's methods of interpreting

Scripture requires us to make such a distinction; and, if
there ever was a discernible difference between the methods
of interpreting Scripture in Palestinian Judaism and
Hellenistic Judaism, it is certainly not to be discerned in
Paul's writings;

(*b*) a leaning towards Wisdom devotion or Wisdom speculation. We have already sufficiently indicated what we mean
by this; it was certainly not at that period at all incompatible with what Paul calls 'being advanced in Judaism
beyond many of my own age among my people' and being
'extremely zealous for the traditions of my fathers' (Gal.
1.14);

(*c*) a 'conversion experience'; whatever be the nature of this
experience, it took the form of a call to be an apostle of the
Son of God among the Gentiles (Gal. 1.15–16).

What then was the content of the teaching which the new
convert received? For clarity's sake, we will divide it under four
headings:

1. *The story of Jesus* This would include his birth as a Jew,
some account of his ministry, since Paul knows enough about
this to regard him as a 'servant' (δοῦλος: Phil. 2.7; διάκονος:
Rom. 15.8), some account of his teaching (of which it is generally
agreed there are echoes in Paul's writings), the institution of the
Eucharist, his passion, death, and resurrection.

2. *Jesus fulfilled the Scriptures* We have mentioned this already
on p. 191 above, and we have suggested that some of the texts
which Paul cites from Scripture had already been chosen for
him by the Christian tradition which he received. Scholars
differ widely in their judgement as to how much teaching on
this subject Paul inherited. Dodd writes that both Paul and the
author of Hebrews give us the impression that in scriptural
exegesis 'they are working upon certain accepted assumptions
and that they have behind them a good deal of fundamental
work upon the subject which must have gone on in very early
days'.[36] Among other passages which he regards as already
chosen by Christians he names Pss. 8; 27; 110; 118; Isa. 53; 61;
Joel 2; Hab. 2; Zech. 9; Deut. 18. Munck would add to this list
Ps. 69 and would add the problem of the unbelief of the Jews

as a heritage passed on from the early Church to Paul.[37] Goppelt, in an extremely interesting article written in 1964, insists that the element of fulfilment of Scripture goes back in some form to Jesus himself: 'He proclaimed himself to be, not just one form of the Jewish expectation of the end, but uniquely, in direct immediacy, as the fulfilment of the Old Testament revelation of God.'[38] Under this heading I would certainly wish to put the identification of Jesus as the servant of the Lord in the Scriptures, and would suggest that this goes back to Jesus in some form.

3. *Jesus is Messiah, Lord, and (probably) Son of Man*   By 'Lord' we mean *Maran* ('our Lord') in Aramaic, as well as $K \acute{v} \rho \iota o s$ in Greek, since we take sides with Cullmann and Delling against Bultmann here (see p. 216 above). We add 'Son of Man' because it helps to explain some of Paul's references to Christ as the 'second man' (1 Cor. 15.47), and also does at least suggest that the title 'Son of Man' was actually used by some Christians about Jesus at some period. The great majority of synoptic scholars seem to hold that Jesus did not use it of himself. Paul does not use it, though equivalents may be detectable. The evangelists attribute its use to Jesus. According to prevailing scholarly opinion, it must have appeared and disappeared within a surprisingly short time. Whether Paul received $v \acute{\iota} o s$ or $v \acute{\iota} o s$ $\Theta \epsilon o \hat{v}$ as a title of Christ in his tradition, it is very difficult to say. He could have simply deduced it from his scriptural proofs; but it is quite possible that this also should be included in his tradition.

A number of scholars have maintained that the doctrine of Christ's pre-existence must have formed part of the tradition which Paul received, among them Delling, as we have observed on p. 216 above. Michel says that the apocalyptic tradition thought of the Messiah as pre-existent in the sense that the Messiah has been hidden since the creation.[39] But he does not think that this is the source of Paul's pre-existence doctrine. This seems just. S-B are surely right in their famous Excursus when they conclude that the Messiah was not really thought of as pre-existent in rabbinic tradition. Paul gained his doctrine of pre-existence through his Wisdom theology and not through Christian tradition. At the same time it may fairly be added that the argument from the Scriptures would easily lead on to the notion of pre-existence: if Jesus fulfilled the figure of the suffering servant in the Psalms, and if that figure is frequently represented in the Scriptures as uttering prayer, protest, and even prophecy, it is an easy step to say that it was the same person who spoke through the Scriptures and fulfilled on earth what he had spoken. The pre-existence doctrine of Hebrews and John is not mere plagiarism from Paul, but a conclusion arrived at independently by each writer.

4. *The end-time has begun, and the Parousia will take place shortly*
Few would dispute this conclusion, though there would be much more debate as to whether this element of tradition goes back to Jesus, a question which does not concern us here. Goppelt maintains that there was a tradition of early Christian apocalyptic which is not identical with anything else, because in it the resurrection began the end-time instead of being the final event.[40] He describes Paul as transforming contemporary apocalyptic expectations from the centre outwards: Christ was the centre. What enabled Paul to do this was his typology. It was, he says, the typology of Abraham, and not the apocalyptic scheme of history, that enabled Paul to break with the Torah and he concludes: 'The central problem of Paul's theology is the relation of typology to apocalyptic methods of handling [scripture].'[41] In other words, Paul's principles of biblical inter-pretation, far from being a mere epiphenomenon of this theo-logical activity, played a crucial part in his thought. If we ask, 'Where did he get his notion of typology from?' we cannot give a simple, unidimensional answer. In a sense we are asking *the* question about the originality of Paul as a theologian. We can, however, point out that typology as such is found in the Old Testament. It is found in rabbinic exegesis in as far as the rabbis regard the Israel of their day as the recipient of the promises made of old and as continuous with the Israel of Scripture. It is particularly close to a homiletic method of treating Scripture; it is impossible not to draw lessons for the contemporary congregation if one is preaching on events in sacred history.[42] It is an obvious conclusion if one is considering salvation-history as relevant to one's own day. For example, we may be sure that the author (or authors) of the Book of Wisdom

did not dilate upon Israel's experiences in Egypt and the wilderness merely out of an interest in history; the way in which, contrary to the general tenor of Scripture itself, Israel is there presented as the innocent party and the Egyptians are denigrated shows a plain desire to relate the predicament of Israel of old to the situation of the Jewish community in Alexandria. Above all, typology was used by the writers of the New Testament to relate the significance of Jesus Christ to the revelation of God in Israel's history. It was the impact of the career of Jesus that impelled them to do this. We have thus arrived at the subject of our next chapter.[43]

Before we move on to that, however, we must briefly examine one more aspect of Paul's theology on which his study of Scripture may throw some light, and that is his eucharistic doctrine. On p. 212 above we quoted Bultmann as saying that 'Christian sacramental theology differs little from that of Gnosticism, if at all'. These are vague terms, for 'Christian sacramental theology' could cover a very wide range of thought indeed, and our knowledge of Gnostic sacramental theology is severely limited and dates from a time well after the close of the New Testament period. But Bultmann does certainly believe that Paul's sacramental theology derives from Gnosticism or from the Hellenistic mystery religions, or both. So it is quite in order to refer to him as we examine this question. We may perhaps be allowed to put aside the suggestion of direct borrowing by Paul from the mystery religions, for two reasons. First, Raymond Brown has made a very strong case for the view that the New Testament language about 'mystery' stems from the Wisdom tradition within Judaism. Its links are with Qumran, not with pagan cults. This does not, of course, preclude the idea that Qumran itself, or its antecedents, may have been influenced by non-Jewish currents of thought. But it does argue against direct borrowing. Secondly, it seems impossible that Paul in 1 Cor. 10.21 would have warned his converts against sharing in the 'cup of demons' and 'the table of demons', if he had consciously borrowed his sacramental theology from the pagan cults. These two phrases must refer to non-Jewish religious feasts. He could not at the same time warn his converts against these feasts and borrow the theology and language of their initiates. If there was borrowing, it must have been indirect and unconscious.

But was there? Can we find no other source for Paul's sacramental language? It seems that we can, to some extent at least. It can be shown that Paul finds in the Scriptures types and analogies for the Christian sacraments; and we can learn something about the sources of his sacramental theology by studying his use of Scripture.

From the careful examination of 1 Cor. 10.1–11 we can learn a certain amount about how Paul understood the sacraments; and with this we can put 2 Cor. 8.15, another passage where Paul refers to the giving of the manna. First and foremost, we learn that these types of the Christian sacraments were the gift of the pre-existent Christ. They were supernatural ($\pi\nu\epsilon\upsilon\mu\alpha\tau\iota\kappa\acute{o}\varsigma$) food and drink; they were so given as to produce neither a sense of scarcity nor superfluity. Next, to use the language of much later sacramental theology, the existence of the sacrament did not destroy the substance of the species. Paul never means to deny the reality of the event which formed the type; and in the scriptural narratives of the giving of the manna and the water from the rock it is made quite plain that the manna did afford physical nourishment and the water did satisfy thirst. In any case the use of Exod. 16.18 in 2 Cor. 8.15 is for the purpose of assuring the Corinthians that in fact nobody will lack that which they really need; if the manna had been regarded by Paul as purely symbolic or immaterial, it would not have served the purpose of his argument. Thirdly, it was possible in Israel of old not to receive these gifts with faith; which means no doubt not to see their supernatural origin, to regard them as purely natural phenomena. This, says Paul, brings judgement and perhaps death.

All this is fairly obvious, and most of it has already been pointed out by editors. But in our treatment of Rom. 11.15f on pp. 108f above we claimed to have traced another quasi-sacramental reference in Paul. Christ is the bread, for which the dough or the grain provides the materials. Christ is also the olive tree. The first fruits of the bread is, according to Scripture to be offered to God. This is a type of Christ's self-offering on behalf of all Christians. And we have suggested that this picture of Christ as the loaf and Christians as the materials for the loaf, coupled with the picture of Christ as the olive tree and Christians as the branches inhering in the tree, affords a parallel to Paul's explicitly eucharistic language in 1 Cor. 10.1–13. It is true of course that olive oil is not wine, but neither is water, and water could serve Paul as a type of the wine in the Eucharist. Already here we have the materials for a sacramental theology which owes nothing to the influence of the pagan mysteries.

From this we proceeded (p. 112 above) to pursue the theme in 1 Cor. 5.6–8, where a connection is established with the paschal offering. The paschal lamb is taken by Paul as a type of Christ's self-giving. Thus it appears that there is a connection between offering and Communion, since the paschal feast was essentially a religious meal. We are still entirely within the ambit of a purely Judaistic circle of thought, but we are already far advanced in a theology which connects the Eucharist with Christ's sacrifice.

The next step is perhaps the most significant, for it leads us to a comparison of 1 Cor. 10.14–21 with Deut. 32.13–14 (see pp. 113f above). Here in Deuteronomy a description is given, which Paul would understand in an eschatological sense, of the good things which Israel could have enjoyed, or would in the future enjoy, through obedience to God. It includes oil, wine, and bread. The lesson is driven home that what prevented Israel from taking advantage of this was their lack of obedience; and words are used which Paul, we know, understood to mean that the Gentiles would in time come to enjoy these benefits. Paul, we may confidently claim, has found in this passage in Deuteronomy a foreshadowing of the Eucharist. The messianic feast that was to have been the prerogative of Israel has, because of Israel's disobedience, been thrown open to the Gentiles as well.

Now this evidence does suggest that Paul drew a great deal of his sacramental theology from his study of Scripture. Basic to it all is his belief that all believers in God have always in some sense been 'in Christ'. It was Christ, pre-existent, who was the author of the promises and threats in Deut. 32. The victims and even the rites of the Torah could be seen as destined types of the perfect sacrifice which Christ was to make in the end-time. (We have noted elsewhere that this application of types, though found here in Paul, is more characteristic of the Epistle to the

Hebrews.) From these passages, and of course in the light of contemporary sacramental practice, Paul draws conclusions about the meaning of the sacraments in the Church of his day, lessons about Christ's presence at the feast, about our sharing in Christ through the Eucharist, about our being incorporated in Christ through baptism, about our offering of ourselves in Christ through the Eucharist, about the dangers of receiving unfaithfully. In fact one begins to wonder whether all of Paul's sacramental theology could not quite easily be explained in terms of his study of these passages of Scripture.

Of course it is not suggested that Paul came to these passages with a mind that was a *tabula rasa*. We have already supposed that Paul had an interest in Wisdom devotion and speculation, and this would certainly make him prone to find in Scripture both the figure of the pre-existent Christ, and also types of Christ's activity in the end-time. But this is not at all the same thing as saying that Paul's concept of the Christian's union with Christ was the same as the concept in the mystery religions of the union of the initiate with the god. Thus Bonnard's conclusion does not seem really justified: 'Consequently a text such as 1 Corinthians 10.1–13 manifestly indicates that the spirit of hellenistic sacramentalism had already penetrated the churches in the time of the apostle Paul.'[44] If Paul's language can be explained in terms of his scriptural study, we are not justified in seeking for its source in some area completely outside Judaism, least of all in a religious tradition which Paul goes out of his way to repudiate.

# 11

## A VINDICATION OF
## PAUL'S INTERPRETATION

All special studies of Scripture should aim at some point to show their relevance to some profound theme of Christian theology. In these studies this theme has quite often been referred to, but always postponed; it is the question of the validity of Paul's interpretation of Scripture. Again and again we have pointed out some piece of Pauline exegesis, and have had to add such words as 'strange though this interpretation may seem to us today'. And again and again the question must have formed itself in the reader's mind: How can such a method of exegesis be justified? Surely this is neither what Scripture originally meant nor what it really means? Now we have at last reached the point where we can face this question and ask ourselves whether Paul's method and principles of biblical interpretation can in any sense be justified today. But this question itself brings up a still deeper one: What is the relation of the Old Testament to the New? Consequently our final question must be dealt with in two chapters. In the first we try to confine ourselves to the question of interpretation. In the second we turn to the deeper question and attempt to pursue one or two themes of importance that seem to emerge out of it. In both chapters, though we begin from Paul's interpretation, we do not hesitate to extend the illustrations and arguments to cover the whole of the New Testament. This is something which has been done by most of the authors whom we shall quote. Since we have no intention of postulating a sharp difference between the principles of interpretation of Paul and of any of the other traditions in the New

Testament, it is something which seems quite justifiable in the circumstances.

We begin by making one point which may seem obvious, but which needs to be made in view of the way in which a number of eminent scholars treat this question. The point is this: if we are to come to any satisfactory solution of the relation of the Old Testament to the New, we cannot simply ignore or rule out of court the solution to this problem adopted by the New Testament writers themselves. In other words, it will not do simply to bypass the New Testament interpretation of Scripture as something which has no relevance for modern Christians. If the men who wrote the New Testament were so mistaken in their approach to the Old Testament that they have nothing here in common with us moderns at all, then our hope of arriving at a satisfactory relation to the Old Testament is dim indeed. It is, however, surprising how many authors who write on this topic do in effect rule out of court the New Testament approach.

We have already noted Bultmann's restriction of the New Testament interpretation of Scripture to the single theme of prediction, and have attempted to show how unjustified this is. But this is not all that Bultmann has to say on the subject. In another essay he considers specifically Paul's interpretation of the Old Testament, and he claims that Paul interprets the Old Testament exclusively in terms of law: 'Thus for Luther, as for Paul, the Old Testament as a whole appears under the concept of Law, that is, as an expression of the demanding will of God.'[1] But this is a complete misunderstanding of how Paul viewed Scripture. It is true that he can very occasionally use νόμος to refer to Scripture as a whole; e.g. 1 Cor. 14.21. But he can also distinguish the Torah from the prophets, as in Rom. 3.21. And he certainly did not view what Bultmann calls the Old Testament, but what Paul thought of simply as Scripture, purely in the light of Law. On the contrary, Paul argues strongly that Scripture contained promise and faith before it contained Law. And as we have seen, he finds Christ, full of grace and truth, frequently in Scripture, even in those parts such as Deuteronomy which would seem on the surface most obviously to be Torah. Starting from this mistaken assumption, Bultmann draws all sorts of conclusions, e.g. that the Old Testament for Paul does not apply to Gentiles. But Abraham, at a crucially important moment in his life, was a Gentile! Bultmann adds: 'Thus the Old Testament is interpreted [by the New Testament writers] out of the eschatological consciousness that all preceding things were provisional and only now receive their true meaning.' This is only true up to a point: the frequent recognition of the pre-existent Christ in Israel's history gives a more permanent significance to the Old Testament than Bultmann appears to allow for. He goes on to say that scriptural proof in the New Testament is no proof at all: 'the faith stood firm without predictive proof'.[2] But, we may ask, what faith? Can it be defined without reference to Israel's religious tradition and therefore to Scripture? Anyway, suppose part of the faith was that Jesus saw himself as fulfilling Scripture? If there are traces of the grace and promise of God in the Old Testament, as Bultmann himself allows, does that not leave room for prophecy, or typology?[3] Eric Voegelin, criticizing Bultmann in the same symposium, says in effect that, no matter how much New Testament or later writers may have overdone the claim, there must be a link between the Old Testament and the New. The New Testament writers 'sensed the link to exist, even though they used inadequate instruments for expressing their conviction'. And he accuses Bultmann of surrendering 'the autonomy of his science to one of the intellectual eruptions of a diseased age'.[4]

Carl Michalson also contributes an article to this symposium which suggests that the New Testament approach to Scripture can be simply laid aside by moderns. He writes: 'On the prophecy-fulfilment model . . . one is more impressed with the discontinuity between the Testaments than with the continuity, unless from a stance from within the New Testament he typologizes or allegorizes the Old Testament faith after the historiographically loose method of the early church.'[5] However, he himself concludes that the real link between the Testaments is God. We may suggest that if this thesis is examined in sufficient depth it will be found to be fundamentally the same as the New Testament approach. But this is yet to be shown. John Bright, we find, does also in effect rule out the New Testament interpretation of the Old Testament in the course of examining the various theories about the relations of the two Testaments which hold the field. He rejects the patristic method of reading a Christian meaning into the Old Testament by means of allegory and typology: he seems, however, to suggest that perhaps the New Testament writers were less guilty in this respect than their successors.[6] The typology of the New Testament he describes as 'a more or less charismatic expression of these writers' conviction that all Scripture—nay, all that had ever happened in Israel—had come to fulfilment in Christ'. And, he adds, this method 'scarcely represents a systematic attempt at exegesis at all'. This off-hand treatment of a profound subject is only too characteristic of the way scholars have viewed New Testament exegesis of Scripture. Had Professor Bright been able to devote more time to studying Paul's methods for instance, he would certainly not have dismissed them as unsystematic. And it seems hardly fair to use the epithet 'charismatic' to mean in fact 'incoherent'.

On the other hand, it is plainly impossible for modern exegetes to accept or themselves adopt the New Testament method of scriptural interpretation in anything remotely resembling a literal manner. In fact very few scholars have attempted to do so. Apart from the conservative evangelicals, many of whom are suspicious of too luxurious a typology anyway, the only scholar who has attempted anything of the sort in recent years is Vischer, whose work we discuss presently. The reasons for our complete inability to adopt the New Testament method of interpretation are not far to seek. In the first place, we are in an essentially different position from theirs: they did not have any 'New Testament'. Their only Bible was the Torah, the Prophets, and the Writings. None of the authors of the New Testament was consciously writing sacred Scripture.[7] Consequently the problem posed itself in different terms to them. We have to reconcile or explain the discrepancies and inconsistencies between the two Testaments; that is, between the two volumes, both accepted as sacred Scripture. The New Testament writers had first to find Christ in the Scripture and only then face the question of inconsistencies between what they knew of Christ and what they read in Scripture—though it is doubtful whether the problem was ever considered by them in terms of discrepancies. So where we have tended to be apologetic, they are aggressive. Where we have tended to see the Old Testament in the light of Christ, they have tended to see Christ in the Old

Testament. We have tended to stress the incompleteness, the obscurity of the Old Testament. They tend to dwell on its prophetic, instructive character. Where we have been negative, they have been positive. And when New Testament writers do stress the incompleteness and imperfection of the Old, it is the old dispensation or the old covenant that they contrast with the new, not the old Scriptures. As we have already pointed out, from about the year A.D. 200 till the present moment, all Christian theologians have been in an essentially different position with regard to the Hebrew Scriptures from that which the New Testament writers occupied.

Secondly, we cannot adopt their method of interpretation because so much of it depends for its validity on assuming that to be history which we must view as legend or myth. We might well cite von Rad's useful distinction between legend (which he calls saga) and history; history, he says, describes a single event; legend casts an aura of typical quality over the event which it enshrines, e.g. Abraham's sacrifice. Legend also narrates events in terms of the narrator's own age, and conveys actual historical information about its own age, though not about the event it narrates.[8] To apply this to a very simple example, Paul in 1 Cor. 10.4 finds the pre-existent Christ present as giver of the water from the rock in the wilderness. Quite apart from the fact that Paul actually follows a non-scriptural legend which represents the rock as following Israel throughout the wilderness period, we cannot be at all confident that the incident of the water from the rock is historical at all. It may, for instance, recall some perfectly natural spring of water. What then becomes of the 'supernatural drink' ($\pi\nu\epsilon\upsilon\mu\alpha\tau\iota\kappa\grave{o}\nu$ $\pi\acute{o}\mu\alpha$)? Again, it seems an inevitable conclusion that Paul identified the pre-existent Christ with the presence of Adonai in the pillar of cloud. But can we have the slightest confidence that the pillar of cloud is historical? Or, to take an example from Romans, Paul makes a great point of the fact that Abraham was justified by faith before he was circumcised. But the utmost we can say about Abraham historically is that he may have existed; details of his being circumcised, his conversation with Adonai, his sacrifice of Isaac, and so on, are the dimmest of dim legend and correspond, if they correspond to realities at all, to historical events that have no relation to Abraham. Thus a vast amount of detailed salvation-history, on which so much detailed typology depends, must be regarded by us as quite incapable of being defended as history. Consequently when we try to make sense of New Testament typology, we must admit that the types, in the shape of persons or events, either never existed, or happened in so different a manner from the way they are related in Scripture, that they become valueless as types

It might be argued that this does not really matter. These events and persons, claimed by Paul and other New Testament writers to be types, may not have been historical, but they witness to the faith of Israel. What the New Testament writers are really doing is claiming that Israel's faith is fulfilled in Christ. After all, the Scriptures of the Old Testament are largely a record of what Israel believed about God. God is revealed in their faith. It is therefore quite legitimate to find cross-connections, foreshadowings, and types between the faith of Israel of old and the faith of the Christian Church.

There is much truth in this argument, as we hope to show presently, but it will hardly stand as a defence of the modern use of typology and 'real presence' as the New Testament writers used it. In the first place, it has removed the typology from the realm of events. We are no longer seeing events, or even historical persons, as foreshadowing the Christian era. We are merely claiming that what Israel (or, to be more accurate certain writers in Israel) believed about God is fulfilled in Christ. This is not what the New Testament writers meant by typology and 'real presence'. For them, the remarkable illumination of the Scriptures consisted in the fact that they found there a record of the pre-existent Christ active in Israel's history; or that a certain pattern of events foreshadowed in a remarkable way the pattern of events revealed in Christ's career. If most of this must be regarded as not having been really connected with historical events, but with the faith of Israel, for the New Testament writers at least it would lose its point. In fact we hope to show that, even on the level of Israel's faith corresponding to Christian faith, this process of foreshadowing and finding of types has significance. But its significance does not consist in the fact that the point which the New Testament writers saw in it is valid. It consists in the reason for their attempting to find types at all. Besides, if we are asked to substitute a schema whereby Israel's faith corresponds to Christian faith for a schema whereby persons and events in Israel's history correspond to the events of the historical career of Jesus, we are at once faced with the question: Are we interpreting rightly the faith of these Old Testament writers? What did they really mean when they wrote their narratives? And here, as we shall be seeing, we encounter fresh difficulties if we try to apply New Testament exegesis literally in the light of what we know about the Scriptures today.

This historical difficulty is well illustrated by a consideration of the work of the one recent scholar who has attempted to apply New Testament methods of exegesis literally, Wilhelm Vischer. He writes a commentary on the Book of Genesis, and this is an excellent model from our point of view, since it brings up the issue of historicity in a sharp and challenging manner. We take his exposition of the significance of Eve, of the meaning of Enoch, and of Noah's blessing in Gen. 9.27.[9] He quotes with approval Luther on Eve: 'And so Eve, the mother of us all, is rightly praised as a holy woman, full of faith and love.' We must protest that Eve is not even legend, she is an eponymous myth, and an eponymous myth cannot be holy, loving, or faithful. Of Enoch Vischer writes: 'In him occurs the amazing miracle that he did not die.' There is nothing amazing in the very early belief that a mythical figure did not die, and there is therefore no miracle at all involved. Take away the history, and you take away all the point of Vischer's exposition. So also with the blessing of Noah. Referring to the light of Christ Vischer writes: 'This light Noah sees by the Holy Spirit, and although he uses obscure words, he none the less prophesies very definitely that the kingdom of the Lord Christ will be built and planted from the tribe of Shem and not of Japhet.' Against this exegesis we must lodge three objections:

(a) Noah never existed; he is a figure of pure myth. He cannot therefore have prophesied anything.

(b) Even if we take it as the work of an early Israelite writer, the word 'prophesy' is inappropriate. 'Prophesy' suggests 'intentionally predict', and the writer did not intentionally predict anything about Jesus Christ.

(c) The names Shem and Japhet do not correspond to any

historical realities, since pre-Abrahamic genealogies have no relation to history.

In short, Vischer comes to grief over the question of history. Type as type, and to a large extent prophecy as prophecy, depends for its validity on actual history. If there is such a thing as a genuine type, it must have been presented in an actual historical context which bears out the character of the type. Thus, for instance, the life of the prophet Jeremiah could well be taken as a type of Christ, because his actual historical experience was to some extent reproduced in the experience of Christ. Genuine prophecy must have something fundamental in common between the prophecy and fulfilment. Thus the account of the servant of the Lord in Isaiah chapters 40–55 could be claimed as a genuine prophecy, since there are important elements in common to it and to the life of Christ. But the great majority of what the New Testament claims as type and prophecy lacks these characteristics.

Amsler actually defends the typological method of exegesis (though not necessarily for use today). He says in the first place that the sense discovered in Scripture by New Testament writers depends on 'the revelational significance of historical events'.[10] This is precisely the difficulty. If they turn out not to be historical events, or not to have the character which Scripture presents them as possessing, how can they still have a revelational significance? Amsler goes on to suggest two advantages which the typological method of exegesis offers: first, it enables us to see in the Old Testament an authorized witness to Jesus Christ. And secondly, it means that the records in the Old Testament, even if now outmoded, can be regarded as words witnessing to the Word.[11] What this comes to is a recommendation of the typological method on the grounds that it Christianizes the Old Testament. We shall be coming to a very similar conclusion presently, but it is no recommendation of this method as suitable for today. We must find a different method, one not incompatible with what we know about the Scriptures.

John Bright's defence of the value of the patriarchal narratives seems to encounter exactly the same difficulty as does Vischer's technique, different though their approaches to the

Old Testament are. Bright defends these narratives on the grounds that in the characters of the Old Testament he frequently recognizes himself, and thus the very shortcomings of these characters can be of value.[12] Abraham, for instance, tried to pass off his wife as his sister, thereby using deceit. Jacob was 'a cheat and a crook', and so on. But we may protest that it is often very doubtful whether the authors of the biblical narratives intend that we should regard their heroes as imperfect and full of shortcoming. For example, is it not much more likely that the writers who describe Abraham's deceitful behaviour about Sarah in Egypt intend us to admire him? Are we not even perhaps intended to admire Jacob for the clever way he tricked his brother? It will not do to say: 'Ah, but we with our higher morality learned from Christ now know that Abraham was a liar and Jacob a crook', because they are not sufficiently solid as historical characters for us to be justified in passing judgement on them. It is like saying that Aeneas in Book IV of the Aeneid was a prig and a hypocrite. What we really mean is that there were elements of the prig and the hypocrite in Virgil. Anyway these patriarchal characters are just as significant for what they meant in the long tradition of Jewish and Christian exegesis; and Jews and Christians agreed, as we shall be seeing, in whitewashing any less amiable characteristics such figures may have shown.

Our difficulty is well expressed by James Barr.[13] The attempt, he says, to formulate the centre of the tradition as an event or series of events which are then described as 'an act or the acts of God' is most unsatisfactory. When one questions the tradition closely, the alleged 'acts of God' dissolve into something very different: 'The "historical" acts of God make sense only because they are set within a framework of conceptions, stories, and conversations which cannot be expressed by any normal use of the word "history".' This is precisely what we meant when we said above that what looks like history turns into the record of Israel's faith. But typology at least does not apply if what is intended is that some element in Israel's faith in the past corresponds to some element in the Christian dispensation.

We might well seem to have said enough to convince the most enthusiastic champion of typology that the New Testament method of scriptural interpretation will not work for us today.

But we should mention three other reasons before we pass on to the next part of our subject. Strictly speaking they are all part of one reason, the fact that our understanding of how Scripture came to be written is different from that of both the New Testament and traditional theology up to about two hundred years ago. But it is worth distinguishing the three implications of this fact. We may set them out as follows:

1. The confident use of typology requires that we assume all the writers of Scripture to have shared a unified outlook. The meaning of what they write is to be judged primarily by the meaning of the type, and not primarily by the immediate circumstances of the writer. Thus in Rom. 9.25–6, Paul quotes Hosea to the effect that God is going to call those his people who formerly were not his people. Paul has no hesitation in applying this to the accession of the Gentiles. We today would insist that, in view of the context in which Hosea wrote it, the prophet meant that Israel, previously rejected by God, is in the future once more to be called his people. It is not that Paul would say: 'Yes, that is the literal meaning, which must be ignored, in favour of the typological meaning.' That would indeed be allegorizing the prophet. Paul rather says: 'The accession of the Gentiles is what the prophet always meant', and he might well go on to claim that Hosea's two children, with their symbolic names, are types of the accession of the Gentiles. The fact that the rabbis could treat the text in a very similar way warns us indeed against rash conclusions about the effect of 'Hellenistic' allegorizing in Paul.[14] But it also shows us the impassable gulf which exists between the exegesis of Paul, of Qumran, and of the rabbis on the one hand, and our modern method of exegesis on the other. The two cannot be reconciled *on the level of exegesis*.

2. The view of inspiration held by the writers of the New Testament is one which we cannot accept today. As we have seen, attempts have been made to rehabilitate New Testament (or at least Pauline) views of inspiration. It has been suggested that Paul held a more flexible, open, charismatic view of inspiration than did those who were under the influence of Greek notions of divine inspiration, whoever we may put into this category. And it is true that various approaches to inspiration

can be found inside the New Testament itself. As we have seen, Paul did not have exactly the same view of inspiration as did the author of 1 Peter. And he in his turn must be distinguished in this respect from the author of 2 Peter. But when all necessary distinctions have been made, every writer of the New Testament is far more like every other writer of the New Testament, and like every rabbi whose opinions have come down to us, as far as the question of inspiration is concerned, than he is like any modern scholar. We do not have the conception, as did all the ancient interpreters of Scripture, of one Spirit carefully directing and co-ordinating God's revelation in Scripture: so that it does not really matter as far as Paul is concerned whether a given utterance is attributed to Moses, or David, or Isaiah, or directly to the Holy Spirit. All is of equal value and authority. The whole conception of the inspiration of Scripture is one which suffers from considerable obscurity among modern scholars and there is a great deal of diversity of opinion. But nobody except the most extremely conservative evangelicals would espouse a conception of inspiration such as Paul held.

3. We, if we are wise, cannot Christianize, moralize, or white-wash Old Testament characters as did the authors of the New Testament. I have carefully inserted the qualification 'if we are wise', because in fact we do, in common homiletic practice at least, commit all these errors. We hold up Abraham as a model of Christian faith, conveniently forgetting that he was a poly-gamist. We extol the wisdom of Solomon, omitting to mention that he was a most oppressive ruler. We praise the courage of Elijah in witness on behalf of God, forgetting that this witness included the massacre of the prophets of Baal. Now the New Testament writers certainly did this: as we have seen, Abraham is presented as the model of the justified sinner. Sarah is held up by the author of Hebrews as another model of faith,[15] though in fact Gen. 18.12 represents her as laughing bitterly in unbelief. Paul joins the rabbis in blackening the character of Ishmael; and so on. But the New Testament writers had much more ex-cuse for this than we have. It was part of the tradition of exege-sis which they had inherited. Moralizing Old Testament characters whose conduct fell short of later standards of be-haviour was the only method they had of making sense of

Scripture as revelation. Christianizing the Old Testament was, as we shall be suggesting presently, an absolute necessity for them if they were to hold a consistent doctrine of God. But these conditions do not apply to us, and inasmuch as they do not apply, we realize our vast distance from their world of thought and the impossibility of our using today their methods of interpreting Scripture.

Does this mean, then, that we must despair of the attempt to find something in common with the New Testament approach to Scripture? Were the writers of the New Testament entirely wrong in imagining that there were any unifying themes uniting the two dispensations? Certainly not. We can, I believe, find common ground with them and understand why they had to interpret the Scriptures on a christocentric basis, if we are willing to stand back to some extent from the problem, and to take a long view. Since this work is primarily concerned with Paul, we will set out our solution in terms of Paul's situation.

Perhaps it may be helpful to approach the question to some extent *ab extra*, not exactly as 'objective' students of religion, but at least as Christians who are aware of what both history and the sociology of religion might have to say about the first century A.D. in the Near East. The great problem posed by late Judaism was how to liberate for the world a religion which had so deep, living, and splendid an apprehension of God. The great obstacle (as it is to this day) was the demand for minute observance of the Torah. One way out would have been the path indicated by Philo, though not followed by him. This would be to isolate the moral teaching and monotheist theology, and to reject the element of scrupulous Torah-observance, and of salvation-history. But the fate of liberal Judaism and Unitarianism alike in our day warns us that this is no satisfactory solution. The 'livingness' of the God of Israel is an essential element in his nature and if you ignore salvation-history you find that this 'livingness' is precisely what you have lost. You are left with a concept of God and with moral and spiritual values. Still looking at the first-century A.D. situation to some extent *ab extra*, one could say that it required some shock, some new force, to effect the catalysis or precipitation of Judaism into the world at large. That shock was administered by the life, teaching, death, and resurrection of Jesus of Nazareth.

But there was a danger that the impetus and new direction given by him might have petered out or developed into an esoteric Judaism. We have the example of the Qumran Community to warn us. The impetus given by the original 'Teacher of Righteousness' petered out into speculations about angels, unbalanced emphasis on correct calendar observance, and wishful dreams about the coming eschatological war. Daniélou in his book on Jewish Christianity has sketched a striking picture of what a pure, unadulterated Jewish Christianity might have been like: a Christology expressed in terms of an angelology; symbols instead of doctrines; *haggadah* developing towards a jungle of legend. All this was averted by the conversion and subsequent career of Paul. Paul was both fully sympathetic to all that was vital in Judaism and fully alive to the implications of the new faith. He was compelled therefore to face squarely the problem of Torah-observance. How could he maintain at one and the same time that he was faithful to the Scriptures and that the ceremonial prescriptions clearly set down in Scripture need no longer be literally observed? He neither allegorized them entirely away nor declared that they were fundamentally mistaken. He maintained instead that what God had now revealed about himself in Jesus Christ had been there all the time and could therefore be discovered in the Scriptures. Without infringing the particularity (Tillich would call it concreteness) of the ceremonial laws of Judaism, without detracting from the uniqueness of the revelation in Christ, he did maintain that the living God of the Old Testament had always been of the same nature as he had now revealed himself to be in Christ. To state it in inaccurate and anachronistic but perhaps expressive language: Paul taught that Adonai had always been the Father and the Son. The way he did this was by his method of interpreting Scripture, and in particular by his doctrine of the pre-existent Christ active in Israel's history.

Schoeps, in discussing just this question, does not seem to have got the elements of the problem exactly in focus. He writes: 'The abolition of the Law is for Paul part of his messianic teaching',[16] and he goes on to say that, since the coming of the Messiah had abolished the Law, Paul had to find another

function for the Torah, and that he found it in the Law's use as
the discoverer of sin. But this is hardly accurate: Paul does not
say: 'The Torah, which fully represented the will of God for the
Jews until the coming of the Messiah, has now been abolished.'
He holds that the Torah as a way of life never was the will of
God for anyone. God had always willed that man should live
by faith; Abraham had actually done so. Moses had pointed
out that the way of faith was what God wanted. The Torah had
never been anything but a *paedagōgos*; it never was a school-
master; it was always more like a policeman. The dispensation
of faith and grace was always in some sense available for
Israel.

No doubt Paul's doctrine of the pre-existent Christ was inspired by what we have called his Wisdom-devotion. But this in
itself is an indication that within Judaism there was already a
feeling of the inadequacy of a monolithic monotheism. To express the living and active God of Judaism some more varied
conception was needed. So we may legitimately claim that
Paul by his exegesis of Scripture, and especially by his doctrine
of the pre-existent Christ active in Israel's history, was doing
what Christians must always be prepared to do: he was expressing the true relation of Christianity to its matrix Judaism. He
was at one and the same time freeing the God of Israel from a
necessary connection with a system of religion which carried an
intolerable burden of primitive practice (taboos, lustrations,
even circumcision), and ensuring that the deepest insights into
God's nature revealed in Christ were not obscured by sub-
Christian elements inherited from Judaism. We today believe
that we can achieve the same result by other methods. We use
the concept of an imperfect and developing revelation, still an
essential feature of modern Christian theology, no matter how
much it may be necessary to purge it from elements of Victorian evolutionary thought. This modern method of ours has
its problems of course, as our ensuing discussion will make
plain. But for good or ill we must make use of it; we cannot
revert to Paul's method. We can however approve the intention
behind Paul's method and accept that intention as our own
today. Paul by his methods was attempting to safeguard what
we, if we are faithful to traditional Christianity, must safeguard
also: the presentation of Christ as the full revelation of the God of

Israel, and the retention of all that is true in the Old Testament.

We can even perhaps follow Paul in rather more detail. We have claimed that Paul appealed to a faith-period before the Law-period, and saw the relation of faith as overlapping the Law-relation at both ends; it had existed before the Law came and continued after the Law was shown to be outmoded. We cannot of course exactly assent to Paul's time-scale; everything must be put much later (still less can we follow the author of Hebrews in tracing the faith relationship back into the mythical period of Abel, Enoch, and Noah). But undoubtedly, before the rise of Judaism as such, there was much more freedom and much more room for faith apart from Torah-observance. The sacralization of the Law, the regrouping of the religion of Israel round the written Torah, was a reaction to the Exile, a movement intended to exclude pagan influences, and to rally Israel as a nation-church. Before it took place, Israel was not a church, and as a nation was by no means immune to foreign influences in its religion. But this vulnerable condition carried with it the possibility of a wider, freer faith and a more immediate relation to God. This can surely be traced in the lives of some of the canonical prophets, Amos perhaps, Hosea certainly, supremely in the life of Jeremiah. We might even, though rather more precariously, go farther back and point out that David, though the quality of his faith may be open to question, was no legalist. What restricted his relation to God is more likely to have been superstition than legalism. The elements in Scripture on which Paul seized in order to show that there was a way of faith before there was a way of the Torah constitute genuine evidence of the existence of a faith-approach to God. In this sense at least, the Christian faith can claim that it is fulfilling some features in Israel's faith (though we cannot call this typology, as we have seen). As has been often pointed out, Deuteronomy is a book of faith as well as a book of the Law. Paul did not invent this evidence; this is not one of the elements provided by the universalizing tendency of the Septuagint, or dependent on Christian hindsight for its validity. It was there in the record of Israel's religion. It means that there were men of faith during the period of the formation of the Pentateuch, though we cannot identify them with either legendary or historical characters quite as confidently as Paul did. This is a point which C. H. Dodd has recognized in his commentary on Romans: 'But Paul is nevertheless so far justified', he writes, 'that the ideal of Deuteronomy is far more inward and spiritual than that of the Law of Holiness and the Priestly Code of which the Law is composed.' Dodd maintains that Paul recognized 'without the aid of modern criticism that there is a stratum in the Pentateuch which goes deeper than the bald legalism of the other faith'.[17] These remarks apply to Paul much more than to other writers of the New Testament, but they do go some way to justify the principles, though not the details, of Paul's interpretation of Scripture.

We must revert to those principles. Paul, we have said, was rightly concerned to emphasize that the historical revelation of God in Jesus Christ was not inconsistent with what was already known of God through Scripture. He was concerned, in fact, for the consistency of God. And surely any Christian theologian must share the same concern. If we believe that anything genuine was known of God through the experience of Israel, then we must believe that the God who was thus known is the God whom we know more fully in Jesus Christ. In this sense, all Christian theologians must 'christianize' the Old Testament. We are so far mesmerized by the historical, critical approach to the Old Testament that we may sometimes be in danger of forgetting that when we speak of the God revealed in the Old Testament, we are still speaking about one, real, living God, who exists and always has existed, and who has made himself known as the same God to Isaiah or Jeremiah, if he has made himself known to them at all. The revelation in the Old Testament may have been imperfect, but the very word imperfect implies that there is a perfect, or at least a less imperfect. He was imperfectly revealed as what? As the God more perfectly known in Jesus Christ, we must answer. This surely is what Paul was fundamentally trying to express by his approach to Scripture. We may well quote with approval Martin Luther here, as himself quoted by Wilhelm Vischer:[18] 'Adam was a Christian long before the birth of Christ . . . He saw not Christ with his eyes; nor do we. He possessed him however in the Word, as we possess him in the Word.' The example of Adam is well chosen, since owing to his completely mythical character, he may stand for any person in the history of Israel who may be regarded as having known God. Anyone to whom God spoke in the Old Testament period heard the God who is revealed in Christ. If you believe that God is supremely revealed in Christ, then any revelation of God which took place in the Old Testament period is in a real sense a revelation of Christ.

We should at this point refer to a theme which we nave traced throughout our study of Paul's interpretation of Scripture, the theme of God-in-Christ. Again and again we have maintained that Paul is not so much saying that God or that Christ spoke or revealed himself or acted, so much as God-in-Christ. Indeed we have at times suggested that in Paul's view the entire history of God's dealings with mankind could be summed up by the formula 'God-in-Christ'. This is a feature of Paul's thought which has often been misinterpreted. Klausner was misled by it into accusing Paul of abolishing the activity of God the Father altogether.[19] Bultmann, on the other hand, is moved by the same phenomenon to conclude that Paul identified the pre-existent Christ with God the Father (he does not make this an accusation against Paul, since he heartily approves of the alleged identification). I quote from the work of André Malet, an interpreter of Bultmann's thought whom the master himself wholly approves: 'Those New Testament expressions which *identify* Christ with God—not which make him equal with God as a second person alongside the first—so that Christ becomes God himself in a different mode of being, make it clear that we must not think of Christ as a hypostasis.'[20] A little later he writes: 'He [Paul] treats God and the Kyrios as interchangeable.'[21] He sums it up on a later page as follows: 'To sum up, the christological titles . . . do not mean that Jesus is a divine hypostasis. If we understand them in that way we rationalise God, blind to the fact that [Christ's] lordship, his divinity, is always sheer event and rules out any sort of objectification. The ancient Church went wrong by interpreting the word of God in terms of Greek metaphysics.'[22]

One of Bultmann's examples to prove this thesis is taken from Rom. 14.9–10, where the alternation between *Christ* judging the living and dead and our all appearing before the judgement seat of *God* seems to tell in favour of Bultmann's argument. But in the last chapter (p. 213 above) we suggested that the distinction between Θεός and Κύριος is based on a distinction which Paul discovered in his Greek version of Isa. 45.25. And we have found no reason to believe that Paul identified the Father and the Son in the way Bultmann suggests. Quite the reverse: we have noted innumerable examples of the pre-existent Christ, especially in the Psalms, being understood as addressing God (Rom. 15.3 is one example out of many). Bultmann would be the first to acknowledge that to address someone is quite incompatible with being identified with him. We have even found examples of dialogue between the Father and the Son. A good instance is 2 Cor. 6.2, which we claim is based on Isa. 49.1–8. In that Isaiah passage, we maintain, Paul discovers just precisely a dialogue between the Father and the Son which puts any notion of identity out of the question. The truth seems to be that Bultmann has let his own rejection of what he calls objectification influence his view of what Paul believed. Bultmann, for reasons which Paul could not possibly have appreciated, objects to the notion of an hypostasis, so he argues that Paul had no such notion either. In fact the work of scholars such as W. L. Knox in the last generation, and A. Feuillet in this, has made it pretty clear that Paul did believe in Christ as an hypostasis of God. He did, strictly speaking, find two divine beings referred to in Scripture. To write, as Bultmann does, 'Christ's lordship, his divinity, is always sheer event and rules out any sort of objectification' may be admirable as existentialist philosophy, but it would have been entirely meaningless to Paul. Nor is it altogether consistent on Bultmann's part to condemn the early Church for interpreting the word of God in terms of Greek metaphysics. In what terms were they to express their doctrine of God? Strictly Hebrew thought either gave them no terms at all, or would have offered language so heavily mythological that the terms which Bultmann wishes to demythologize look simple and literal in comparison. Besides, in turning to Greek metaphysics, the early Church was only doing in its day what Bultmann is doing in his, attempting to express its doctrine of God in language comprehensible to contemporary man. It is difficult not to conclude that, justified or not, the early Church was more successful in its expression than Bultmann has been. The traditional trinitarian doctrine of three Persons in one substance seems better fitted to express the relation of the Father to the Son than is Bultmann's formula 'Christ becomes God himself in a different mode of being',[23] which appears to be old-fashioned modalism.

We claim therefore that Paul was prepared to apply his formula 'God-in-Christ' to the utmost limit. God was in Christ not only in the incarnation reconciling the world to himself. He was also in Christ in his activity throughout Israel's history. He was even acting in Christ when he created the world. However Paul arrived at such a doctrine, it is not one which can be described as jejune, crude, or (to use a favourite epithet of Bultmann's) primitive. It implies the existence and activity of a God whose nature consists in active self-giving love (whom Paul in Rom. 9.16 calls 'the God of mercy'), a love which culminates in the supreme act of redemption carried out by Jesus Christ on the plane of history. We seem to have arrived at a conception of God startlingly like that of traditional Christianity, except for one omission. There does not seem to be any hint of a Three-in-One. Remarkably enough, Bultmann, despite his rejection of objectivization, does make room for a sort of modalist trinitarianism in his account of Paul's theology. Malet represents Paul as thinking of the Spirit as 'a third mode of being'.[24] Is this really representative of Paul's thought? Does he regard the Spirit in the same way as he regards the Son?

This is a far-reaching question. To answer it thoroughly one would have to go far beyond the limits of this study. But we may say that, in Paul's interpretation of Scripture, there are no traces of his regarding the Spirit as he regarded the pre-existent Christ, that is, as something like a distinguishable hypostasis. Paul nowhere suggests that the Spirit, like the Son, can be detected as active in Israel's history, referred to by some specific title such as Κύριος. He does of course believe, as every Jew believed whether he was orthodox or sectarian, that the prophets spoke by the Holy Spirit. But this is nothing like as distinctive as his doctrine of the pre-existent Christ. In the two places where he cites a Scripture passage that seems to mark out the spirit of the Lord as something like an hypostasis (1 Cor. 2.16 and Rom. 11.34) he identifies the *rūach Adonai* with Christ. We may well remind ourselves that Wisdom in the Book of Wisdom is a spirit; and the great passage in praise of Wisdom in Ben Sira by implication identifies Wisdom with the spirit of the

Lord that brooded over the waters of creation (Ecclus. 24.3). But Paul identifies Wisdom with Christ, not with the Spirit. The only place where Paul gives the impression of finding the Spirit as a separate hypostasis in Israel's history is 2 Cor. 3.17, and this is one of the most obscure passages in all his works.[25] In any case, those who argue that Paul means by the words ὁ δὲ Κύριος τὸ Πνεῦμά ἐστιν 'and in that passage in Exodus 34 the word Κύριος means the Holy Spirit', have the very greatest difficulty in avoiding the conclusion that Paul identifies Christ with the Holy Spirit. Indeed, if it comes to a question of identification, a much better case could be made out for the thesis that Paul identifies the Son with the Spirit than that he identifies the Father with the Son. There is not in Paul as firm a basis for the doctrine of the Trinity as there is for the cosubstantiality of the Father and the Son.

But we have no reason to conclude from this that the later doctrine of the Trinity is incompatible with Paul's account of the relation of the Son to the Father. Paul in fact devoted much more thought to the question of the relation of the Son to the Father than to the question of the relation of the Spirit to Christ or to the Father. We might perhaps draw an analogy with the later development of Christology in the Church. Just as Christian theologians could only give proper attention to the status of the Holy Spirit in the godhead after they had come to a decision about the status of the Son, so with Paul. His first concern was with Christ and his relation to God. He inherited a purely soteriological doctrine of Christ: Christ was the great act of God redeeming mankind. Without in any way lessening the importance of Christ as God's redeeming act, he did go a long way towards establishing the ontological relation between Christ and God. In this process the question of the Spirit's status was not immediately involved, and in fact Paul left it undecided. One could conclude that Paul identified the Spirit with Christ; but there is also evidence that he distinguished the two. We may not commit Paul either to a consciously binitarian or a consciously trinitarian doctrine of God. All we can say on the basis of the evidence is that, in order to safeguard the reality of God's redeeming action in Christ, Paul was compelled to postulate a distinction within the godhead. The later doctrine of the cosubstantiality of the Spirit, and therefore the doctrine of the Trinity as such, was not within Paul's theological horizon. But it could well be argued that it was by no means incompatible with his intentions. In order to safeguard the conception of a God who comes forth in redeeming love to enter human history, it is by no means arbitrary to claim that he must be also regarded as returning to himself 'bringing many sons to glory'. And such a claim implies the cosubstantiality of the Spirit.

We have suggested that Paul may well have thought of all redeemed mankind as having been 'in Christ' from the beginning. This prompts another reflection: May not this concept of Christ as the norm of God's activity throughout history help to some extent to account for Paul's surprising lack of references to the details of Jesus' historical career? We today are accustomed to the thought of the 'scandal of particularity'. How could a brief period of thirty years make a crucial, even a cosmic, difference to the entire history of mankind, before and after the event? Admittedly the ancients did not have our vast perspective of human history; and admittedly the prospect of the Parousia cut off for the earliest Christians any unlimited panorama of future history. But Paul shows no sign of being embarrassed by our 'scandal of particularity'. For him the scandal is the scandal of the cross, the scandal of a crucified Messiah who had lived the way of faith and not the way of Torah-observance. He gives no sign of being scandalized (or aware that others were scandalized) by the thought that God has in Christ intervened in history during a period of thirty years, and that this was God's only intervention in history. May this not be because he did not hold that this was God's only intervention in history? Certainly as far as the history of the Jews is concerned, Paul held that God had constantly revealed himself as active to redeem, to judge, to warn, to guide. And equally certainly Paul held that such revelations were revelations of God-in-Christ. It is true that the appearance in what we call the incarnation was unique, because it was 'in the flesh' as none of the other appearances had been, and because in it God's redeeming action was supremely, effectively, finally, and permanently to be apprehended. But the newness of the new covenant was not an absolute newness in time. Something had been known about it in the period of Israel's former history.

Perhaps Paul was aware of the need to present a doctrine of God's relation to human history that did not confine itself absolutely to those thirty years of history. Certainly he was not entirely christocentric in the sense that he confined himself to the Christ of history exclusively. We must remind ourselves also that, according to Paul, Abraham was justified (perhaps justified in Christ) while he was still a Gentile, and that this opens the theoretical possibility of a theology of the history of the Gentiles as well as of the history of Israel. It is a possibility of which, as far as we know, Paul did not avail himself, though the author of Hebrews did. In Heb. 11 Abel, Enoch, Noah, Abraham, are all represented as knowing God by faith, all technically Gentiles when they came to faith; all, except Abraham, remaining Gentiles all their lives. In fact neither Paul nor the author of Hebrews gives us a theology of history in full; but perhaps one motive for Paul's scanty references to the details of the historical life of Christ is that he was anxious to preserve the full perspective of history. If so, this is a motive which we ought to respect.

Since our main theme in this chapter is the validity of Paul's interpretation of Scripture, we must now give some attention to those scholars who tend to defend his interpretation. We begin with K. Weiss. Writing on the theme of Paul's use of cult language from the old dispensation, Weiss maintains that Paul does not simply spiritualize Temple sacrifice, etc., in the sense of making them remote from history or actuality.[26] On the contrary, he believes that everything which was foreshadowed in the old dispensation, faith, circumcision, the Torah, only receives its true reality and force in the new. One should speak, he suggests, not of a typological or spiritualizing of the cult, but of a saving or eschatological realization of it. One may welcome this emphasis, in as far as it suggests that Paul did not ignore the historical reality of what was recorded in Scripture. But one may well ask whether Weiss has made sufficient allowance for the reality of Christ's presence in Israel's history. For example, Paul believed that before circumcision was instituted Abraham had already been justified by faith. There does not seem, therefore, much scope for an eschatological fulfilment of circumcision in baptism or anything else. In Hebrews the apparatus of the cult gives as imperfect a foreshadowing of the true sacrifice as Adam does of Christ in Paul. And, in Paul at any rate, salvation

was not only realized in the *eschaton*. Christ appeared for redemption as well as for judgement in the wilderness, though it
was at best a temporary salvation.

Von Rad, in an essay in Westermann's book, makes an interesting point: the New Testament, he says, does not provide
'any norm, any handy rule for its [the Old Testament's] interpretation'.[27] He can only suggest that for New Testament
writers the solution is 'in Christ', precisely the conclusion to
which our study of Paul has led. But after all, difficult though
this solution may be to apply, it is a solution. The christocentric
interpretation of the Old Testament is not at all a 'handy rule',
but it is a criterion. Von Rad goes on to claim that the typological interpretation of the Old Testament is justified because
there is a real correspondence between the events of the Old
Testament and of the New. This he attributes to the fact that
it is the same God who is revealed in both Testaments. In view
of the necessary warning by Barr referred to above (p. 233), we
may well be wary of justifying typology on the basis of a real
correspondence of events. But we can certainly agree that the
link between the Testaments is to be found in the nature of
God. This will be largely the theme of our last chapter. Smart
comes to very much this conclusion also: 'The faithfulness of
God, on which everything depended for Israel, was the consistency of his nature in his relation with Israel in past, present
and future',[28] and he guards himself against the danger of too
much reliance on alleged history in the Old Testament by adding later on that what provides the pattern in salvation-history
is the character of God, not the character of history.[29]

Goppelt, in an article in *New Testament Studies* (Dec. 1966),
brings together the findings of a seminar held in Heidelberg in
1966.[30] He says that, though we cannot follow Paul's rabbinic
methods of proof, we can claim that his interpretation follows
the main drift of the Old Testament Scriptures. Thus Paul's
interpretation of the Red Sea incidents is as true to their meaning as is the description of the incidents themselves in Scripture.
This is in effect to give up the claim that in typological exegesis
real event corresponds to real event, and to fall back on a
correspondence of faith to faith—perfectly legitimate, as we
have seen, as long as we do not claim that it is typology. He goes
on to reject the view that the connection between the Testaments

is one of historical continuity or of cyclic pattern: what connects the two is the promise and fulfilment of God.[31] This is certainly what Paul would have said. But can we moderns be so confident about the promise? It would seem wiser to say that the promise is one form of revelation. This is how one important tradition in Israel expressed in terms of fulfilment shows that it is the same God who is revealing himself. In his most recent work Bring discusses the validity of Paul's exegesis, and finally concludes that in effect we must not ask what the text originally meant, but what God meant by it.[32] Paul's method of exegesis meant in practice putting the Old Testament in its proper context of salvation-history culminating in Christ. We would only be inclined to assent to this way of putting it if it were expressed in the most general terms. No doubt, for instance, those who understand the character of God as revealed in Christ believe that God, when he inspired Hosea to utter the prophecy about *Lō'-'ammi* and *Lō'-rūchāmah*, intended that ultimately the Gentiles should be given as full knowledge of himself as the Jews had received. But is this the same thing as saying that this is what God really meant by Hos. 2.23? Surely we must distinguish between what Hosea meant by the words he uttered and what God meant by his whole dispensation in Christ. To confuse the two does not help matters.

We turn now to those writers who are more sceptical of the possibility of finding any link between New Testament interpretation and the modern approach to the Old Testament, although we shall discover that there is often much ground in common between the two groups. Schrenk in *TWNT*, commenting on the origin of the rabbinic method of interpretation of Scripture, writes: 'Hillel's seven rules are only the beginning of a system of schematic, syllogistic, scholastic mishandling of the text.'[33] This seems unduly severe. Only looked at from the point of view of moderns, who want to find out primarily what the text meant when it was written, can rabbinic exegesis be called 'mishandling'. The rabbis needed to expound the text primarily for the purpose of *Halakah*. Christians needed it primarily for instruction about Christ. Neither tradition was consciously ignoring the original meaning, but neither was primarily interested in that. Later on in the same article, Schrenk writes about the early Christian interpretation of

Scripture. He says that 'the peculiar problem of scriptural interpretation for the early Christians was that in one sense the Scriptures were outmoded, and in another they were still absolutely authoritative'.[34] As we have seen, as far as Paul is concerned, this is not the case. The Scriptures were not outmoded at all; the covenant on Sinai, recorded in the Scriptures, was. The problem was therefore more restricted than Schrenk suggests, how to explain those parts of Scripture which appeared to command Torah-observance as the way of life intended by God for the Jews. E. L. Wenger asks in a brief article the very relevant question: Does typology give us real information? 'Is it a genuine pattern of relationships equally valid with the pattern of causal relationships?'[35] He writes primarily with Austin Farrer's treatment of Mark's Gospel in mind, where the question of historicity is very sharply posed. He concludes that we may have to demythologize typology. That would at least be better than simply dismissing it as Bultmann does; and perhaps the contents of this chapter may constitute such an enterprise.

W. Pannenberg, in his important study of the doctrine of the incarnation, has some relevant remarks on Paul's use of the doctrine of the pre-existent Christ.[36] We must retain the concept of the pre-existent Son, he says, as a witness to Jesus' eternal unity with God. He actually believes that the doctrine pre-dates Paul, and he rejects Bultmann's thesis that it originated in a Gnostic redeemer-myth. He therefore considers that the Wisdom-tradition has had no influence on Paul, and can be traced only in John. He thinks pre-existence is a logical conclusion from the belief that the Son was sent by God. Pre-existence, he suggests, can be defended as a symbol of the fact that the Christ-event and Jesus' eternal relation with God must be held together. We do not think that Pannenberg has fully appreciated the evidence that Paul did have a doctrine of Christ as the pre-existent Wisdom; but fundamentally we must agree with this, though this is hardly the way we would want to put it. Pre-existence, we would rather say, is a witness to the fact that God as he is known in Christ has always manifested himself as such a God. We would, in fact, wish to demonstrate the God of self-giving love as revealed in Israel's history. Pannenberg seems to acknowledge this when he adds that it was dangerous when incarnation theology cut loose from Old Testament history.[37]

Michalson, in an article already quoted, suggests that thoroughgoing typology is really 'creeping Marcionism'. When Samson taking the gates of Gaza and Elisha raising the widow's child are types of the resurrection, then we have abandoned the reality of the Old Testament altogether.[38] Michalson wants to see Samson, Elisha, and Isaac (often taken as types of Christ) 'as figures of real historical life, undergoing real moral crises, real human pathos, real trust in the faithfulness of God'. If this is his argument, his examples are not well chosen: Isaac is hardly a figure of history at all; Samson has far too much of a solar cult about him to be a suitable subject for biographical study, and even Elisha is surrounded with a halo of legend. We do not know nearly enough about these characters to be able to appreciate their moral struggles. Perhaps it is better to emphasize the faithfulness of God, which is, after all, historically manifested in the faith of those who wrote the Old Testament narratives. If all we want is moral crises and human pathos, we can probably find better (and often more historical) examples in Plutarch's *Lives*.

This is perhaps a proper place to note a comment of Barr's on typology.[39] He says that 'New Testament writers use typology mostly to explicate "a mainly christological kerygma", and that this is why they tend to concentrate on events'. There is much truth in this, but it does not always apply. For example, in his citation of Exod. 33.19 in Rom. 9.15, the citation is used mainly to show that God's mercy is of the very essence of his nature, not to show that he has mercy on some and not on all. Admittedly, if this is typology, the type consists in the theophany to Moses; but the main point of the type is to show the consistent character of God. Similarly the citations of Isaiah and Job in Rom. 11.34–5 seem to refer to the eternal being of the Son rather than to any particular event, unless the creation of the world be regarded as such.

Baumgärtel's book *Verheissung* has a valuable discussion of the New Testament interpretation of Scripture.[40] As the title of his book indicates, he views the relation between the two Testaments under the category of promise and fulfilment. Christ is the Yes to the Old Testament for its covenant, though not for its method. We Christians are part of salvation-history; the Old Testament therefore speaks to us as much as Jesus Christ does.[41] The Old Testament does not help us with Christology. It is only related to Christ through the claim: 'I am the Lord thy God'.[42] Baumgärtel constantly emphasizes that the Old Testament is promise, not prediction. He admits that there is an element of prediction in the New Testament, but claims that it is confined to the function of recognition;[43] and he adds that for Paul typology largely takes the place of prediction-fulfilment. The types, he says, were intended for us and not for Israel of old.[44] He concludes that we cannot use the method of typology today, but that the principle behind it is still valid.[45]

There is much that is refreshingly true here, particularly Baumgärtel's emphasis on the character of God as that which affords the ultimate link between the old dispensation and the new. His suggestion that in the New Testament fulfilment of prediction is usually recognition, is a profound one. We may question, however, whether 'promise and fulfilment' can safely be given so fundamental a part in the relation between the Testaments. It is certainly true that Paul, for example, sees many promises in Scripture which he claims are fulfilled in Christ. But can we always be sure that this is really what the promise in question means? 'It does not say, "And to off-springs", referring to many; but, referring to one, "And to your offspring", which is Christ' (Gal. 3.16). Is it not safe to bring the whole relationship back to the character of God? Paul could not have found God-in-Christ reflected in the Old Testament if there had not been something there corresponding to God-in-Christ. We need not tie ourselves to how Paul thinks it is revealed. We can hardly agree with Baumgärtel when he claims that the types were meant for us and not for Israel of old. Looking at the matter for once from Paul's point of view, we must say that there was only one event or set of events comprising each type. It was valid in its own right, and its full meaning could have been understood at the time. The reason why so many Israelites fell in the wilderness was that they did not have faith (1 Cor. 10.5f; Heb. 4.2). If they had had faith they would have recognized the pre-existent Christ. Perhaps those who did not fall recognized him. Moses certainly did.

Eichrodt, in an essay in Westermann's *Essays on Old Testament Interpretation*, cites Baumgärtel's objection to typology as such: 'The Old Testament facts are not facts at all; thus the

Old Testament history of salvation is not history of salvation at all.'[46] Eichrodt answers first that one need not be so sceptical about Old Testament history. And secondly that 'If Israel's faith in deliverance deceives us about every particular revelatory act of God, then the basic promise "I am the Lord thy God", which supposedly stands behind it, can be no more than an imaginary reality, a treacherous and dangerous guide'. This particular debate reminds us strangely of the similar debate concerning the historicity of the Gospels. But we can agree with Eichrodt that we need not suppose that there were no acts of God and no revelation in the events of Israel's history. Very often, however, we would look for those events and those acts in quarters quite different from where the New Testament writers found them. Where the New Testament writers found such revealing acts in the patriarchal stories and the history of the desert wandering, we would be more inclined to look to more recent events: the great Assyrian crisis in the eighth century B.C.; the decline and fall of the Judean state in 620–587; the exile and the return; even in the Maccabean period. The New Testament writers did not wholly ignore these events (witness Heb. 11), but they bestowed their main attention elsewhere. We, however, claim that the principle is the same. We, like them, see God's character disclosed in the events of history.

One of the great merits of Professor Barr's recent work *Old and New in Interpretation* is that he does not hesitate to put penetrating and even disturbing questions about convictions that have long gone without challenge. At one point in his work he puts just such a question, one very relevant to the subject of this chapter: Does the New Testament, he asks, really provide the true fulfilment of the Old, or is the New Testament form of fulfilment purely arbitrary?[47] We hope to try to answer this question more fully in our last chapter, but in the meantime it may usefully serve as an introduction to the last topic to be treated in this chapter. We have attempted to show that the New Testament writers in general and Paul in particular gave to the Scriptures of the Old Testament a christocentric interpretation.[48] This was not, to put it mildly, the only conceivable interpretation and it was rejected by the great majority of those who were the authorized interpreters of those Scriptures. Does it not seem a very impudent claim in the light of history? Nietzsche, with his usual penetration, has seen this point and expressed it with quite characteristic bitterness. He wrote:

> What can one expect of the after-effects of a religion which in the centuries of its foundation performed this unheard-of philological farce in regard to the Old Testament? I mean the attempt to withdraw the Old Testament from the Jews by asserting that it contains nothing but Christian doctrine and belongs in truth to the Christians as the true people of Israel, whereas the Jews had merely arrogated its possession to themselves. The Christians gave themselves up to a passion for re-interpretation and substitution— a process which cannot possibly have been compatible with a good conscience. However much Jewish scholars protested, it was affirmed that everywhere in the Old Testament the theme was Christ and only Christ.[49]

Any honest Christian scholar who has read, for example, Justin's *Dialogue with Trypho* will feel much sympathy for this point of view. Again and again Justin insists on a Christian interpretation of the Old Testament in passages where all modern scholars will side with Trypho, especially when Justin backs up his arguments with texts which rely for their demonstrative force on the LXX translation claimed as superior to the MT. But in fact, when we examine more carefully than Nietzsche, at any rate, did both the Hebrew Scriptures and the Jewish interpretation of them, we shall see that he has unduly simplified the issue. It is not a simple question of which interpretation is right, Jewish or Christian. We cannot take for granted that there is any one self-authenticating interpretation of the Old Testament that will ultimately be accepted by the sheer force of its simple appropriateness. In the first place, the Old Testament is not one homogeneous corpus of writings belonging to the same period. There is a great deal of reinterpretation to be found inside the Old Testament itself. Von Rad, for instance, points out that, since there was a conviction in Israel that no words of a prophet could be without effect, some of Hosea's words against Northern Israel have been reinterpreted to apply to Judah. Indeed he claims that the prophets were constantly engaged in interpreting the tradition.[50] Thus what Christians call 'the Old Testament' is neither homogeneous, nor, as we shall be emphasizing presently, is it clearly defined in either content or time. Once we realize that we are dealing not with a corpus of documents but a religious tradition, we must concede that the process of reinterpretation never ceased right up to the time of the writing of the New Testament.

Secondly, the rabbinic interpretation of Scripture, which is presumably what Nietzsche meant by his reference to the Jewish understanding of the Old Testament, was, in its own way, just as 'arbitrary' as the Christian one. Christians interpreted it on a christocentric basis. The rabbis interpreted it on a Torah-centric one. Both interpretations involved considerable exegetical manoeuvres. If the Christians had to find Christ in the desert wanderings, the rabbis had to find the Torah in the story of Abraham. If the Christians thought they saw Jesus every time the Psalms mentioned the anointed one, the rabbis thought they saw the Torah every time Proverbs mentioned light. It is true that there is more in the Hebrew Scriptures about the Torah than there is about the anointed one, but even so a great deal remained that had to be explained or explained away: Elijah's behaviour on Mount Carmel, quite illegal by even the laws of Deuteronomy; the free way in which the early kings of Israel (Saul, David, Solomon) offered sacrifice even though they were not priests; Amos' strange failure to condemn the Northern Kingdom for not obeying the Torah's rules about the central altar; and so on. The rabbis in fact had to carry out a task of reinterpretation of the Scriptures which was as great as that which Christians undertook, not so much because (as was the case with the Christians) it was not always easy to find their central theme in the Scriptures, but because they had to cover the whole Scriptures. Even Esther and the Song of Songs (indeed, reading the Talmud, one is tempted to say 'especially Esther and the Song of Songs') had to be explained in a Torah-centric sense. The New Testament writers, because they were much more confined in time, did not have so huge a task.

In this respect surely J. D. Smart is unfair to the rabbis when he writes: 'The rabbis focussed their attention upon the law and had little appreciation of the prophets.'[51] One ventures to suggest that he can hardly have read very much of the rabbis to make so partial a judgement. The rabbis had as much appreciation of the prophets as had the writers of the New Testament,[52] but their preoccupation with the Torah meant that the freedom, almost the iconoclasm, of the greatest prophets could not really influence them. The writers of the New Testament, with their relatively free attitude towards the Torah could appreciate this element better. Equally misleading is Smart's claim that typology is not found in orthodox Jewish exegesis.[53] Typology is already found in the Old Testament itself. Von Rad points out that within the Old Testament the wilderness period had already become typical of disobedience, punishment, and forgiveness, and he refers to Pss. 78,106, and Ezek. 20.[54] We have already pointed out that there is incipient typology in the Book of Wisdom, and that it is to be found, though not eschatologically applied, in the Talmud and elsewhere. Bläser has much better expressed the rabbinic principle of Scripture interpretation: 'According to the rabbinic view, the Law is the contents and the deeper meaning of the entire Scriptures.'[55] His final judgement in the same article is equally true: 'It is not that Scripture leads Paul to Christ; but on the contrary through Christ Paul recognises the Scripture as a witness to Christ.'[56] In other words, Christians brought to Scripture a principle of interpretation partly, it is true, derived from Scripture itself, but partly derived from outside Scripture, from the career of Jesus of Nazareth. Rabbinic Judaism brought to Scripture a different principle of interpretation. This principle, Torah-observance, was much more obviously derived from Scripture, but was not for all that the only possible principle, nor was it one that was self-authenticating. In order to apply it consistently the Scripture often had to be supplemented, adapted, and even sometimes wrested from its original meaning.

The point we are making becomes clearer still when we turn to other interpretations of Scripture apart from those of rabbinic Judaism and Christianity. We can point to at least three. The first is of course that of Qumran. Qumran's interpretation differed from that of rabbinic Judaism not in being less Torah-centric, but in claiming that the true community of the Torah was their sect and not the nation of the Jews based on the Temple cultus in Jerusalem. They also differed in their belief as to how the Torah ought to be obeyed, especially in the matter of calendar observances. Above all, they interpreted the prophets in a way quite different from that of either orthodox

Judaism or Christianity. The prophets had in fact spoken about the historical events surrounding the origin of the sect, the persecution of the original 'Teacher of Righteousness' and so on— events which were apparently mostly already fulfilled when the sectarian commentators wrote. This principle of interpretation, invented no doubt by the original 'Teacher of Righteousness', has no more intrinsic claim to be the right one than have the other two.

Secondly, there was Philo. Philo no doubt regarded himself as a Jew of unimpeachable orthodoxy, but in fact his principle of interpretation of Scripture was totally different from that of orthodox Judaism, Christianity, or Qumran. He wanted to show that Moses had incorporated into his writings all the philosophy which contemporary Greek culture could provide. His technique for achieving this end was allegory. Of all the principles of interpretation which we have considered so far, this is least likely to receive from anyone today the epithet 'self-authenticating'. But it was an interpretation and was not without its influence on later Christianity.

Lastly, there is Islam. Islam does not of course regard the Hebrew Scriptures or the Christian New Testament with anything like the reverence it accords to its own Scripture, the Qur'an. But in the Qur'an there is undoubtedly implicit a principle of interpretation of the Bible as a whole. That principle derives from the conception of Mohammed as the last and greatest of the prophets. No one who was not an orthodox Muslim would claim that this principle of interpretation has very much foundation in either Hebrew Scriptures or Christian New Testament. But it is as well to remind ourselves that here is, very much alive today, still another tradition of interpretation of our Scriptures.

We would be wrong to suggest that, even in the matter of re-interpretation, any given tradition must proceed upon one principle only. In fact all the five distinct methods of interpretation we have enumerated do proceed upon one general principle each. The exception might seem to be Qumran, but we could subsume Qumran's exegesis reasonably enough under the heading: 'the Sect is the true Israel and therefore to the Sect alone is the true method of Torah-observance revealed'. We must remember that any attempt to moralize the more primitive parts of Scripture, any desire to whitewash scriptural characters, is in fact a move towards making Scripture as a whole more consistent, and therefore implies a principle of interpretation. When the Chronicler, dealing with David's census, represents Satan and not God as inciting David to commit the sin of organizing a census, he is in fact attempting to present a more consistent picture of God (cf. 2 Sam. 24.1 with 1 Chron. 21.1). When the rabbis and Paul represent Ishmael as persecuting Jacob in Gen. 21.9, they are in fact trying to justify Abraham for his apparently harsh conduct towards Hagar, and thereby perhaps they are attempting to present a more consistent picture of the God of Abraham.

We must conclude therefore that the New Testament interpretation of the Old Testament cannot be justified by us today in detail, but that it can be justified in principle. No single tradition can legitimately claim that its principle of interpretation is obvious, demonstrative, or self-authenticating. All must be justified, if they are to be justified at all, by something more than the fact that they can appeal to the contents of the Old Testament. As far as the New Testament writers' interpretation is concerned, they can appeal to the character of God as he has revealed himself to Israel and in Jesus Christ. In our last chapter we must try to estimate the validity of this appeal.

# 12

# THE RELATION BETWEEN
# THE TESTAMENTS

Though our main theme now is the attempt to find the best
scheme for relating, as Christians, the Old Testament to the
New, we cannot approach this theme directly. This is because
'the Old Testament' is not a clear-cut concept which all can
refer to and hope to understand each other at once. We have
committed ourselves to approach this theme, so to speak,
through the eyes of the writers of the New Testament. We must
in this chapter cease to look at the Old Testament through their
eyes and make our own assessment of it. But we cannot do this
until we have fully acknowledged what it is that we are dealing
with. We are in fact dealing with a religious tradition rather
than with a corpus of ancient writings. It is true that ultimately
we as Christians today must relate ourselves to that corpus of
ancient writings which we call the Old Testament. But we can
only do so adequately when we have satisfied ourselves that we
can understand what it was that the New Testament writers
were doing when they expounded the Scriptures and can find
sufficient common ground with them to serve as our starting-
point.

We begin this chapter therefore with a discussion of the element of continuity between the Old Testament and the New,
which means in effect the extent to which early Christianity can
be viewed, in this respect, as a continuation in one direction of
late Judaism. We say 'in this respect' because the continuity is
more obvious in the area which we are examining, interpretation of Scripture, than in other areas; and we would not suggest
that Christianity as a whole is *merely* a continuation of one side

of Judaism. The question of continuity will lead us to ask whether Christianity represented in any sense a 'return to the prophets'. From that we go on to consider the New Testament treatment of stock Old Testament figures. This brings us to the centre of the question, and we go on to propound our theory of how the Old Testament should be related to the New, basing our argument on a critique of Professor James Barr's book *Old and New in Interpretation*.

From the New Testament point of view, what we are considering is the sacred Scripture. We do not know its exact limits, in Paul's eyes anyway. Did he regard Qoheleth or the Song of Solomon as Scripture? He had evidently read the Book of Wisdom but did he regard it as part of Scripture? Moreover, quite apart from formal questions of what was or was not regarded as Scripture by Paul, it is vitally important that we remember how he thought of Scripture. To a large extent, this means that we have to come to terms with the religious tradition of the Judaism of the first century of our era. It was this religious tradition in which Jesus was born, which influenced him more than anything else probably, and which early Christians took for granted despite their christocentric assumptions. But we must not forget that those very assumptions were partly taken from the religious tradition itself.

The temptation at this point is to say in effect: 'We as Christians are not bound to any tradition of Judaism. We are competent as Christians to judge both the Scriptures of the Old Testament and Judaism as a whole for ourselves. We believe, for example, that we can find a great deal more of value and significance in the teaching of some of the canonical prophets than Judaism ever found.' But if we reflect for a moment we shall realize that the only reason we can pass this judgement on the prophets is because we have been enlightened by what we know of God in Jesus Christ. Anything that we know about them, apart from what we know through Jesus Christ, may have an indirect relevance to this revelational knowledge, but does not enable us to judge them. It is strictly speaking *Religionsgeschichte*, and has no direct bearing on the relation of the Old Testament to the New.

We find ourselves thus in a tension between two poles: on the one hand, we cannot regard Christianity as a clean break as far

as its antecedents are concerned. We can trace a very real continuity, especially in methods of scriptural interpretation. On
the other hand, the religious tradition has thrown up in Jesus
Christ an absolute criterion by which it can be judged. We say
'thrown up', but this is not to suggest that the process was a
random one. On the contrary, as Christians we regard the
emergence of the criterion as constituting revelation. It is God's
action, God's plan, the unique focus of his redemptive movement towards mankind. It is because of these two poles that we
find ourselves so often, in discussing the relation of the Old
Testament to the New, to be apparently arguing in a circle.
Christ, we say, is the criterion for judging the Old Testament,
because in him God's character and action is uniquely and
supremely expressed. But who is Christ, and how can we recognize him as God? We must refer to the Old Testament itself, the
very object which we are using Christ in order to assess! Such
circular arguing seems inevitable in the nature of the case. The
two other alternatives are *either* to present Jesus Christ as a
complete intrusion with no antecedents at all, in which case he
will be quite incomprehensible; *or* so to assimilate the significance of Jesus Christ to the Judaism in which he was born that
he loses all originality and simply becomes a feature of later
Judaism. According to this alternative, Christianity itself becomes quite incomprehensible. We must therefore be content
with an apparently circular argument. We may console ourselves with the reflection that on the one hand the tradition of
Judaism is able to explain a great deal about Jesus, and indeed
may in the future have even more to tell us; but on the other it
may well happen that this very process serves equally to underline the originality of Jesus. The more we know of his background, the more we admire his originality! This is reflected in
the fact that, when we come to use him as a criterion for judging the Old Testament, we find that a great deal in it must be
regarded as outmoded and negated by the revelation of God
which we encounter in him.

    This point, the tension between continuity and transcend-
ence, is well appreciated by Professor James Barr. He writes:
'the formation of the tradition is soteriologically functional . . .
It is the shape of the tradition that leads Jesus to the finding of
his obedience, but it is also the shape of the tradition that leads

his enemies to see him as a blasphemer and to demand that he should be put to death.'[1] He goes on to say that the New Testament originated in a situation of late Judaism, and that this was not identical with the Old Testament at every point in its development. This is precisely the point that we would underline. The tradition of Judaism as Paul, for example, received it was not identical with the Old Testament, as if that could be handed over complete with the ink fresh on the last line of Malachi. It had undergone hundreds of years of development and rehandling. No writer of the New Testament could fail to be influenced by what had happened during those centuries. Barr expresses this very clearly when he writes (op. cit., p. 118): 'one of the ways in which the Old Testament is related to salvation in Christ is in its production of the situation in which it itself was understood in the first century A.D.'

On the other hand, later in the same book Barr suggests that it was because they possessed written Scriptures that the New Testament writers could appeal to an earlier stage in the tradition: 'Thus for the New Testament men, within the limits of the way in which they perceived the sense of the past texts, the possession of a written Scripture was the means by which an appeal to the earlier stages against the latest tradition could be made, the potential for a fresh grasping of what had been historically given in the past.'[2] This is true, but it is expressed very much from our modern point of view. Paul would certainly not have viewed it like this. In the first place, he was not consciously appealing from a recent tradition to an earlier one. For him, all was of equal authority, so his problem was one of interpretation not of weighing authorities. He maintained that the element in Scripture which was decisive had always been there and was there side by side with the Torah-observance element. It is true that he is anxious to establish the priority in time of the way of faith. But he does not believe that the way of faith was altogether eclipsed by the way of the Law. Secondly, the method which Paul used to establish the priority of the way of faith was one which had been elaborated by the later tradition, and a great deal that he took for granted in his exposition was in fact the product of this later development. We can confidently claim that Paul could never have written as he did, had he not been the heir of the tradition of scriptural interpretation of late Judaism. There was no question of Paul 'rediscovering the Scriptures'. Christ discovered him, and he used the tradition of exegesis in which he had been educated to interpret the Scriptures christocentrically. Thirdly, it is important to realize that the very texts which Paul used were not, so to speak, preserved in ice waiting for him to vindicate them. On the contrary, the very way in which the texts were handed down (tradition of LXX translation, influence of Targums, peculiarities of Paul's own version) itself influenced his interpretation in no small degree. It is quite true that the existence of written Scriptures enabled Paul, so to speak, to lift his head from an entirely rabbinic tradition of theology, but it also meant that he was in many respects committed to a rabbinic method of interpretation.

There is therefore a certain danger in the claim made by many Christian theologians that the Old Testament is in itself the natural and true preliminary to the New Testament. It is the danger of introducing an artificial discontinuity. Such a view runs the risk of ignoring all that happened 'between the Testaments'. Thus H. W. Wolff propounds three possible answers to the question: 'What is the context of the Old Testament as a whole?'[3] The first is: 'It is a strange, ancient, oriental religious document.' He rejects this on the grounds that it is different from all other ancient oriental religious documents and must be put in a category of its own. The second possible answer is: 'It is the Bible of Judaism.' He rejects this on the grounds that it can only be this if it is removed from its true context. 'The absolutising of the Law in the synagogue tears it out of the context in the Pentateuch in which it is firmly surrounded by God's saving deeds for Israel, and his covenant with Israel and is given as God's help in life.' The third answer is: 'It is the preliminary to the New Testament.' This he accepts. But such a way of solving the problem does seem to involve an element of discontinuity. Surely if we are to find a context for the Old Testament it must be woven together (*contextum*) with the Old Testament itself. The New Testament was written more than two hundred years after the latest book in the Old Testament. Again, the New Testament writers did not intend to propound a new context for the Old Testament. They too accepted it as the Bible of Judaism. They only differed from contemporary Jews in the question as to what was Judaism, or what should it be. Nor can the introduction of eschatology ease his problem, as he seems to suggest, when he writes: 'The constant consideration of the New Testament *eschaton* helps the expositor to interpret the Old Testament texts in a way that is true to the material, in a forward direction, in the direction of the actual witnessing intent of the texts in their context.'[4] The eschatological interpretation of the texts does indeed point towards Christ, and thereby reminds us of the criterion by which we judge them. But that very interpretation is itself in part a product of the 'intertestamental period' and would certainly have been impossible without what happened between Malachi and Matthew. We can only go back to the texts in order to interpret them christocentrically by means of going back through history. We cannot bridge the gap between the Old Testament and the New by making a backward leap in time. The New Testament writers did not intend to do this; they were applying contemporary methods of exegesis in the light of Christ. We can only understand them, and therefore come to terms with them as Christians, in as far as we realize the extent to which their christocentric interpretation was conditioned by the tradition of exegesis in which they stood.

It is sometimes suggested that Christianity represents, in part at least, a movement within Judaism back to the prophets. We have already observed that there is some truth in this, in the sense that the relative freedom which New Testament writers possessed *vis-à-vis* the Torah enabled them to appreciate better much of the prophets' message. They were not compelled to interpret them in a Torah-centric sense. Might it not be said, however, that they succeeded in doing this only by means of substituting a christocentric interpretation for a Torah-centric one, and that the New Testament writers were just as much blinded by their christocentric approach to some aspects of the prophets' message as orthodox Judaism was by its Torah-centric approach? For example, Paul only quotes Hosea in Romans in order to show that God's choice has fallen on the Gentiles. If he had been fully alive to the prophet's message, would he not have quoted Hos. 11, that wonderful chapter in which God's wrath is overcome by his love? This would seem very relevant indeed to what Paul writes in Rom. 11.22 about 'the kindness

and the severity of God'. Might we not say that his determination to find references in Hosea to the Christian dispensation
blinded Paul to some of the deepest elements in the prophet's
thought? Or again, is it not remarkable that Paul quotes Jeremiah so relatively little? We have indeed traced the olive tree
figure back to Jeremiah, and have even suggested that the
appeal to God by the prophet which follows the passage about
the olive tree may have influenced Paul's thought (Jer. 11.16–
20). But there is a great deal else in Jeremiah that might well
have appeared in Paul's works: the intimate protestations that
the prophet utters to God, very closely akin to the relation
between the believer and Christ that Paul describes, the rejection of Temple and sacrifice, and so on. Could it not be reasonably said that, because Paul could not find christological
references in such passages as those, he ignored them?

These are weighty considerations, and should warn us
against an easy assumption that Christianity as a religion of
freedom appealed back over the centuries to the free prophets
of the pre-legal era. It was not as simple as that. The New
Testament writers could only appeal back to the Scriptures
against contemporary Torah-centric interpretation on the
basis of their christocentric assumptions. They were not free, as
the 'liberal' theologians of the last century thought themselves
free, to construct a new religion out of the moral teaching of
Jesus and the moral teaching of the canonical prophets. But
there is a real sense in which Christianity did represent a return
to the prophets. Pauline Christianity at least was based on the
concept of justification by faith. And here we can find a link
with the prophets.

Von Rad has pointed out that the pre-exilic prophets were
fundamentally opposed to the pattern of salvation-history which
is to be found in so much of the Pentateuch.[5] Up to the exile, he
says, Israel's creed was salvation-history ('an Aramean ready
to perish etc.'). And after the return the Chronicler attempted
to resume the theme: the restored Temple was only a continuation of what David had planned and so on. But the prophets
spoke in a completely different vein: Jahweh has broken off
salvation-history and intends to establish a new relationship in
the future. Now, we may legitimately argue, the old theory of
salvation-history had depended very much on institutions, the

Temple, the cult, the priesthood, the kingship. Hence the Chronicler's emphasis on Temple, cult, and priesthood. Salvation history is certainly part of Paul's belief, as we have seen, but it is much more like what the prophets had looked for than what the Chronicler imagined. The new relationship has been established in Christ; there is no new Temple, cult, or priesthood in a strictly institutional sense. There is certainly the people of God, continuous with Israel of old. But then Paul would say that the new element was also somehow to be traced in Israel's history of old. Because the new relationship of man to God (though not altogether new, as we have seen) is one of faith, both the consummation of salvation-history in Christ and the freedom from institutions which the prophets envisaged are possible. This great principle of justification by faith, which Paul sees supremely manifested in the cross, enables Christianity to establish a real link with the prophets, and also to contain in itself a principle of self-criticism which has enabled it time and time again in its history to free itself from the narrowness of recent tradition. This freedom does not mean an iconoclasm which attempts to dispense with tradition altogether. No New Testament writer could have succeeded in doing this, even had he wished to. But it does mean an essential element of freedom. Since this emphasis on the way of faith undoubtedly goes back to the teaching of Jesus himself, it was no quirk of Paul's. It is embedded in the very heart of Christianity. Compared with Christianity, therefore, the Qumran Sect, despite the prominence it gave to the study of the prophets, is not really a movement back to the prophets at all. It had no real means of freeing itself from historical institutions, and when Temple, cult, and priesthood went down with the wreck of the Jewish state, the Qumran Sect disappeared also.

But the element of discontinuity must not be overemphasized. The New Testament writers rarely explicitly or consciously repudiate the religious tradition in which they were brought up. Mark 7.1–13 (parallel in Matt. 15.1–9) is an exception to this, where Jesus explicitly repudiates the *Halakah*. But the repudiation is supported by a quotation from the prophets. Certainly we never find New Testament writers repudiating the tradition of scriptural interpretation which they had received. Indeed in this respect the Qumran Sect shows a much more marked tendency

towards discontinuity. Otto Betz has argued that, according to
the tradition of the Sect, the Torah was actually hidden for
a period between the death of Joshua and the finding of the
book in the Temple during the reign of Josiah.[6] They emphasized certain teachers in the course of Israel's history over
against others. Thus Hilkaiah and Ezra were magnified, the
historical Jerusalem priesthood perhaps played down. The
original 'Teacher of Righteousness' was viewed as standing in
a succession with Moses, Hilkaiah, and Ezra rather than with
the official teachers of Israel of his day. The transactions on
Mount Nebo were so understood as to constitute a new revelation of how the Torah was to be followed, a revelation entrusted
to a small group and handed down till the appearance of the
original 'Teacher of Righteousness'. We do not find anything
corresponding to this in the New Testament.

It cannot even be said that the New Testament writers were
particularly interested in magnifying, or reading a special
significance into, individual Old Testament characters. We do
not find anything like the stock apocalyptic technique of choos-
ing a character from Scripture, Enoch, Isaiah, or Ezra for
example, and making him the recipient of special secrets, thereby giving him a significance greater than he possesses in Scripture. Nor is there much sign of the contrary tendency to blacken
the character of some figure in Scripture not already blackened
by tradition. The only place where such a tendency to devote
special attention to some one figure appears is Hebrews, where
the author gives very great prominence to Melchisedech despite
his very brief appearances in Scripture. We now know from
the Qumran documents that there was much speculation about
Melchisedech. The Sectaries seem to have regarded him as a
superior angel. It is perhaps no coincidence that in Stephen's
speech in Acts 7 we have what is probably a disparagement of
Solomon: he should have known that God does not dwell in
houses built by men; but, we are to understand, God's true
dwelling-place is Christ. There does seem to be a connection
between Acts 7 and Hebrews. But the author of Hebrews does
not in fact develop his exposition of the significance of Melchisedech as he would have liked to, and we do not find anything
else like it in the New Testament.

Noth is therefore hardly accurate when he says that New

Testament writers do not exhibit Old Testament characters as ethical models, heroes of faith, or examples of true humanity.[7] One would have thought that a short perusal of Heb. 11 would have dissipated this idea. The truth is that the writers of the New Testament treated scriptural characters exactly as contemporary rabbinic exegesis did. They shared the same tendency to whitewash characters of whom Scripture approves and blacken those whom it condemns. It is easy to cite a whole string of examples: the Epistle of James praises the patience of Job (an example which Noth concedes), though we know that in fact Job was anything but patient. James also exalts Elijah's ability to hold up rain and to call it down, which he attributes to Elijah's righteousness (Jas. 5.11,16–18). He also notices the righteousness of Rahab in receiving the spies. If we had more information about the list of worthies of the old dispensation which the author of Hebrews gives, it is certain that we would find a great deal of whitewashing or moralizing of scriptural characters. Even as it is, we can detect a number of moralizing details: Abel is preferred to Cain because he is righteous (11.4), a point which the scriptural account omits. Isaac's blessing of Jacob is regarded as a morally commendable act (11.20). In 11.27, though we are told in Exod. 2.14 that Moses was afraid, Hebrews describes him as 'not being afraid of the anger of the king'. When we see the names of Samson and Jephthah in the list of heroes, we cannot be blamed for suspecting that the author of Hebrews must have heavily moralized, and even Christianized, them in his mind before he could fit them into such a context. Similarly the author reflects the rabbinic tendency to give Esau a bad character (see 12.16, where he is described as 'immoral and irreligious'). We find the same moralizing of the story of Cain and Abel in 1 John 3.12; compare also Jude 11. An admirable example occurs in 1 Pet. 3.5–6, where Sarah is held up as an example of Christian women, and the wives of the patriarchs are described generally as 'holy women'. This is of course because they are scriptural characters, not because Scripture attributes any special holiness to them. There is a tendency in 1 Tim. 2.13–14 to blacken Eve in comparison with Adam. The two latest books in the New Testament are particularly rich in this sort of moralizing: in 2 Peter and Jude we meet an encomium on Lot, who suffered moral agonies because of what he witnessed in Sodom, and a condemnation of Balaam entirely in the rabbinic tradition (see 2 Pet. 2.7,15–16; Jude 11).

In Paul such moralizing is not very frequent, but it is certainly present. An obvious example is Ishmael, who is described in Gal. 4.29 as persecuting Isaac. It is possible that Hagar is also represented as morally inferior; she comes from Egypt, which is traditionally the source of evil and temptation (see Rev. 11.8). In one sense most of the great characters of the Scriptures whom Paul mentions are Christianized, since Abraham, Moses, Isaiah, and the other prophets all knew God by faith and therefore in some sense knew God in Christ. But it must be said that Noth's observation is more true of Paul than of later New Testament writers.

In fact the moralizing tendency is an inevitable one. Quite apart from later Judaism, we can see it at work inside the Old Testament itself. The pious David of the Chronicler is much more of a plaster saint than the figure of flesh and blood whom we meet in the succession narrative in the Books of Samuel. We find this tendency present in Ben Sira, though he is remarkably restrained: Enoch is described as an example of repentance in 44.16, and Aaron is described as 'a holy man' in 45.6 despite his part in the incident of the golden calf. We find it in the Book of Wisdom, where Jacob's flight after his shameless deception of his brother is narrated in the words 'When a righteous man fled from his brother's wrath, she [sc. Wisdom] guided him on straight paths' (Wisd. 10.10). We think of Philo's treatment of Jacob, who is always represented as a character of surpassing wisdom and righteousness. No doubt many more examples could be culled from the pages of Josephus. An unusual example occurs in the *Biblical Antiquities* of Pseudo-Philo, where attempts are made to present Tamar as an example of later Jewish morality.[8] This work seems to have been written towards the end of the first century A.D., and may therefore suitably point to the Epistle of Clement, its contemporary. This Epistle affords the perfect epitome of the moralizing of Old Testament characters: a whole gallery of them is paraded as examples of modest, self-effacing Roman gentlemen. It is interesting to see that even Jonah could be represented in rabbinic tradition as an example of heroic self-sacrifice: 'R. Nathan says: Jonah

made his voyage only in order to drown himself in the sea . . .
And so you also find that the patriarchs and the prophets
offered their lives in behalf of Israel.'[9]

In fact this whitewashing and blackening, as we have already
observed, is really a method of presenting a consistent picture
of God in the Scriptures. These people were either approved or
disapproved by God, and must therefore be represented as acting according to the highest concept of God which has been
revealed—or else to have offended against it. The fact that the
writers of the New Testament quite unconsciously accepted this
moralizing process, and made no very serious attempt to reverse traditional moral judgements of scriptural characters,
underlines the extent to which they accepted the God of Israel
as their God. It indicates an important element of continuity
between the tradition of late Judaism and the New Testament.

Through our discussion of continuity we seem to have arrived
at the conclusion that the relation of the Old Testament to the
New can best be defined in terms of the revelation of the character of God. This theme we must now elaborate, and this is best
done by first giving some consideration to other views which
scholars have put forward about the relation between the
Testaments. Some of them we have encountered and discussed
already; but it will be convenient to mention them again so as
to be able to place in the right perspective the view we are
attempting to defend.

We have already examined Bultmann's thesis that the Old
Testament represents another religion. 'The Old Testament
[he writes] is for Christians "a closed chapter" . . . To us the
history of Israel is not history of revelation.'[10] Bultmann does
not, of course, deny that the Old Testament is of value to
Christians in many ways, but not, he maintains, in terms of
revelation. This view encounters a difficulty when we come to
give an account of how we know God through the New Testament. Bultmann would claim indeed that we know God by
faith alone. But this surely implies that the faith-act is an act of
recognition: faith enables us to recognize God, indeed to recognize God in Christ. How can we recognize God in Christ if we
do not know something about him already? The only place
where that (previous) knowledge can have come from, on

Bultmann's assumptions, is the Old Testament, since Bultmann would strongly repudiate the notion that we can know anything whatever about God by studying the structure of the universe, or by aesthetic contemplation, or by religious experience, etc. Thus, short of claiming that we recognize God in Christ by means of a completely irrational intuition, Bultmann would seem to be compelled to acknowledge some sort of revelation in the Old Testament. A similar attitude to that of Bultmann is taken up by F. Hesse, but here it is buttressed by a most fallacious argument; having stated that in the Old Testament we really have another religion, he writes: 'here we are facing the situation which Paul characterises by speaking of the veil that hangs before the hearts of those who read the Old Testament without Christ'.[11] Here is a double confusion: he assumes that in 2 Cor. 3.14 ἡ παλαιὰ διαθήκη refers to the Torah, the Prophets, and the Writings, a view which has only to be brought into the light to be seen to be indefensible. And secondly, he actually suggests that for Paul of all people the religion of Israel appeared as another religion to his own.

Next comes the group of scholars who still maintain that in a true sense the New Testament is the fulfilment of the Old. None of them (except Vischer, to whose views we need not revert) claims that everything in the Old Testament finds its natural fulfilment in the New. They would all qualify their fulfilment thesis by saying that only the most important elements in the Old Testament are fulfilled; or even that of all the competitors for the title of fulfilment of the Old Testament, Christianity has the best claim. But they would all make the claim in some form. The views of some we have considered already, e.g. those of Baumgärtel and Wolff, but to the list we may add the names of John Bright and G. E. Wright. Bright maintains that there is, despite all internal divergencies, a recognizably distinct faith of Israel and a recognizably distinct faith of the New Testament; and concludes on the basis of this that 'We have the right to affirm, as the New Testament affirmed, that the true conclusion of Israel's history, and the fulfilment of her faith, lies in Christ and his gospel—not in the Talmud'.[12] Wright expresses essentially the same view when he says: 'From a purely descriptive standpoint, the canonical Bible, taken as a whole, displays an inner movement and an interrelatedness of

its parts which are far more characteristic of itself than anything either of its two main sections has in common with their
environment.'[13] The difficulty with this view is twofold: first,
as we have already pointed out, Christianity is not demonstratively superior to Judaism (or even the Qumran creed) as the
fulfilment of the Old Testament. Some other criterion must be
brought in to decide the issue. But secondly, this view takes it
for granted that there is an 'Old Testament religion', or theology or creed, or even piety (Baumgärtel's word)[14] which, so to
speak, stands out on its own. This is most questionable. It depends for its validity on divorcing the Old Testament from the
religious tradition in which it was written and which continued
unbroken till the emergence of Christianity. If it is claimed that
by 'fulfilment of the Old Testament' is meant 'fulfilment of the
religious tradition out of which Christianity emerged' the
claim becomes even more difficult to vindicate.

A third school sees the Old Testament fundamentally in
terms of salvation-history. They argue that the most just way
in which to sum up the significance of the Old Testament is as
the record of the redemptive acts of God. Thus Cullmann
writes that what matters is the 'event-character' of the Old
Testament revelation and its connection with real history in
Jesus.[15] Von Rad similarly says that the Old Testament religion
consists not in ideas about God but in God's redemptive acts.[16]
Alan Richardson expresses it as 'a kerygma concerning God's
saving action in the history of his people'.[17] McKenzie seems to
maintain the same view when he writes: 'It is the history of
Israel that sets Jesus apart from all culture heroes, king-saviours,
cosmic men, and mythological bearers of life',[18] and he goes on
to claim that it is the history of Israel, not the doctrine of the
Old Testament, that is relevant. The difficulty with this view
has already been well pointed out by Barr. These 'redemptive
acts of God' in Israel's history too often on closer inspection
dissolve into legend or myth; and we are driven to defining
them not in terms of Israel's history but of Israel's faith. What
is more, those acts on which both Israel of old and the New
Testament writers laid greatest stress are often those which we
are least inclined today to treat as history. Admittedly, the
fact that we must often speak of Israel's faith rather than
Israel's history does not prevent us from thinking in terms of

revelation. But it certainly does put a considerable question mark against the 'salvation-history' schema.

Perhaps we may just glance at Brunner's suggestion, more because of the greatness of his name than because of the soundness of the suggestion. In an essay originally published in 1932 he suggests that the Old Testament is important for us today because it avoids the Hellenism which even the Greek of the New Testament imported; this Hellenism led to such horrid things as 'idealism, rationalism, and mysticism . . . in the Old Testament we come upon a world completely unaffected by the whole Hellenic spirit'.[19] This approach suffers from the fallacy of discontinuity to which we referred above. What is the use of a 'pure' Hebrew tradition (if it ever existed), if by the time it reaches the New Testament it has been 'contaminated' with Hellenism or with anything else? In any case, the discovery of the Qumran documents, and the research on the Wisdom literature of Judaism which has taken place since Brunner wrote, make his assertion that the Old Testament world was unaffected by the Hellenic spirit extremely doubtful.

The great merit of James Barr's approach to the question of the relation between the Testaments is that he does not ask us to confine ourselves to any one principle or any one formula in order to characterize the Old Testament revelation as a whole. He writes: 'We are unlikely to find any single conception which will be adequate to state the character of the tradition.'[20] This is a liberating conclusion, since it frees us from the necessity of forcing the Old Testament into one mould, whether it be salvation-history or promise, and of subsequently explaining away any elements that cannot be fitted into the mould. In view of our comparison with the other religious traditions that claim to be the true fulfilment of the Old Testament, Judaism, Qumran etc., we do not want to find ourselves in a position where we seem to have to claim that the majority of the Old Testament, or the most important elements in the Old Testament (still less everything in the Old Testament), is really ours and does not properly belong to the Jews or the Muslims or anyone else. It will be quite enough for us if we can show that certain important elements in the Old Testament tradition find their true fulfilment in Christianity. If we may use a figure to explain our position: it should be quite enough if we can show that the Old

Testament is the quarry from which essential New Testament materials were taken. We should not be concerned to claim that it is the source or spring from which the river that is the New Testament tradition originated, for that would suggest that there is only one source and only one river. A quarry on the other hand is a place from which various builders can draw their materials in order to build, perhaps, a great variety of houses.

On the other hand, if we are to be faithful to the basic New Testament assertions about the Scriptures as known to the writers of the New Testament, we cannot forgo the conception of revelation in the Old Testament. This is a point where we must differ from Professor Barr. He objects to what he calls a 'revelational model' as a way of understanding the Old Testament.[21] This is partly because he is very rightly aware of the great variety of ways by which the revelation must be said to have been mediated in the Old Testament tradition if revelational language is to be used: not just revelation through history, but also through myth, legend, story, legal codes, and so on. But it is also because, if a revelation in the Old Testament is to be claimed, it will have to be described as having been provided, at certain points at any rate, by Near Eastern cultural patterns, only thinly disguised as Hebrew religion. He refuses, rightly no doubt, to accept the plea commonly made on behalf of such material that it has been 'historicized', the original pastoral festival of the Passover has been connected with the deliverance from Egypt, and so on.

In fact, as we shall be suggesting presently, neither of these objections to the language of revelation is necessarily fatal. It depends on what (or rather who) is revealed, and how the revelation is understood as having been apprehended. The first objection may be held over for the moment, since we shall be suggesting that, if revelation is rightly understood, the great variety of media of revelation does not matter. But the second objection should be squarely faced. In principle, there does not seem to be anything incompatible with the traditional faith of Christians in admitting that Near Eastern cultural patterns may have been among the media of revelation. Professor Barr himself has had a great part in destroying the oversimple contrast between Hebrew and Greek modes of thought. It can no longer be maintained that there ever was a 'pure' Hebrew tradition, uncontaminated by contiguous religion or alien culture. In fact, of course, there never has been such a thing as an absolutely 'pure' religious tradition anywhere and certainly the religious tradition from which Christianity originated cannot possibly be described as 'pure' religious tradition in the sense of wholly Hebrew, uninfluenced by oriental or Greek thought. Despite the exclusion of the Samaritans, despite the *Halakhah* of the Pharisees, the Judaism of the first century A.D was already deeply influenced by non-Hebrew currents of religious thought, Iranian, Egyptian, Hellenistic. That every religious tradition should be something of a syncretism is an inescapable fact of history. Far better to conclude that God, where he reveals himself in history, uses this syncretism for his own purposes, than to attempt to deny the fact of syncretism. Instead of lamenting, or denying, the composite character of Israel's religious tradition at any point in its history, we should go on the principle of *finem vide*. The tree is known by its fruits. In reaction against the sometimes superficial Hellenism of the Victorian divines, we must not be pushed into a totally unrealistic Hebraism. When one studies the picture of a purely Jewish Christianity presented, for example, by Daniélou in *Théologie du Judéo-Christianisme*[22] one is inclined to say: Thank God for the Greeks!

But in fact Professor Barr himself, despite his distaste for a 'revelational model', often comes very close to using the concept, though not the language, of revelation. He cannot avoid using the concept of 'knowing God'. Thus he writes: 'The coming of Christ, like the Old Testament incidents, is a further (and amazing) act of one who is known; it is not a first disclosure of one who is not known.'[23] If God is at any point to be described as being known or as having made himself known, it is very hard to avoid the conclusion that there is a revelation there. We can readily agree with Professor Barr that this revelation in Christ is not unprecedented, or made in a vacuum, but it would still seem to merit the term revelation, and so, by the same argument, would any of the other occasions on which God was known to men in Israel's history, by whatever means that knowledge was conveyed. Again, though the disclosure in Christ was not the first disclosure of God, the call of Abraham might very well merit the description of the first disclosure of God. As we have seen, Paul apparently regarded Abraham as being in effect a Gentile when God called him; and in the New Testament Gentiles are often characterized as not knowing God. We find Barr using very similar language a little later on: 'There is the sending of the incarnate Son into the world by the Father; but this is not the unveiling of one unknown, but a new deed of one known because in Israel God was known.'[24] Paul would, of course, entirely agree with this sentiment. Indeed he would go further and say that Christ was already known to some in Israel. But the point here is, to speak of Israel as already knowing God is in fact to posit some sort of revelation. It is most unlikely that Barr would envisage Israel as having discovered God for itself, as if the people had had to go out and seek for God, eventually finding him by their own efforts. He would no doubt agree with the witness of both Testaments that God is one who makes himself known to man. This does then imply that God, by whatever means, did reveal himself to Israel of old.

Finally, we may point to one other passage where Barr uses the language of 'knowing God'. He writes: 'that which can be known of our God [i.e. the Christian God] is known only when we consider the Old Testament as a place in which he is known'.[25] He is here concerned to make the entirely valid point that we cannot understand the God of whom the New Testament writers speak unless we concede that the same God was known in some sense to Israel of old. But once again the language of knowing God seems inevitably to lead to a doctrine of revelation, in the Old Testament as well as the New, even though the word 'revelation' is not used. Incidentally, it is surprising to find Professor Barr using such inexact language here, seeing that he has so often in this book and elsewhere reproved others for using language in an imprecise way. What he calls the Old Testament is not a 'place' at all, not at least in the sense in which Barr means it to be understood. The Old Testament is a record of how God made himself known to Israel of old. The last thing that Professor Barr would wish is that we should treat the record as being itself the revelation. The revelation was made by very various means to men in Israel of old, and has been recorded by them in an equally varied manner.

We may conclude therefore, first, that anyone who, like Professor Barr, would maintain that God is known by means of the Old Testament as well as by means of the New is thereby committed to some sort of a doctrine of revelation. And secondly, that the actual account of the media by which that revelation was communicated to Israel of old is not a matter of first importance, and may imply the use of a great many different means, both as regards variation between oral and written methods, and as regards the cultural elements inseparable from the means of revelation.

We are now in a position to state fairly succinctly what is, for Christians, the relation between the Old Testament and the New. The connecting factor is the revelation of God's character. Knowing God as recorded in the Old Testament means knowing the sort of person he is, what his will is likely to be in any given set of circumstances, what is his strategy, or manner of dealing with men. In this sense, God was certainly known by Israel in the period of which the Old Testament is the record. If it is objected that this character of God as recorded in the Old Testament is not consistent with itself, and is not always compatible with God's character as recorded in the New Testament, we must readily admit this. But we must add two essential qualifications: first, within the Old Testament itself we can see the understanding of God being corrected and purified. Secondly (and this is essential both in order to safeguard the specifically Christian understanding of God, and so that those words 'corrected' and 'purified' should have a specific content), we must use the revelation of God in Jesus Christ set out in the New Testament as the criterion by which we judge what in the Old Testament is truer knowledge of God and what is less true. In this respect we can use Christ as the screen through which alleged knowledge of God recorded in the Old Testament must be passed. What is not compatible with Christ is thereby rejected and eliminated. What is compatible with Christ is now seen in what Christians must regard as its true light. This does leave us with a real doctrine of the fulfilment of the Scriptures, even though it is not identical with the doctrine on which the writers of the New Testament worked. We cannot do without the revelation of God recorded in the Old Testament, since, as Professor Barr has pointed out, we must be able to *recognize* God in Christ. In Christ we do not meet God for the first time. On the other hand, we must use the revelation recorded in the New Testament as our control for the Old Testament. The eschatological approach to the Old Testament is justified in as much as *finem vide* must be our guide when we wish to know what is true in the Old Testament. But the pragmatic, *a posteriori* approach is justified in as much as we do not need, and should not desire, to claim that everything in the Old Testament finds its true meaning in Christ.

We ought now to be able to see clearly the point at which our modern understanding of the Old Testament and the New Testament understanding of the Old Testament coincide. Both interpretations agree that the God who is revealed in Jesus Christ is the same God who was known to Israel of old. Thus both lay great emphasis on the consistency and unchanging character of God. Because of his revelation of himself in Christ, we now know that 'his nature and his name is love'. But if so, it has always been so: if God did in any sense reveal himself to Moses in the burning bush, or to Isaiah in the Temple, the God who revealed himself was the God of self-giving love, the God who was prepared to send his only Son, the God whom Christians worship as One in Three. This profound truth is expressed by the two greatest theologians of the New Testament in strikingly similar terms, which we may translate as 'grace and truth'. In John 1.14 that phrase πλήρης χάριτος καὶ ἀληθείας is, we believe, deliberately designed to recall Exod. 34.6, where God reveals himself to Moses hidden in the cleft of the rock as 'abounding in steadfast love and faithfulness'. The χάρις of John (*chesed* in the Hebrew) represents the innermost character of God, self-giving love. The ἀλήθεια has here what (*pace* Professor Barr) we must be allowed to call its Hebrew meaning of 'faithfulness, consistency' ('*emeth* in the Hebrew). God is in his true nature all *chesed*, love, and always manifests himself as such; he is therefore also true. But Paul reverts to the same Old Testament episode at a crucial point in his argument in Romans. Does God really show partiality, Paul asks in Rom. 9.14, when he considers that Jacob was preferred to Esau while they were both still in the womb? No, he answers, the solution to this problem is to be found in the revelation of his true character. He is one who has mercy, whose nature it is to have pity. This is the motive behind his choice of Jacob. And six chapters further on Paul actually brings this mercy (ἔλεος) into juxtaposition with his faithfulness in Christ (ἀλήθεια). In 15.8–9 he writes:

> Christ became a servant to the circumcised to show God's truthfulness (ἀληθείας), in order to confirm the promises given to the patriarchs, and in order that the Gentiles might glorify God for his mercy (ἐλέους).

Thus at the very deepest level modern Christians can agree with Paul and John and the other writers of the New Testament in their interpretation of the Old Testament. The God who is revealed in Jesus Christ is the same God who is known in the Old Testament. We cannot possibly adopt their methods of interpretation but we can, and must, agree with their intention. We, like them, if we are prepared to admit that anything whatever can be known of God by means of the Old Testament record, must agree that the God known there by that means is the God known in Jesus Christ. No matter how much we must dissent from their methods of exegesis, we must applaud their determination to present a consistent picture of God, one which is judged by the criterion of Jesus Christ, one which does not repudiate the Old Testament revelation.

# NOTES

## Chapter 1

1 H. von Soden, *Hand Commentar z. N.T.* (Freiburg 1891), vol. III.

2 See my *Studies in the Pastoral Epistles* (London 1968), p. 70.

3 C. H. Dodd, *The Epistle of Paul to the Romans* (London 1932).

4 G. B. Caird, *Principalities and Powers* (Oxford 1956), p. 41.

5 H. Schlier, art. δειγματίζω in *TWNT* (Stuttgart 1935), vol. II.

6 The rabbis were not very sure whether הוקע meant hanging, but very reasonably decided it by reference to 2 Sam. 21.6. They show a tendency to vindicate divine justice by so rendering the passage that it is not the rulers who are punished (since there is no evidence in the text that they indulged in idolatry), but the people: 'Take the chiefs of the people (and appoint them as judges) and hang up those (whom the judges shall condemn).' See *Tractate Sanhedrin* I, 220–1. There are traces of this interpretation in the Targum of Palestine (see Etheridge, p. 433).

7 See *Tractate Sanhedrin* II, 724.

8 See *De Spec. Leg.* I, 56; *De Somniis* I, 88f; *De Mut. Nom.* 107. The last is the passage containing the allegory.

9 *The Targums of Onkelos and Jonathan ben Uzziel on the Pentateuch*, ed. and tr. J. W. Etheridge (London 1865), p. 433.

10 G. Kurze, art. 'Die στοιχεῖα τοῦ κόσμου, Gal. 4, und Kol. 2' in *Biblische Zeitschrift* 15 (1918–21), 335–7.

11 A. J. Bandstra, *The Law and the Elements of the World* (Kampen 1964), pp. 19–62.

12 E. Y. Hincks, art. 'The meaning of the Phrase τὰ στοιχεῖα τοῦ κόσμου in Gal. 4.3 and Col. 2.8' in *JBL* 15 (1896), 183–92.

13 W. H. P. Hatch, art. 'τὰ στοιχεῖα τοῦ κόσμου in Paul and Bardaisan' in *JTS* 28 (1927), 181–2.

14 G. H. C. MacGregor, art. 'Principalities and powers: the Cosmic Background of Paul's Thought' in *NTS* 1 (1954–55), 17–28. See also B. Reicke's art. 'The Law and the World according to Paul' in *JBL* 70 (1951), 259–76. He strongly affirms that τὰ στοιχεῖα τοῦ κόσμου are the evil world powers conquered by Christ. He would also identify them with the angels of Gal. 3.19. He does not make clear whether he agrees with the view rather favoured by Schlier that the angels were the

*authors* of the Law. He says on pp. 262 and 268 that they 'ordained' the Law; but on p. 263 that they 'established' it.

15  T. K. Abbott, *The Epistles to the Ephesians and Colossians* (Edinburgh 1909).

16  E. Lohmeyer, *Die Briefe an die Philipper, an die Kolosser, und an Philemon* (8e., Göttingen 1961).

17  M. Dibelius, *Der Brief an die Kolosser* (Tübingen 1953).

18  J. B. Lightfoot, *The Epistles of Paul: Colossians and Ephesians* (London 1897).

19  C. F. D. Moule, *The Epistles to the Colossians and Philemon* (Cambridge 1958). Caird also accepts a change of subject (op. cit., p. 43).

20  J. A. T. Robinson, *The Body* (London 1952), p. 41.

21  J. Rutherford, art. 'Note on Colossians 2.15' in *ET* 18 (1906–7), 565–566.

22  E. Larsson, *Christus als Vorbild* (Uppsala 1962), p. 85. This view is also held by P. X. Vallisoleto in an art. 'Delens chirographum' in *Verbum Domini* 13 (1933), 181–5 and 'Et spolians principatus et potestates' in ibid., 187–92.

23  H. A. A. Kennedy, art. 'Two Exegetical Notes on St Paul; II: Colossians 2.10–15' in *ET* 28 (1916–17), 363–6.

24  G. Megas, art. 'Das χειρόγραφον Adams' in *ZNTW* 27 (1928), 305–320.

25  Op. cit., p. 85

26  *From First Adam to Last*, p. 86.

27  The substance of this chapter was read as a paper at the Fourth Congress of NT Studies, Christ Church, Oxford in September 1969.

## Chapter 2

1  C. K. Barrett, *A Commentary on the Epistle to the Romans* (London 1957).

2  *According to the Scriptures*, p. 58 (London 1932).

3  E. Grässer, art. 'Der Historische Jesus im Hebräerbrief' in *ZNTW* (1965), pp. 63–91.

4  Midrash on the Psalms I, 198; see also on Ps. 2.9. Ed. W. G. Braude, 2 vols. (Yale 1959).

5  Midrash on the Psalms I, 233.

6  Midrash on the Psalms II, 97.

7  M. Mansoor, ed. and tr., *The Thanksgiving Hymns* (Leiden 1961). See also E. L. Sukenik, ed., *The Dead Sea Scrolls of the Hebrew University* (Jerusalem 1955), for the Hebrew text.

8  *Paulus und das Judentum* (Stuttgart 1935), p. 69.

9  M-J. Lagrange, *Saint Paul: Épitre aux Romains* (Paris 1915).

10  *The Epistle to the Romans*, in loc. 15.3, E. T. 6e., E. Hoskyns (London 1933).

11 O. Michel, *Der Brief an die Römer* (Göttingen 1957).

12 *New Testament Apologetic*, pp. 103–4.

13 For a fuller discussion of this, see *The Pioneer Ministry*, pp. 76–8.

14 W. Sanday and A. C. Headlam, *A Critical and Exegetical Commentary on the Epistle to the Romans* (5e., Edinburgh 1902).

15 F. Leenhardt, *L'Épitre de Saint Paul aux Romains* (Neuchâtel and Paris 1957).

16 The LXX translates with ἔκστασις, literally 'ecstasy', of course, though it can mean 'distraction of mind' caused by terror, astonishment, or anger. The Hebrew verb חפז which it translates means 'to hurry away in alarm'; exactly the same phrase, in Hebrew and Greek, occurs in Ps. 31.23 (LXX 30.23; RSV 31.22), where the RSV translates 'I had said in my alarm, I am driven far from thy sight'. In both Psalm contexts the word indicates alarm, even indignation. But of course Paul might take ἐν ἐκστάσει as indicating that the prophet David was about to speak an inspired utterance, since ἔκστασις could certainly mean this; cf. Acts 11.5; 22.17, where it is used of a trance or condition fit for divine communications. Philo has a considerable discussion of the meaning of ἔκστασις, where it occurs in the LXX of Gen. 15.12. He describes it as ἔνθεος κατοχωχή τε καὶ μανία ᾖ τὸ προφητικὸν γένος χρῆται, and insists that the fact of Abraham being seized by ecstasy here proves that he was a prophet. See *Quis Rev. Div. Heres*, 249–58. See also J. Lindblom, *Gesichte und Offenbarungen* (Lund 1968), p. 40, for the connection between ἔκστασις and τὸ πνεῦμα.

17 See *Tractate Ta'anith*, ed. J. Rabbinowitz, in BT (London 1938), p. 49.

18 S. Lyonnet, art. 'La Notion de Justice de Dieu en Rom. 3.5 et L'Exégèse Paulinienne du "Miserere"' in *Sacra Pagina* 2 (ed. J. Coppens, Paris and Gembloux 1959), p. 342.

19 Though in fact, as pointed in the MT, it is ambiguous: בְּדָבְרֶךָ and F. Buhl in Kittel's *Bibl. Heb.* thinks that the singular may be original.

20 See *Paulus und seine Bibel* (Gütersloh 1929), p. 80. So also Ulonska, p. 168. H. Ulonska *Die Funktion der alttestamenlichen Zitate und Ausspielungen in der paulischen Briefen* (Diss, Münster 1963).

21 L. Koehler and W. Baumgartner, *Lexicon in Veteris Testamenti Libros* (London 1953), *sub.* עלמות.

22 The same translation occurs in the title of Ps. 46 (LXX 45) where the LXX renders עַל־עֲלָמוֹת with ὑπὲρ τῶν κρυφίων. Liddell and Scott give the meaning 'occult, mysterious' as a possible one for κρύφιος.

23 M-J. Lagrange, *Saint Paul : Épitre aux Romains*.

24 A. Nygren, *Commentary on Romans* (E.T. London 1952, Swedish e. of 1944).

25 The Hebrew is ואדע כי לא יצדק מבלעדיך. It is interesting that the author of the *Hodayoth* also has slightly misquoted the Hebrew.

26 W. Diezinger, art. 'Unter Toten Freigeworden' in *Nov. Test.* 5 (1962), 268–98.

27 Most editors take the Heb. נָשָׂאתִי, tr. LXX ὑψωθείς, as meaning 'I endured', and the word tr. by ἐταπεινώθην, אֵמֶיךָ, as meaning 'thy terrors'. But the Hebrew is obscure.

28 *Paulus*, p. 178. H. J. Schoeps, *Paulus: die Theologie des Apostels im Lichte der judischen Religionsgeschichte* (Tübingen 1959).

29 Cf. also Vg. 'memorare quae mea substantia'.

30 The LXX has missed the point here and translates with ἐγχρονίζει.

31 Midrash on the Psalms I, 513 on Ps. 60.

32 The point is that the phrase in Rom. 4.25 ὃς παρεδόθη διὰ τὰ παραπτώ-ματα ἡμῶν καὶ ἠγέρθη διὰ τὴν δικαίωσιν ἡμῶν probably derives from Isa. 53 (*sic* Michel, Euler (*Die Verkündigung vom Leidenden Gottesknecht aus Jes. 53 in der Griechischen Bibel* (Stuttgart–Berlin 1934), p. 141) and Lindars (op. cit., p. 82)). In the LXX verse 10e runs: δικαιῶσαι δίκαιον εὖ δουλεύοντα πολλοῖς. There is thus good reason to believe that Paul found the justification of the Messiah here.

33 The word I have translated 'taunter' is παραλαλεῖν, which really means 'talk at random'. The LXX seems to have given the wrong Greek words to the Hebrew, because it translates חרג which means 'taunt', with ὀνειδίζειν, which means 'abuse', and גדף 'abuse' with παρα-λαλεῖν 'make fun of'. But there is a v.l. καταλαλοῦντος which would give the sense 'talk against, abuse'.

34 The Hebrew phrase thus rendered by the LXX is שׁיר ידידת, which the MT punctuates as a plural. The RSV, probably correctly, tr. 'a love song'. But Jedidah was Solomon's name. If Paul had access to the Hebrew here, he would see Solomon as a type of Christ, and so probably did the author of Hebrews.

35 C. K. Barrett sees in Rom. 8.32 a reference to Gen. 22.16 οὐκ ἐφείσω τοῦ υἱοῦ σου τοῦ ἀγαπητοῦ. We may therefore with equal probability see a reference to the phrase τοῦ ἀγαπητοῦ in the title of Ps. 45.

36 G. Kittel, art. 'πίστις Ἰησοῦ Χριστοῦ bei Paulus' in *Theol. Stud. u. Krit.* (1906), 419f.

37 Karl Barth, *The Epistle to the Romans*, in loc. 1.17.

38 T. F. Torrance, art. 'One Aspect of the Biblical Conception of Faith' in *ET* 68 (1957), 111, 157, 221.

39 P. Vallotton, *Le Christ et la Foi* (Geneva 1960), pp. 46–7, 69–72.

40 The main tenor of my argument about this text has already appeared in *Paul's Understanding of Jesus*, pp. 8–9. But, as that lecture had only a very limited circulation and as I did not give any references, I make no apology for reproducing it here.

41 K. E. Kirk, *The Epistle to the Romans* (Oxford 1937); J. A. Sanders, art. 'Habakkuk in Qumran, Paul, and the Old Testament' in *Journal of Religion* xxxix, Note (Oct. 1959), 232–44; A. Feuillet, art. 'La Citation d'Habacuc 2.4 et les Huit Premiers Chapitres de L'Épitre aux

Romains' in *NTS* 6 (1959), 52–80. The greatest degree of emphasis in embracing the 'fashionable' translation is reached by W. Grundmann in *Paul and Qumran*, ed. J. Murphy-O'Connor (London 1968), p. 100, who accuses Paul of altering the Habakkuk quotation from 'the just shall live by faith' to 'he who through faith is just shall live'. It is worth noting that the Vg. gives no countenance to the 'fashionable' rendering. It offers 'justus autem in fide sua vivet'.

42 J. Calvin, *Ioannis Calvini in Novum Testamentum Commentarii*, ed. A. Tholuck (Berlin 1834, vols. i–vii) in loc.

43 E. E. Ellis, *Paul's Use of the Old Testament* (Edinburgh 1957), p. 118.

44 T. W. Manson, art. 'The Argument from Prophecy' in *JTS* xlvi (1945), 129–36.

45 G. Schrenk, art. δίκαιος in *TWNT* ii (Stuttgart 1935).

46 C. H. Dodd, *According to the Scriptures*, p. 41.

47 J. Z. Lauterbach, *The Mekilta de Rabbi Ishmael* (Philadelphia 1933), vol. i, p. 254.

48 Quoted by W. Rudolph in Kittel's *Bibl. Heb.*, sub Jerem. 23.5.

49 H. Dechent, art. 'Der "Gerechte"—eine Bezeichung für den Messias' in *Theol. Stud. u. Krit.* (1927–8), 439–43.

50 Op. cit., p. 230.

51 Art. cit., *passim*.

52 I do not necessarily want to suggest that the Teacher of Righteousness always refers to one and the same individual. There is much to be said for the suggestion that it refers to an office, held by a succcession of people. See J. Weingreen, art. 'The title Moreh Sedek' in *Journal of Semitic Studies* 6 (Autumn 1961), 162–74.

53 See *Tractate Makkoth*, ed. H. M. Lazarus, in BT (London 1935), p. 173. S-B refer to this interpretation, but suggest it may have been prompted by anti-Christian polemic, ad. loc. Rom. 1.17.

54 אוּמָנוּת (handiwork) for אֱמוּנָה (faithfulness). See S-B, ad loc. Gal. 3.11.

55 Wᶜ, third hand in the Freer Ms., now in Washington.

56 See *The Wrath of the Lamb*, pp. 73f and *Paul's Understanding of Jesus*, pp. 4–8.

57 Martin Luther, *Commentary on the Epistle to the Galatians* (E.T. of 1575, London 1953), p. 236.

58 J. B. Lightfoot, *St Paul's Epistle to the Galatians* (10e., London 1890), in loc.

59 H. Schlier, *Der Brief an die Galater* (Göttingen 1962).

60 M-J. Lagrange, *Saint Paul: Épitre aux Galates* (Paris 1950), in loc.

61 Etheridge, op. cit., p. 534.

62 See *Tractate Sotah*, ed. A. Cohen, in BT (London 1936), pp. 184f.

63 E. Lohmeyer, art. 'Probleme Paulinischer Theologie' in ZNTW 28 (1929), 177–207.

64 R. Bring, *Commentary on Galatians* (E.T., Philadelphia 1961). See also his *Christus und das Gesetz* (London 1969), pp. 43–54. A. Müller, in his unpublished dissertation 'Die Auslegung alttestamentlichen Geschichtsstoffs bei Paulus' (Halle 1960), p. 120, is much nearer the mark when he maintains that the law is presented as an alternative (though impossible) way of life.

65 U. Holzmeister, art. 'De Christi Crucifixione Quid e Deut. 21.22 et Gal. 3.13 consequatur' in *Biblica* xxvii (1946), 18–29. *J. Hoad*, art. 'Some New Testament References to Isaiah 53' in *ET* 68 (May 1957), 244–5.

66 See *Tractate Sanhedrin* i, ed. J. Schachter and H. Freedman, in BT (London 1935), p. 300. See also S-B in loc. The Targum refs. in Etheridge, op. cit., are pp. 522 and 622.

67 Schoeps, op. cit., p. 184, The Hebrew is תלוי.

68 H. Vollmer, *Die Alttestamentlichen Citate bei Paulus* (Freiburg und Leipzig 1899), p. 29.

69 It is hardly necessary to point out that it is not irrelevant to cite Symmachus' version, even though he lived after Paul's day. The Qumran documents have now made it plain that Aquila, Symmachus, and Theodotion all revised previously existing translations, and did not translate *de novo*. See D. Barthelémey, art. 'Chainon Manquant de l'Histoire de la Septante' in *RB* 60 (1953), 18f.

70 A. W. F. Blunt, *The Epistle of Paul to the Galatians* (Oxford 1925).

71 E. D. Burton, art. 'Redemption from the Curse of the Law—an exposition of Gal. 3.13, 14' in *American Journal of Theology* ii (1907), 624–46.

72 E. Larsson, *Christus als Vorbild*, p. 49.

73 R. A. Lipsius, *Briefe an de Galater, Römer, Philipper* (Freiburg 1891).

74 H. Lietzmann, *An die Galater* (Tübingen 1911).

75 P. Benoit, art. 'La Loi et la Croix d'après Saint Paul' in *RB* 47 (1938), 475–509.

76 F. Büchsel, art. κατάρα in *TWNT* (Stuttgart 1949).

## Chapter 3

1 M. R. James, ed. and tr., *The Biblical Antiquities* of Pseudo-Philo [*Bibl. Ant.*] (London 1917) xix, 6.

2 The LXX is numbered Ps. 31 of course.

3 The LXX actually renders this as a prayer:
   Rescue me from those who encircle me.

4 The Hebrew here hardly makes sense. It runs literally: 'shouts of deliverance thou dost encompass me'. The LXX has taken the Heb.

רְעִי (? 'shouts of') as meaning 'my shout of joy', hence 'my joy'; and פלט (apparently a noun meaning 'escape' in the MT) as a verb meaning 'rescue'. Then תְּסוֹבְבֵנִי has been taken as a participle (presumably dropping the ת by haplography with the previous ט) to give the sense 'those who encircle me'.

5  See P. I. Hershon *A Rabbinical Commentary on Genesis* (London 1885), pp. 91–2.

6  U. Wilckens, art. 'Die Rechtfertigung Abrahams nach Römer 4' in *Studien zur Theologie der alttestamentlichen Überlieferung* (Neukirch 1961), 112f.

7  The suggestion was originally made by Michel in his commentary; he suggests it may be a reference to the LXX of Gen. 18.3.

8  See C. Westermann, *Essays in O.T. Interpretation*, p. 118.

9  L. Cerfaux, *Le Christ dans la Théologie de Saint Paul* (Paris 1951), p. 161.

10  *From First Adam to Last*, pp. 32–4.

11  A. Kolenkow, art. 'The Ascription of Romans 4.5' in *Harvard Theological Review* 60 (1967), 228–30.

12  *Comm. in Gal.*, pp. 236–7 (E.T., 1575 e., London 1953).

13  This reference is noted by Kirk in loc.

14  Vol. I, p. 220.

15  Midrash on the Psalms I, 408.

16  Ibid., 434–5.

17  See *Tractate Aboth*, ed. J. Israelstam, in BT (London 1935), p. 59.

18  G. Vermes, *Scripture and Tradition in Judaism* (Leiden 1961), p. 67.

19  M. R. James, op. cit., p. 18.

20  *Archaeologia* I, 7, 1 in S. A. Naber, ed., *Josephus Opera Omnia* (Leipzig 1888).

21  Vermes, op. cit., pp. 79–80.

22  Hershon, op. cit., p. 66. This book is in fact a translation of part of the book called *Tsᵃ'eynah urᵃ'eynahi*, a popular commentary on the Pentateuch.

23  *Legum Allegoriae* III, 228f.

24  *Quis Rev. Div. Heres* 90–5.

25  πίστις γάρ, ὡς ὁ παλαιὸς λόγος, τῶν ἀδήλων τὰ ἐμφανῆ.

26  *De Mig. Abrahami*, 44. It is followed by a citation of Gen. 15.6.

27  *De Praemiis et Poenis* 28–30.

28  See *De Opific. Mund.* 34, of dawn: ἡ μὲν προευαγγελίζεται μέλλοντα ἥλιον ἀνίσχειν 'it gives the first intimation of the good news of the coming rising of the sun'. *De Mut. Nom.* 158, of a fledgling bird: τὴν ἐλπίδα τοῦ πέτεσθαι δυνήσεσθαι προευαγγελιζόμενος '[he shakes his wings] anticipating the splendid hope of his being able to fly'. *De*

*Abrahamo* 153: καὶ προσιόντι μὲν φιλῷ προευαγγελίζεται τὸ τῆς εὐνοίας πάθος εὐοδίῳ καὶ γαληνῷ βλέμματι 'as a friend approaches, he learns beforehand the happy news of one's feeling of good will towards him by one's cheerful and calm expression' (my trans.).

29 It comes in his commentary on Rom. 4.3f. A. Müller in his unpublished dissertation describes Abraham's faith as a *Vorabbildung* of Christian faith, which approximates to the view maintained here (p. 114).

## Chapter 4

1 Though I do not think that Paul wrote Ephesians, I believe it comes from the pen of a close disciple.

2 See T. W. Manson, art. ἱλαστήριον in *JTS* 46 (Jan. Apr. 1945), 1f.

3 In loc. Rom. 4. 17–22.

4 In *Le Christ dans la Théologie de St Paul* (Paris 1951), p. 161.

5 I have elaborated this point in *Jesus Christ in the Old Testament*, pp. 23f. Apart from any other considerations, one of the events to which Paul refers here is the manifestation of Christ as the giver of water from the rock: Christ cannot be a type of himself!

6 In *Jesus Christ in the Old Testament*, pp. 133f. I suggested that the author of 1 Peter actually had Hab. 2.1–4 in mind when he wrote these verses. I have also discussed some of these passages in *Studies in the Pastoral Epistles*, pp. 42–55.

7 *According to the Scriptures*, p. 44.

8 *New Testament Apologetic*, p. 226.

9 L. Goppelt, art. 'Apokalyptic und Typologie bei Paulus' in *Theologische Literaturzeitung* 89 (May 1964), 322–43.

10 See *Quod Deus Sit Immort.* 4.

11 See *Archaeologia* I, 13, 1.

12 *Bibl. Ant.* XVIII, 5 and XXXII, 1–5.

13 See *Tractate Sotah*, p. 151.

14 I, 220f.

15 See *Tractate Baba Kamma*, ed. E. Kirzner, in BT (London 1935) I, pp. 287–8.

16 Hershon, pp. 125 and 127.

17 See *H. J. Schoeps*, art. 'The Sacrifice of Isaac in Paul's Theology' in *JBL* 65 (1946), 385f. He repeats the arguments without very much addition in *Paulus*, pp. 144f.

18 *Scripture and Tradition in Judaism*, pp. 195–225.

19 Op. cit., pp. 120–1.

20 J. E. Wood, art. 'Isaac Typology in the New Testament' in *NTS* 14 (July 1968), 583–9.

21  *From First Adam to Last*, pp. 26–9.

22  *Paulus und seine Bibel*, p. 46.

23  J. W. Doeve, *Jewish Hermeneutics in the Synoptic Gospels and Acts* (Assen 1954), p. 107.

24  *New Testament Apologetic*, p. 226.

25  *Scripture and Tradition in Judaism*, p. 220.

26  See *Tractate Sanhedrin*, ed. J. Schachter and H. Freedman, in BT (London 1935) ii, pp. 595–6. The same tradition is found in the Palestinian Targum. See R. le Déaut, art. 'Traditions Targumiques dans le Corpus Paulinien' in *Biblica* 42 (1961), 38.

27  See J. P. Lightfoot, *The Apostolic Fathers: the Epistle of Barnabas* (London 1891), p. 251 (my trans.). There is, however, a possibility that the *Testaments of the Twelve Patriarchs* may provide a still earlier Christian mention of the 'Aqedah. In Test. Levi 18.6 we read: 'The heavens shall be opened, And from the temple of glory shall come upon him sanctification, With the Father's voice as from Abraham to Isaac' (see R. H. Charles, *Apocrypha and Pseudepigrapha of the O.T.*, vol. ii, p. 314). If the *Testaments* (or this part of them is) are Christian, then this is probably earlier than the Epistle of Barnabas. I owe this reference to an art. by I. H. Marshall, 'Son of God or Servant of Yahweh?' in *NTS* 15 (Apr. 1969), 334.

## Chapter 5

1  G. W. H. Lampe, ed., *A Patristic Greek Lexicon* (Oxford 1961+).

2  It is surprising that neither *TWNT* nor Cremer so much as mentions κοίτη in their dictionaries, far less give it any detailed treatment.

3  *Tractate Yebamoth*, ed. W. Slotki, in BT (London 1936), pp. 428–9.

4  Hershon, p. 88.

5  *Bibl. Ant.* xxxii, 5, a reference noticed by J. Munck, art. 'Christus und Israel, eine Auslegung von Röm. 9–11' in *Acta Jutlandica* xxviii (1956), Theology Series 7, p. 33.

6  R. P. C. Hanson, *Allegory and Event* (London 1959), p. 81.

7  G. A. Dannell, art. 'Did Paul know the Tradition about the Virgin Birth?' in *Studia Theologica* 4 (1950), 94–101.

8  In this and the four quotations which follow I have given my own translation.

9  See my art., 'Philo's Etymologies' in *JTS* xviii NS (1967), 128–39.

10  All my examples of post-Pauline usage come from the *Patristic Greek Lexicon*, sub. ἀλληγορεῖν. I have given my own translation of all of them. The references are Hipp. *Haer.* 8.14; Clem. *Strom.* 7.12; Or. *Cels.* 4.44; Theod. *Gal.* 4.24.

11  Perhaps one might suggest one more contrast. Hagar, immediately fruitful, but with a posterity of no significance, contrasted with Sarah,

long barren, but ultimately bearing a progeny which is ultimately of immense significance. Ulonska would see a typological treatment in verses 22 and 28–9, and an allegorical one in verses 24–7. See H. Ulonska, op. cit., p. 66. A. Müller in his dissertation (pp. 129–9) has an excellent discussion of this passage. He treats verses 24–7 as a parenthesis, and argues that here we have allegory rather than typology, because it is not what happened to Hagar and Sarah that is significant, but what they stand for: Hagar stands for slavery, Sarah for freedom. He adds that Paul does not use his allegory in order to abstract from it and build up a philosophical or ethical principle, but rather to illuminate the eschatological situation of the contemporary church.

12  S-B in loc. Rev. 11.8.

13  *St Paul and the Church of the Gentiles* (Cambridge 1939), p. 97.

14  J. Klausner, *From Jesus to Paul* (E.T., London 1944), p. 456. The various readings in the text witness to the uncertainty of meaning.

15  *Jewish Hermeneutics in the Synoptic Gospels and Acts*, p. 202.

16  Equally misleading is the suggestion, based on the Vulgate and adapted by Luther, that συστοιχεῖ means 'is geographically one with', on the (quite mistaken) assumption that there is a range of hills which can be traced from the Sinai peninsula to the Judean massif.

17  See *Tractate Berakoth*, 51–2.

18  The words 'with her son Isaac' are not in the MT but are supplied by the RSV from the LXX.

19  See *Tractate Pesahim*, ed. H. Freedman, in BT (London 1938), p. 616. *Yigmol* 'be manifest' is connected with the verb GML 'to wean'.

20  Hershon, p. 117.

21  Quoted by Lipsius in loc.

22  See *Essays on Typology* (London 1957), p. 15.

23  See *Allegory and Event*, p. 82.

24  See *L'Ancien Testament dans L'Église* (Neuchâtel 1960), p. 171.

25  See *Die Alttestamentlichen Citate bei Paulus*, p. 64. Vollmer is very slightly inaccurate here, for he writes: 'Paulus nennt die Erzahlung eine Allegorie.' Bläser must be added to the list of those who take this passage as typology, not allegory. See P. Bläser, art. 'Schriftverwertung und Schrifterklärung in Rabbinentum und bei Paulus' in *Theologische Quartalschrift* 132 (1952), 152–69.

26  See *Typos*, p. 168.

27  See *Paulus und seine Bibel*, p. 108.

28  See *Paul's Use of the Old Testament*, p. 53.

29  See *Paulus und das Judentum* (Stuttgart 1935), p. 64. It is very amusing to note that, writing in 1935, Windisch goes on in a footnote to accuse Karl Barth of treating Paul as Paul treated Genesis!

30  See *Paulus*, p. 252, n. 1.

31  See *De Cherubim* 8–9; *De Post. Caini* 130.

# Chapter 6

1  E. Dinkler, art. 'The Historical and Eschatological Israel in Roms. 9–11' in *Journal of Religion* xxxvi (1956), p. 123.

2  *Christus und Israel*, p. 89.

3  *Paul and the Salvation of Mankind* (E.T., London 1959), p. 45.

4  In Deut. 7.25 the LXX uses πταίειν to translate MT ישׁק where Israel is described as being made to stumble by idols. This is the same Hebrew word as is rendered by σκάνδαλον in Paul's version of Ps. 69.22 in Rom. 11.9 above.

5  See *Paulus*, p. 256.

6  *Christus und Israel*, p. 95.

7  G. Delling, art. ἀρχή in *TWNT*, vol. 1 (Stuttgart 1949).

8  D. E. H. Whiteley, art. 'St Paul's Thought on the Atonement' in *JTS* 8 NS (1957), 245.

9  *De Spec. Leg.* IV, 179–80. The Greek is: διότι τοῦ συμπάντος ἀνθρώπων γένους ἀπενεμήθη οἷά τις ἀπαρχὴ τῷ ποιητῇ καὶ πατρί. My trans.

10  *De Sacrif. Abel et Cain* 108. The Greek is: τὸ τοίνυν φύραμα κυρίως, εἰ χρὴ τἀληθὲς εἰπεῖν, ἡμεῖς ἐσμεν αὐτοὶ συμπεφορημένων καὶ συγκεκριμένων πλειστῶν οὐσιῶν, ἵνα ἀποτελεσθῶμεν. My trans.

11  See *Tractate 'Orlah*, ed. J. Israelstam, in BT (London 1948), p. 364.

12  But there is a well attested v. l. ἀπ' ἀρχῆς which RSV actually adopts.

13  Etheridge, op. cit., p. 388.

14  H. Lietzmann, *An die Korinther I and II* (4e. rev., Tübingen 1949).

15  Lampe and Woollcombe, op. cit., p. 55.

16  E. B. Allo, *Saint Paul: Première Épitre aux Corinthiens* (Paris 1956).

17  Euler, op. cit., p. 142. Conzelmann denies that there is any Exodus typology here. See H. Conzelmann, *Der Erste Brief an die Korinther* (Krit. Exeg. Komm., Göttingen 1969).

18  C. K. Barrett, *The First Epistle to the Corinthians* (London 1968).

19  H. L. Goudge, *The First Epistle to the Corinthians* (London 1903).

20  A. Robertson and A. Plummer, *A Critical and Exegetical Commentary on the First Epistle of Saint Paul to the Corinthians* (Edinburgh 1911).

21  J. Héring, *La Première Épitre de Saint Paul aux Corinthiens* (Neuchâtel-Paris 1949).

22  See G. V. Jourdan, art. 'κοινωνία in 1 Cor. 10.16' in *JBL* 67 (1948), 111f.

23  See *Tractate Kethuboth*, ed. W. Slotki, in BT (London 1936) III, p. 721.

24  The Targum of Onkelos omits the reference to wine. Is this perhaps a sign of anti-Christian polemic? An indication that this was for early Christians a proof text about the Eucharist? But it is retained by the

Targum of Palestine and the Targum of Jerusalem, which show fewer signs of the influence of the controversy with the Church. See Etheridge, op. cit., pp. 549, 664, 665.

25 See *Quis Rev. Div. Heres* 279. The Greek is: ἀφ' οὗ καθάπερ ἀπὸ ῥίζης τὸ σκεπτικὸν καὶ θεωρητικὸν τῶν τῆς φύσεως πραγμάτων ἀνέβλαστεν ἔρνος, ὄνομα Ἰσραήλ. My trans.

26 C. Maurer, art. ῥίζα in *TWNT* VI (Stuttgart 1959).

27 Charles here reads מִמֶּנּוּ שׁוֹרֶשׁ. He says that the Hebrew is 'almost wholly obliterated' (op. cit. in loc.). Lévi accepts the same reading. It means literally 'a root from himself' (R. H. Charles, *The Apocrypha and Pseudepigrapha of the Old Testament* (Oxford 1913) in loc. Ecclus. 47.22).

28 The translation of וַיַּעַל by ἀνηγγείλαμεν is puzzling. Both Ottley (R. R. Ottley, *The Book of Isaiah according to the Septuagint* (Cambridge 1909), in loc. Isa. 53.2) and Maurer suggest that the original rendering was ἀνέτειλεν. Euler (op. cit., p. 53) denies that ἀνηγγείλαμεν can have been caused by a misreading of the MT because there is no Hebrew word whose radicals could be mistaken for a Hebrew word meaning 'proclaim'. It must be a case of change taking place within the Greek; perhaps ἀνάγειν or ἀνατέλλειν was misread. Nevertheless one might very tentatively suggest that it may have been a dittography for the last word in verse 1 נִגְלָתָה; the dittography then displaced the first word of verse 2.

29 Euler, op. cit., pp. 12, 29, 33, 37.

30 It is true that the reading is uncertain in Rom. 11.17 and a reading which omits ῥίζα altogether is supported by P⁴⁰, Codex Claromontanus, and other authorities (this reading is actually adopted in the RSV text). But even if verse 17 is discounted, verse 18 gives us this sense.

31 The MT of Isa. 60.21 reads נֵצֶר מַטָּעַ. Kittel in *Bibl. Heb.* points out the Targum ('the plant of my joy' נִצְבַּת דַּחְדוּת ), the Syr., and the Vg. ('germen plantationis meae') seem to have read נֵצֶר מַטָּעַי 'the shoot of my planting'. He himself suggests נֵצֶר מַטַּע יהוה 'the plant of the Lord's planting'. But this is not supported by the LXX, which has simply τὸ φύτευμα. *Hodayoth* vi. 15 has מַטָּעַה עוֹלָם, but this does not necessarily claim to be a translation.

32 See Otto Betz, *Offenbarungen und Schriftforschung in der Qumransekte* (Tübingen 1960), pp. 41f.

33 This is easily explained; it read הַמּוּלָה as הַמּוּלָה 'the circumcision' instead of as הַמּוּלָה 'uproar'

34 It is less easy to see why this should be. But, having once turned 'uproar' into the 'circumcision', the translator would find himself with גְּדוֹלָה untranslated. It would have made nonsense to have attached it to 'circumcision' and offered 'the great circumcision' (besides

requiring הגדולה in the Hebrew). Perhaps the translator thought that by putting together גדולה and עליה he could be justified in inserting θλῖψις to explain it.

35 It has ἐμβαλῶμεν ξύλον εἰς τὸν ἄρτον αὐτοῦ 'let us throw a piece of wood into his bread', a phrase which is completely meaningless in the context.

36 *Paul's Use of the Old Testament*, p. 123.

37 See *Tractate Menahoth* I, ed. E. Cashdan, in BT (London 1948), pp. 321–33.

38 See *Stromata* VI, cap. xv, 120, 1 in Clemens Alexandrinus, ed. O. Stählin, rev. E. Früchtel (Berlin 1960). The Greek is: Δύναται δὲ ὁ ὑπὸ τοῦ ἀποστόλου γενόμενος ἐγκεντρισμὸς εἰς τὴν καλλιέλαιαν γίγνεσθαι, τὸν Χριστὸν αὐτόν, τουτέστι τῶν εἰς Χριστὸν πιστευόντων.

39 See P. E. Hughes, art. 'The Olive Tree of Romans 11' in *Evangelical Quarterly* 20 (1948), 22–45.

40 *Church Dogmatics* II (E.T., Edinburgh 1957), pp. 214 and 285.

41 It is just possible that a secondary (very secondary) passage behind Rom. 11.17–24 may be Hos. 14.5–7, where Israel is compared, among many other figures, to an olive. P. Humbert, 'Le Messie dans le Targum des Prophètes' (monograph from *Révue de Théologie et de Philosophie* (Lausanne 1911)), points out that the Targum sees in this verse a reference to the Messiah and to the resurrection of the just.

## Chapter 7

1 See J. Kallas, art. 'Romans 13.1–7: An Interpolation' in *NTS* 11 (July 1965), 365f.

2 It tr. ומצא as if it was ומצאת *waw* consecutive. Note that the LXX is quite capable of translating *waw* with an imperative literally, as its treatment of שכל shows. This suggests that there was a Hebrew text known to the LXX translators, perhaps to Paul, and to the Vg., which read מצאת.

3 He has read שכל as if it was שָׂכִיל (Qal.) or שִׂכֵּל (Pi'el) instead of שֶׂכֶל, as MT. Both these forms are very rare, particularly the Qal, but they are found. It is remarkable that in Prov. 3.4 Aquila used περινοεῖν. This sort of translation of *sēkel* in this text must have been a firmly fixed tradition.

4 *Tractate Shekalim*, ed. M. H. Segal, in BT (London 1938), p. 10.

5 See Rom. 11.35; where the Targum on the verse quoted here, Job 41.11 (MT and LXX 41.3), runs 'Who hath been before me on the day of creation that I should repay him?' (quoted by W. L. Knox, *St Paul and the Church of the Gentiles*, p. 118). Thus the sense of the verse assumed by Paul is much the same as that assumed by the Targum.

6 Ed. J. Israelstam, in the BT, pp. 19–21.

7 He quotes ἱλαρὸν γὰρ δότην ἀγαπᾷ ὁ Θεός, a line absent altogether from the MT

8 W. Klassen, art. 'Coals of Fire: Sign of Repentance or Revenge?' in *NTS* 9 (July 1963), 337f.

9 He also refers to Herford's suggestion that these phrases describe R. Eliezer's sufferings as a result of the excommunication pronounced against him by the rabbis.

10 The Hebrew is singular, עָקְרָב and 'vengeance' in the Greek is ἐκδίκησις.

11 Compare W. D. Davies, *The Setting of the Sermon on the Mount* (Cambridge 1964) and B. Gerhardsson, *The Good Samaritan—the Good Shepherd?* (Lund 1958).

12 D. Daube, *The New Testament and Rabbinic Judaism* (London 1956), pp. 90–7.

13 C. H. Talbert, art. 'Tradition and Redaction in Romans 12.9–21' in *NTS* 16 (Oct. 1969), 83–94.

## Chapter 8

1 P. W. Schmiedel, *Die Briefe an die Thessaloniker und an die Korinther* (Hand. Comm., Freiburg 1891).

2 A Plummer, *A Critical and Exegetical Commentary on the Second Epistle of St Paul to the Corinthians* (I.C.C., Edinburgh 1915).

3 R. H. Strachan, *The Second Epistle of St Paul to the Corinthians* (Moff. Comm., London 1935).

4 E. B. Allo, *Seconde Épitre aux Corinthiens* (Paris 1956). Compare for precisely the same confusion S. Del Paramo, who translates τῆς παλαιᾶς διαθήκης here as 'los libros del Antiguo Testamento'. See his art. 'La Citas de los Salmos en S. Pablo' in *Analecta Biblica* 18 (Rome 1963), 229.

5 J. Héring, *La Seconde Épitre de Saint Paul aux Corinthiens* (Neuchâtel and Paris 1958).

6 R. F. Weymouth, *The New Testament in Modern Speech* (London 1902).

7 J. Moffatt, *A New Translation of the Bible* (London e. of 1934).

8 R. A. Knox, *The New Testament of our Lord and Saviour Jesus Christ* (London 1945).

9 J. B. Phillips, *Letters to Young Churches* (London 1947).

10 A. Jones, ed., *The Jerusalem Bible* (London 1966).

11 *Good News For Modern Man: the New Testament; Today's English Version* (American Bible Society, New York 1966).

12 W. Barclay, *The New Testament*, vol. ii (London 1969).

13 To him we should add the name of J. Behm in whose art. on διαθήκη in *TWNT* there is no suggestion that ἡ παλαιὰ διαθήκη in Paul could

mean 'the Hebrew Scriptures' (see *TWNT* II (Stuttgart 1950), pp. 106f.

14 Vollmer, op. cit., p. 50.

15 See *Paulus und seine Bibel*, pp. 142–3.

16 See *Paulus*, pp. 176–7.

17 Westermann, *Essays in Old Testament Interpretation*, pp. 300–1 (E.T., London 1963, of German e. 1960).

18 Bandstra, op. cit., p. 88.

19 See Bring, *Christus und das Gesetz*, p. 7. A similar view is put forward by C. H. Renard in an art. 'La Lecture de l'Ancien Testament par Saint Paul' in *Analecta Biblica* 18 (Rome 1963), 210.

20 Amsler, op. cit., pp. 48, 54.

21 p. 97.

22 See *Paulus und das Judentum*, p. 70.

23 The word which LXX translates as κατάλειμμα and Paul as ὑπόλειμμα here is שְׁאָר. But in Mal. 2.15 LXX translates the same word with ὑπόλειμμα, so we are not justified in assuming that Paul's version did not have ὑπόλειμμα in Isa. 10.22.

24 The passage Paul quotes from Isa. 8.14 here is correctly translated by the RSV thus: 'And he will become a sanctuary, and a stone of offence, and a rock of stumbling to both houses of Israel, and a trap and a snare to the inhabitants of Jerusalem.' The LXX largely misses the sense, because it translates the word in Hebrew that means '*for* a stone of offence and *for* a rock of stumbling' as if it was the word that means 'not', thus giving exactly the opposite meaning to what Isaiah wishes to convey: 'not as a stone of offence will you encounter him, nor as a rock of stumbling'. In addition it turns 'both houses of Israel' into 'the house of Jacob' and translates 'for a trap and a snare' with ἐν παγίδι καὶ ἐν κοιλάσματι, giving the meaning 'and the house of Jacob [are] in a snare, and [so are] those who sit in the interior of Jerusalem'. No doubt the LXX read Isa. 8.14a as לֹא אֶבֶן נֶגֶף וְלֹא צוּר מִכְשׁוֹל. Seeligman ranks this among passages in which the LXX translator 'forcibly tries to wrench, from passages which he cannot understand, some signification, either by adding a negation not occurring in the Hebrew text, or by neglecting a negation which does occur in the Hebrew original' (see I. L. Seeligman, *The Septuagint Version of Isaiah: a discussion of its problems* (Leiden 1948), p. 57).

25 The evidence for this is found in what Etheridge calls 'the Jerusalem Targum', but what others, notably Bowker, describe as a version of the Palestine Targum. Etheridge reserves the name 'Palestine Targum' for the Targum ascribed to Jonathan ben Uzziel (which Bowker calls 'Pseudo-Jonathan'. See J. Bowker, *The Targums and Rabbinic Literature* (Cambridge 1969), pp. 16–28). Till recently the Targum in question was found only in fragments (though one fragment covers Deut.

30.12–14), but a complete Ms., called the Neofiti Ms., has now turned up, but has not yet been published. The relevant passage runs thus· 'The law is not in the heavens, that thou shouldest say, O that we had one like Mosheh the prophet to ascend into heaven and bring it to us, and make us hear its commands, that we may do them! Neither is the law beyond the great sea, that thou shouldest say, O that we had one like Jonah the prophet, who could descend into the depths of the sea, and bring it to us, and make us hear its commands' (Etheridge, pp. 654–5).

26  E. E. Ellis, art. '*A Note on Pauline Hermeneutics*' in *NTS* 2 (1955–56), pp. 131–2.

27  Von J. Schmid, art. 'Die alttestamentliche Citate bei Paulus und die Theorie vom sensus plenior' in *Biblische Zeitschrift* 3 (1959), 161–73.

28  The Midrash on the Psalms offers a most elaborate exegesis of Ps. 19.2, only two verses previous to the verse cited by Paul in Rom. 10.18. The first line, it claims, refers to Moses' sojourn on Sinai while he was receiving the Torah, and the second line refers to a whole series of critical nights in Israel's history (see Midrash 1, 276–9). If traditional rabbinical exegesis could find such remarkable implications in verse 2 of Ps. 19, there would be nothing arbitrary or unreasonable from Paul's point of view in finding that verse 4 refers to the evangelistic activity of apostles and prophets.

29  See *Typos*, p. 153 n.

30  *Jesus Christ in the Old Testament*, chapter 2.

31  See W. L. Knox, op. cit., p. 118.

32  *From First Adam to Last*, p. 67.

33  Ibid., p. 82.

34  *L'ancien Testament dans l'Église*, p. 56. Vollmer had made precisely the same claim much earlier when he said that in Paul's view Israel's history took place primarily for the instruction of Christians (op. cit., p. 77).

35  In *Jesus Christ in the Old Testament* I have argued that J. Jeremias is mistaken in regarding Moses as a type of Christ in 2 Cor. 3 (op. cit., p. 33).

36  Though Paul mentions specifically neither Moses nor Jonah in Rom. 10.6–8, the evidence of the Palestine Targum (using Bowker's terminology) makes it extremely likely that he regarded them as types of Christ's resurrection and *descensus ad inferos* respectively. The evidence of Matt. 12.39–40 suggests that Paul did not invent this typology himself, but that it was current in the early Church. E. Käsemann notes the reference in the Targum but considers that Baruch 3.29 is nearer to Paul's thought background. See *Perspectives on Paul* (E.T., London 1971, of German e. of 1969), pp. 160–1. Käsemann describes what Paul is doing here as taking over 'motifs from the Sophia myth'. It may be questioned whether this is a true description of Rom. 10.6–8. It would seem simpler and more accurate to describe it as a typological midrash on Deut. 30.12–14.

37 Amsler, op. cit., p. 57.

38 *Paulus und seine Bibel*, pp. 104, 106.

39 Op. cit., p. 82.

40 See *Paulus*, p. 246.

41 J. D. Wood, *The Interpretation of the Bible* (London 1959), pp. 21–2, 168.

42 F. Baumgärtel, in Westermann, op. cit., p. 143.

43 J. A. Fitzmeyer, art. 'The Use of Explicit O.T. Quotations in Qumran Literature and in the N.T.' in *NTS* 7 (1960–61), 297–333.

44 A. Müller, art. 'Der Qal-Wachomer Schluss bei Paulus' in *ZNTW* 58 (1967), 73–92.

45 See Vermes, *The Dead Sea Scrolls in English*, pp. 102–3. The proper singular of 'staves' is 'staff'.

46 See Vermes, op. cit., p. 104. In fact the meaning of the two words סכות and כיון is by no means certain. Many modern scholars believe they are the names of Assyrian gods. But, whatever their original meaning, no one suggests that of themselves they have any connection with the Books of the Law and of the Prophets.

47 Midrash on the Psalms 1, 30, 81, 368, 422–3, 441.

48 *Bibl. Ant.* xxiii, 6–7.

49 See *Tractate Gittin*, 266.

50 לא תחסם שור בדישו.

51 See Moulton and Milligan, *sub* φιμόω.

52 LXX less accurately uses κέντρον.

53 E. Evans, *The Epistles of Paul to the Corinthians*. Clarendon Bible (Oxford 1930).

54 P. A. Lipsius, *Briefe an die Korinther* (Freiburg 1891).

55 C. K. Barrett, *The First Epistle to the Corinthians*.

56 Etheridge, p. 632; S-B note this passage.

57 See I. Porusch, ed., *Tractate Me'ilah* in BT (London 1948).

58 See H. Freedman, ed., *Tractate Baba Mezi'a* in BT (London 1935), pp. 509f and M. Simon, ed., *Tractate Gittin* in BT (London 1936), p. 290.

59 My trans.

60 See H. B. Swete, *An Introduction to the Old Testament in Greek* (Cambridge 1914), p. 576. My trans.

## Chapter 9

1 Paul writes παιδευόμενοι καὶ μὴ θανατούμενοι echoing the LXX:
παιδεύων ἐπαίδευσέν με ὁ Κύριος
καὶ τῷ θανάτῳ οὐ παρέδωκέν με.

Ps. 118 was of course a psalm widely used in the early Church; cf. 118.22 so often quoted in the NT and also verse 26 quoted in the Gospels. 118.18 was represented by the rabbis as having been uttered by Abraham, Isaac, Jacob, Moses, and David as a thanksgiving for the miracles which God wrought on their behalf (Midrash on the Psalms II, 242). Paul must have applied it first to Christ and then to Christians in Christ.

2 Quoted in S-B in loc. 2 Cor. 8.15.

3 R. P. C. Hanson, *II Corinthians* (Torch Series) (London 1954).

4 Unless Paul is referring in the previous verses to the other Gentile churches, who are not yet ready with their contributions. Paul hopes the Corinthians will supply the immediate needs of the collection and that the others will equalize the position later by sending in their contributions. As far as concerns the point we are studying here, it does not matter which interpretation we favour.

5 *Quis Rer. Div. Heres* 191. My trans. The Greek is:

ἔτι δὲ τοίνυν τὴν οὐράνιον τροφήν—σοφία δὲ ἐστιν—
τῆς ψυχῆς, ἣν κο λεῖ μαννά—διανεμεῖ πᾶσιν τοῖς
χρησομένοις θεῖος λόγος ἐξ ἴσου πεφροντικῶς
διαφερόντως ἰσότητος. μαρτυρεῖ δὲ Μωϋσῆς λέγων . . . κτλ.

6 C. S. C. Williams, ed., 2 Corinthians in Peake's *Commentary on the Bible*, new e. (London 1962).

7 J. J. O'Rourke, ed., 2 Corinthians in the *Jerome Bible Commentary* (London 1968).

8 The LXX uses the non-classical word πολυωρεῖν 'treat with much care'. The MT is וְהוֹתִירְךָ.

9 The MT is יֵשׁ מְפַזֵּר וְנוֹסָף עוֹד

וְחוֹשֵׂךְ מִיֹּשֶׁר אַךְ־לְמַחְסוֹר

10 See *Tractate Berakoth*, ed. M. Simon, in BT (London 1948), p. 396.

11 The MT is טוֹב עַיִן הוּא יְבֹרָךְ

12 On the other hand, the LXX of Prov. 22.8cd looks very much as if it was translated from a Hebrew original:

ἄνδρα ἱλαρὸν καὶ δότην εὐλογεῖ ὁ Θεός,
ματαιότητα δὲ ἔργων αὐτοῦ συντελέσει.

The second line is very Septuagintal Greek and could hardly have been anything but a translation. It is not easy to understand what it means. LXX has used συντελέσει just before this in 8b, where it renders MT יְכַלֶּה (though the Hebrew is obscure; G. Beer in Kittel's *Bibl. Heb.* suggests that it should read יְכַהוּ), so 8d may mean 'and will remove the vanity of his works', i.e. (?) compensate for his previous vain works by this good work. It may be a misplaced doublet: LXX 22.8c = MT 22.9a and LXX 22.8d = MT 22.8b.

13 See *Tractate Nedarim* 118, ed. H. Freedman, in BT (London 1936).

14 Braude II, 210.

15 Paul also echoes other texts in this passage: e.g. Isa. 55.10; Hos. 10.12. Vollmer suggests that these texts, together with Deut. 28.12, were already combined in rabbinic tradition by the word מָטָר 'rain', a link only valid in the Hebrew (see Vollmer op. cit., p. 41).

16 See Bultmann's essay in Westerman, op. cit., pp. 51f.

17 Ibid., p. 55.

18 *Old and New in Interpretation* (London 1966), p. 124.

19 Op. cit., p. 51.

20 For this and the previous reference, see op. cit., p. 52.

21 Compare C. H. Dodd, *According to the Scriptures*, p. 127, where he makes the point that in the (oral) *testimonia* which he recognizes exact predictive fulfilment is not a prominent feature at all.

22 Op. cit., p. 145.

23 Diezinger, art. cit., pp. 232–3.

24 See Clement XII, 7, ed. J. B. Lightfoot, in *The Apostolic Fathers*.

25 LXX: Δεῖξόν μοι τὴν σεαυτοῦ δόξαν.

26 See *De Specialibus Legibus* I, 41–50. My trans. The Greek is:
πέπεισμαι μὲν ταῖς σαῖς ὑφηγήσεσιν ὅτι οὐκ ἂν ἴσχυσα δέξασθαι τὸ τῆς σῆς φαντασίας ἐναργὲς εἶδος. ἱκετεύω δὲ τὴν γοῦν περί σε δόξαν θεάσασθαι.

27 Chapter 4: 'Inspired Scripture'.

28 *Bibl. Ant.* XXVIII, 6, 10.

29 Braude I, 455.

30 *Ibid.*, II, 88.

31 Vollmer, op. cit., p. 73.

32 See *Paulus und seine Bibel*, p. 69. In his commentary on Rom. 10.20 he writes: 'It has nothing to do with the subjectivity of Isaiah, but only with the importance of the utterance.'

33 See *The Interpretation of Scripture*, p. 188.

34 Amsler, op. cit., pp. 222–5.

35 *According to the Scriptures*, p. 126.

36 *Paulus und seine Bibel*, p. 54.

37 Doeve, op. cit., p. 116.

38 See W. Windfuhr, art. 'Der Apostel Paulus als Haggadist' in *ZATW* 44 (1926), 327–30.

39 Vollmer thinks these texts were already conflated when Paul used them (op. cit., p. 36).

40 This charge is made very explicitly by Vollmer, op. cit., p. 59.

41 *Paulus und seine Bibel*, p. 82.

42 James Barr, op. cit., p. 142n.

43 H. Ulonska, op. cit.

44 See *Tractate Sotah*, ed. A. Cohen, in BT (London 1936), p. 150.

45 See my art. already referred to, 'Philo's Etymologies'.

46 See *W. Bacher*, art. 'Gamaliel I' in the *Jewish Encyclopedia* (New York 1904). The Talmud reference that follows is *Tractate Shabbath*, ed. Freedman, in BT (London 1938) III, p. 565.

47 A. S. van der Woude and J. van der Ploeg have published articles about this Targum, which they are editing. See A. S. van der Woude 'Das Hiobtargum Aus Qumran Höhle XI', Supplement to *Vetus Testamentum* 1962 (Leiden 1963), pp. 322–31; J. van der Ploeg 'Le Targum de Job de la Grotte 11 de Qumran' (Amsterdam 1962). It is in Aramaic. It does not appear to cover the verse cited by Paul in Rom. 11.35 (Job 41.3, MT). Both scholars refer to the story of Gamaliel ordering the Targum on Job to be buried. van der Ploeg suggests it may have been this one; van der Woude is more doubtful. van der Ploeg suggests that Gamaliel may have disapproved of a sacred text being translated into the vernacular, or that the Targum may have contained heterodox teaching, though none has yet been traced in this one. It has apparently no connection with the much later *Targum on Job*. The author of the newly discovered Targum shows a tendency to 'rationalise the mythological terminology of the Hebrew text' (van der Woude, p. 331).

48 MT קללת אלהים תלוי.

49 It is true that Aquila and Theodotion render the Hebrew with κατάρα Θεοῦ κρεμάμενος, but this only strengthens our argument (see Vollmer, op. cit., p. 29). We can hardly suppose that Paul was acquainted with two Greek versions of the same text.

50 Vollmer, op. cit., p. 10.

51 *Paulus und seine Bibel*, p. 68.

52 S. Brock's review of *The Septuagint and Modern Society*, by S. Jellicoe, in *JTS* 20 (2) (October 1969), 579.

53 See Westermann, op. cit., p. 53. His example of Isa. 7.14 must now be qualified by Qumran evidence which suggests that the Christians were not the first to understand *'almah* as 'virgin'.

54 Ulonska, op. cit., pp. 27, 64.

55 See *De Mutatione Nominium* 48. Philo quotes Job 14.4: τίς γάρ, ὡς ὁ Ἰώβ φησι, κάθαρος ἀπὸ ῥόπου, κἂν μία ἡμέρα ἐστὶν ἡ ζωή; This is no doubt based on the LXX of Job. 14.4–5, which is by no means a literal trans. of the MT: τίς γὰρ κάθαρος ἔσται ἀπὸ ῥόπου; ἀλλ' οὐθείς. ἐὰν καὶ μία ἡμέρα ὁ βίος αὐτοῦ . . . εἰς χρόνον ἔθου. Philo has misunderstood the application of the second clause, which LXX here correctly following the Heb. attaches to the following sentence.

56 See his comm. in loc. 11.35.

L. Wilson, *Gnosis and the New Testament* (London 1968),

. 144.

*Christ in the Old Testament*, pp. 141f.

W. D. Davies in *Christian Origins and Judaism* (London 1962),
'The Scrolls have shown that much that has been labelled
tic may well have been native to Judaism.'

*Christ dans la Théologie de Saint Paul*, pp. 186–7.

lmann, *The Christology of the New Testament* (E.T., London 1959,
man e. of 1957), p. 168.

elling, art. 'Zum Neueren Paulus-verständnis' in *Nov. Test.* 4
), 99, 100–1, 106.

this view is still maintained by H. Conzelmann. See an article by
called 'The Mother of Wisdom' in the collection *The Future of Our
igious Past*, ed. J. M. Robinson (E.T., London 1971, of the German
of 1964), pp. 230–43.

e *St Paul and the Church of the Gentiles*, pp. 100, 108.

ee *Paul's Use of the Old Testament*, p. 124.

See *Le Christ, Sagesse de Dieu*, p. 397.

See *According to the Scriptures*, p. 23.

See art. 'Christus und Israel', pp. 22, 19.

L. Goppelt, art. 'Apokalyptik und Typologie bei Paulus' in *Theologische Literaturzeitung* 89 (May 1964), 337. Dodd also concludes that the
argument from Scripture in some form goes back to Jesus himself
(*According to the Scriptures*, pp. 109–10).

9 See art. cit. 'Der Christus des Paulus', p. 8.

40 See art. 'Apokalyptik und Typologie bei Paulus', pp. 324–7.

41 Ibid., p. 328.

42 Might one not justly claim that there is a certain prophet-typology in
the Qur'ān? Mohammed seems to regard himself as the fulfilment of
all prophetic types.

43 It might be maintained that such non-Pauline formulas as are to be
found in Phil. 2.6–9; Col. 1.15–18; Eph. 5.14 are to be attributed to the
tradition which he received. But it seems to me to be more satisfactory
to regard them as contemporary with Paul rather than as part of his
tradition.

44 See P. Bonnard, art. 'Mourir et vivre avec Jésus-Christ selon Saint
Paul' in *RdHPR* 2 (1956), pp. 101f.

## Chapter 11

1 See Bultmann's essay: 'The Significance of the Old Testament for the
Christian Faith' (1933). E.T. in B. W. Anderson's *The Old Testament
and Christian Faith*, p. 14.

57  See A. G. Wright, *M.* .......
    For details see note 4.......

58  See *Paul's Use of the Ol.......*

59  I here retain Etheridge.......
    Targum of Palestine' an.......

## Chapter 10

1   *Comm. in Gal.*, 34–6.

2   A. Marmorstein, art. 'Paulus u.......
    271–85.

3   O. Michel, art. 'Der Christus des.......

4   See *From Jesus to Paul*, p. 204.

5   I have noted one in John 5.35 in.......
    pp. 12–14.

6   Klausner, op. cit., pp. 54–5.

7   Doeve, op. cit., p. 292.

8   Ibid., p. 99.

9   Ibid., p. 64.

10  Amsler, op. cit., p. 55.

11  This is not to suggest, of course, that the Tor.......
    one period. A very similar point is made by C........
    'La Lecture de l'Ancien Testament par Saint Pa.......
    18 (Rome 1963), 207–15.

12  Op. cit., p. 42.

13  Ibid., p. 66.

14  Ibid., p. 67; see also p. 143.

15  Compare also Lietzmann's description of Paul writing.......
    p. 202 above.

16  Op. cit., pp. 83–4.

17  Op. cit., pp. 238–9.

18  See R. E. Brown, art. 'The Pre-Christian Semitic Concept of.......
    in *Catholic Biblical Quarterly*, vol. 20 (1958); also 'The Semit.......
    ground of the New Testament Mysterion I and II' in *Biblica* 39.......
    426–48 and 40 (1959), 70–89.

19  We must not forget that John quite explicitly identifies the pre-exi.......
    Christ with *Adonai-Sabaoth* who reveals himself to Isaiah in the Temp.......
    see John 12.37f.

20  Op. cit. (E.T., London 1965), I, p. 187.

21  Ibid., I, p. 298.

22  See *Primitive Christianity in its Contemporary Setting*, p. 190.

23  Ibid., p. 197.

24  Ibid., p. 201.

300

25  See R. M.......
    *passim.*

26  Op. cit.,.......

27  See *Jesus*.......

28  Compar.......
    p. 108:.......
    Helleni.......

    See *Le*.......

29  O. C.......

30  of G.......

    G. I.......

31  (196.......

32  But.......
    hin.......
    *Re*.......
    e.......

33  S.......
    S.......

34

35

36

37

38

57 See A. G. Wright, *Midrash: the Literary Genre* (New York 1967), p. 85. For details see note 47.
58 See *Paul's Use of the Old Testament*, p. 15.
59 I here retain Etheridge's terminology. Bowker would call them 'the Targum of Palestine' and 'Pseudo-Jonathan' respectively.

## Chapter 10

1 *Comm. in Gal.*, 34–6.
2 A. Marmorstein, art. 'Paulus und die Rabbinen' in *ZNTW* 30 (1931), 271–85.
3 O. Michel, art. 'Der Christus des Paulus' in *ZNTW* 32 (1933), 7–31.
4 See *From Jesus to Paul*, p. 204.
5 I have noted one in John 5.35 in my *Studies in the Pastoral Epistles*, pp. 12–14.
6 Klausner, op. cit., pp. 54–5.
7 Doeve, op. cit., p. 292.
8 Ibid., p. 99.
9 Ibid., p. 64.
10 Amsler, op. cit., p. 55.
11 This is not to suggest, of course, that the Torah was all composed in one period. A very similar point is made by C. H. Renard in an art. 'La Lecture de l'Ancien Testament par Saint Paul' in *Analecta Biblica* 18 (Rome 1963), 207–15.
12 Op. cit., p. 42.
13 Ibid., p. 66.
14 Ibid., p. 67; see also p. 143.
15 Compare also Lietzmann's description of Paul writing *Haggadah*; see p. 202 above.
16 Op. cit., pp. 83–4.
17 Op. cit., pp. 238–9.
18 See R. E. Brown, art. 'The Pre-Christian Semitic Concept of Mystery' in *Catholic Biblical Quarterly*, vol. 20 (1958); also 'The Semitic Background of the New Testament Mysterion I and II' in *Biblica* 39 (1958), 426–48 and 40 (1959), 70–89.
19 We must not forget that John quite explicitly identifies the pre-existent Christ with *Adonai-Sabaoth* who reveals himself to Isaiah in the Temple: see John 12.37f.
20 Op. cit. (E.T., London 1965), I, p. 187.
21 Ibid., I, p. 298.
22 See *Primitive Christianity in its Contemporary Setting*, p. 190.
23 Ibid., p. 197.
24 Ibid., p. 201.

25  See R. McL. Wilson, *Gnosis and the New Testament* (London 1968), *passim.*

26  Op. cit., p. 144.

27  See *Jesus Christ in the Old Testament*, pp. 141f.

28  Compare W. D. Davies in *Christian Origins and Judaism* (London 1962), p. 108: 'The Scrolls have shown that much that has been labelled Hellenistic may well have been native to Judaism.'

29  See *Le Christ dans la Théologie de Saint Paul*, pp. 186–7.

30  O. Cullmann, *The Christology of the New Testament* (E.T., London 1959, of German e. of 1957), p. 168.

31  G. Delling, art. 'Zum Neueren Paulus-verständnis' in *Nov. Test.* 4 (1960), 99, 100–1, 106.

32  But this view is still maintained by H. Conzelmann. See an article by him called 'The Mother of Wisdom' in the collection *The Future of Our Religious Past*, ed. J. M. Robinson (E.T., London 1971, of the German e. of 1964), pp. 230–43.

33  See *St Paul and the Church of the Gentiles*, pp. 100, 108.

34  See *Paul's Use of the Old Testament*, p. 124.

35  See *Le Christ, Sagesse de Dieu*, p. 397.

36  See *According to the Scriptures*, p. 23.

37  See art. 'Christus und Israel', pp. 22, 19.

38  L. Goppelt, art. 'Apokalyptik und Typologie bei Paulus' in *Theologische Literaturzeitung* 89 (May 1964), 337. Dodd also concludes that the argument from Scripture in some form goes back to Jesus himself (*According to the Scriptures*, pp. 109–10).

39  See art. cit. 'Der Christus des Paulus', p. 8.

40  See art. 'Apokalyptik und Typologie bei Paulus', pp. 324–7.

41  Ibid., p. 328.

42  Might one not justly claim that there is a certain prophet-typology in the Qur'ān? Mohammed seems to regard himself as the fulfilment of all prophetic types.

43  It might be maintained that such non-Pauline formulas as are to be found in Phil. 2.6–9; Col. 1.15–18; Eph. 5.14 are to be attributed to the tradition which he received. But it seems to me to be more satisfactory to regard them as contemporary with Paul rather than as part of his tradition.

44  See P. Bonnard, art. 'Mourir et vivre avec Jésus-Christ selon Saint Paul' in *RdHPR* 2 (1956), pp. 101f.

## Chapter 11

1  See Bultmann's essay: 'The Significance of the Old Testament for the Christian Faith' (1933). E.T. in B. W. Anderson's *The Old Testament and Christian Faith*, p. 14.

2  Ibid., pp. 32–3.

3  See op. cit., pp. 20–8. Of course Bultmann's failure to distinguish typology from allegory further obscures the issue.

4  Op. cit., pp. 74, 81.

5  Op. cit., p. 54.

6  See J. Bright, *The Authority of the Old Testament* (London 1967), pp. 79, 92.

7  Exceptions might be made in favour of the authors of 2 Peter and Revelation respectively. But they are not exceptions which make any difference to our argument here.

8  See *Theology of the Old Testament* (E.T., Edinburgh 1962, 1965), p. 420.

9  W. Vischer, *The Witness of the Old Testament to Christ* (E.T., London 1949, of German e. of 1936) I, pp. 82, 87, 105.

10  'le sens révélationnel des évènements historiques', see *L'ancien Testament dans l'Église*, p. 185.

11  Ibid., p. 216.

12  See *The Authority of the Old Testament*, pp. 207, 231.

13  See *Old and New in Interpretation*, pp. 207, 231.

14  See the opinions of R. Johanan in *Tractate Pesahim*, 463.

15  To be exact we must add *si vera lectio*, Heb. 11.11.

16  See *Paulus*, pp. 177, 181.

17  See his Commentary on Rom. 10.4f, pp. 165–6.

18  See *The Witness of the Old Testament to Christ*, p. 68.

19  See *From Jesus to Paul*, p. 495.

20  See A. Malet, *The Thought of Rudolf Bultmann* (E.T. of Fr. e. of 1962, Shannon 1970), p. 163.

21  Ibid., p. 164.

22  Ibid., p. 165. The quotation is from *Glauben und Verstehen*, by R. Bultmann, 2, p. 258.

23  Strictly speaking this is Malet's formula, not Bultmann's. But Bultmann must have approved it.

24  Op. cit., p. 164.

25  The problems of the passage are well discussed in Ingo Hermann's *Kyrios und Pneuma* (Munich 1961). See also Feuillet's *Le Christ, Sagesse de Dieu*, pp. 114f.

26  See his art. 'Paulus—Priester der Christlichen Kultgemeinde' in *Theologische Literaturzeitung* 79 (1959), 355f.

27  See von Rad's art. in Westermann's *Essays in Old Testament Interpretation*, pp. 22, 37.

28  See *Interpretation of Scripture*, p. 100.

29  Ibid., p. 102.

30  See art. 'Paulus und die Heilsgeschichte', in *NTS* 13 (Dec. 1966), 35–6.

31  Ibid., pp. 37–8.

32  See *Christus und das Gesetz*, p. 159.

33  G. Schrenk, art. γράφω in *TWNT*, vol. 1 (Stuttgart 1949), 755.

34  Ibid., p. 759.

35  E. L. Wenger, art. 'The Typological Hypothesis' in E.T. 68 (Apr. 1957) 222–3.

36  W. Pannenberg, *Jesus God and Man* (E.T., London 1968, of German e. of 1964), pp. 151–6.

37  Ibid., p. 157.

38  C. Michalson, art. cit. in B. W. Anderson, *The Old Testament and Christian Faith*, pp. 62–3. Incidentally, did Elisha raise a widow's daughter? I can find no trace of it in the Scriptures.

39  See Barr, op. cit., pp. 108–9.

40  D. F. Baumgärtel, *Verheissung* (Gütersloh 1952).

41  Ibid., pp. 64–5.

42  Ibid., p. 69.

43  Ibid., pp. 71–5.

44  Ibid., pp. 78–9.

45  Ibid., p. 85.

46  W. Eichrodt, art. in C. Westermann's *Essays on Old Testament Interpretation*, pp. 236–8.

47  See *Old and New in Interpretation*, pp. 141f.

48  This is in effect the conclusion of J. Coppens in an art. in which he summarizes recent work on this subject: 'Paul élabore une exégèse christologique de l'Ancien Testament qui en impose par son originalité et par sa profondeur des vues.' See his art. 'Les Arguments Scriptuaires et leur Portée dans les lettres Pauliniennes' in *Analecta Biblica* 18 (Rome 1963), p. 233.

49  Quoted by J. J. Schoeps in *Paulus*. I have taken the quotation from the E.T. of his work, though everywhere else I have quoted direct from the German edition. The passage comprises Aphorism 84 in 'Morgenröte'.

50  See *Old Testament Theology*, II, pp. 45, 333.

51  See *The Interpretation of Scripture*, p. 106.

52  Compare, for example, R. Johanan's splendid exposition of Hosea to be found in *Tractate Pesahim*, 460–2. This is noted in S-B.

53  Op. cit., p. 94.

54  *Old Testament Theology*, I, p. 284.

55  Art. 'Schriftverwertung und Schrifterlärung in Rabbinentum und bei Paulus', p. 163 in *Theologische Quartalschrift* 132 (1952), 152–69.

56  Art. cit., p. 169.

## Chapter 12

1 *Old and New in Interpretation*, p. 27; see p. 118 for the quotation at the end of this paragraph.

2 Ibid., p. 137.

3 A. W. Wolff, art. in Westermann's *Essays on Old Testament Interpretation*, pp. 166–70.

4 Ibid., p. 184.

5 See *Theology of the Old Testament* I, p. 128.

6 See *Offenbarungen und Schriftforschung in der Qumransekte*, pp. 10, 14, 41.

7 M. Noth, art. in Westermann, op. cit., p. 86.

8 See *Bibl. Ant.* IX, 6. The author of the first Gospel, by including Tamar in his genealogy of Christ, seems to be boldly pointing in the opposite direction. Perhaps another small example of this counter-tendency is to be found in John 1.47, where the description of Nathanael as 'an Israelite, in whom is no guile' might seem to suggest that in the original Israel there had been guile.

9 See *Mekilta*, ed. and tr. J. Z. Lauterbach, vol. I, p. 10.

10 See B. Anderson, op. cit., p. 31.

11 See Westermann, op. cit., pp. 300–1.

12 J. Bright, op. cit., pp. 123, 126.

13 G. E. Wright, art. in *The Old Testament and Christian Faith*, ed. B. Anderson, p. 178.

14 See Westermann, op. cit., pp. 148–9.

15 See O. Cullmann, art. in B. Anderson, op. cit., p. 121.

16 See von Rad, art. in Westermann, op. cit., p. 32.

17 A. R. Richardson, art. in Anderson, op. cit., p. 44.

18 J. L. McKenzie, art. in Anderson, op. cit., pp. 109, 111.

19 E. Brunner, art. in Anderson, op. cit., p. 269.

20 *Old and New in Interpretation*, p. 15.

21 Op. cit., pp. 77–88, 98. His latest book is now (1973) *The Bible in the Modern World* (London 1973); but he does not in it add anything to what he has said about revelation in earlier works.

22 J. Daniélou, *Théologie du Judéo-Christianisme* (Paris 1957).

23 *Old and New in Interpretation*, p. 81.

24 Ibid., p. 101.

25 Ibid., p. 149.

# BIBLIOGRAPHY

## BOOKS REFERRED TO IN TEXT

Abbott, T. K., *The Epistles to the Ephesians and Colossians*. I.C.C., Edinburgh 1909.

Allo, E. B., S. Paul: *Première Épitre aux Corinthiens*. Paris 1956. *Seconde Épitre aux Corinthiens*. Paris 1956.

Amsler, S., *L'Ancien Testament dans l'Église*. Neuchâtel 1960.

Bandastra, A. J., *The Law and the Elements of the World*. Kampen 1964.

Barclay, W., *The New Testament*. Vol. II. London 1969.

Barr, J., *Old and New in Interpretation*. London 1966. *The Bible in the Modern World*. London 1973.

Barrett, C. K., *From First Adam to Last*. London 1962. *A Commentary on the Epistle to the Romans*. Black's Series. London 1957.

Barth, Karl, *The Epistle to the Romans*. E.T. 6e., London 1933.

Baumgärtel, D. F., *Verheissung*. Gütersloh 1952.

Baumgartner, W., see Koehler, L.

Betz, O., *Offenbarungen und Schriftforschung in der Qumransekte*. Tubingen 1960.

Blunt, A. W. F., *The Epistle of Paul to the Galatians*. Oxford 1925.

Bowker, J., *The Targums and Rabbinic Literature*. Cambridge 1969.

Braude, W. G., ed. and tr., *The Midrash on the Psalms*. Yale 1959.

Bright, J., *The Authority of the Old Testament*. London 1962.

Bring, R., *Commentary on Galatians*. E.T., Philadelphia 1961. *Christus und das Gesetz*. Leiden 1969.

Bultmann, R., *Theology of the New Testament*. E.T. London 1965. *Primitive Christianity in its Contemporary Setting*. E.T., London 1956.

Caird, C. B., *Principalities and Powers*. Oxford 1956.

Cashdan, E., ed., *Tractate Menahoth* in BT. London 1948.

Cerfaux, L., *Le Christ dans la Théologie de S. Paul*. Paris 1951.

Charles, R. H., *The Apocrypha and Pseudepigraphia of the OT*. London 1913.

Cohen, A., ed., *Tractate Sotah* in BT. London 1936.

Conzelmann, H., ed., *Der Erste Brief an die Corinther Krit- Exeg. Komm.* Göttingen 1969.

Cullmann, O., *The Christology of the New Testament*. E.T., London 1959.

Daniélou, J., *Théologie du Judeo-Christianism*. Paris 1957.

Daube, D., *The New Testament and Rabbinic Judaism*. London 1956.

Davies, W. D., *The Setting of the Sermon on the Mount*. Cambridge 1964. *Christian Origins and Judaism*. London 1962.

Dibelius, M., *Der Brief an die Kolosser Handbuch z. N.T.*, ed. D. H. Greeven. Tübingen 1953.

Doeve, J. W., *Jewish Hermeneutics in the Synoptic Gospels and Acts*. Assen 1954.

Dodd, C. H., *The Epistle to the Romans*. Moffatt Commentaries. London 1932. *According to the Scriptures*. London 1952.

Ellis, E. E., *Paul's Use of the Old Testament*. Edinburgh 1957.

Etheridge, J. W., *The Targums of Onkelos and Jonathan ben Uzziel on the Pentateuch*. London 1865.

Euler, K. F., *Die Verkündigung vom Leidenden Gottesknecht aus Jes. 53 in der Griechischen Bibel*. Stuttgart–Berlin 1934.

Evans, E., *The Epistles of Paul to the Corinthians*. Clarendon Bible. Oxford 1930.

Feuillet, A., *Le Christ, Sagesse de Dieu*. Paris 1966.

Freedman, H., ed., *Tractate Shabbath in BT*. London 1938 and see Schachter J. Ed., *Tractate Pesahim in BT*. London 1938. Ed., *Tractate Baba Mezi'a in BT*. London 1935. Ed., *Tractate Nedarim in BT*. London 1936.

Gerhardsson, B., *The Good Samaritan—the Good Shepherd*. Lund 1958.

*Good News for Modern Man*. American Bible Soc., New York 1966.

Goppelt, L., *Typos*. 1966 e., Darmstadt.

Goudge, H. L., *The First Epistle to the Corinthians*. London 1903.

Hanson, A. T., *The Wrath of the Lamb*. London 1957. *The Pioneer Ministry*. London 1961. *Paul's Understanding of Jesus*. Hull 1963. *Jesus Christ in the Old Testament*. London 1965. *Studies in the Pastoral Epistles*. London 1968.

Hanson, R. P. C., *Allegory and Event*. London 1936. *II Corinthians*. Torch Commentaries. London 1954.

Héring, J., *La Première Épitre de S. Paul aux Corinthiens*. Neuchâtel and Paris 1958.

Hermann, I., *Kyrios und Pneuma*. Munich 1961.

Hershon, P. I., *A Rabbinical Commentary on Genesis*. London 1885.

Humbert, P., Le Messie dans le Targum des Prophetes, monograph in *Révue de Théologie et de Philosophie*. Lausanne 1911.

Israelstam, J., ed., *Tractate Aboth in BT*. London 1935. Ed., *Tractate 'Orlah in BT*. London 1948.

James, M. R., ed and tr. *The Biblical Antiquities* of Pseudo-Philo. London 1917.

Jones, A., ed., *The Jerusalem Bible*. London 1966.

Käsemann, E., *Perspectives on Paul*. E.T., London 1971.

Kirk, K. E., *The Epistle to the Romans*. Clarendon Bible. Oxford 1937.

Kirzner, E., ed., *Tractate Baba Kamma* in BT. London 1935.

Klausner, J., *From Jesus to Paul*. E.T., London 1944.

Knox, R. A., *The New Testament of Our Lord and Saviour Jesus Christ*. London 1945.

Knox, W. L., *St Paul and the Church of the Gentiles*. Cambridge 1939.

Koehler, L. and Baumgartner, W., *Lexicon in Veteris Testamenti Libros*. Leiden 1953.

Lagrange, M-J., *S. Paul: Épitre aux Romains*. Paris 1915. *Épitre aux Galates*. Paris 1950.

Lampe, G. W. H., and with Woollcombe, K., *A Patristic Greek Lexicon*. Oxford 1961. *Essays in Typology*. London 1957.

Lauterbach, J. Z., *The Mekilta de Rabbi Ishmael*. Philadelphia 1933.

Lazarus, H. M., ed., *Tractate Makkoth* in BT. London 1935.

Leenhardt, F., *L'Épitre de S. Paul aux Romains*. Neuchâtel and Paris 1957.

Lévi, I., *The Hebrew Text of the Book of Ecclesiasticus*. Leiden 1969.

Liddell, H. G., and Scott, R., *A Greek-English Lexicon*. 9e., Oxford 1940.

Lietzmann, H., *An die Römer* in *Handbuch z. N.T.* 3e., Tübingen 1928. *An die Galater*. Tübingen 1911. *An die Korinther I and II*. 4e. rev., Tübingen 1949.

Lightfoot, J. B., *The Epistles of Paul: Colossians and Ephesians*. London 1961. *St Paul's Epistle to the Galatians*. 10e., London 1880. Ed. *The Apostolic Fathers*. London 1891.

Lindars, B., *New Testament Apologetic*. London 1961.

Lindblom, J., *Gesichte und Offenbarungen*. Lund 1968.

Lipsius, R. A., *Briefe an die Galater, Römer, Philipper* in *Hand-Comm. z. N.T.* Freiburg 1891.

Lohmeyer, E., ed., *Die Briefe an die Philipper, an die Kolosser, und an Philemon* in *Krit-Exeg. Komm. ü. d. N.T.* 8e., Göttingen 1961.

Luther, M., *Commentary on the Epistle to the Galatians*. E.T. of 1575. London 1953.

Malet, A., *The Thought of Rudolf Bultmann*. E.T., Shannon 1970.

Mansoor, M., *The Thanksgiving Hymns*. Leiden 1961.

Michel, O., ed., *Der Brief an die Römer* in *Krit-Exeg. Komm. ü. d. N.T.* Göttingen 1957. *Paulus und seine Bibel*. Gütersloh 1929.

Milligan, G., see Moulton, J. H.

Moffat, J., *A New Translation of the Bible*. London e. 1934.

Moule, C. F. D., *The Epistles to the Colossians and Philemon*. Cambridge Greek Testament. Cambridge 1958.

Moulton, J. H., *The Vocabulary of the Greek Testament*. London 1930. See also Milligan, G.

Munck, J., *Paul and the Salvation of Mankind.* E.T., London 1959.

Naber, S., ed., Josephus *Opera Omnia.* Leipzig 1888.

Nygren, A., *Comm. on Romans.* E.T., London 1952.

Ottley, R., *The Book of Isaiah according to the Septuagint.* Cambridge 1909.

Pannenberg, W., *Jesus God and Man.* E.T., London 1968.

Phillips, J. B., *Letters to Young Churches.* London 1947.

Plummer, A., see Robertson, A. *A Crit. and Exeg. Commentary on the Second Epistle of St Paul to the Corinthians.* I.C.C., Edinburgh 1915.

Porusch, I., ed., *Tractate Me'ilah* in BT. London 1948.

Rabbinowitz, J., ed., *Tractate Ta'anith* in BT. London 1938.

Robertson, A., and Plummer, A., *A Crit. and Exeg. Commentary on the 1st Epistle of Paul to the Corinthians.* I.C.C., Edinburgh 1911.

Robinson, J. A. T., *The Body.* London 1952.

Sanday, A., and Headlam, A. C., *A Critical and Exegetical Comm. on the Epistle to the Romans.* I.C.C., 5e. Edinburgh 1902.

Schachter, J., and Freedman, A., ed., *Tractate Sanhedrin* on BT. London 1935.

Schlier, N., ed., *Der Brief an die Galater* in *Krit. Exeg. Komm.* Göttingen 1962.

Schmiedel, P. W., *Die Brief an die Thessaloniker und an die Korinther* in *Hand Comm.* Frieburg 1891.

Schoeps, H. J., *Paulus: die Theologie des Apostles im Lichte der Judischen Religionsgeschichte.* Tübingen 1959.

Scott, R., see Liddell, H. G.

Seeligman, I. L., *The Septuagint Version of Isaiah.* Leiden 1948.

Segal, M. H., ed., *Tractate Shekalim* in BT. London 1938.

Simon, M., ed., *Tractate Gittin* in BT. London 1946.

Slotki, W., ed., *Tractate Yebamoth* in BT. London 1936.

Smart, J. D., *The Interpretation of Scripture.* London 1961.

Stählin, O., ed., *Clemens Alexandrinus*, rev. E. Früctel. Berlin 1960.

Stenning, J. F., *The Targum of Isaiah.* Oxford 1949.

Strachan, R. H., *The Second Epistle of St Paul to the Corinthians.* Moffat Commentaries. London 1935.

Strack, H. L., and Billerbeck, P., *Komm. z. N.T. aus Talmud und Midrasch.* 3 vols. 3e. Munich 1961.

Sukenik, E. L., ed., *The Dead Sea Scrolls of the Hebrew University.* Jerusalem 1955.

Swete, H. B., *An Introduction to the Old Testament in Greek.* Cambridge 1914.

Tholuck, A., ed., *Ioannis Calvini in Novum Testamentum Commentarii.* Vols. I–VII. Berlin 1834.

Vallotton, P., *Le Christ et la Foi.* Geneva 1960.

van der Ploeg, J., *Le Targum de Job de la Grotte 11 de Qumran.* Amsterdam 1962.
van der Woude, A. S., *Das Hiobtargum aus Qumran Höhle XI*, supplement to *Vetus Testamentum.* Leiden 1963.
Vermes, G., *Scripture and Tradition in Judaism.* Leiden 1961.
Vischer, W., *The Dead Sea Scrolls in English.* London 1962. *The Witness of the Old Testament to Christ.* E.T., London 1949.
Vollmer, H., *Die Alttestamentlichen Citate bei Paulus.* Freiburg and Leipzig 1899.
Von Rad, G., *The Theology of the Old Testament.* E.T., Edinburgh 1962, 1965.
Von Soden, H., *Hand-Commentar z. N.T.* Vol. III. Freiburg 1891.
Weymouth, R. F., *The New Testament in Modern Speech.* London 1902.
Wilson, R. McL., *Gnosis and the New Testament.* London 1968.
Windisch, H., *Paulus und das Judentum.* Stuttgart 1935.
Wood, J. D., *The Interpretation of the Bible.* London 1959.
Wright, A. G., *Midrash: the Literary Genre.* New York 1967.

## ARTICLES REFERRED TO IN THE TEXT

Bacher, W., 'Gamaliel I' in *The Jewish Encyclopedia* (New York 1904).
Barthelémcy, D., 'Chainon Manquant de L'Histoire de la Septante' in *RB* 60 (1953), 18f.
Baumgärtel, F., art. in C. Westermann's *Essays in OT Interpretation* (E.T., London 1963), p. 143.
Behm, J., art. διαθήκη in *TWNT* II (Stuttgart 1950), 106f.
Beer, G., ed., Proverbs in Kittel's *Bibl. Hebr.*
Benoit, P., 'La Loi et le Croix d'après Paul' in *RB* 47 (1938), 475–509.
Bläser, P., 'Schriftverwertung und Schrifterklärung in Rabbinentum und bei Paulus' in *Theologische Quartalschrift* 132 (1952), 152–69.
Bonnard, P., 'Mourir et vivre avec Jésus-Christ selon S. Paul' in *RdHPR* 2 (1956), 101f.
Brock, S., Review: *The Septuagint and Modern Society* by S. Jellico in *JTS* 20 (2) (Oct. 1969), 579.
Brown, R. E., 'The Pre-Christian Semitic Concept of Mystery' in *Catholic Biblical Quarterly.* 'The Semitic Background of the NT Mysterion I and II' in *Biblica* 39 (1958), 426–48.
Brunner, E., art. in B. W. Anderson's *The OT and Christian Faith* (E.T., London 1964), p. 269.
Buhl, F., ed., Psalms in Kittel's *Bibl. Heb.*
Bultmann, R., art. in Westermann's *Essays in OT Interpretation* (E.T., London 1963), pp. 51f.; art. 'The Significance of the OT

for the Christian Faith' in Anderson's *The OT and Christian Faith* (E.T., London 1933).

Burton, E. D., 'Redemption from the Curse of the Law' in *American Journal of Theology* 11 (1967), 624–46.

Conzelmann, H., art. 'The Mother of Wisdom' in *The Future of Our Religious Past*, ed. J. M. Robinson (E.T., London 1971), pp. 231–243.

Coppens, J., 'Les Arguments Scriptuaires et leur Portée dans les lettres Pauliniennes' in *Analecta Biblica* (Rome 1963), 233.

Cullmann, O., art. in Anderson's *The OT and Christian Faith* (E.T., London 1964) p. 121.

Dannall, G. A., 'Did Paul Know the Tradition about the Virgin Birth?' in *Studia Theologica* 4 (1950), 94–101.

Dechent, H., 'Der "Gerechte" —eine Bezeichung für den Messias' in *Theol. Stud. u. Krit.* (1927–28), 439–43.

Delling, G., art. ἀρχή in *TWNT* (Stuttgart 1949). 'Zum Neueren Paulus-verständnis' in *Nov. Test.* 4 (1960), 100–1, 106.

Del Paramo, S., 'La Citas de los Salmos en S. Pablo' in *Analecta Biblica* 18 (Rome 1963), 229.

Diezinger, W., 'Unter Toten Freigeworden' in *Nov. Test.* 5 (1962), 268–98.

Dinkler, E., 'The Historical and Eschatological Israel in Romans 5. 9–11' in *Journal of Religion* xxxvi (1956), 123.

Eichrodt, W., art. in Westermann's *Essays in OT Interpretation* (E.T., London 1963), pp. 236–8.

Feuillet, A., 'La Citation d'Habacue 2.4 et les Huit Premiers Chapitres de l'Épitre aux Romains' in *NTS* 6 (1959), 52–80.

Fitzmeyer, J. A., 'The Use of Explicit OT Quotations in Qumran Literature and in the NT' in *NTS* 7 (1960–61), 292–333.

Goppelt, L., 'Apokalyptic und Typologie bei Paulus' in *Theologische Literaturzeitung* 89 (May 1964), 322–43. 'Paulus und die Heilsgeschichte' in *NTS* 13 (Dec. 1966), 35–6.

Grässer, E., 'Der Historische Jesus im Hebräerbrief' in *ZNTW* 56 (1965), 63–91.

Grundmann, W., art: 'The Teacher of Righteousness of Qumran and the Question of Justification by Faith in the Theology of the Apostle Paul' in *Paul and Qumran*, ed. J. Murphy O'Connor (London 1968), pp. 85–114.

Hanson, A. T., 'Philo's Etymologies' in *JTS* xviii NS (1967), 128–139.

Hatch, W. H. P., 'τὰ στοιχεῖα τοῦ κόσμου in Paul and Bardaisan' in *JTS* 28 (1927), 181–2.

Hesse, F., art. in Westermann's *Essays in O.T. Interpretation* (E.T., London 1963) pp. 300–1.

Hincks, E. Y., 'The meaning of the phrase τὰ στοιχεῖα τοῦ κόσμου in Gal. 4.3 and Col. 2.8' in *JBL* 15 (1896), 183–92.

Hughes, P. E., art. 'The Olive Tree of Romans 11' in *Evang. Quarterly* 20 (1948), 22–45.

Hoad, J., 'Some NT References to Isaiah 53' in *ET* 68 (May 1957), 254–5.

Holzmeister, U., 'De Christi Crucifixione Quid e Deut. 21.22s et Gal. 3.13 consequatur' in *Biblica* xxvii (1946), 18–29.

Jourdan, G. V., art. 'κοινωνία in 1 Cor. 10.16' in *JBL* 67 (1948), 111f.

Kallas, J., art. 'Romans 13. 1–7—An Interpolation' in *NTS* 11 (July 1965), 365f.

Kennedy, H. A. A., 'Two Exegetical Notes on St Paul: ii Colossians 2.10–15' in *ET* 28 (1916–17), 363–5.

Kittel, G., 'πίστις ᾿ησοῦ Χριστοῦ bei Paulus' in *Theol. Stud. u. Krit.* (1906), 419f.

Kittel, R., ed., Isaiah in his own *Biblia Hebraica*.

Klassen, W., art. 'Coals of Fire—Sign of Repentance or Revenge' in *NTS* 9 (July 1963), 337f.

Kolenkow, A., 'The Ascription of Roms. 4.5' in *Harvard Theological Review* 60 (1967), 228–30.

Kurze, G., 'Die στοιχεῖα τοῦ κόσμου Gal. 4 und Kol. 2' in *Biblische Zeitschrift* 15 (1918–21), 335–7.

Le Déaut, R., 'Traditions Targumiques dans le Corpus Paulinien' in *Biblica* 42 (1961), 38.

Lohmeyer, E., 'Probleme Paulinischer Theologie' in *ZNTW* 28 (1929), 177–207.

Lyonnet, S., 'La notion de Justice de Dieu en Rom. 3.5 et l'Exégèse Paulinienne du "Miserere"' in *Sacra Pagina*, vol. 2, ed. J. Coppens (1959), 342f.

Macgregor, G. H. C., 'Principalities and Powers: the Cosmic Background of Paul's Thought' in *NTS* 1 (1954–5), 17–28.

McKenzie, J. L., art. in Anderson's *The OT and Christian Faith* (E.T., London 1964), pp. 109–11.

Manson, T. W., 'The Argument from Prophecy' in *JTS* xlvi (1945), 129–36.

Marshal, I. H., 'Son of God or Servant of Yahweh?' in *NTS* 15 (Apr. 1969), 334.

Maurer, C., art. ῥίζα in *TWNT* vi (Stuttgart 1959).

Megas, G., 'Das χειρόγραφον Adams' in *ZNTW* 27 (1928), 305–20.

Michalson, C., art. in Anderson's *The Old Testament and Christian Faith* (E.T., London 1964), p. 54.

Michel, O., 'Der Christus des Paulus' in *ZNTW* (1933), 7–31.

Müller, A., 'Der Qal-Wachomar Schluss bei Paulus' in *ZNTW* 58

(1967), 73–92. 'Die Auslegung Alttestamentlichen Gesichtsstoffs bei Paulus' diss. (Halle 1960).

Munck, J., 'Christus und Israel—Eine Auslegung von Römer 9–11' in *Acta Jutlandica* XXVIII (1956), Theology Series, 7, 33.

Noth, M., art. in Westermann's *Essays in OT Interpretation* (E.T., London 1963), p. 86.

O'Rourke, J. J., ed., 2 Corinthians in the *Jerome Bible Commentary* (London 1968).

Reicke, B., 'The Law and the World according to St Paul' in *JBL* 70 (1951), 259–76.

Renard, C. H., 'La Lecture de l'Ancien Testament par S. Paul' in *Analecta Biblica* 18 (Rome 1963), 210.

Richardson, A. R., art. in Anderson's *The OT and Christian Faith* (E.T., London 1964), p. 44.

Rudolph, W., ed., Jeremiah in Kittel's *Bibl. Hebr.*

Rutherford, J., 'Note on Colossians 2.15' in *ET* 18 (1906–07), 565–6.

Sanders, T. A., 'Habakkuk in Qumran, Paul, and in the OT' in *Journal of Religion* XXXIX, No. 4 (Oct. 1959), 232–44.

Schlier, H., art. δειγματίζω in *TWNT* II (Stuttgart 1935).

Schmid, von J., 'Die Alttestamentliche Citate bei Paulus und die Theorie von sensus plenior' in *Biblische Zeitschrift* 3 (1959), 161–73.

Schoeps, H. J., 'The Sacrifice of Isaac in Paul's Theology' in *JBL* 65 (1946), 385f.

Schrenk, G., art. δίκαιος in *TWNT* II (Stuttgart 1935). art. γράφω in *TWNT* I (Stuttgart 1949), 755.

Talbert, T. H., art. 'Tradition and Redaction in Romans 12. 9–21' in *NTS* 16 (Oct. 1969), 83–94.

Torrance, T. F., 'One Aspect of the Biblical Conception of Faith' in *ET* 68 (1957), 111, 157, 221.

Ulonska, H., diss. 'Die Funktion der alttestamentlichen Zitate und Ausspielungen in die Paulischen Briefen' (Münster 1963).

Vallisoleto, P. X., 'Delens Chirographum' in *Verbum Domini* 13 (1933), 181–5 and 'Et spolians principatus et potestates' in ibid., 187–92.

Voegelin, E., art. in Anderson's *The Old Testament and Christian Faith* (E.T., London 1964), p. 74.

Von Rad, G., art. in Westermann's *Essays in O.T. Interpretation* (E.T., London 1963), p. 22.

Weingreen, J., 'The Title Moreh Sedek' in *Journal of Semitic Studies* 6 (Autumn 1961), 162–74.

Weiss, K., 'Paulus-Priester der Christlichen Kultgemeinde' in *Theologische Literaturzeitung* 79 (1959), 355f.

Wenger, E. L., 'The Typological Hypothesis' in *ET* 68 (Apr. 1957), 222–3

Whiteley, D. E. H., art. 'St Paul's Thought on the Atonement' in *JTS* 8 NS (1957).

Wilckens, U., 'Die Rechtfertigung Abrahams nach Römer 4' in *Studien z. Theologie der Alttestamentlichen Überlieferung* (Neukirch 1961), 112f.

Williams, C. S. C., ed., 2 Corinthians in Peake's *Commentary on the Bible* (new e., London 1962).

Windfuhr, W., 'Der Apostel Paulus also Haggadist' in *ZATW* 44 (1926), 327–30.

Wolff, A., art. in Westermann's *Essays in OT Interpretation* (E.T., London 1963), pp. 166–70.

Wood, J. E., 'Isaac Typology in the NT' in *NTS* 14 (July 1968), 583–9.

Wright, G., art. in Anderson's *The OT and the Christian Faith* (London 1964), p. 178.

Zimmerli, W., art. in Westermann's *Essays in OT Interpretation* (E.T., London 1963), p. 118.

# INDEX OF NAMES

# INDEX OF
# SCRIPTURE REFERENCES

# INDEX OF REFERENCES
# TO NON-CANONICAL JEWISH
# AND CHRISTIAN BOOKS